THE BALLADE

BY

HELEN LOUISE COHEN, Ph.D.

New York
COLUMBIA UNIVERSITY PRESS
1915

Printed from type April, 1915

Press of
The New Era Printing Company
Lancaster, Pa.

This Monograph has been approved by the Department of English and Comparative Literature in Columbia University as a contribution to knowledge worthy of publication.

A. H. THORNDIKE,

Executive Officer

PREFACE

This work, begun as a study of the *ballade* in English and eventually outgrowing its narrower limits, undertakes to give the history of that verse form from its origins in Romance lands through its career in France and England up to the present day. An attempt is made to show what modifications the form underwent at the hands of the *trouvères*; how, in the course of poetic competitions, the envoy came to be added, and how the formal *ballade,* in the end, became unalterably reduced to three stanzas with identical rime scheme and refrain. The account given of the course of this lyric in France illustrates the typical ideas that pervaded *ballade* literature and calls attention also to the function of the *ballade* in the drama. A minute examination of the Middle English *ballade* is made possible by the comparatively small number of specimens in that language. The selections in Chapter III, brought together for the first time from rhetorical and critical treatises of the fourteenth, fifteenth, sixteenth, and seventeenth centuries, will be found useful for the detailed study of this fixed form and as a means of gauging its changing popularity as reflected in current literary criticism. The last chapter deals with the *ballade* in the nineteenth century and after. My obligations to previous research I have made plain in the footnotes and in the Bibliographies. The latter contain lists of all the manuscripts and of most of the books which I have consulted.

There is little that is original in my account of the beginnings of French poetry, except as the various theories of the origin of the Romance lyric are applied to the *ballade.* Neither do the sections in Chapter IV, devoted to Chaucer and to Quixley, pretend to be more than a summary of the results of recent scholarship. Where I have copied *ballades* from manuscripts, I have sought to make a faithful transcription rather than a critical text, and have rarely supplied more than punctuation. The following material is, I believe, printed for the first time:

CHAPTER II.

"Ave douce dame de paradis," British Museum *Ms. Additional 15224.*

Ballade en la Personne de la Vierge, Bibliothèque Nationale Ms. Fr. 24408.

"Ma mère où ma face est empraincte," same manuscript.

"Les payens versificateurs," same manuscript.

"Le grant yver par sa froidure," *Bibliothèque Nationale Ms. Fr. 19369.*

"Au verger de dieu ordonée," *Bibliothèque Nationale Ms. 24408.*

Oraison par Manière de Ballade, same manuscript.

Sur la Peche Dorgueil, Bibliothèque Nationale Ms. Fr. 2306.

"Pecheur qui scez qui morir doiz," British Museum *Ms. Harley 4397.*

Ballade de la Mort, Bibliothèque Nationale Ms. Fr. 1707.

CHAPTER IV.

Balade upon the Chaunce of the Dyse, Bodleian *Ms. Fairfax 16.*

Balade Coloured and Reuersid, British Museum Ms. Arundel 26.[1]

Triple Ballade, Cambridge University Library *Ms. Fg. 1.6.* and Bodleian *Ms. Tanner 246.*

[1] This was printed by H. N. MacCracken a year after I had transcribed it. Cf. p. 286 below.

Balade fet de la Reygne Katerine Russel, Trinity College *Ms. R 14.5.*

APPENDIX I.

"Gentilz gallans faictes armée" and "Les dames ont vue la requeste," Bodleian *Ms. Douce 479.*

With printed material I have followed the text given except in the case of early printed books, where I have occasionally supplied punctuation. The following selections are reprinted from books in no case later than the seventeenth century:

CHAPTER II.

Oraison à la Vierge Marie, Les Faictz et Dictz de Sieur Jehan Molinet (Paris, 1531).

Balade de la Morte, Jehan Bouchet, *XIII Rondeaulx Avec XXV Balades Differentes* (Paris, 1536).

La Morte Parle a Lhomme Humain, Les Lunettes des Princes (Paris, 1539).

Balade contre Folles Amours, Jehan Bouchet, same title and date as above.

Le Sexe Masculin, two *ballades* with this title, Gracien Dupont, *Les Controverses des Sexes Masculin et Feminin* (Toulouse, 1584).

Balade de Mazarin Grand Joueur de Hoc (Paris, 1649).

CHAPTER III.

On the theory of the *ballade* from:

Gracien Dupont. *Art et Science de Rhetoricque Metriffiee* (Toulouse, 1539).

Francoise de Pierre Delaudun Daigaliers, *L'Art Poétique François* (Paris, 1598).

Pierre de Deimier, *L'Académie de L'Art Poétique* (Paris, 1610).

Francois Colletet, *L'Escole des Muses* (Paris, 1656).

Envoy, Court of Sapyence (printed by Wynkyn de Worde, 1510).

Outside the faculty of Columbia University, I wish especially to thank M. Joseph Bédier, M. Pierre Champion, Professor H. N. MacCracken of Smith College, Professor K. C. M. Sills of Bowdoin College, and Professor John M. Burnam of the University of Cincinnati for their kindly advice; and M. Alfred Jeanroy, Mr. Austin Dobson, Mr. Edmund Gosse, and Andrew Lang—though in his case it is now too late—for their generous letters, now incorporated in the text.

I am glad to acknowledge the courtesy of the authorities of the British Museum and of the *Bibliothèque Nationale,* and to record the help received from Mr. Falconer Madan and Mr. R. A. Abrams of the Bodleian Library, from M. Georges Ritter of the library at Rouen, Mr. T. J. Kiernan of the Harvard Library, and Miss P. V. Fullerton of the New York Public Library. I am also under obligations to Mr. Frederick W. Erb and Miss A. M. Erb of the Columbia Library for their most expert and painstaking services.

To my friend and former fellow student, Professor Frank H. Ristine of Hamilton College, I am indebted for the assistance he has given me in preparing my manuscript for the press and in reading the proof. Professor Raymond Weeks, Professor C. S. Baldwin, Professor H. M. Ayres, Professor F. A. Patterson, all of Columbia University, have read my manuscript and have made many valuable suggestions. I take this opportunity of expressing my gratitude to them for their coöperation. To Professor William W. Lawrence, who suggested the subject of this study, and who has throughout my work acted as counselor and critic, I owe most.

H. L. C.

Washington Irving High School,
New York, 1 February, 1914.

INTRODUCTION

Several contemporary critics, notably Benedetto Croce, condemn those scholars who try to separate and identify literary types as if they were so many labeled and distinct specimens in a museum of literary history. It is the contention of Croce and his followers that the terms, "tragedy," "romance," "lyric," and the like, are employed merely as a rough attempt at classification and not in conformity to genuine definitions.[1] Every piece of literature is thus to be looked upon as a law unto itself. This conception of criticism would, for example, put the ban on any consideration of the technique of poetry as distinct from its substance. The *ballade,* however, by its very nature, is regulated by laws outside itself. Its construction is determined by arbitrary requirements. Though a tragedy is a tragedy, whether it observe the unities or ignore them, whether it be *Samson Agonistes* or *King Lear,* a *ballade* depends upon its three stanzas, its identical rimes, and its refrain for its very being.

The similarity in sounds between the terms, *ballade* and *ballad,* has sometimes led English-speaking people to misconceive the character of the former. The fixed verse form, now known as the *ballade,* is as great a contrast as could well be imagined to the traditional narrative or lyric poems of uncertain dimensions, or in fact to any verse forms not fixed, that go under the name of *ballad.* But antithetical as a popular ballad like *The Twa Sisters o' Binnorye* and

[1] Benedetto Croce, *Estetica,* translated as *Aesthetic as Science of Expression and General Linguistic,* by Douglas Ainslee (London, 1909), p. 63.

any *ballade* are in length, in subject matter, and in purpose, they have, nevertheless, two features in common, repetition and refrain, both of which point to a popular origin in the choral song of early times. At least some of the refrains in the *ballettes,* which were in all probability the immediate progenitors of the French *ballade,* are fragments of early popular lyrics, though transmitted through an aristocratic medium.

The *ballade* in its most highly developed artistic form, is defined in Rostand's *Cyrano de Bergerac,* in a familiar scene between Cyrano and the Vicomte de Valvert. The nobleman contemptuously salutes the "cadet de Gascogne" as "Poète!" and an altercation follows:

CYRANO

"Oui, monsieur, poète! et tellement,
Qu'en ferraillant je vais—hop!—à l'improvisade,
Vous composer une ballade.

LE VICOMTE

Une ballade?

CYRANO

Vous ne vous doutez pas de ce que c'est, je crois?

LE VICOMTE

Mais. . . .

CYRANO, récitant comme une leçon.

La ballade, donc, se compose de trois
Couplets de huit vers . . .

LE VICOMTE, piétinant.

Oh!

CYRANO, continuant.

Et d'un envoi de quatre . . .

LE VICOMTE

Vous . . .

CYRANO

Je vais tout ensemble en faire une et me battre,
Et vous toucher, monsieur, au dernier vers.

LE VICOMTE

Non!

CYRANO

Non?

(Déclamant.)

"Ballade du duel qu'en l'hôtel bourguignon
Monsieur de Bergerac eut avec un bélître!"

LE VICOMTE

Qu'est-ce que c'est que ça, s'il vous plaît?

CYRANO

C'est le titre.

* * * * * * * * * * *

CYRANO, fermant une seconde les yeux.

Attendez! . . . je choisis mes rimes . . . Là, j'y suis.

(Il fait ce qu'il dit, à mesure.)

Je jette avec grâce mon feutre,
Je fais lentement l'abandon
Du grand manteau qui me calfeutre,
Et je tire mon espadon;
Élégant comme Céladon,
Agile comme Scaramouche,
Je vous préviens, cher Mirmydon,
Qu'à la fin de l'envoi je touche!

(Premiers engagements de fer.)

Vous auriez bien dû rester neutre;
Où vais-je vous larder, dindon? . . .

Dans le flanc, sous votre maheutre? . . .
Au cœur, sous votre bleu cordon? . . .
. . . Les coquilles tintent, ding-don!
Ma pointe voltige: une mouche!
Décidément . . . c'est au bedon,
Qu'à la fin de l'envoi, je touche.

Il me manque une rime en eutre . . .
Vous rompez, plus blanc qu'amidon?
C'est pour me fournir le mot pleutre!
. . . Tac! je pare la pointe dont
Vous espériez me faire don;—
J'ouvre la ligne,—je la bouche . . .
Tiens bien ta broche, Laridon!
A la fin de l'envoi, je touche.

(Il annonce solennellement:)

Envoi

Prince, demande à Dieu pardon!
Je quarte du pied, j'escarmouche,
Je coupe, je feinte . . .
(Se fendant.)
Hé! là donc,
(Le vicomte chancelle; Cyrano salue.)
A la fin de l'envoi, je touche.[2]

[2] With this masterpiece of Rostand's should be compared Lafontaine's "Ballade pour le second Terme," written in 1659 and dedicated to Foucquet in return for financial assistance. (See H. Regnier, *Œuvres de J. de La Fontaine,* Paris, 1883, Vol. I, p. lx).

"Trois fois dix vers, et puis cinq d'ajoutés,
Sans point d'abus, c'est ma tâche complète;
Mais le mal est qu'ils ne sont pas comptés.
Par quelque bout il faut que je m'y mette;
Puis, que jamais ballade je promette,
Dussé-je entrer au fin fond d'une tour,
Nenni, ma fois, car je suis déja court,

Here we have, at one and the same time, a definition and an example of the *ballade*. It was this fixed form which, in the late Middle Ages, captured the taste of France and even had a certain vogue in England. In the former

Si que je crains que n'ayez rien du nôtre.
Quand il s'agit de mettre une œuvre au Jour,
Promettre est un, et tenir est un autre.

Sur ce refrain, de grace, permettez
Que je vous conte en vers une sornette.
Colin, venant des universités,
Promit un jour cent francs à Guillemette.
De quatre-vingts il trompa la fillette,
Qui, de dépit, lui dit pour faire court:
Vous y viendrez cuire dans notre four!
Colin répond, faisant le bon apôtre:
Ne vous fachez, belle; car, en amour,
Promettre est un, et tenir est un autre.

Sans y penser j'ai vingt vers ajustés,
Et la besogne est plus d'à demi faite.
Cherchons-en treize de tous côtés,
Puis ma ballade est entière et parfaite.
Pour faire tant que l'ayez, toute nette,
Je suis en eau, tant que j'ai l'esprit lourd,
Et n'ai rien fait se par quelque bon tour
Je ne fabrique encore un vers en *ôtre;*
Car vous pourriez me dire à votre tour:
Promettre est un, et tenir est un autre.

Envoi

O vous, l'honneur de ce mortel séjour,
Ce n'est pas d'hui que ce proverbe court;
On ne l'a fait de mon temps ni du vôtre:
Trop bien savez qu'en language de cour
Promettre est un, et tenir est un autre.''

J. de la Fontaine, *Œuvres Complètes* (Paris, 1820), Vol. XIII, p. 215. Cf. also, Brander Matthews, *Recreations of an Anthologist* (New York, 1904), p. 35.

country, from the end of the fourteenth to the beginning of the sixteenth century, it attained incredible popularity. Eustache Deschamps (1320–1415), for example, alone wrote at least eleven hundred and seventy-five *ballades*.[3] Moreover, the *ballade* like the sonnet, its successor in favor, came to be written in more or less closely connected sequences.[4] With the importation into France in the sixteenth century of new ideas derived ultimately from the literature of classical antiquity, the vogue of the *ballade* grew less pronounced, so that we find it a matter of indifference, if not of positive contempt, to the members of the Pléiade.[5] French poets, however, unlike the English, never altogether discontinued the use of this lyric, although it was more or less sporadic in French literature until the nineteenth century.[6] Then Banville and his followers[7] cultivated the form once more; but the number composed by them is insignificant compared with the thousands of *ballades* written by the fifteenth century poets. In England, the *ballade* vanished with the generation after Chaucer, not to reappear there until the closing years of the century just past.

When once the poetic guilds of Northern France had prescribed a *ballade* like Cyrano's improvisation, the essential features of that form were no longer a matter of choice.

3 Marquis de Queux de Saint-Hilaire, *Œuvres Complètes de Eustache Deschamps, Société des Anciens Textes Français* (Paris, 1891), Vol. I, p. x.

4 See Chapter II, below.

5 Cf. Du Bellay's characterization of the *ballade*, cited in Chapter III, below.

6 Voiture, Sarrazin, Mme. Deshoulières, and La Fontaine wrote *ballades* in the first half of the seventeenth century. Cf. Chapter II, below.

7 Musset, Coppée, Rollinat, Verlaine, Tailhade, etc. Cf. Chapter V, below.

A poet who set out to write a *ballade* had to find a subject which could be treated in a kind of verse distinguished for its rigid and repetitious rime scheme. He deliberately limited his range of ideas by his decision to conform to elaborate restrictions. Technique was distinctly the poet's problem. The success of his *ballade* depended upon his ability to temper his inspiration to a type of poetry that had been definitely described. If we are charmed by the great *ballades* of Chaucer and of Villon, of Banville and of Swinburne, it is because these poets found in the *ballade* a form uniquely harmonious with certain ideas that they wished to express.

CONTENTS

THE BALLADE

CHAPTER I

ORIGINS OF THE BALLADE

Until the nineteenth century, the words *ballad* and *ballade* were used more or less interchangeably in English. The *New English Dictionary,* discussing the history of *balade, ballat, ballad, ballade,* and cognate forms, refers them to the late Latin *ballare* (to dance) and to the Provençal *balada.* In our current usage, both *ballad* and *ballade* are used consistently as technical terms; the first is usually applied to traditional narrative and lyric poetry, the second to the fixed verse form which is the subject of the present inquiry. The earliest example given in the *New English Dictionary* of the use of the word *balade* in English is in the Prologue to Chaucer's *Legend of Good Women* (1394), where it is employed to describe the three-stanza poem imitated from the French. The passage in question reads:

> "And after that they wenten in compas,
> Daunsinge aboute this flour an esy pas,
> And songen, as it were in carole-wyse,
> This balade, which that I shal yow devyse."[1]

Up to the end of the eighteenth century, the word, whether

[1] W. W. Skeat, *The Complete Works of Geoffrey Chaucer* (Oxford, 1894), Vol. III, p. 82: Prologue AG, ll. 199–202.

it be spelled *balade, ballat, ballad,* or *ballade,* is associated by English writers generally with song. In England, in the nineteenth century, poets who used the fixed French verse form have for the most part called their poems *ballades.* In Gleeson White's collection[2] that spelling is used. But a glance at the table of contents in a volume of Swinburne's poems will show that even at the present day *ballad* is used as a title for the short fixed verse form derived from the French.

The word *balade,*[3] then, appeared in England at the end of the fourteenth century, and was originally used to describe the imitation of the French lyric with fixed form. Chaucer, of course, is likely to have been familiar with the Italian word *ballata,* but since he was adapting the French art form he naturally took over the native term. *Balade* continued to be definitely associated with songs or with lyric poetry in England until the nineteenth century, when one variant, *ballade,* came to be generally connected with a specific kind of lyric poetry and another variant, *ballad,* with traditional narrative and lyric poetry.

In France, at the present time, the same word *ballade* serves for the English or Scottish popular ballad and for a certain kind of narrative poem, written in imitation of German authors like Uhland, as well as for the artificially fixed lyric poem. It is plain, however, that until the nineteenth century there was no necessity in France for pressing the word into service to distinguish any kind of verse but the three-stanza poem with fixed rime-scheme and refrain. The history of the word, therefore, involves the history of the form of poetry it designates, and throws some light on the origin of the form.

The *New English Dictionary,* as we have seen, derived

2 Gleeson White, *Ballades and Rondeaus* (London, 1887).

3 For further discussion of the use of *balade,* see Chapter IV.

the French word *balade*,[4] now naturalized in England in several forms, from the Provençal *balada*. The earliest known French use of the word *balade* is to be found in a poem of the *trouvère* Hubert Kaukesel, who flourished shortly after the middle of the thirteenth century, in the lines of the envoy:

> "A ma dame, *barade* presenter
> Te voil; di li par moi sans celer,
> Ke de sa cose empirier et grever
> *N'est ce pas cortoisie.*
> *Diex! ki a boine amor,*
> *S'il s'en repent nul jor,*
> *Il fait grant villonie.*"[5]

This form *barade* is curious. Paul Meyer has told us that the scribe wrote it as two words, *bara-de,* as though he were not clear in his own mind just what the term was. The question is, did he transcribe the original correctly, or did he mistake an "l" for an "r"?[6]

Another early example of the use of the word, the next in point of time, indeed, is supplied by a character in the *Jeu du Pèlerin,* composed shortly before 1300, in which Adan de la Hale is mentioned:

[4] The modern spelling in both English and French is with two l's. "*Balade*" is the usual spelling in the Middle Ages.

[5] P. Meyer, *Des Rapports de la Poésie des Trouvères avec celle des Troubadours* (*Romania,* 1890), p. 30.

[6] See P. Meyer, *Opus Cit.*, p. 31: *Barade,* as Meyer points out, may be a Gascon form. But since *MS fr. 844,* where the same piece occurs, is mutilated on fol. 155 just at the critical point in the envoy, we cannot be sure. Speaking of the poem from which the envoy is quoted, he says: "C'est bien en effet une ballade, qui toutefois a cinq couplets et non trois."

"... savoit canchons faire,
Partures et motés entés;
De che fist-il à grans plantés.
Et *balades,* je ne sai quantes."[7]

And at least one of Adan's *chansons* has every characteristic of the *ballade* before the envoy was added and the refrain reduced.[8]

In the *Dit de la Panthère,* written sometime between 1290 and 1328,[9] the author, Nicole de Margival, makes use of the terms *balade* and *baladele* to name three-stanza poems with common rimes and refrains. Two other illustrations of the early use of the word appear, one in the *Roman de Fauvel* (c. 1313), in the lines:

"Et tout autour i avoit pointes
Motez, chançons, *balades,* maintes";[10]

the other in the *Comte d' Anjou* (1316):

"Li auquant chantent pastourelles,
Li autre dient en vielles
Chançons royaus et estempies,
Danses, noctes et baleries,
. . . .
Lais d'amours, descors et *balades,*
Pour esbatre ces genz malades."[10]

Before the middle of the thirteenth century, a three-stanza poem with refrain and with common rimes was described in northern France as *ballete,* if we may rely on

[7] E. de Coussemaker, *Œuvres Complètes du Trouvère Adam de la Halle* (Paris, 1872), p. 418.

[8] See below.

[9] H. A. Todd, *Le Dit de la Panthère par Nicole de Margival* (Paris, 1883), p. xxvii.

[10] P. Meyer, *Opus Cit.,* p. 31.

the writer of *MS. Douce 308*. The opinion has been advanced that in this MS. *ballete* is a deliberate formation on the part of a scribe or of an author. The word seems to have been a compromise between *ballade,* of Provençal origin,[11] and the French *ballet,* a diminutive of *bal* meaning dance.[12]

Nothing is to be gained, in considering the origin of the *ballade,* by a study of the various theories advanced concerning the obscure beginnings of the Romance lyric. The *ballade* has no mark of a popular origin, if we except its name—borrowed probably from the Provençal *balada,* which was itself an artistic and not a folk dance song—and the refrain, which is associated with the procedure of choral song. It has been conjectured that a primitive Romance *ballade,*[13] a dance song in three stanzas, may have

11 G. Eckert, *Über die bei Altfranzösischen Dichtern Vorkommenden Bezeichnungen der Einzelnen Dichtungsarten* (Heidelberg, 1895), p. 15. Cf. E. Stengel, *Der Strophenausgang in den Ältesten Französischen Balladen und sein Verhältnis zum Refrain und Strophengrundstock, Zeitschrift für fr. Sprache u. Literatur,* XVIII, p. 86: "Dazu kommt nun noch dass die dritte Strophe eines der Lieder (Nr. 14) unserer Abteilung beginnt '*Balaide, sans demoreir Vai ou je t'envoie,*' also die sonst übliche Bezeichnung verwendet. Sollte die Form *ballete* daher etwa nur eine schlechte Schreibung für *balaide* sein?"

12 Examples of the use of *balader* are given in Godefroy, *Dictionnaire de l'Ancienne Langue Françoise* (Paris, 1902), Vol. I, p. 559.

13 E. Stengel, *Ableitung der Provenzalisch-französischen Dansa- und Virelay-Formen, Zeitschrift für Romanische Sprache und Literatur,* XVI, p. 100. Cf. L. Biadene, *La Leggenda dello Sclavo Dalmasino* (Bologna, 1894), p. 24, note: "Cosicchè anche senza estendere le ricerche parrà lecito conchiudere che lo schema XX-AAAX di versi alessandrini è uno degli schemi fondamentali, se pur non è lo schema fondamentale della Ballata italiana, anzi si dovrà forse dire, della Ballata romanza." Cf. also, F. Flamini, *Studi di Storia Letteraria Italiana e Straniera* (Livorno, 1895), pp. 148–149.

Analogues of the *ballade* are found in other Romance languages. Cf. A. Jeanroy, *Les Origines de la Poésie Lyrique en France au*

been the archetype from which the Provençal *balada* and *dansa,* and the French *ballete* and *ballade* sprang. The theory is that this primitive dance song[14] was probably composed of single lines of text alternating with a re-

Moyen Age (Paris, 1904), pp. 403–405: ''Cette forme de la ballette [cf. Bartsch, *Chréstomathie,* 546] a eu beaucoup de succès à l'étranger: les trois quarts des pièces portuguaises du recueil du Vatican, tant les chansons purement courtoises que les pièces semi-populaires, sont des ballettes assez librement traitées.

''C'est elle aussi qu'a employée la lyrique semi-populaire de l'Italie de la fin du xiiie au xve siecle: seulement le nombre des couplets n'est pas limité, le refrain ne correspond presque jamais exactement à la fin du couplet; il n'y correspond pas du moins par les rimes, dont une seule l'y rattache, et ce n'est que peu à peu qu'on s'astreignit à donner à ses vers la même dimension qu' aux derniers du couplet. La dénomination française elle-même a passé les Alpes. Ces pièces reçoivent souvent les noms de *ballata, ballatetta, ballatina, canzonetta ballatella* (Carducci, [*Cantilene e Ballate*] pp. 211, 213, 215, 219, 222, *et passim*). . . . En somme, ces pièces italiennes se relient, du moins par leur forme, aux ballettes françaises du xiie et xiiie siècles.''

Consult A. Jeanroy, *Opus Cit.,* pp. 432–433, for the *dansa* in Italy, Portugal, and Spain.

An early word on these relationships is spoken on p. vi of the Introduction in K. Bartsch, *Denkmäler der Provenzalischen Litteratur* (Stuttgart, 1856).

14 Cf. E. Stengel in G. Groeber, *Grundriss der Romanischen Philologie* (Strassburg, 1902), II Band, 1. Abteilung, p. 91: ''Die italienische *ballata,* welcher Dante (*De vulg. eloq.* II, 3) den Vorzug vor dem Sonett zuerkennt, zeigt zumeist denselben Bau, wie die analogen provenzalischen und altfranzösischen volkstümlichen Dichtungen. Doch zerfällt der erste, bedeutend entwickeltere Strophenteil zumeist in zwei gleichartige Absätze von je zwei, drei oder vier Zeilen. Darin ist offenbar eine Einwirkung der Canzonenstrophe zu erkennen. Die vorweg geschickte *Ripresa* wird bei den weiteren *Coblen* nicht wiederholt. Meist sind die *ballate* überhaupt nur einstrophig. Petrarca hat im ganzen sieben, Dante zehn (darunter aber drei unregelmässige) verfasst. . . . Auch in Spanien zeigen schon zwei Bettellieder des Erzpriesters von Hita genau denselben Bau: *aa ab BB* (Vgl. F. Wolf, *Studien,* S. 129 Anm.).''

frain. In course of time, the number of lines was, in all likelihood, increased, and one or more of them made to rime with the refrain. This process went on no doubt because verses that went hand in hand with the dance would naturally be adapted to the music. The repetition of a favorite tune would compel those supplying the words to furnish successive line groups necessarily alike in structure. The building up of a dance song may be thus described. To provide variety, the refrain was gradually introduced into the stanza itself. But at first, there were no rules governing either the form of the refrain or its place in the stanza; only the exigencies of the rime in any way affected its position. In the end, however, a fixed stanza was developed, a stanza of eight lines in which the first line was repeated three times and the second line twice:[15]

SOLISTE,	
puis CHŒUR:	"*Hareu! li maus d'amer* *M'ochist!*
SOLISTE:	Il me fait desirer,
CHŒUR:	*Hareu, li maus d'amer;*
SOLISTE:	Par un douch regarder Me prist.
CHŒUR:	*Hareu! li maus d'amer* *M'ochist.*"[16]

It can not be definitely said that the *ballade,* any more than several other verse forms, owes its origin to the archetypal dance song from which the stanza quoted above may have been evolved. But when we examine the development of the *balada* of Provence and the *ballete* of northern France, the evolution of a stanza like that employed in the early

15 A. Jeanroy in Petit de Julleville, *Histoire de la Langue et la Littérature Française* (Paris, 1896), Tome I, p. 360.

16 A. Jeanroy, *Les Origines de la Poésie Lyrique en France au Moyen Age* (Paris, 1904), p. 406.

ballades is reasonably accounted for by means of this hypothesis of Jeanroy.

In Provençal, the *balada* and the *dansa,* in all probability analogues of the *ballade,* must be taken into consideration. Bartsch says: "Both consisted, generally speaking, of three stanzas preceded by a verse unit which was repeated in the manner of a refrain at the end of every stanza."[17]

At least seven Provençal lyrics, all anonymous, are given the designation *balada* in the manuscripts.[18] The fact that the word *balade* appears to be derived from the Provençal *balada* does not imply that there is any direct connection between the lyric of the south, the surviving examples of which show only slight resemblances to one another, and the fixed form developed in northern France, with its three stanzas, persistent rime-scheme, and refrain. An examination of the *balada* furnishes conclusive proof that in Provence

[17] K. Bartsch, *Grundriss zur Geschichte der Provenzalischen Literatur* (Elberfeldt, 1872), p. 35. But cf. E. Stengel, *Ableitung der Provinzalisch-Französischen Dansa- und der Französischen Virelay-Formen, Zeitschrift für Französische Sprache und Literature,* XVI, p. 97: "keinen zweifel darüber dass die *Dansa* als eine Abart der *Ballada* anzusehen ist und zwar der Hauptsache nach jüngeres Gepräge und gekünsteltere Formen als diese aufweist. Nur in einem Punkte, darin nämlich, dass sie die Angleichung des Strophenabschlusses an den Strophenanfang unterlässt, stellt sie sich als Abkömmling gerade der ältesten Balladenform dar."

[18] K. Bartsch, *Die Provenzalische Liederhandschrift Q, Zeitschrift für Romanische Philologie,* IV, p. 503. The following list gives the location of certain examples of the *balada in the manuscripts: Codex Riccardi 2909, fol.* 46, "Qvant escaualcai l'autrer"; *fol* 5a, "Morte man li semblan q ma donam"; *fol.* 5f, "Damor mestera ben e gent"; *fol.* 6d, "Qvant gilos er fora bels ami"; *Bibliothèque Nationale Ms. fr. 20050, fol.* 79, "A l'entrada del tems clar"; *Ms. Vatican, 3206, fol.* 105a, "Pres soi ses faillencha." *Codex Riccardi 2909* and *Ms. Vatican 3206* are of the fourteenth century; *Ms. fr. 20050* is of the thirteenth century.

the term was in general used to describe almost any kind of artistic dance song, irrespective of form, and was not applied to any one variety.

The most primitive form of the *balada* is thought to be represented by "Mort m'an li semblan."[19]

It is a three-stanza poem, riming A A a a a a,[20] in which the two-line refrain should, according to Bartsch, be repeated after the first and second lines of each stanza. The most primitive feature is the recurrence of the same rime throughout. The best known *balada* is the one which begins "A l'entrada del tens clar."[21] This spring song, refrain apart, exhibits very little that is characteristic of the *ballade* stanza, though the refrain was at first perhaps of two lines only. According to Stengel, the *ballade* stanza was first plainly indicated in "D'amor m'estera,"[22] a poem whose rime-scheme is a a b B B, with the refrain repeated in part after the first line of all six stanzas. The fundamental popular *ballade* scheme may have been, according to the same authority, B B a a b B B. The second a-line would, under the influence of the opening of the stanza, be modified from a b-line, so that originally the form may have been B B a b b B B, from which it would appear that the stanza was composed of what the Germans call a stanza nucleus (*Strophengrundstock*), *a*, and a stanza conclusion (*Strophenausgang*), *b*, which was built on the analogy of the refrain.[23]

19 C. Bartsch, *Chréstomathie Provençale* (Elberfeldt, 1880), 243.

20 In the indications of rime schemes, capitals are used to designate the rimes of the refrain.

21 V. Crescini, *Manualetto Provenzale* (Verona-Padua, 1905), p. 243.

22 K. Bartsch, *Chréstomathie Provençale* (Elberfeld, 1880), 245.

23 E. Stengel in G. Groeber's *Grundriss der Romanischen Philologie*, II, 1, p. 89; Stengel, discussing the *balada*, further analyzes the structure of "Quant lo gilos" and "Coindeta sui" (*B. Chr.* 245–6): "Ebenso verhält es sich bei der weit volkstümlicheren 5-strophigen Ballade *Coindeta sui* (*B. Chr.*[4] 245–6) mit dem Strophenschema:

But there are two views of the development of the *ballette* stanza, Jeanroy's and Stengel's. Jeanroy, though he believes in the existence of Romance lyrics, sets up no archetypal *ballade* as progenitor alike of *balade* and *ballette*. His theory is that the *ballette* stanza borrowed its sophisticated form from the *chanson savante* and added thereto a refrain which was joined to the body of the stanza by means of another line riming with a single line of the refrain or

a a a b und Refrain *B B*. Die Wiederholung der ersten Refrainzeile nach der ersten Zeile jeder Strophe halte ich auch hier für sekundär. Die Strophenform wird hier ursprünglich *B B*]*a a b b B B* gelautet haben. Charakteristisch für die späteren Balladen der Provenzalen wie Italiener, und auch für die ihnen entsprechenden altfranzösischen *baletes,* ist eben die konstante Gewohnheit den Strophenabschluss an den Strophengrundstock derart anzugleichen, dass der Anfang des ersteren mit dem Schluss des letzteren in Übereinstimmung gebracht wird. Jeanroy, der die Balladenform überhaupt nicht scharf genug von der des Rondel u. Virelai sondert, hat diesen Sachverhalt verkannt. Er spricht (S. 402) von einer Verlängerung der Strophe '*d'un vers ayant la même rime que le refrain tout entier ou que l'un de ses vers.*' Dass meine Auffassung die richtige ist, ergibt schon der analoge Bau der italienschen Balladen, ergibt aber auch die volkstümliche 3-Strophische Ballade *Quant lo gilos* (B. *Gr.* 461, 201, gedr. Zs. IV., 503), deren Schema lautet a_6 a_6 a_6 b_3 b_5 + Refrain B_{10} B_5. Scheinbar lässt sich hier die Abweichung des Strophenabschlusses vom Refrain befriedigend nur auf Jeanroy'sche Weise erklären, die zweite B-Zeile wäre einfach angefügt, wegen B_5 des Refrains. (Sonderbar genug fasst Jeanroy aber dies Schema ganz anders auf, nämlich als a_6 a_6 a_6 b_8 B_{10} B_5 und will, indem er auf die Wiederholung der ersten Refrainzeile nach der ersten und zweiten Zeile jeder Strophe Wert legt, dieses wie die beiden letztgenannten Gedichte, als frei behandelte Rondels auffassen, obwohl gerade diese drei sich im Texte ausdrücklich selbst also Balladen bezeichnen; Vgl. Abschn. 202, 203). Aber wie wäre dann die erste b-Zeile zu erklären? Das Rätsel löst sich, wenn wir sie mit der dritten á-Zeile zu einen 10-Silbner mit schwachem archaischen Reihenschluss kombinieren. Durch Binnenreim wurde dieser zerlegt um so die erforderliche Angleichung des Strophenabschlusses an den Strophengrundstock nich nur hinsichtlich des

with the whole refrain. He believes that the number of syllables in the line that joined the refrain with the rest of the stanza was not necessarily altered to conform to the number in the refrain. On the contrary, the connection

Reimes, sondern auch hinsichtlich der Versart zu ermöglichen. a_6 a_6 b_3 b_5 B_{10} B_5 ist also abgeändert aus a_6 a_6 b_{10} b_5 B_{10} B_5. Der Text der ersten Strophe mag das veranschaulichen:

''Ballada cointa e gaia
Faz cui pes ne cui plaia
Pel doez cant qui m'apaia;| Queus audi
Seir e de mati.
Quant lo gilos er fora, bels ami,
Venes vos a mi.''

Jeanroy's theory, in part challenged by Stengel, should be here given. It is found in *Les Origines,* pp. 397–402 *passim:* ''La forme la plus simple et la plus ancienne de toutes était composée de couplets que chantait un soliste et que suivait un refrain repris par le choeur . . . le couplet y est de trois, quatre ou cinq vers sur une même assonance, et ces différentes dimensions correspondent probablement à des époques différentes. Quand au refrain il a pu se composer à l'origine d'onomatopées ou de syllabes imitant le son d'un instrument de musique . . . Mais on eut de bonne heure, l'idée de rattacher le refrain au couplet par la rime: pour cela on enleva au refrain son premier vers rimant avec le second, et on le fit rimer avec le couplet: le chœur était ainsi averti du moment où son rôle allait commencer. (a a a b B) . . . Un perfectionnement de cette forme consiste à couper le refrain en deux parties qui riment respectivement avec les premiers et le dernier vers du couplet (a a a b A B) . . . Mais dans le chanson à danser proprement dite, il n'en est point comme dans la strophe dont il vient d'être question: le refrain y subsiste toujours, et n'est jamais remplacé par deux vers ordinaires. Sa forme la plus habituelle était donc un couplet monorime suivi d'un refrain qui y était rattaché d'une façon quelconque. . . . Elle [la ballette] ne s'en tint pas non plus aux strophes monorimes, qui parurent sans doubt monotones: elle emprunta aux chanson leur formes savantes, et fit suivre les couplets d'un refrain qu'elle y rattacha ordinairement en allongeant ceux-ci d'un vers ayant la même rime que le refrain tout entier ou que l'un de ses vers.''

between the stanza and the refrain was often made in an exceedingly loose way. Stengel, on the other hand, postulates the archetypal *ballade,* which he describes as a three-stanza form in which the stanzas show plainly the threefold division of stanza nucleus, stanza conclusion, and refrain. He holds, moreover, that in the *ballade* stanza, that is, the stanza of the *balade* or *ballete,* there was a sharp separation alike between the stanza nucleus (*Strophengrundstock*) and the end of the stanza (*Strophenabschluss*). Originally, he believes, the end of the stanza corresponded exactly to the refrain, but was, in the majority of cases, made similar to the stanza nucleus. Then the stanza nucleus was itself divided into two parts, each of which at first consisted of one line. As these lines became longer, the tendency was for them to break into shorter lines, and thus the two halves of the stanza nucleus became longer. In the same way the number of lines in the end of the stanza (*Strophenausgang*) and in the refrain multiplied. Briefly, where Jeanroy sees a deliberate attempt to connect an isolated refrain, sung originally by a chorus, with a line or with several lines, sung by soloists, Stengel recognizes a stanza nucleus and a stanza conclusion, the latter corresponding in form with the refrain and tending to become less like the refrain and more like the stanza nucleus.[24]

[24] E. Stengel, *Der Strophenausgang in den Ältesten Französischen Balladen und sein Verhältniss zum Refrain und Strophengrundstock,* in *Zeitschrift für Französische Sprache u. Litteratur,* XVIII, p. 113. See this article *passim* for evidence with which Stengel supports his theory. Ph. Aug. Becker, in a review of F. Noack's *Der Strophenausgang,* etc., in *Litteraturblatt für Germanische u. Romanische Philologie* (1902), p. 143, summarizing the theories of Stengel and of Noack, who follows him, writes: "Diese Eigenart der Ballette, die auch den Reigen der anderen romanischen Nationen nicht fremd gewesen zu sein scheint, begreift sich leicht aus dem Umstand das der Chor auf dem Sologesang mit einem Rundtanz antwortete, wobei

The date of the various specimens of the *balada*, in connection with which the subject of the general *ballade* stanza has been examined, cannot definitely be assigned; their form and language point to the end of the twelfth and the beginning of the thirteenth century. As to the *dansa*, another Provençal form of three stanzas connected with the *ballade*, examples are given in *Las Joyas del Gay Saber*.[25] They had been presented at the Poets' Court at Toulouse from 1451–1471. In every stanza there is a group of lines that do not rime with the refrain and a group of lines that do. In the collection there are only two specimens where the last line of the refrain is repeated at the close of each stanza and of the *tornada*. One of these is as follows:

Dansa d'Amors am Refranh

"Neyt et jorn, dins en la pessa
Ne m puesc tenir d'alegrar,

er den Schlusstheil der vorgesungenen Melodie wiederholte; sein Refrain musste demgemäss mit dem Strophenausgang in der Länge und Disposition der Verszeilen genau übereinstimmen. Der Reim hingegen hatte im Grunde nun mnemonischen Wert; eine teilweise Aufgabe der Gleichheit war also von geringerem Belang, so lange sie das Reimgeschlecht nicht berührte; *ein* Gleichklang reichte am Ende aus. Die Aenderung der Versform bedeutet hingegen den Verzicht auf die gleiche Melodie und lässt sicher auf einer Verliterarisierung des Tanzliedes schliessen.''

25 The rules for the *dansa* given in the *Leys d'Amors* (1356) are: ''La danse est un ditié gracieux qui contient un refrain, c'est à dire un répons, seulement, et trois couplets semblables à la fin, pour la mesure comme pour les rimes, au répons; et la *tornada* doit être pareille au répons; et le commencement de chaque couplet doit être de même mesure, et au choix, sur les mêmes rimes ou sur des rimes différentes; mais ces rimes doivent être entièrement différentes de celles du répons. . . . Le répons doit être de la mesure d'un demi-couplet, à deux vers près en plus ou en moins. Les vers de la danse ne doivent pas dépasser huit syllabes.'' [Translation from Provençal found in P. Meyer, *Les Derniers Troubadours de la Provence* (Paris, 1871), p. 114.]

Quant my sove la noblessa
De la Flor que m fay pensar.
En mon joven me comensa
Amors de far mortalz jocs;
Tant m'art he 'mflama sos focs,
Que n passi greu penedensa,
Dolor mortal e destressa,
Et no puesc alz cossirar,
Sino que la gentilessa
De la Flor que m fay pensar.

Helas! no m puese ben deffendre
Que ne senta la dolor
Que passi per fin' amor,
Don cuda lo mieu cor fendre,
Dolens et plens de tristessa,
Qui no cessa de plorar,
Per tal sos volers aguessa
De la Flor que m fay pensar.

Prec humilment, test' enclina,
Eysausisqua men desir,
Car, ne y a plus medecina
Per me far tost engausir;
No's creatura que sabessa
Autra milhor cogitar,
Que surmontes la princessa
De la Flor que m fay pensar.

Tornada

Ma blancha Flors e mestressa,
Sus trastot quan es ses par,
Datz me l secors e l'endressa
De la Flors que m fay pensar."[26]

[26] A. F. Gatien-Arnoult, *Monumens de la Littérature Romane* (Paris-Toulouse, 1841–1849), Vol. IV, *Las Flors del Gay Saber,* p. 214.

Other specimens of the *dansa* show, in those parts of the poem where the refrain would come in the *ballade* stanza, end-words with the same rime, but no recurring burden, as may be seen, for example, in the *Dansa de Nostra Dona*.[27] Other examples of the *dansa* might be cited to establish its place in the ballade family.

The Old French analogue of the *balade*, as we have said, was the *ballette*. At least one hundred and eight of these *ballettes*, so-called, are contained in a single manuscript, which is, as a matter of fact, the only place where the word has been discovered.[28] The surviving *ballettes*, like the surviving examples of the *balada*, are not, in reality, popular poetry. Alfred Jeanroy,[29] generously answering some inquiries of mine, wrote me, under the date of 23 July, 1910: "I have not found any *ballades* earlier than those generally known, but I have tried to show that the refrains interpolated in certain *chansons*, *pastourelles* and elsewhere belonged originally to *chansons à danser* or *ballettes*. . . . I am firmly persuaded that the *ballettes* (those in the Oxford Ms. and the others, too) were sung; that they were sung is proved by those texts in which the refrains (these refrains being fragments of *ballettes*) seem to regulate the dance as in *Guillaume de Dôle*, for example."

The fragments of dance songs that are left are not older than the thirteenth century. They are to be found in the *romans aristocratiques*, like *Guillaume de Dôle* or *La Violette*, that describe seigneurial celebrations, or in *chansons*, *motets*, and *pastourelles*, upon which these fragments are grafted in the manner of refrains. While the dance

27 A. F. Gatien-Arnoult, *Opus. Cit.*, Vol. IV, pp. 205–207.

28 Bodleian *Ms. Douce 308.*

29 I was enabled to correspond with M. Jeanroy through the kind offices of M. Joseph Bédier, who was visiting New York in the spring of 1910.

songs of the thirteenth century reflect the manner of the old popular dance songs of the peasants, it is certainly true that in the form in which we know them, the form given them by courtly poets, the form that was made to accompany the dance in the halls of great nobles, they were aristocratic and not popular.[30] The repetition of a refrain in these popular Old French dance songs was suggested, of course, by the repetition of identical movements in the dances they accompanied. In the extant refrains, recognized as fragments of an older, though only rarely of a folk poetry, the allusions to the dance are innumerable.[31] The oldest text to contain such refrains is *Guillaume de Dôle*, written between 1210 and 1215.[32] This *roman* is interspersed with lyric fragments.[33] Similar lyric fragments came to serve as refrains in the *ballettes*.

The French analogue of the *balada* is, as noted, the *bal-*

[30] Joseph Bédier, *Les Plus Anciennes Danses Françaises, Revue de Deux Mondes*, January 15, 1906, p. 424. Cf. also Jeanroy, *Les Origines*, p. 113: "Nos refrains ne sont que de fragments, mais ils jouaient dans les morceaux auxquels ils appartenaient, le rôle de nos refrains actuels, et ils y étaient répété (à l'origine probablement par ce chœur répondant au soliste). C'est ce qui explique qu'ils se soient imprimés plus profondément dans la mémoire, et qu'ils aient seuls survécu."

[31] See Jeanroy, *Les Origines*, pp. 394–396.

[32] Godefroy, *Dictionnaire de L'Ancienne Langue Française* (Paris, 1898), Vol. 1, p. 559, quotes under *Bal:*

Souz un chastel q'en apele Biaucler
En mont poi d'eure i ot granz bauz levez:
Cez damoiseles i vont por caroler,
Cil escuier i vont por bohorder,
Cil chevalier i vont por esgarder.
(*G. de Dôle*, Vat. Chr., 725, f. 89.)

[33] Jeanroy, *Les Origines*, pp. 115–116.

lette.[34] In the *ballette* are embedded, as we have just said, some of the older refrains. In the course of the development of the *ballette,* we find the stanza progressing from one rime to several, whether the method be that described by Stengel or Jeanroy; we observe, too, a strong tendency to reduce the number of stanzas to three. The *ballettes* of

[34] P. Meyer, *Documents Manuscrits de l'Ancienne Littérature de la France Conservés dans les Bibliothèques de la Grande-Bretagne* (Paris, 1871), pp. 150–154 *passim:*

''Le manuscrit, Douce 308 est un volume in-folio de 297 feuillets, écrit par diverses mains, et à ce qu'il semble, vers le second quart du XIVe siècle. La première partie du moins, qui contient les *Vœux du Paon,* ne saurait être antérieure à 1312. Il a dû être exécuté en Lorraine, car il offre d'un façon, passablement marquée les caractères du dialecte, de cette province. . . . Ce qui donne la plus grande importance au manuscrit Douce 308, c'est le recueil de poésies lyriques qui s'y trouve compris. . . . Le manuscrit Douce est le seul qui ait adopté le classment par genres. . . . ce qui est intéressant c'est l'idée du classement et non son exécution. Cette idée est celle d'un homme curieux et exact, ayant déjà le sentiment de la critique. Que cet homme soit le scribe qui a exécuté le manuscrit ou un autre, c'est ce que nous ne pouvous guère savoir; mais il y a apparence que l'auteur d'un tel classement vivait plutôt au XIVe siècle qu'au XIIIe, et cette présomption se change en certitude s'il est vrai que l'une des pièces du recueil n'est pas antérieure à 1320.

''Une autre remarque qui a son importance est que ce recueil a été fait dans une intention purement littéraire, pour être lu et non pour être chanté. De tous les chansonniers français il est, je crois, le seul qui ne soit pas noté. En cela il ressemble aux chansonniers provençaux, qui à une exception près, sont également depourvus de notation musicale.''

Cf. also R. A. Meyer, *Französische Lieder aus der Florentiner Handschrift, Beihefte zur Zeitschrift für Romanische Philologie,* 8 Heft (Halle, 1907), p. 37: ''E. Stengel hat . . . nachgewiesen, dass die Bezeichnung ''Ballette'' auf recht schwachen Füssen steht, indem die Wortform ''ballette'' nur einmal in der HS Douce 308 vorkommt. Daneben ist einmal in derselben HS. die Form ''balaide'' belegt, . . . Es ist mehr als zweifelhaft ob die Form ''ballette'' ein altfranzösisches Wort ist.''

the *Douce* MS. appear to belong to about the middle of the thirteenth century, although at least one of the *ballettes* may be as late as 1320. In these poems it is certain that the refrain was repeated at the end of every stanza, though the manuscripts rarely show this repetition because scribes were most economical with their parchment. The manuscripts that contain *ballettes* ordinarily place the refrain at the head of the piece (doubtless it was in reality sung and taken up in chorus at the beginning); then the refrain is sometimes repeated, often entire, at the end of the last stanza; and the first few words of the refrain are occasionally given at the end of the first and second stanzas. The place of the refrain is plainly indicated, however, by the fact that the last line of every stanza has a rime corresponding with the refrain rime.[35]

What appears to be one of the earliest *ballettes*, in point of form, is reprinted below.

> "Amors ne se donne mais elle se uant. il nest nuns ki soit ameis si nait argent.
>
> I Cil est. .I. uiellars pansus. tezis deuant. et kil ait estei truans tot son uiuant. cil ait aikes a doner on i antant. et lautre lait on aler qui point ni tant.
>
> II Ceu puet on moult bien prouer certainne|| ment. Car il nest nuns ki tant ainme loialment. cil nait pooir de doneir ki puist niant. an amor monteplier de son talant.

[35] Jeanroy, *Les Origines*, p. 402, Cf. E. Stengel *Die Refrains der Oxforder Ballettes, Ztschr. für Fr. Spr. und Lit.*, XXVIII, p. 72: "Dass die Voranstellung des Refrains nichts besonderes zu besagen hat, zeigen Doppeltexte [in the *Douce MS.*] wie 11 (= 115), 15 (= 117), wo derselbe Refrain ein Mal nur am Strophenschluss, ein Mal nur im Eingang geschrieben ist."

III Leaulteis est tote morte simplement. an feme son
li aporte elle lou prant. Qui nait riens noist a la porte
a uuelz lou uant. en si desoiuent les femes bone gent."[36]

The stanza form of this *ballette* is similar to that of a *chanson pieuse* in *MS. fr. 12483,* "Pour s'amour ai en douleur lonc temps esté." Both the *ballette* and the *chanson pieuse* probably had the same model.[37]

The refrains of the *ballettes* in the Oxford manuscript have been grouped in six classes by Stengel.[38] In the first class, he places those refrains that occur at the end of the stanzas and not at the beginning of the whole poem. The idea seems to be that a refrain like this is more intimately connected with the sense of each stanza. In the second group of refrains, he places those that have no connection with the stanzas in sense, but are expressions of the lover's emotion. The third class is much like the second in containing a variety of refrains that are nothing more than terms of endearment. The fourth class, too, includes the lover's exclamations, rhetorical questions, or a statement of his desires. In the fifth class, Stengel includes refrains that are also common maxims. And in the sixth group, he places utterances of girls and of women.

Other *ballettes* which belong to the last half of the twelfth century, and are therefore older than those of the *Douce MS.* are contained in a Florentine manuscript.[39] Here are

[36] George Steffens, *Die Altfranzösische Liederhandschrift der Bodleiana in Oxford, Douce 308,* Herrig's *Archiv für das Studium der Neueren Sprachen* (Braunschweig, 1897), Vol. 99, p. 343.

[37] A. Jeanroy, *Les Chansons pieuses du MS. fr. 12483 de la Bibliothèque Nationale, Mélanges Wilmotte* (Paris, 1910), p. 255. Other *chansons* in this collection exhibit an early form of the *ballette* stanza. See pp. 261, 265.

[38] G. Steffens, *Opus Cit.,* pp. 339, 340, 342, 343, 372, 377.

[39] R. A. Meyer, *Französische Lieder aus der Florentiner Handschrift Strozzi-Magliabecchiana cl. vii, 1040* (Halle, 1907), p. 37.

found specimens of the two types of songs with refrain, the kind in which the close of the stanza is structurally connected with the refrain, and the kind in which the refrain appears to be independent of any part of the stanza. R. A. Meyer, the latest editor of the manuscript, believes that the structure of early Latin hymns is responsible for the Romance songs with refrain, and his answer to Stengel's theory is that the similarity between the close of the stanza and the refrain, far from betokening a development earlier than the stanza where the refrain is structurally independent, really may indicate a more primitive state of things. He presents for examination hymns where similarity between the close of the stanza and the refrain is obviously not obligatory.

As an example of what may have led to the stanza of the *ballette,* Meyer cites the following hymn:

1. "Veris ad imperia
Renascuntur omnia,
Amoris prooemia
Corda premunt saucia
Quaerula melodia
    Gratia praevia,
    Corda marcentia
    Media.
Vitae vernat flos
Intra nos.

2. Suspirat luscinia,
Nostra sibi conscia
Impetrent suspiria,
Quod sequatur venia,
Dirige, vitae via,
    Gratia praevia,
    Viae dispendia
    Gravia.

Vitae vernat flos
Intra nos."[40]

Of the two *ballettes* quoted immediately below from the Florentine manuscript, the first, according to Meyer, shows a stanza conclusion harmonizing with the refrain, whereas the second shows that the end of the stanza has been assimilated to the stanza nucleus.

"*De quant bone ore fu nés*
chi s'amie tient au pré
en l'erba giolie!

I.

'Or ma trés douse amie,
dieus vous dont le bon giort;

[40] G. M. Dreves and C. Blume, *Analecta Hymnica Medii Ævi* (Leipzig, 1886 ff), XXI, No. 40. Cf. R. A. Meyer, *Französische Lieder aus der Florentiner Handschrift Strozzi-Magliabecchiana cl. vii, 1040* (Halle, 1907), pp. 35–36: "Wir haben jedenfalls den Refrain als ein der römischen Kunstpoesie unbekanntes Stilmittel zu bezeichnen. Ob der Refrain in der römischen Volkspoesie vorhanden war, darüber wissen wir nichts. Wenn wir nun nachweisen können, dass die Formen der Refraingedichte, wie sie uns in französischer Sprache zuerst am 1200 (Guillaume de Dôle) überliefert werden, mit älter überlieferten Formen der lateinischen Kirchenpoesie in allerengste Verbindung stehen, wie ja eine absolute Zusammengehörigkeit der Melodieen die über diesen französischen und lateinischen Texten stehen, nicht geleugnet wird, wenn wir ferner glauben dürfen, nachweisen zu können, dass die erwähnten lateinischen Gedichte ihre Formen nicht von hypothetischen 'urromanischen Refraingedichten' sondern aus anderer Quelle erhalten haben, so wird sich die Theorie, welche die Formen der seit 1200 überlieferten Refraingedichte auf eine urromanische Grundlage zurückführt, als anfechtbar erweisen. Dabei bleibt natürlich unbestreitbar, dass in früherer Zeit vielleicht einmal französische volkstümliche Gedichte existiert haben, die formal mit vulgärlateinischen Liedern in Zusammenhang standen, doch wir wissen nichts von solchen Gedichten."

vos estes aviséa,
se n'amaris o non?'
'Nani voyr, mon dous amis,
le parti en est tout pris:
ne vos amerai mie.'
De quant bone ore fu nés
chi s'amie tient au pré
en l'erba giolie!

II.

'Or ma trés douse amie,
era a dieu vos chomant,
ge vos ai . . . servie
e amé mot lielmant.'
'Il est voir, mon dous amis,
Vos etes gay e giolis,
e ge sui plus jolie.'
De quant bone ore fu nés
chi s'amie tient au pré
en l'erba giolie!

III.

Quant ge le vi . . .
sur son cival monter,
e sendre s'espeia,
ses gans glans enformer:
En sospirant ge li dis:
'revenés, mon dous amis,
ge serai vostre amie.'
De quant bone ore fu nés
chi s'amie tient au pré
en l'erba giolie!"[41]

"*Per ont m'en iroye,*
ma douse dame,
se aler m'en voldroie?

[41] R. A. Meyer, *Opus Cit.*, p. 42, No. V

I.

Se je m'en voy par les cians,
les ciardons i sont trop grans:
Je me ponheroie,
ma douse dame,
se aler m'en voldroye!

II.

Si je m'en voy par les boys,
les boysons i sont estroys:
Je me mangeroye,
ma douse dame,
se aler m'en voldroye!

III.

Se je m'en voy par le pré
mes ciauses sont semelés:
Je me banheroye,
ma douse dame,
s'aler m'en voldroie!"[42]

Meyer's theory that the *ballette* stanza shows in its structure the influence of the Latin hymn may or may not be true. This influence would not affect the hypothesis of an archetypal dance song which led to the *balada,* the *dansa,* the *ballette,* and the *ballade.* Nor would it invalidate the supposition that some of the refrains found in *ballettes* may be descended from those of popular poetry. Whether the *ballade* developed directly from such *ballettes* as those first discussed, or whether it is merely a parallel growth, cannot be exactly determined. The present writer believes that the evidence is in favor of the direct descent of the *ballade* from the *ballette.* As will be presently observed, the earliest *ballades* were three-stanza poems with a common

[42] R. A. Meyer, *Opus Cit.,* p. 48, No. V.

rime-scheme throughout and a refrain. The first *ballades* have no envoy. The *ballettes,* it is to be remembered, show a marked tendency to three stanzas; they also show a uniform rime-scheme throughout and a refrain. There seems every reason to believe that the *ballade* took its three stanzas and refrain from the *ballette.* The *ballettes* are not, however, the only poems written in the thirteenth century that show a uniform rime-scheme throughout. Consider the *chanson pieuse,* attributed to Guillaume le Vinier,[43] for which no model among the profane lyrics has yet been found:[44]

I. " Vierge pucele roiaus,
Es cui li dous Jhesucris,
Li dous gloriëus joiaus
Fu conçeüs et nouris,
Bien fu vos cuers raemplis
De sa grase et de s'amour
A cel jour
Que Sains Esperis
I eut le fil Dieu assis.

II. Douce dame emperiaus,
Esmeree flour de lis,
Dous vergiers especiaus
Ou li sains fruis fu cueillis,
Souverains rosiers eslis,
Vous aportastes la flour
Et l'oudour
Par coi paradis
Nous fust ouvers et pramis.

[43] E. Ulrix, *Les Chansons Inédites de Guillaume le Vinier d'Arras, Mélanges Wilmotte* (Paris, 1910), p. 796.

[44] J. Bédier, *Un Feuillet Recémment Retrouvé d'un Chansonnier Français du xiiie Siècle, Mélanges Wilmotte* (Paris, 1910), p. 897.

III. Vous estes amours loiaus
Dont li mort cuer sont espris,
Li sourgons et li ruisiaus
Ki arouse le païs,
Li confors et li delis,
La fontaine de douçour
    Ou li plour
  Sont puisié et pris
Par coi pechié sont remis.

IV. Ha! sanctuaires trés haus,
Sor tous autres conjoïs,
Trés dous precïeus vaissiaus,
De toutes vertus garnis,
Sains tresors ou Dieu a mis
De virginité l'ounour,
    Tel valour,
  Dame, avés conquis,
Nule n'est vers vous en pris.

V. France dame naturaus,
Ki savés les desconfis,
Vers tous pechiés et tous maus,
Soiiés moi confors toudis,
Et qant mes cors ert faillis,
Proiiés vostre Creatour,
    Cui j'aour,
  K'aveuc ses amis
Mete n'ame en paradis.

VI. Cançon, rent grés et mercis
La nonper et la meillour,
    K'a cest tour
  M'a s'aïe apris
De li a faire aucuns dis."[45]

[45] E. Järnström, *Recueil de Chansons Pieuses du XIIIe Siècle* (Helsinki, 1910), Vol. I, p. 133. Cf. also the *Histoire Littéraire*, Vol. XXIII, p. 596: "... la ballade de Guillame le Vinier, composée de six couplets. Voici le quatrième, dont les trois derniers vers forment le refrain:

But we have to guard against reasoning in a circle. Indeed one *chanson pieuse,* that shows a refrain and two stanzas with the same rimes, is thought to have been composed to a *ballette* air.[46]

"De la mere Dieu chanterai
Et en chantant li prierai
Qu'ele me soit, quant je morrai,
Procheinne,
La douce pucelle de touz biens plainne.

S'ele m'est près, seürs serai,
Quant de cest siecle partirai,
Que je de m'ame a Dieu ferai
Estrainne
La douce pucelle de touz biens plainne.

III. Dame d'onneur et de valour
Et la mieudre de la meillour,
Fluns de pitié et de douçour
Fontainne;
La douce pucelle de touz biens plainne.

IV. Mieudre qu'on ne porroit penser,
Souviegne vos de nos tenser,
Quant vostre filz fera sonner
S'erainne,
La douce pucelle de touz biens plainne.

"Un tout seul basier
De cuer, à loisir,
Porroit mon vouloir
Grant piece accomplir;
Mais de desirrier
Me verrois morir,
Le plus n'en avoie.
Bone est la doulours
De quoi naist docours
Et soulas et joie."

[46] E. Järnström, *Opus Cit.*, p. 15.

V. Or te [illegible] oli damas,
Si ch[illegible] ceste dame as,
Que c[illegible] r ne te soit gas
N[illegible]
La do[illegible] de touz biens plainne."[47]

To another *tro*[illegible] ierekins de la Coupele, is attributed a five-stan[illegible] with refrain and identical rimes, one stanza of which is the following:

I. "A mon pooir ai serui
Ma dame et de volenté.
Dex doint, qu'il me soit merri,
Et qu'ele m'en sache gré.
Mis i a[i] tot [mon] aé
Cuer et cors (et) pensée ausi.
Se par li n'ai recouré
Santé, dont sai je de fi:
Ja de mes maus ne gar[i]rai.
Dex, que ferai, de l'amor n'ai
De la bele, ou mon cuer nis ai?"[48]

In the Modena manuscript of French *chansons,* the first forty-nine pieces of which were written before 1254, a poem (number 39 in the series), attributed to Moniot d'Arras, shows the same rimes in all stanzas:

[47] E. Järnström, *Opus Cit.*, p. 59. Jeanroy, reviewing Järnström's book in *Romania* for January, 1911, says of this poem (p. 84): "Le No. XX (R 664) a la même structure qu'une chanson à refrain, tout à fait dans la manière de Colin Muset (R. 144); il y a identité, non pas entre toutes les rimes, mais entres celles du refrain et du petit vers qui rattache celui-ci au couplet. Peut-être cette forme très simple et d'allure populaire, était-elle empruntée à une chanson antérieure, qui paraît perdue."

[48] F. Noack, *Der Strophenausgang in seinem Verhältnis zum Refrain u. Strophengrundstock in der Refrainhältigen Altfranzösischen Lyric, Ausgaben und Abhandlungen aus dem Gebiete der Romanischen Philologie* (Marburg, 1899), XCVIII, p. 127.

"Quant jo voi le dolc tans d'esté
Venir, che cantent roscenaus,
Adonc a Amors poesté
Plus seur bons che seur delloiaus;
Molt part ont cest(e) siecle amusé;
Nus ne se puet tenir a aus;
Dame, si vos gardez de çaus.

Tant a en vos sens et belté,
Por Deu, ne soiés comunaus
A tel gent com vos ai nomé;
Vostre ami(s) jetés de travaus;
Trop ai lonc tans cest fais porté
D'ensi vivre, que m'est noaus;
Si per vos mor, donc serai saus.

A ço pert que j'ai tant amé:
Dame, si jo fusse des faus
Je eüsse ma volenté,
Mais miels aem vivra con loiaus
E mel voil [vers] vos recovrer,
Por plus alegier de mes maus,
Che gehagner por estre baus."[49]

The earliest *ballades* were always three-stanza refrain poems with the same rime-scheme throughout, the latter feature being thus common to *chansons* other than the *ballette*. The many *ballades* attributed to Adan[50] de la Hale (1237–1287) have not survived. The *chansons* assigned to Adan by Guy include a poem which is like a *ballade* except that it has four stanzas. Its two-line refrain recalls, of course, the extended refrains in the *ballettes:*

"Li dous maus mi renouvèle,
Avoec le printans

[49] A. Jeanroy, *Les Chansons Françaises, Inédites du Manuscrit de Modène,* Supplement of *Revue des Langues Romanes* (1896), p. 254.

[50] The spelling now preferred.

Doi iou bien estre chantans,
Pour si jolie nouvêle
C'onques mais nus pour si bele,
Ne plus sage ne meillour,
Ne senti mal ne dolour
  Or est ensi
Que j'atenderai merchi."[51]

The earliest *ballades* are found, often with the music to which they were sung, in the *romans* of the late thirteenth and early fourteenth centuries and in the works of Jehannot de Lescurel. Such *romans* are the *Roman de Fauvel,*[52] the *Dit de la Panthère, La Prise Amoureuse, Le Romans de la Dame a la Lycorne et du Biau Chevalier au Lyon,* and *Li Regret Guillaume.*

Todd assigns the composition of the *Dit de la Panthère* to some time between 1290 and 1328. Two lyrics in Margival's work, one called in the text a *Baladele,* the other a *Balade,* are among the earliest *ballades.* In the *Baladele,* the monorimes are very primitive; and in the *Balade,* the stanza recalls the structure of a *ballette* stanza, as it is made up of five lines of seven syllables, followed by five lines of five syllables, the last of which is the refrain, the rime-scheme being a b a b b c c. The text of one of these poems will serve as an example:

" Anuis meslez a contraire
M'a si mué mon afaire

51 E. de Coussemaker, *Œuvres Complètes du Trouvère Adam de la Halle* (Paris, 1872), pp. 40–42.

52 Pierre Aubury, *Le Roman de Fauvel* (Paris, 1907). This is a photographic reproduction of *MS. fr. 146* of the *Bibliothèque Nationale.* The date of Bk. I is 1310, of Bk. II, 1314. (See R. Hess, *Der Roman de Fauvel, Romanische Forschungen,* XXVII, p. 295.) The *ballades* interpolated in the *Roman* in this particular MS. do not appear in the other MSS., and are, in all probability, by various authors.

Qu'il m'a fait longuement taire
De chanter et de chant faire.

Car la bele au dous viaire
Que j'aing defuit mon repaire;
N'est assez pour moy retraire
De chanter et de chant faire?

Bone amour, veilliez atraire
Tant que je puisse a li plaire,
Si arai bon examplaire
De chanter et de chant faire."[53]

Another of Margival's lyrics, called in the text simply *chançonete,* is in reality a *ballade* of the early type with irregular lines and a two-line refrain. A stanza will suffice to show the structure:

"Biautez, bontez, douce chiere,
Sens et avenans maniere,
Et grace m'ont si conquis
En monstrant dame de pris
Soudainement
Qu'a li servir me rent
Outreement."[54]

Le Roman de la Dame a la Lycorne et du Biau Chevalier au Lyon contains more *ballades.* This poem, too, dates from the end of the thirteenth or the beginning of the fourteenth century.[55] It contains fourteen *ballades,* one of them, however, a fragment. In the text the word *balade* is used

[53] H. A. Todd, *Le Dit de la Panthère d'Amours par Nicole de Margival* (Paris, 1883), p. 87.

[54] H. A. Todd, *Opus Cit.*, p. 84.

[55] F. Gennrich, *Le Romans de la Dame a La Lycorne et du Biau Chevalier au Lyon, Gesellschaft für Romanische Literatur* (Dresden, 1908), XVIII, p. 93.

three times;[56] the other *ballades* introduced are designated as *canchonnette, canchon,* and *chant.* Eleven of the *ballades* rime a b a b b c c, and vary in number of syllables to the line from seven to ten. The fragmentary *ballade* rimes a b a b b c c, and is made up of ten-syllable lines. Two other *ballades* are constructed differently. One rimes a a b a a b b a a a a, with a two-line refrain and seven-syllable lines; the other rimes a b a b c c d d, with a one-line refrain and ten-syllable lines. Two of the *ballades* have a two-line refrain. The *ballade* quoted below is the earliest example known to me of the distribution of the stanzas of a *ballade* between two speakers.[57] The first two stanzas here are spoken by the Chevalier au Lyon; the third is the Lady's answer.

"Quant sui seuls et a par moi,
Lors est toute ma pensee
En vous, dame, a qui j'ay
De fin coer m'amour donnee.
Seur toutes coses m'agree
Le grant bien de vous penser,
Quant a vus ne puis parler.

Onques femme tant n'amai,
Con vous ai tous jours amee;
Puis l'eure, que je vus ai
Premierement acointee,
Douce, plesant, savouree;
Ne fai que vous regreter,
Quant a vus ne puis parler.

Biaus sire, bien vous en croi
Et m'en tieng si apaÿe,
Que sachies en bonne foy,

[56] Lines 3712, 5163, 3770.
[57] Cf. p. 81 below.

M'amour vus aie otroïe
Que tant aves desiree.
Ce vous doit bien conforter,
Quant a vous ne puis parlër."[58]

In *La Prise Amoureuse*,[59] composed about 1332 by Jehan Acart de Hesdin, there are nine *ballades*.[60] The author of these poems, whether he be Jehan Acart or some other,

[58] F. Gennrich, *Opus Cit.*, ll. 3715–3728; ll. 3751–3757. Cf. Chapter II, below, on *ballade* in dialogue.

[59] Ernest Hoepffner, *Jehan Acart de Hesdin, La Prise Amoureuse, Gesellschaft für Romanische Literatur* (Dresden, 1910), XXII, p. xiv.

[60] E. Langlois, *Les Manuscrits du Roman de la Rose, Les Travaux et Mémoires de l'Université de Lille* (1910), pp. 110–116. There exists one MS. (Arras 897) in which these *ballades*, with one exception, do not appear in the text. It is probable that their absence is due to their suppression by the Arras copyist. Cf. G. Raynaud, *Hoepffner's La Prise Amoureuse, Romania* XL (1911), p. 130: "Langlois serait assez porté à croire que le MS. d'Arras (qui du reste est daté de 1370) represente quand même un ancient état de l'ouvrage et que les ballades et rondeaux, ajoutés après coup, ne sont pas l'œuvre de Jean Acart. Sauf vérification à faire sur le MS. nous pensons au contraire qu'il y a eu suppression de la part du copiste d'Arras, car, s'il est vrai que certaines de ces pièces adressées à la dame, et insérés dans le text de Paris ne s'y attachent pas étroitement, il est aisé à constater d'autre part que la moitié d'entre elles (huit exactement) sont annoncées par contexte; ce sont autant de corrections délicates que le copiste de Paris eût dû faire au texte primitif pour justifier l'hypothèse de M. Langlois. La présence d'ailleurs de poésies courtes, de rhythm différent, dans les poèmes de cette epoque est fréquente. Comment aussi expliquer autrement la ballade finale qu'a conservée le MS. d'Arras? Bien entendu l'examen de ce MS. donnera la vraie explication; mais que ce soit Jean Acart, comme nous le croyons, ou tout autre, l'auteur des rondeaux et ballades figurant dans la *Prise Amoureuse* ne joue pas moins, après la démonstration de Hoepffner, un rôle à part dans l'histoire de la poésie française au XIVe siècle, tenant encore des ses devanciers certains traits charactéristiques que répudient plus tard Machaut et ses disciples, et faisant dejà voir plusieurs tendances que ceux-ci adopteront."

serves as a link between the *trouvères,* who produced *ballettes* or *chançons* with certain features of the *ballades,* and the first prolific writers of the *ballade,* Machaut, Froissart, and Deschamps. These *ballades* of the *romans* and of Lescurel are all, in a sense, transitional types, but the *ballades* in *La Prise Amoureuse* are especially so. They differ from the later *ballades* in the proportionate frequency of the two-line refrain. There are two with the two-line refrain and seven with the one-line refrain, whereas in Machaut only ten *ballades* show the two-line refrain to two hundred and forty that have the one-line refrain, and in Froissart, where two have the longer refrain, thirty-eight have not. The percentage of *ballades* having two-line refrains is even smaller in the work of Deschamps. On the other hand, among the *ballettes* in the *Douce MS.* only four have the single-line refrain, and in the *Dit de la Panthère,* two of the *ballades* (not those so named) have a two-line refrain.

The seven-syllable line is most frequent in the *ballades* of the *Prise Amoureuse,* of the *Roman de Fauvel,* and in the poems of Lescurel. The eight-syllable line is next in point of frequency. In contrast, four-fifths of Machaut's *ballades* use the ten-syllable line, and it is equally popular with his school. The earliest *ballades,* like the Oxford *ballettes,* rarely introduce the ten-syllable line. The *ballades* in the *Prise Amoureuse* show great variety of line structure within the stanza, and in this particular range themselves with the older generation.

The *ballades* in the *Prise Amoureuse,* in the matter of the relation of the refrain to the stanza, also exhibit features of the earlier *ballette.* In the *ballades* of Deschamps, Machaut, and Froissart, the refrains are closely connected in syllable-count and rime with one or more lines of the stanza. Only three of the *ballades* (I, V, and IX) in the

Prise Amoureuse show this intimate connection of refrain and stanza; the other four have a refrain, which, while riming with some previous line in the strophe, shows a different syllable-count. The case is similar with the two *ballades* that have a two-line refrain. They rime with some previous line of the stanza, but only the first of the two lines resembles the other lines. One of the *ballades* attributed to Jehan Acart follows:

Balade I.

"Si plaisamment m'avés pris
Et espris,
Mes dous cuers, que li miens prise,
Qu'a vous me renc, et com pris
Ai compris
En ceste Amoureuse Prise,
Es dous biens qu'Amours m'envoie,
D'estre en voie,
Pour vostre amour desservir,
Flours du mond, a vous servir.

Donc ne doi estre repris,
S'ai empris
Voloir de si noble emprise,
Car ja pour venir a pris
Senc apris
Mon cuer de si douce aprise,
Que, se ja merci n'avoie,
Si s'avoie
Mes cuers, sanz ja messervir,
Flours du monde, a vous servir.

Gens corps ou rien n'a mespris,
Et pourpris
Ou toute honnours est pourprise,
Ancois que mors m'ait souspris
N'entrepris,

Par grace soiéz esprise,
Que vo pitiéz me pourvoie,
  Et si voie
Moi a ma vie asservir,
Flours du monde, a vous servir."[61]

The *ballades* of Jehannot de Lescurel, a little known poet of not later than the middle of the fourteenth century, are also of the early type.[62] Eleven *ballades* survive, one of which, given below, shows the two-line refrain and irregularity of line structure common to the earlier *ballades:*

"Belle, com loiaus amans,
Vostres sui: car soiez moie.
Je vous servirai touz tans,
N'autre amer je ne voudroie,
Ne ne puis; se le povoie,
N'i voudroie estre entendans.
Et pour ce, se Dex me voie,
Dame, bon gré vous saroie,
Se voustre bouche riant
Daignoit toucher à la moie.

Li dons est nobles et grans;
Ca, se par vou gré l'avoie,
Je seroie connoisanz
Que de vous amez seroie,
Et mieus vous en ameroie.
Pource, biaus cuers dous et frans,
Par si qu'aviser m'en doie,
Dame, bon gré vous saroie
Se vostre bouche riant
Daignoit toucher à la moie.

61 E. Hoepffner, *Opus Cit.*, p. 1.

62 He could not have lived later than the middle of the fourteenth century, because the MS. of his poems is of that period.

Vostre vis est si plaisans
Que jà ne me souleroie
D'estre à vo plaisir baisans
S'amez de vous me sentoie;
A mieus souhaidier faudroie.
Pour ce que soie sentant
Quelle est d'amer la grant joie,
Dame, bon gré vous saroie
Se vostre bouche riant
Daignoit toucher à la moie."[63]

In *Li Regret Guilaume Comte de Hainault,* written in 1339[64] by Jehan de le Mote, are thirty *ballades,* put into

[63] A. de Montaiglon, *Chansons Ballades et Rondeaux de Jehannot de Lescurel* (Paris, 1855), p. 29.

[64] A. Scheler, *Li Regret Guillaume Comte de Hainault par Jehan de Mote* (Louvain, 1882), p. viii. The rime schemes and line structure (the lines vary occasionally within the same *ballade*), of the thirty *ballades* is indicated below:

(1) a b a b b c c 10 syllables	(11) a a b b 8 syllables
(2) a b a b b c b c 8 syllables	(12) a b a b c c d d 10 syllables
(3) a b a b b c c 8 syllables	(13) a b a b b c c 8 syllables
(4) a b a b b c b c 10 syllables	(14) a b a b b c c 10 syllables
(5) a b a b b c c d c d 7 syllables	(15) a b b a c c d d 8 syllables
(6) a b a b b c c 10 syllables	(16) a b a b b c c 10 syllables
(7) a b a b b c b c 7 syllables	(17) a b a b b c c 8 syllables
(8) a b a b c c 10 syllables	(18) a b a b c b c 10 syllables
(9) a a a a a b b 10 syllables	(19) a b a b b c c b b 8 syllables
(10) a b a b b c c 8 syllables	(20) a b a b b c c 8 syllables

the mouths of as many abstract qualities, who are with one accord mourning the good count. All these *ballades* have a single-line refrain; five show seven-syllable lines; thirteen, eight-syllable lines; one, nine-syllable lines; and eleven use the ten-syllable line. Both the frequent use of the ten-syllable line, and the single-line refrain, show the author to belong decidedly to the generation of Machaut rather than of Margival. The *ballade* that follows, the first in the poem, is in all respects like many of Deschamps:

Cançon

"On ne poroit penser ne souhaidier
Plus grant tourment ne plus aspre dolour,
Qui s'est en mi venue hierbegier,
Jou qui soloie iestre dame d'onnour,
Car j'ai bien cause en mi d'avoir tristour,
Ne me faura jamais tant con je dure,
Puis c'ai pierdu le flour de douçour pure.

Car ceste flour a osté dou rosier
Pires que coers mesdisans plains d'errour,
Car mesdisans poet on bien apaisier,
Mès ne voi ci ne voie ne retour
Pour quoi joie aye, ainsçois arai gringnour
Painne, et c'est drois: d'autre cose n'ai cure,
Puis c'ai perdu le flour de douçour pure.

(21) a b a b b c c
8 syllables
(22) a b a b b c b c
8 syllables
(23) a b a b c c d d
7 syllables
(24) a b a b b c c
10 syllables
(25) a b a b c b c
7 syllables
(26) a b a b b c c
8 syllables
(27) a b a b b c b c
8 syllables
(28) a b a b b c c
10 syllables
(29) a b a b b c c
7 syllables
(30) a b a b b c c
9 syllables

Et non pour quant Nature voel pryer
Que le bouton qu'il laissa pour savoir
Sour l'oudourant grascieus englentier,
Voelle nourir en parfaite valour,
Que de par li raie aucunne douçour,
Car li espoirs de li me raseüre
Puis c'ai perdu le flour de douçour pure."[65]

In this "roman," *Li Regret Guillaume,* the *trouvère* hero, at the opening of the poem, is hastening to a *puy d'amour* in order to submit a "*cançon amoureuse.*"[66] It was, indeed, in these very *puys d'amour* and in the earlier religious *puys,* both poetic guilds of the thirteenth century and later, that the *ballade* of three stanzas with common rimes and a refrain came to be diversified and complicated in line structure and rime. In the *puys,* too, the envoy, which had hitherto been a feature of several kinds of *chansons,* became attached to and identified with the *ballade,* so that after the opening of the fourteenth century a *ballade,* whether composed in a *puy* or not, almost inevitably contained a conventional address to the "Prince" in the first line of the envoy. These same *puys* saw the development of the *serventois,*[67] of the *chant royal,*[68] and of other forms with envoy, as well as of the *ballade.*

[65] A. Scheler, *Opus Cit.,* p. 20.

[66] A. Scheler, *Opus Cit.,* p. 4:

"Singneur, jou qui ai fait ce livre
Dormoie une nuit à delivre
En mon lit ù couciés estoie.
En dormant melancholioie
A une cançon amoureuse,
Et par samblance grascieuse
Dis k'à .i. puis la porteroie
Pour couronner, se je pooie."

[67] See Appendix II.

[68] See Appendix III.

Since certain final stages in the evolution of the *ballade* were accomplished in the *puy,* it will be well to give some consideration to this institution. The history of the word *pui* or *puy* is uncertain. It has been derived from the Latin *podium* meaning "elevation," and in this sense has been supposed to refer to the platform on which the officials of the concourse sat.[69] Other critics have derived the word from the name of the town in Velay. Some of the supporters of this latter theory believe that pilgrims from every part of France spread the fame of the Virgin of Le Puy in Velay until religious societies named in her honor sprang up in northern France. Others, among whom is Paul Meyer, believe that a literary society actually existed in the town of Le Puy which was the model for similar societies in the North.[70] A third explanation, that offered by Guy, goes back to the more usual meaning of the Latin *podium,* namely, mountain. Guy recalls the allegory of Muses residing on a remote peak, and in commenting on the antiquity of the notion,[71] supposes that the term *puy,* sig-

69 See H. Guy, *Adan de la Hale* (Paris, 1898), p. xxxiv, and notes.

70 P. Meyer, *La Chanson de la Croisade contre les Albigeois,* (Paris, 1879), Vol. II, p. 39: "Quant à la cour du Puy, dont il est ici question, elle nous est connue principalement par deux témoignages qu'on a souvent rapprochés. L'un est emprunté à la vie du Moine de Montaudon; il y est dit que ce religieux, ayant obtenue de son abbé la permission de mener la vie mondaine, fut seigneur de la cour du Puy et conserva ce titre tant que cette cour dura. . . . L'autre témoignage est la soixante quatrième des *cento novelle antiche.* . . . En outre, quatre *approvatori* étaient institutés pour examiner les chansons qui leur étaient soumises, signalant les bonnes, et rendant les autres à leurs auteurs pour être corrigées. La célèbre chanson de Guiraut de Calanson (commencement du XIIIe siècle) sur le 'menor ters d'amors' fut selon Guiraut Riquier, qui l'a longuement commentée, presentée à la cour du Puy (Mahn *Werke d. Troub.* IV, 199)".

71 H. Guy, *Opus Cit.,* p. xxxiv, criticizes the derivation of *puy* from *podium* meaning a platform, on the ground that, in the first place,

nifying mountain, represented to religious and secular poets the heights to which they aspired to raise the subject which they were treating.[72] As early as 1051, there was authorized a *confrérie* of *jongleurs* at the Sainte-Trinité

podium is really unfamiliar in the sense of platform, and, in the second place, because the societies would hardly have been named from so unimportant an accessory. Paul Meyer's hypothesis he questions (p. xxxvi) on the ground that other early societies of similar nature probably existed. He thinks that the numerous literary societies could scarcely all have sprung from the one in the capital of Velay. "Il est vraisemblable," he writes, "que l'établissement des puys répondait à une tendance générale et presque instinctive de la société d'alors."

The origin of the institution as curiously viewed by Abbe de la Rue in his *Essais Historiques sur les Bardes, Les Jongleurs et les Trouvères Normands et Anglo-Normands* (*Caen*, 1834), p. 28, is as follows: "L'origine des Puys d'amour ne nous est pas connue, mais elle doit être très ancienne; elle pourrait bien être celtique, du moins on trouve ces jeux poétiques en usage au vi[e] siècle; le Barde Taliesin reconnait que son fils lui est supérieur en poésie, et que cette supériorité a été proclamée dans les jeux littérares établis pour juger et couronner les meilleures poésies; ces jeux subsistaient encore au xiie siècle dans le pays de Galles et même au xve. Les Bretons les avaient probablement importés de la Gaule, leur première patrie; les peuples de nos provinces du Nord avaient pu en maintenir l'usage ou tout au moins en conserver le souvenir; le souvenir des hommes subsiste longtemps, surtout quand il s'agit d'institutions agréables et utiles; dans ce dernier cas, les jeux poétiques auront été rétablis dans le Nord de la France, lors de la Formation du Roman Wallan."

[72] H. Guy, *Opus Cit.*, pp. xxxviii. In a review of Guy's *Adan de la Hale* in *Romania*, xxix (1900), p. 294, Jeanroy says: "Sur l'origine même et l'acception primitive du mot M. J. a soumis à une pénétrante critique les opinions émises; la théorie qu'il y oppose n'est pas non plus absolument satisfaisante." On pp. 298–299 of the same review, Jeanroy cites some interesting references to *puis* found in lyric poetry.

de Fécamp in Normandy.[73] According to their charter, the purpose of their association was masses, alms, vigils, and prayers. Yearly on St. Martin's Day they walked in a procession with the monks. At a later date *puys* are known to have existed in Valenciennes, Arras, Rouen, Caen, Amiens, Abbéville, Dieppe, Douai, Cambray, Evreu, Lille, Bethune, and London. It will be unnecessary, in the interests of a full account of the *ballade,* to do more than touch on the history of a typical *puy* in France, and of the one known English *puy.*

All the *puys* of the Middle Ages were originally religious in character. Their foundation was usually attributed to clerks who had had miraculous visions of the Virgin.[74] Gradually these religious fraternities evolved into literary societies, chambers of rhetoric, and academies, with only a faint coloring of their religious purpose left. The "confrérie de Notre-Dame des Ardents"[75] at Arras is said to go back to the Virgin's gift of a healing candle to two minstrels during a pest in 1105. Early in the thirteenth century, so the account runs, a religious guild was founded at Arras in memory of this miracle. The statutes of the society[76] express its purpose to save the "ardans qui ardoisent du fu d'enfer." Each member was to attend the meetings held three times a year, to pay dues, to succour his comrades in poverty, to follow them to the grave, and to pay a forfeit if any of these duties was neglected. In this society,

73 Leroux de Lincy, *Recueil de Chants Historiques Français* (Paris, 1841), p. xxix, p. xxx, and by the same author, *Essai Historique et Littéraire sur l'Abbaye de Fécamp* (Rouen, 1840), p. 378. Cf. Joseph Bédier, *Richard de Normandie, Romanic Review,* I, p. 122.

74 See Appendix 1, E.

75 H. Guy, *Adan de la Hale* (Paris, 1898), pp. xxvii–xxxiv, *passim.*

76 Cf. *MS. B. N. 8541.* For the statutes of the *puy* at Amiens, see Victor de Beauvillée, *Recueil de Documents Inédits Concernant la Picardie* (Paris, 1862–1882), Vol. 1, p. 189, ff.

in which, as in the others the members were classified, the *trouvères* were held first in dignity. This society, moreover, never lost its original religious character.[77] Now, as to the literary organization of this *puy* at Arras, which is so intimately connected with the activity of Adan de la Hale, the president of the association was called "Prince," and to him, as representing the whole corporation, the envoys of poems, composed before and after the vogue of the *ballade,* were frequently addressed. This office was probably elective, and would be held only by a rich man, because a "Prince" was expected to pay the expenses of any dramatic enterprises, to fee the clergy who officiated

[77] H. Guy, *Opus Cit.*, p. xxxiii. "S'ils font bande à part, quand il s'agit de s'occuper de leur gaie science, ils entendent pourtant escorter aux procession le saint cierge." See also L. Passy, *Fragments d'Histoire Littéraire à Propos d'un Nouveau Manuscrit de Chansons Françaises, Bibliothèque de l'Ecole des Chartes,* 4e série, Vol. V (Paris, 1859), p. 492: "J'aimerais à definir un Puy, et en particulier le Puy d'Arras, une confrérie littéraire. A prendre dans leur sens littéral les paroles de Vilain, on pourrait croire que de son temps les puys avaient perdu leur premier caractère, et substitué la culte de l'amour au culte de la Vierge. Dès l'origine, il est vrai, l'esprit littéraire disputa à l'esprit religieux la direction des Puys. . . . La vie du moyen âge était si ennuyeuse et si monotone! . . . Comment ne pas saisir la première occasion de se distraire, et quelle occasion plus naturelle que d'honorer la mère d'un Dieu par les lettres et les arts, la musique et la poésie? La confrérie tourna en académie, et le Puy Notre-Dame devint un Puy d'amour. Les poètes s'habituèrent à célèbrer la beauté de leurs maîtresses dans une réunion où ils n'auraient dû célébrer que la vertu de la Vierge; et les mêmes voix sur les mêmes airs chantèrent de pieux cantiques et de legères chansons. Le sentiment religieux ne fut cependent jamais étouffé: il survécut dans l'objet même de l'assemblée et dans les details de la fête. Lorsqu'on retrouve au seizième siècle les Puys constitués et fonctionnant sous la haute influence de l'Eglise, on ne peut pas supposer qu'au treizième,

Pour sostenir amour, joie et jovent,

il se soient dérobés à cette influence."

at ceremonies, and to entertain generously. From the remark of the father of the fool in Adan's *La Feuillee,* namely, "Tasiés pour les Dames," it may be assumed that ladies were occasionally, if not frequently, present at the sessions.

In this study, the literary forms other than the *ballade* which engaged the attention of the *puys* need not be discussed. The *puy* at Arras, like the other poetic guilds, turned its attention to the subject of our study only after the middle of the fourteenth century.[78] The brotherhood of the *puy* founded in London at the close of the thirteenth or at the beginning of the fourteenth century,[79] was, of course, modelled on these French *confréries.*

The society received from the city great privileges in connection with the Chapel of St. Mary near Guildhall, which was built towards the close of Edward I's reign. The society was religious, convivial, and literary.[80] Whether its models were the *confréries* of Normandy and Picardy, or a particular *confrérie* at Le Puy in Velay, cannot be certainly determined. The editor[81] of the *Liber Custumarum,* which contains the Statutes[82] of the English *puy,* be-

78 There is no evidence for the exact date at which any *puy* took up the *ballade* as an exercise.

79 H. T. Riley, *Memorials of London and London Life* (1276–1419), (London, 1868), p. 42: 27 Edward I. A. D. 1299. Letter-Book E., first fly-leaf. (Latin.)

"Common Pleas holden on Monday the morrow of Holy Trinity in the 27th year of the year of the reign of King Edward, son of King Henry.—

At this Court, Henry le Waleys gave and granted unto the Brethren of the Pui 5 marks of yearly quit-rent to be received from all his tenements in London, toward the support of one chaplain, celebrating divine service in the new Chapel at the Guildhall of London." The Henry le Waleys here mentioned had been mayor both of London and Bordeaux.

80 See Appendix I, A.

81 H. T. Riley.

82 See Appendix I, A.

lieves that during the period of the organization of the English guild, the interruption of England's commercial relations with Normandy and Picardy made it probable that merchants from Gascoigne and Guyenne, neighbors of Le Puy, imported from thence the main features of a religious-literary guild. Although the majority of members were foreigners, the name of the "third Prince" of the fraternity, the only person named in the documents of the *Liber Custumarum,* which, as we have said, contains the statutes of the society, is English. Its convivial aspects, feasts, and processions seem most prominent, but masses and almsgiving also are prominent, not to speak of the yearly literary contest. On this occasion a crown was awarded to the composer of the best *chancoun reale.*[83] Search of promising manuscript collections has failed to reveal any of the poems presented to the English *puy*. It is not unlikely, however, that both the *ballade* and the *chant royal* may have figured in its latest contests, if not in English, perhaps in French. The sessions of this *puy* seem to have ceased after the fourteenth century.[84]

The last important contribution to the structure of the *ballade* was thus the envoy, added in the *puys* in the late fourteenth century, in the course of such poetical contests as have been described. Thereafter, chambers of rhetoric and individual poets might vary the length of the line, con-

[83] See Appendix II.

[84] H. T. Riley, *Munimenta Gidhallae Londoniensis* (London, 1860), Vol. II, Pt. I, p. LI: "As to the place of meeting of the companions of the Puy, we are not informed; if, indeed, they had any such fixed place, which seems doubtful. The Vintry which we know to have been extensively inhabited by merchants of Bordeaux and other localities of Gascoigne and Guyenne, seems not unlikely to have been their favorite place of resort." We are tempted to wonder whether the illustrious poet, son of a vintner, was familiar with the latest findings of the English *puy*.

trive elaborate rime ornaments, or adapt the *ballade* to express various ideas and perform many functions, but, with the addition of an envoy, the form was fixed in its essential features.

Apparently, then, the *ballade* took roughly about four centuries to develop. There seems no reason to doubt that the word itself came from the Provençal *balada. Ballette,* used to describe what was probably a direct predecessor of the *ballade,* is, we may assume, a corruption. The *ballade* stanza was well developed by the fourteenth century, whatever the process; whether the procedure was according to the method suggested by Stengel, by Jeanroy, or by R. A. Meyer is still to be determined. We see the *ballade* stanza in various stages of development in the *balada* and in the *ballette.* To the latter the *ballade* owes probably its three stanzas and refrain. The *ballettes,* composed in the thirteenth century, were artistic dance songs. They incorporated refrains which, copied from those of traditional poetry, had become the stock-in-trade of the *trouvères.* Many of the *ballettes* consisted of only three stanzas, with a refrain at least two lines in length, loosely connected with the stanza. There are three conspicuous ways in which this thirteenth century dance song differs from its successor or analogue, for the earlier verse form shows a refrain of several lines which is frequently independent of the rest of the stanza and which often has every mark of being popular in character. It is the refrain in all of these forms, in the *balada* as well as in the *ballette* and the *ballade,* that points to an ultimate popular origin, and establishes their kinship with earlier Romance songs composed in connection with the dance. Practically nothing remains of that primitive Romance literature which has become a postulate of literary critics. The primitive dance songs survive only in refrains modelled on those of popular tradition. Though the *ballade* has, as might be supposed, its analogues in Spanish, Italian, and Provençal, in no one of these languages did so rigid a verse form as the French develop.[85] Other probable contributions to the form of the *ballade* are to be found in the *chansonniers* of the thirteenth century, which contain poems with the same rimes running through a number of stanzas; there were, too, especially in verses composed for presentation in the *puys,* envoys in which *trouvères,* judges, and other notabilities were addressed by name. In the late thirteenth century, three-stanza refrain poems, with the same rimes throughout, were written and named *balades,* and as the fourteenth century progressed, the refrains of many lines that had characterized the *ballade,* in the *romans* and elsewhere, were generally reduced to one line. At length, at the close of the same century, the envoy, with its conventional salute to the "Prince," was annexed, and the *ballade* became in France a favorite poetic type for at least two centuries to come.

85 In the fifteenth century, however, the Provençal *dansa* showed a structure similar to that of the *ballade.*

CHAPTER II

THE *BALLADE* IN FRANCE FROM THE END OF THE FOURTEENTH CENTURY TO THE MIDDLE OF THE SEVENTEENTH CENTURY

It would obviously be an impossible task to make a list of all the writers who have produced *ballades,* and still more so to register all the occurrences of the type in early times. The great frequency of the *ballade* form in medieval France has already been noticed. And, with the exception of the eighteenth century, it has been in constant use in that country since the days of Lescurel. So, while the history of its origins must be made relatively complete, its long career in France necessitates limiting an account of its further development to its more significant phases.

In the preceding chapter, the history of the early *ballade* referred to its increasingly complex versification. As time went on, not only did the form become modified, but there accumulated gradually a fund of *ballade* ideas,[1]

[1] F. J. A. Davidson, *Über den Ursprung und die Geschichte der Französischen Ballade* (Leipzig, 1900), p. 73: "Sie ist damals die eigentliche Ausdrucksform für alle Arten von Gedanken. Sie beschränkt sich nicht auf irgend eine Schattierung und hängt von keiner besonderen Eingebung ab. Man bedient sich ihrer für politische sowohl wie für religiöse, für satirische als auch für Liebesgedichte, und zwischen diesen Extremen giebt es keine Nuancierung des Gedankens, die sie nicht ausdrücken kann. Der Grund hierfür ist jedenfalls der, dass ihr Charakter allein in Rhythmus liegt und durchaus nicht vom Gegenstand der Dichtung selbst abhängt." It is wholly true, of course, that the *ballade* is distinguished from other lyrical poetry by its metrical peculiarities more than by its content. Davidson is prefectly justified, too, in emphasizing the very wide application of the *ballade.* But to grant the *ballade* this extensive range is not to deny that *ballade* literature had certain favorite themes.

which was steadily drawn on from the days of Lescurel and Deschamps down to the time of La Fontaine. *Ballades* on these themes were occasionally grouped in sequences, and, more commonly still, became a favorite ornament of the early religious and secular drama. The *ballade,* likewise, continued to be favored by poets in the *puys,* and also in the more or less informal poetical concourses like those held at Blois under the auspices of Charles d'Orléans. On one such occasion at Blois, for instance, the paradox, "Je meurs de soif auprès de la fontaine," was announced as the refrain for *ballades* to be written in competition.[2] Charles and his poet guests tried their hand on *ballades* based on this idea.[3] Charles had indeed at least as early as 1451[4] played with the same sentiment:

> "Je meurs de soif en cousté la fontaine,
> Tremblant de froit ou feu des amoureux.
> Je gaigne temps et pers mainte semaine
> Je joue et ris quant me sens douloureux,
> Desplaisance j'ay d'esperance plaine,
> J'actens boneur en regret angoisseux,
> Rien ne me plaist et si suis desireux,
> Je m'esjois et courre a ma pensée,
> En bien et mal par Fortune menée."

[2] A *ballade* beginning, "Ma doulce dame en qui jay ma fiance," and bearing as refrain, "Je meurs de soif auprès de la fontaine," appears on sig. tiii[v] of the *Jardin de Plaisance* of A. Vérard, as republished by the *Société des Anciens Textes Français* (Paris, 1910).

[3] P. Champion: *Le Manuscrit Autographe de Poësies de Charles d'Orléans* (Paris, 1907), p. 25, note 5: "Ce tournoi poétique ne peut avoir eu lieu avant 1456, car on y voit figurer *Gilles des Ormes* qui paraît seulement dans la maison du duc en 1456 (comptes de 1456). . . . Mais je ne crois pas que l'on puisse préciser cette date. L'inscription de la pièce de Villon ne peut pas être antérieure au 19 décembre 1547. A vrai dire, il n'y eut jamais un concours, mais seulement un thème à développer."

[4] Pierre Champion, *Vie de Charles d'Orléans* (Paris, 1911), p. 652.

Somewhat later, in another *ballade,* he modified the theme to, "Je n'ay plus soif, tarie est la fontaine." Then eleven of his friends took up the idea and developed it. The names of five of these are lost; but Montbeton and Robertet, Bertaut de Villebresme, Jean Caillau, Gilles des Ormes, Simonet Caillau, and François Villon are known to have written *ballades* around the sentiment, "Je meurs de soif auprès de la fontaine."[5]

In the fifteenth century, when a number of very different ideas were finding expression in *ballades,* there was also great variety within the form itself.[6] Many things could be done with a type of poetry the only fixed features of which were three stanzas, a refrain, the same rime-scheme in every stanza, and, under some circumstances, an envoy. By actual count, however, the most frequent stanzas were either that of eight lines, made up of octosyllabics and riming a b a b b c b c, or that of ten lines composed of decasyllabics, riming a b a b b c c d c d. Every stanza was a metrical unit, for the sense was seldom allowed to run over from one stanza to the next. It is noteworthy, too, that there were no breaks in sense even in the longest stanzas. Stanzas, moreover, in which two or more distinct ideas were elaborated were unusual, although every line in all three

[5] Pierre Champion, *Opus Cit.*, p. 653.

[6] H. Chatelain, *Recherches sur le Vers Français au XVe Siècle,* (Paris, 1908). In Chapter X of this work, Chatelain treats fully the variations of the *ballade* form in the fifteenth century. His summary is complete for the golden age of the *ballade;* the numerous metrical modifications of the type worked out in that century were, for all practical purposes, never augmented. Chatelain has done his work so thoroughly that it is only necessary to refer to his summary. The subject of the metrical structure of the *ballade* in the treatises on poetics of the fourteenth, fifteenth, sixteenth, and seventeenth centuries is discussed below in Chapter III.

stanzas might contain an illustration of the theme of the whole *ballade*.[7]

The metrical form of the *ballade* had originally, as has been shown, been conditioned to a certain extent by popular dance airs.[8] And from the evidence of certain manuscripts it seems certain that at least as late as the close of the fifteenth century *ballades* were written to be sung. A manuscript of Lescurel's gives a musical accompaniment for the first stanza of every *ballade*.[9] In a British Museum manuscript of Charles d'Orléans's poems, there is some musical notation of the sixteenth century.[10]

What little has been said so far about the externals of the *ballade* has applied to the normal examples of the type; but at an early date French poets taxed their ingenuity in turning out what may well be called freak *ballades*. The abnormal complication and absurd ornamentation of the form was not confined to the school of the "Grands Rhétoriqueurs." Deschamps and Christine de Pisan were both guilty of trying to see to what strange contortions they might subject this poetic form. Deschamps wrote at least two *ballades* that he claimed in the title might be read in

7 Compare the *ballades* composed of popular proverbs, cited below.

8 Cf. Pierre Aubry, *Trouvères et Troubadours* (Paris, 1910), pp. 58–62.

9 A. de Montaiglon, *Chansons Ballades et Rondeaux de Jehannot de Lescurel* (Paris, 1855), pp. viii–ix.

10 This fact was given to me by M. Pierre Champion in a kindly personal interview in the summer of 1910, in Paris. See also P. Champion, *Vie de Charles d'Orléans* (Paris, 1911), p. 260: "Toute poésie était encore, en partie, dépendante de la musique et de la facile banalité qui en découle. Au temps de Guillaume de Machault, cinquante ans environ avant que Charles composât ses première poésies, on chantait les rondeaux, les chansons, et même les ballades. Au temps de la jeunesse de Charles d'Orléans, les chansons seulement demeuraient des compositions musicales et de ce fait se distinguaient des rondeaux."

eight different ways. The first stanza of one of these will serve to show that the poet's assertion was not extravagant:

"Virginité, Beauté, Bonté, Saincté,
Amoureuse, precieuse, agreable,
Humilité, Pitié, Eternité,
Glorieuse, piteuse, charitable,
Vertueuse, doucereuse, honourable,
Tressainctement pour nous tous destinée,
Divinité, Verité inmuable,
Certainement le siecle ains ordenée."[11]

The artifice of Christine's *Balades d'Estrange Façon* is quite as painful. She furnished a *balade retrograde qui se dit a droit et a rebours,* the first stanza of which is:

"Doulçour, bonté, gentillece,
Noblece, beaulté, grant honnour,

[11] Le Marquis de Queux de Sainte-Hilaire, *Œuvres Complètes de Eustache Deschamps* (Paris, 1887), Vol. I, p. 81. On p. 82 are given the directions for reading the *ballade* here printed:

"*Comment ceste Balade se diversifie en .viii. ordres et se list par huit manieres differans l'une de l'autre, tout par bonnes rimes et tousjours revenans a une meisme sentence et conclusion si comme il apparra aux lisans.*

La premiere, elle se list de l'ordre droit en descendant aval;

La seconde, elle se retrograde du premier ver en reversant contremont;

La tierce, en lisant l'un vers a droit et l'autre tout arrebours;

La quarte, en prenant au ver de la rubriche par-dessus, en remontant amont;

La quinte, en prenant dessoubz, au piet de laditte rubriche et retrogradant contremont jusques au commencement;

Le sixte, chacune couple se couppe parmi desseure;

Item semblablement par dessoubz servent a laditte rubriche;

La .vii^{e}., les vers se croissent de l'un en l'autre;

La .viii^{e}., ou neuvyme, les mos des vers se raportent l'un contre l'autre en bonne substance sanz y muer la matere.

Deschamps was guilty of another *ballade* similarly constructed. See *Opus Cit.*, Vol. I, p. 95.

Valour, maintien et sagece,
Humblece en doulz plaisant atour,
Conforteresse en savour.
  Dueil angoisseux secourable,
  Acueil bel et agreable."[12]

And she also contrived a *balade a Rimes Reprises.* Its intricacies are evident in the stanza given:

"Flour de beaulté en valour souverain,
Raim de bonté, plante de toute grace,
Grace d'avoir sur tous le pris a plain,
Plain de savoir et qui tous maulz efface,
Face plaisant, corps digne de louenge,
Ange en semblant ou il n'a que redire,
D'yre vuidié a vous des preux ou renge,
Renge mon cuer qui fors vous ne desire."[13]

A peculiarly ornamented *ballade* was discovered by Paul Meyer in a manuscript of the end of the fifteenth century in the Hunterian Museum. He calls it a *ballade tantogramme,* and cites three lines and the refrain:

"Poure Prouvence, pueple peu plantureux
Par pestillence pugni presentement,
Perséquté, perdu, plaintif, parouреux
. . . .
Paradis paint, peneux pelerinage."[14]

A mere *tour de force* of a different variety is that *ballade* of Deschamps's on the books of the Bible. Proper names

[12] M. Roy, *Œuvres poétiques de Christine de Pisan* (Paris, 1886), Vol. I, p. 119.

[13] M. Roy, *Opus Cit.*, Vol. I, p. 120.

[14] Paul Meyer, *Documents Manuscrits de L'Ancienne Littérature de la France Conservés dans les Bibliothèques de la Grande-Bretagne* (*Extraits des Archives des Missions Scientifiques et Littéraires 2e série*), (Paris, 1871), p. 119. The *MS.* is *Q. 7.12* (*Haenel, 7.126*).

have at times contributed to the effect of great poetry, as in Milton's *Paradise Lost* and in Shakespeare's *King Henry the Fifth;* but the discords of a single stanza are sufficient to indicate the dullness of this *ballade* by Deschamps:

"Paraboles, Ecclestiastes rent,
Cantiques lors, sapience verras;
L'Ecclesiastiques a nous s'estent,
Ysaie, puis vient Jheremias,
Treuves Baruch, Ezechie, et si as
De Daniel, Osée, Joel, s'as
Amos après, Abdye ainsis a nom,
Jonas Micheas, et ensuit Naom,
Abbacuth, Sophonie, Aggeus, Zacharie,
Malachias, Machabée, s'escrie:
L'ordre sçavoir du lire n'est que bon."[15]

Jehan Meschinot's four *ballades* on love must have been very difficult to put together. The four deal severally with "amour sodale," "amour vertueuse," "amour folle," and "amour viceuse." Each is composed of three stanzas of ten-syllable lines and an envoy of six lines. After the fourth syllable of every line there is an abrupt break. The first half of every line in all four *ballades* associates some action or quality with love, as "Amour loue," "Amour blâme," and in all four *ballades* the portions of lines preceding the break are identical. The second part of the line, however, changes in every *ballade* according to the special character of the love that is being described. A glance at the first three lines and the refrain of all the *ballades* will illustrate Meschinot's scheme:

[15] Le Marquis de Queux de Saint-Hilaire, *Œuvres Complètes de Eustache Deschamps* (Paris, 1882), Vol. III, p. 289. In Gower's *Cinkante Balades,* XLIII, and in the *Traitié* of the same author, VII, VIII, IX, X, XI, definitely employ lists of proper names as poetic ornaments.

Amour sodale

"Amour commande aux gens estre loyaux.
Amour deffend compaignie maulvaise.
Amour acquiert grans biens à ses féaux.
. . . .
Amour blasme qui sans mal ne veult vivre."

Amour vertueuse

"Amour commande aux gens estre parfaicts.
Amour deffend tous deshonnestes faicts.
Amour acquiert aux amans los et prix . . .
. . . .
Amour blasme Les meschans et infaicts."

Amour folle.

"Amour commande à tous estre joyeux.
Amour deffend qu'on ait dueil ne souci.
Amour acquiert bruit d'estre gracieux.
. . . .
Amour blasme ceux qui n'ont robe neufve."

Amour viceuse

"Amour commande aux gens vivre en luxure.
Amour deffend chasteté nette et pure.
Amour acquiert enfin damnation . . .
. . . .
Amour blasme les vivans sans laidure."[16]

Eccentricities of rime, too, were in order. Clément Marot wrote "du jour de Noel, sur l'air j'ai veu le temps que m'estoie à Basac," a *ballade* in which all rime words end in *c*, as the first stanza here given shows:

[16] Arthur de la Borderie, *Jean Meschinot, sa Vie et ses Œuvres, Bibliothèque de l'École des Chartes,* t. 56 (Paris, 1895), p. 620. Cf. with these *ballades,* the *Balade* [de l'Amour] in *Le Prisonnier Desconforté* (ed. by P. Champion, Paris, 1908, p. 14), in which every one of the twenty-eight lines begins with the word "Amour."

"Or est Noël venu son petit trac:
Sus donc aux champs, bergieres de respec:
Prenons chascun panetiere & bissac,
Flute, flageol, cornemuse, & rebec:
Ores n'est pas temps de clorre le bec,
Chantons, sautons, & dansons ric à ric:
Puis allons veoir l'Enfant au povre nic,
Tant exalté d'Helie, aussi d'Enoc,
Et adoré de maint grand Roy, & Duc:
S'on nous dit nac, il faudra dir noc:
Chantons Noel tant au soir, qu'au des-jucs."[17]

Acrostic *ballades* were not uncommon. The envoy of Villon's prayer on behalf of his mother spells out his name. So does his *Balade des Contre-Verités.* The "balade que Villon donna à un gentilhomme nouuellement marié pour l'envoyer à son epouse par luy conquise à l'espée," embodies the lady's name in an acrostic that runs through the first two stanzas. Jean Marot wrote a "ballade de la Parangonne des Dames dont le nom est escript par le commencement des lettres capitales."[18]

17 *Œuvres de Clement Marot avec les Ouvrages de Jean Marot son Pere ceux de Michel Marot son Fils & les Pièces du Different de Clement avec François Sagon* (A la Haye, 1731), Tome II, p. 25. The *c* rimes are used again in the *Ballade du Mazarin Grand Joueur de Hoc,* given below with the historical *ballades.*

18 *Opus Cit.,* Tome IV, p. 326. The first two stanzas follow:

"Au Catalogue des Dames vertueuses
Nous voyons or ceste Dame excellente,
Noble en tous faitz, qui par gestes heureuses
En nostre sexe tout bon bruyt represente;
De sens, d'honneur c'est l'addresse & la sente
Enumerée entre les parangonnes;
Bonne, belle, liberalle, prudente,
Royne d'honneur, exemplaire des bonnes.

Elle a ce cueur qu'œuvres ambicieuses
Tient soubz le pied & les humbles augmente.

The *ballade* in dialogue was a popular diversion with the French poets of three centuries. It owes some of its features to the *débat* of earlier French poetry, which arose, doubtless, from a very simple principle of social intercourse. It might happen that some advocate of his own opinion would persist in supporting his peculiar views, till his wearied opponent retired from the field. Such an argument was the essence and origin of the lyrical *débat*.[19] The *ballade* dialogue resembles quite closely that variety of the *débat*, known technically as the *tenso*, which has been defined as a real or fictitious dialogue in poetic form between two poets or two persons, or between two personifications. The tone of these dialogues varied from hostility to tempered urbanity, and the altercation led to no decision. Some of these *tensos* were real dialogues in the sense that the debate had actually occurred between two poets. The fictitious *tenso* was the work of one author.[20]

Some such early literary tradition should account for the frequent use of dialogue give-and-take by *ballade* writers. At any rate the practice was common.[21] Sometimes the

Aux povres gens parolles gracieuses
Joyeusement avecques dons presente;
Grande en vertuz & de vices absente
Nous la tenons, car de toutes personnes
Elle est dicte par raison très decente,
Royne d'honneur exemplaire des bonnes.''

The lady in question is ''Anne de Bretaigne, Royne de France.''

[19] Cf. A. Jeanroy, *Les Origines de la Poésie Lyrique en France au Moyen Âge* (Paris, 1904), Pt. I, Ch. II, *passim*. Cf. also T. H. Hanford, *The Mediaeval Debate between Wine and Water*, *Publications of the Modern Language Association*, XXI, pp. 315–367.

[20] H. Knobloch, *Die Streitgedichte im Provenzalischen und Altfranzösischen* (Breslau, 1866), p. 13.

[21] Cf. A. Jeanroy, *Les Origines de la Poésie Lyrique en France au Moyen Age* (Paris, 1904), p. 479. Here we have a *ballette dialoguée*.

speakers divide the line, as in Christine's *balade a responses:*

"Mon doulz ami.—Ma chiere dame.
—S'acoute a moy.—Trés volentiers.
M'aimes-tu bien?—Ouïl, par m'ame.
—Si fais je toy.—C'est doulz mestiers.
—De quoy?—D'amer.—Voire, sanz tiers.
—Deux cuers en un.—Sanz decepvoir.
—Voire aux loiaulz.—Tu as dit voir."[22]

Sometimes each speaker is given a complete line, and they alternate, as in the same author's *Balade a vers a responses:*

"Amours, escoute ma complainte?
—Or dis: qu'as tu? de quoy te plains?
—De toy par qui je suis destraintte.
—Tort as quante de ce te complains?
—Non ay voir, car majoye estains.
—Joye en aras s'en toy ne tient?
—Trop crain le grant mal qui en vient.
—Pense au bien, non pas au dommage?
—Vueille ou non, d'un seul me souvient."[23]

In another *ballade* each speaker is given a group of lines in the stanza, as in some of the *Cent Ballades* (58); in the same collection a whole *ballade* is more frequently assigned to a single disputant. Christine, again, in *Le Livre du Duc des Vrais Amans,* has a *ballade* in which the characters, a lady and her lover, speak in alternating stanzas thus:

22 M. Roy, *Œuvres Poétiques de Christine de Pisan* (Paris, 1886), Vol. I, p. 121, st. 1. This type of dialogue *ballade* is very common; see British Museum *MS. Landsdowne 380,* f. 258r, and J. Quicherat, *Les Vers de Maître Henri Baude* (Paris, 1856), p. 26.

23 M. Roy, *Opus Cit.,* Vol. I, p. 122, st. 1.

"Belle, il me fault departir
Et esloignier vo presence,
Dont grant dueil me fault sentir,
Car je mourray de pesance
Puis que plus n'aray l'aisance
De veoir vostre doulz vis
Qui est, a ma congnoiscence,
Le plus perfait qu'onques vis.

—Amis, ne puis consentir
De bon gré vostre partence,
Car sans vous sera martir
Mon cuer en grief penitence,
Si me fait mal quant je pense
Qu'ainsi soit de moy ravis
Cil qui est par excellence
Le plus perfait qu'onques vis.

—Dame, bien doit amortir
Tout mon bien quant souffisance
Avions tous .II. et partir
La convient sans qu'aye offense
Faitte, et si n'y puis deffense
Mettre, dont j'enrage vifs
Pour vous, cuer plein d'essience,
Le plus perfait qu'onques vis.

—Ou que faciez residence,
Foy, amis, je vous plevis,
Car vous estes sans doubtance
Le plus perfait qu'onques vis."[24]

An amusing *débat* situation is found in two seventeenth century *ballades* by Madame de Deshoulières and M. le Duc de Saint Aignan. The second stanza and the envoy of the

[24] M. Roy, *Œuvres Poétiques de Christine de Pisan* (Paris, 1896), Vol. III, p. 189.

lady's *ballade* and the second stanza of her opponent's follow:

"Riches atours, table, nombreux valets,
Font aujourd'hui, les trois quarts du mérite.
Si des amants soumis, constants, discrets,
Il est encore, la troupe en est petite:
Amour d'un mois est amour décrépite.
Amants brutaux sont les plus applaudis.
Soupirs et pleurs feroient passer pour grue:
Faveur est dite aussitôt qu'obtenue.
On n'aime plus comme on aimoit jadis.

Envoi

Fils de Vénus, songe à tes intérêts;
Je vais changer l'encens en camouflets:
Tout est perdu, si ce train continue:
Ramène-nous le siècle d'Amadis.
Il est honteux qu'en cour d'attraits pourvûe,
Où politesse au comble est parvenue.
On n'aime plus comme on aimoit jadis."[25]

Reponse de M. Le Duc de Saint-Aignan.

St. 2

"Nul riche atour, nul nombre de valets,
Ne contribue à mon peu de mérite;
Toujours me tiens au rang des plus discrets:
Tant mieux pour moi si la troupe est petite.
Amour chez moi n'est jamais décrépite;
Et quand les sots sont les plus applaudis,
Dûsse-je en tout passer pour une grue,
Faveur se cache aussitôt qu'obtenue,
Tant j'aime encor comme on aimoit jadis."[26]

[25] *Œuvres de Madame et de Mademoiselle Deshoulières* (Paris, 1753), Vol. I, p. 153.
[26] *Opus Cit.*, Vol. I, p. 155.

A certain type of dialogue popular in the Middle Ages[27] has its analogues in *ballade* literature. The older conversations between body and soul reappear in modified form, as is seen in the following *ballade* of Deschamps (*dialogue entre la tête et le corps*):

"Malade suy, dist le chief a son corps,
Tant que ne sçay que je devenir doye.
—C'est a bon droit, vous avez bouté hors
Les droiz membres dont je vous soustenoie,
D'estranges mains aidier ne vous pourroye,
Ce dist le corps, car vous n'avez osté
Jambes et bras et le destre costé
Et m'avez, joint membres d'autre paraige
Qui m'ont destruit et a vous la santé.
—Corps, doulz amis, dy moy donc que feray ge?"[28]

A reported dispute of similar character is found in a *balade* in which "le coeur reproche au corps d'aimer en trop haut lieu":

Stanza 1.

"Mon cuer au corps chascun jour se combat,
En lui blasmant son penser, sa folie,
Et ce qu'il veult amer en hault estat,
En noblie lieu, en treshaulte lignie,
Veult que le corps lui tiengne compangnie,
En le menant par tout ou il vourra,
Ou se ce non le cuer dit qu'il mourra
Et que par ce fera le corps perir
Puisque veoir sa dame ne pourra:
Ainsi ont trop cuer et corps a souffrir.

[27] In *Romania* for 1880, p. 311, G. Paris, in a review of G. Kleinerts's *Über den Streit zwischen Leib und Seele* (Halle, 1880), writes: "Le véritable dialogue où le corps renvoie à l'âme ses reproches apparaît dans un poème français." Cf. Wright, *Poems attributed to Walter Mapes*, p. 321.

[28] Le Marquis de Queux de Saint-Hilaire, *Œuvres Complètes de Eustaches Deschamps* (Paris, 1887), Vol. V, p. 344, st. 1.

Stanza 3.

L'un pour l'autre languit en ce debat;
Force est de corps par le cuer afeblie,
Dont le corps dit: Pourquoy me fais tu mat?
Le cuers respont: Tu ne me sequeurs mie.
Mouvoir me veulx; mayne moy vir m'amie.
Le corps tremblant a dit: Qui te croira,
Je seray mors, aussi l'en t'occira;
De si hault lieu ne te deust souvenir.
—Tu pers ton temps, autrement n'en sera.
Ainsi out trop cuer et corps a souffrir."[29]

Villon's well known *ballade, Debat du Cuer et du Corps,* has four stanzas and envoy. Here the poet's heart assumes the rôle usually played by the soul in more serious controversy with the body.[30]

Le Debat du Cuer et du Corps de Villon.

" Qu'est-ce que i'oÿ?
—Ce suis.
—Qui?
—Ton cuer.
Qui ne tient mais qu'à vng petit filet.
Force n'ay plus, substance ne liqueur,
Quand ie te voy retraict ainsi seulet,
Com poure chien tappy en reculet.
—Pour quoy est ce?
—Pour ta folle plaisance.
—Que t'en chault-il?
—Ien ay la desplaisance.

29 Le Marquis de Queux de Saint-Hilaire, *Opus Cit.*, Vol. III, p. 385.

30 For other French versions of the debate between soul and body, cf. G. Kleinert, *Über den Streit zwischen Leib und Seele* (Halle, 1880), p. 51, p. 53. Cf. too, C. Ruutz-Rees, *Charles Sainte-Marthe* (New York, 1910), pp. 333–334.

—Laisse m'en paix!
—Pour quoy?
—I'y penseray.
—Quand fera ce?
—Quant feray hors d'enfance.
—Plus ne t'en dis.
—Et ie m'en passeray.
Que penses tu?
—Estre homme de valeur.
—Tu as trente ans.
—C'est l'aage d'vng mullet.
—Est ce enfance?
—Nennil.
—C'est donc folleur.
Qui te saisist?
—Par où?
—Par le collet.
Riens ne congois.
—Si fais; mouches en let:
L'vng est blanc, l'autre noir, c'est la distance.
—Est ce donc tout?
—Que veulx tu que ie tance?
Se n'est assez, ie recommenceray.
—Tu es perdu!
—I'y mettray resistance.
—Plus ne t'en dis.
—Et ie m'en passeray.

. . . .

Envoi

—Veulx tu viure?
—Dieu m'en doint la puissance!
Il te fault—
Quoy?
—Remors de conscience;
Lire sans fin.
—En quoy lire?
—En science;

Laisser les folz!
—Bien i'y aduiseray.
—Or le retien!
—I'en ay bien souuenaice.
—N'atens pas tant que viengne à desplaisance.
Plus ne t'en dis.
—Et ie m'en passeray."[31]

Thus the form of the *ballade* became more and more diversified. Nevertheless, whatever external features were added to its structure, the original three stanzas, persistent rimes, and refrain remained unaltered. The fund of ideas, from which those who used the form drew, was fairly limited. These ideas, embodied in the main themes employed by the writers of French *ballades,* suggest a method of classification, which is not inevitable but merely convenient. What follows, therefore, is in the nature of a survey of French *ballade* literature, grouped, so far as possible,[32] according to subject.

The Religious Ballade

The shaping of the *ballade* in the *puy* must have meant its early adaptation to religious themes. It is not surprising, therefore, to find French poets during three centuries piously inclined to make this fixed form do service for prayer and praise. The *ballades* given in this section are chiefly concerned with the worship of Mary. Sometimes

[31] A. Longnon, *Œuvres Complètes de François Villon* (Paris, 1892), p. 113. Swinburne's translation of this and of the other Villon *ballades* is noteworthy. Cf. P. Champion, *François Villon, Sa Vie et Son Temps* (Paris, 1913), Vol. II, pp. 130–132.

[32] Under the two headings, "*Ballade* Sequences," and the "*Ballade* in the Drama," there has, obviously, been a departure from the method of arrangement by subject. It is also true that the doctrines of Courtly Love inform practically all the *ballades* cited.

she is addressed in the terms of profane love; sometimes the special doctrines connected with her are set forth. But other religious ideas as well are contained in *ballade* literature. The persons of the Trinity[33] are duly celebrated, the Saviour is ceremonially enshrined, and sin and salvation are reverently treated.

Undoubtedly the most beautiful of the *ballade* prayers to the holy mother is Villon's "feit a la requeste de sa mere pour prier Nostre-Dame":

Ballade

"Dames des cieulx, regente terrienne,
Emperiere des infernaux palus,
Recevez moy, vostre humble chrestienne,
Que comprinse soye entre vous esleus,
Ce non obstant qu'onques rien ne valus.
Les biens de vous, Ma Dame et Ma Maistresse,
Sont trop plus grans que ne suis pecheresse,
Sans lesquelz biens ame ne peut merir
N'avoir les cieulx, je n'en suis jangleresse.
En ceste foy je vueil vivre et mourir.

A vostre Filz dictes que je suis sienne;
De luy soyent mes pechiez abolus;
Pardonne moy comme a l'Egipcienne,
Ou comme il feist au clerc Theophilus,
Lequel par vous fut quitte et absolus,
Combien qu'il eust au deable fait promesse.
Preservez moy que face jamais ce,
Vierge portant, sans rompure encourir,
Le sacrement qu'on celebre a la messe.
En ceste foy je vueil vivre et mourir.

33 A *balade* (?) of thirteen stanzas and envoy addressed to "Mon Dieu" and beginning with the line "O eternelle Trinité" appears in *Le Prisonnier Desconforté* (ed. by P. Champion, Paris, 1908, p. 53).

Femme je suis povrette et ancïenne,
Qui riens ne sçay; oncques lettre ne leus.
Au moustier voy dont suis paroissienne
Paradis paint, ou sont harpes et lus.
Et ung enfer ou dampnez sont boullus:
L'ung me fait paour, l'autre joye et liesse.
La joye avoir me fay, haulte Deesse,
A qui pecheurs doivent tous recouvrir,
Comblez de foy, sans fainte ne paresse.
En ceste foy je vueil vivre et mourir.

V ous portastes, digne Vierge, princesse,
I esus regnant qui n'a ne fin ne cesse.
L e Tout Puissant prenant nostre foiblesse,
L aissa les cieulx et nous Vint secourir,
O ffrit a mort sa tres chiere jeunesse;
*N*ostre Seigneur tel est, tel le confesse.
En ceste foy je vueil vivre et mourir."[34]

A prayer to the Virgin,[35] probably of the fifteenth century, offers a contrast to the foregoing:

"Ave douce dame de paradis,
Toute pleine de grace et de douchour,
Pour nous auons lautaine ioie aquiz,
Bien heureuse de nostre uraie amour,

[34] *François Villon, Œuvres,* editées par un Ancien Archiviste (Paris, 1911), p. 40. Cf. P. Champion, *François Villon, Sa Vie et Son Temps* (Paris, 1913), Vol. I, p. 16 ff.

[35] British Museum *MS. Additional 15,224, fol.* 49^r. Paul Meyer, *Extraits du MS. Additional 15224 du Musée Britannique, Bulletin de Societé des Anciens Textes Français* (Paris, 1882), p. 69, describes this MS. as "un petit volume écrit sur parchemin d'une écriture italienne, vers la fin du XV siècle ou plus probablement au commencement du XVI. . . . L'intérêt de ce recueil consiste pour une grande part à avoir été fait en Italie. . . . Il porte témoignage de l'état qu'en ce pays on faisait de notre poésie au temps de la Renaissance."

Dez pecheours estez port et seiour,
En nouz sort la fontaine de tout bien,
Douce mere, pries per nous, amen.

Salue fleur odorant de touz esliz,
Du quel fruit auons tres noble pascour,
A nous fesons nostre reclaim tout diz,
Esperance que nous done uigour.
Pleine de grace entendez ma clamour,
Quar tressouvent empleurant me souien.
Douce mere, pries pour nous, amen.

Gale sans per secourez ce chetiz,
Qui sui en nef sans auiron dentour,
Et auouglez par mon peche porriz,
Humble dame a qui ie faz mon plour.
Prier uostre dolx fil nostre segnour
Quil ait merci de ce poure cristien,
Douce mere, pries pour nous, amen.

O yhesu crist nostre uray creatour,
Aiez misericorde ama folour,
Pour amour de ta mere aqui me tien,
Douce mere, pries pour nous, amen."

Another and earlier "balade de Nostre Dame moult belle" was written by Deschamps about 1380. In the first stanza the poet prays:

" Secourez moy, douce vierge Marie,
Port de salut que l'en doit reclamer;
Je sens ma nef foible, provre et pourrie,
De sept tourmens assaillie en la mer;
Mon voile est roupt, ancres n'y puet encrer;
J'ay grant paour que plunge ou que n'affonde
Se voz pitiez envers moy ne se fonde."[36]

[36] Le Marquis de Queux de Saint-Hilaire, *Œuvres Complètes de Eustache Deschamps* (Paris, 1878), Vol. I, p. 258.

Deschamps's "autre balade de Nostre Dame" contains an answer to the preceding:

"Presente suis, je te viens faire aie,
Mais il te fault mon filz, ton Dieu, amer
Et delaissier t'erreur et ta folie
Et ce monde qui te fait tourmenter;
Pour .vii. tourmens qu'il convient rebouter,
Pran .vii. vertus qui font la vie monde,
Se ma pitié veulz que vers toy se fonde.

Humilité et Chastité n'oublie
Et Charité, qui tant fait a louer;
Abstinance soit en ta compaignie,
Pacience, pour tous maulx endurer.
De ton avoir doiz, aux povres donner
Pour eschiver d'enfer la mort seconde,
Se ma pitié veulz vers toy que se fonde.

Par ces vertus yert ta nef redrecie,
Et si pourras ton voile asseurer,
Ne les tourmens ne te mefferont mie,
Que ne puisses a droit port arriver;
Ton voile est droit, vueille toy ordener
Si que peché en ton vaissel n'abonde,
Se ma pitiez veulz que vers toy se fonde."[37]

Comparable with this last, is Jean Marot's monologue, another poem in which the Virgin herself speaks:

"Parlant en form de Ballade
le jour de son Assomption.

Devant que la cause premiere
Fist la terre & la mer jadis,
Devant que Dieu crea lumiere,
Ne qu'il formast ses Benedicts,

[37] Le Marquis de Queux de Saint-Hilaire, *Opus Cit.*, Vol. I, p. 259.

Devant ce temps que je vous dis,
Sentence estoit desja donnée,
Que je seroye en Paradis
Sur tous les angelz couronnée.

Maintenant je suis Tresoriere
Des hautz biens de gloire assouvis;
Maintenant je suis emperiere
Triumphante en royal devis;
Maintenant les benoitz ravis
Me disent fleur sans courroux née.
Vous estes selon nostre advis,
Sur tous les angels couronnée.

Après que boys, prez & rivieres
Seront de leurs estres bannys;
Après que par loy droicturiere
Humains seront par mort finis,
Des haults trones d'honneur garnys
Comme Royne, preordonnée
Vivray par siecles infinis
Sur tous les angels couronnée.

Envoy

Prince en ce jour dire je puys,
Puisque telle gloire m'est donnée.
J'ay esté, je serai & suys
Sur tous les angels couronnée."[38]

The Virgin speaks for herself, too, in an anonymous *ballade,* probably of the fifteenth century:[39]

[38] *Œuvres de Clement Marot avec les Ouvrages de Jean Marot son Pere ceux de Michel Marot son Fils & les Pièces du Different de Clement avec François Sagon* (A la Haye, 1731), tome IV, p. 353.

[39] See note on p. 71 below. The *ballade* is found in *MS. p. 24408,* f. 50^v–51^r, of the *Bibliothèque Nationale.*

Argumentum

Nigra sum sed formosa filia Jerusalem. Canticorum 1°.

"Ballade en la personne de la Vierge

Or sus levez hault la veue,
Deuotes filles de syon,
Voyez comment dieu ma preueue,
Ains du ciel la perfection
Tant que par preelection;
Et oultre la forme mortelle,
Je suis par sa protection
Noire en couleur mais toute belle.

Noire en couleur mauez congneue,
Portant vostre condition,
Dhomme et de femme ainsy venue,
Et subiecte en affliction.
Mais sentez que sans fiction,
De dieu suis mere naturelle,
Tost direz ma conception,
Noire en couleur mais toute belle.

Nolite me considerare quod fusca sim, quia decolaravit me sol. Canticorum 1°

Ne vous artz si mauez veue,
Pale et sans consolation,
Car le vray soleil ma rendue
Sans couleur par compassion.
Quand lay veu souffrir passion
Pour lohmme quj luy fut rebelle,
La fuz en desolation,
Noire en couleur mais toute belle.

Envoy

Prince cest vostre Intencion
Que Marie humble columbelle
Soit dicte par preuention
Noire en couleur mais toute belle."

NICOLAS BAUDRY.

Molinet's *Oraison a la Vierge Marie* belongs to the second half of the fifteenth century, and has all the decorative effect of that ornate period:

"O recouurance moult plaisant!
Deuãt vous me suys presente,
En ce lieu a genoulx disant
Des maulx quay fait la verite.
Pour ce que en suys desherite,
Vers dieu dont poure me reclame.
Pour moster de ma pourete
Ayez pitie de ma poure ame.

O esclarboucle reluysant!
Nuyct et iour sans obscurite,
Esmeraulde trescler luysant,
Et saphir de securite;
Dyamant de mundicite
Rubis rayant cler comme flame,
Je vous requiers en charite
Ayez pitie de ma poure ame.

O cypres aromatisant!
Palme de grant suauite,
Cedre sus tous resplendissant,
Oliue de fertilite;
A matres grant necessite
Vous prie et requier saincte dame,
Quant a mourir seray cite,
Ayez pitie de ma poure ame.

O rose odoriferant!
Et vray lis de virginite,
Violette tres flourissant,
Marguerite dhumilite,
Mariolaine de purite,
Romarin flairant comme basme,
Par vostre clemence et pitie,
Ayez pitie de ma poure ame.

Prince eternal en trinite,
Trois personnes ie vous reclame,
Et vous requiers en vnite
Ayez pitie de ma poure ame."[40]

Praise of the Virgin spoken by her own son is also found in *ballade* form:[41]

Argument

Ballade en laquelle est escript
Comme le fameux Jesuchrist
Ont a sa mere toute belle
Quelle est pour luy et luy pour elle.

"Ma mere ou ma face empraincte,
Subiect ou mon corps fut emprainct,
Nayez ennuy soucy ne craincte
Du peche que homme faict crainct,
Car vostre concept nest attainct
Du crime de commune loy;
Ne doubtez de peche le tainct,
Je suis pour vous et vous pour moy.

Vostre pudique chair et saincte
Pour moy qui suis des sainctz le sainct
Fut par grace vestue et ceincte,
De purite le sacre sainct ceincte,
Et plus je fais que laspid sainct,
Est mys par vous en desarroy,
Vela comment soubz secret mainct,
Je suis pour vous et vous pour moy.

[40] *Les Faictz et Dictz de Feu de Bonne Memoire Maistre Jehan Molinet* (Paris, 1531), Sig. Pii^r.

[41] *MS. fr. 24408*, fol. 49^v–50^r, of the *Bibliothèque Nationale*. This is a collection of *chants royaux, ballades* and *rondeaux* in honor of the Virgin Mary (sixteenth century). There are twenty-two *ballades*.

Vous nauez oz, sang, nerf ne joincte,
Que grace nayct au corps conjoinct,
Diuinite fut en vous joincte,
Cest moy a dieu mon pere joinct,
Jay tousiours este vostre adioincte,
Comme tienct saincte eglise et foy,
Par quoy mere ne craignez point,
Je suis pour vous et vous pour moy.

Envoy

Se aucun de erreur vous mord ou poinct,
Nen soyez pourtant en esmoy,
Car pour premier et dernier poinct,
Je suis pour vous et vous pour moy."
JEHAN COUPPEL.

The idea of the Immaculate Conception is touched on in the following *ballade,* in which the Virgin is addressed as a substitute for the antique muse:[42]

Ballade

"Les payens versificateurs
Pryent le muses benignement,
Mais noz prudentz predicateurs
Oyent quilz ont failly grandement,
Quj font maintenant aultrement,
Invocant de premiere assiete
En leurs sermons treshumblement,
La saincte nymphe au grand poete.

Ingenieux compositeurs,
Prennons tous manifestement
Aux malingz[43] preuaricateurs

[42] *MS. fr. 24408,* fol. 69^v–70^r, of the *Bibliothèque Nationale.* It seems to be of the sixteenth century.

[43] Not in Godefroy.

Quilz sabusent totalement,
Disant la vierge faulsement
En peche amour este faicte,
Veu quelle estoit diuinement
La saincte nymphe au grand poete.

Subtilz et facondz orateurs
Venez par escriptz amplement,
Dire comme vrays amateurs
Quelle est amant tout element,
Sans peche generalement,
De dieu premier discrete,
Par grand honneur specialement
La saincte nymphe au grand poete.

Enuoy

La vierge fut benignement
Dicte par loraison celeste,
De Gabriel certainement
La saincte nymphe au grand poete."

ROBERT BELLENGER.

A *ballade*[44] contained in a manuscript of the *Bibliothèque Nationale* which is described as "sur l'Immaculée Conception," merely touches on that aspect of the subject. The poet uses elaborate similes drawn from the miracles of spring to illuminate the doctrines of original sin and salvation:

"Le grant yuer par sa froidure
Du beau verger dhumanite
Hatta les fleurs et la verdure,
Luy ostant toute amenite.

44 *MS. fr. 19369, fol.* 78^v–79^r, of the *Bibliothèque Nationale.* This manuscript contains twenty-seven *ballades.* The librarian whom I consulted believed the handwriting to be of the early sixteenth century.

Jusques a ce que en dignite
Zephire vent delicieux,
Engendra par benignite
Le doulx printemps solatieux.

Par lyuer de froide nature
Jentens dadam la vilite,
Qui gasta la belle ornature
De toute sa posterite.
Fors de la fleur de purite,
Que dieu son cher filz gracieux
Esleut en grace et dignite,
Le doulx printemps solatieux.

Jamais en ceste creature
Vil peche neust activite,
Pour tant que diuine ornature
La preseruoit deprauite.
En la saincte festivité
De sou sainct concept precieux,
Qui la prenne en suauite,
Le doulx printemps solatieux.

Enuoy

Prince, pour non vtilite,
Malgre sathan fallatieux,
Elle este en toute humilite,
Le doulx printemps solatieux."

A similar parallel between the solace of spring and the alleviating power of divine intercession is found in the same manuscript, from which three other illustrations have been drawn:

Ballade[45]

"Au verger de dieu ordonne,
Logis des humains et repere,

[45] *MS. fr. 24408*, fol. 51v–52r, of the *Bibliothèque Nationale.*

Se apparoit le desordonne
Serpent quj suprent nostre pere.
En ce lieu set rien ny prospere,
Quand en sourt au printemps seulette
Pour adam quj plus biens ne espere
La blanche fleur de violette.

Au frays moys de Mars obstine;
Sourt la fleur quj rigeur tempere
Comme est de dieu predestine
Faisant abysmer la vipere.
Dieu par dessus nature opere
Quand sa vertu rend si complete,
Quon voit contre tout impropere
La blanche fleur de violette.

Vierge, je me suis ordonne,
Figurer toy saincte nom prospere
A ceste fleur tu as donne
Dodeur quj tous aultres supere.
Il te plaist et ton filz limpere,
Supporte donc ma plume necte,
Quj te painct voulant te complere
La blanche fleur de violette.

Enuoy

Prince, la vierge est nostre mere,
Quj son filz doulcement allecte,
Que je nomme sans coulpe amere
La blanche fleur de violette."

PIERRE BEUARD

In a *ballade* of Clément Marot the familiar parallel between Mary's Son and the devoted pelican is drawn:

"Le pellican de la forest celique,
Entre ses faictz tant beaulx et nouvelletz,
Après les cieulx et l'ordre archangelique
Voulut créer ses petis oyselletz,

Puis s'envola, les laissa tous seuletz,
Et leur donna, pour mieulx sur la terre estre,
La grand' forest de paradis terrestre,
D'arbres de vie amplement revestue,
Plantez par luy, qu'on peult dire en tout estre
Le pellican qui pour les siens se tue.

Mais ce pendant qu'en ramage musique
Chantent aux boys comme rossignolletz,
Un oyseleur cauteleux et inique
Les a deceuz à glus, rhetz et filletz,
Dont sont banniz des jardins verdeletz,
Car des haultz fruictz trop voulurent repaistre,
Parquoy en lieu sentant pouldre et salpestre
Par plusieurs ans mainte souffrance ont eue,
En attendant hors du beau lieu champestre
Le pellican qui pour les siens se tue.

Pour eulx mourut cest oysel deifique,
Car du hault boys plein de sainctz Angeletz
Vola ça bas par charité pudique,
Où il trouva corbeaux trèsordz et laydz,
Qui de son sang ont faict maintz ruysseletz,
Le tourmentant à dextre et à senestre.
Si que sa mort, comme l'on peult congnoistre,
A ses petis a la vie rendue.
Ainsi leur fait sa bonté apparoistre
Le Pellican qui pour les siens se tue.

Envoy

Les corbeaux sont ces Juifs exilez
Qui ont à tort les membres mutilez
Du Pellican, c'est du seul Dieu et maistre.
Les Oyseletz sont Humains, qu'il feit naistre,
Et l'Oyseleur, la Serpente tortue
Qui les deceut, leur faisant mescongnoistre
Le Pellican qui pour les siens se tue."[46]

[46] Pierre Jannet, *Œuvres Complètes de Clément Marot* (Paris, 1873), Vol. II, p. 76.

The deity himself speaks in Molinet's *Oraison par Maniere de Ballade:*[47]

"Nous, dieu damours, createur, Roy de gloire,
Salut à tous vrays amans dhumble affaire.
Comme il soit uray que, depuis la victoire
De nostre filz sur le monte de caluaire,
Plusieurs souldars par peu de congnoissance
De noz armes font au dyable aliance.
Si vous faisons pour vostre bien mander
Lescu dargent au chief dor luysant cler,
A cinq playes que quant prescheurs ou carmes,
Com vrays heraulx les vouldront blasonner
Loyaulx amans recongnoissez ces armes.

Divinite du chief dor pouez croire
Pare innocence est largent ou pourtraire,
Voulurent iuifz les plays et encoire
Parfist longis louuraige necessaire;
Pour vrays amans deliurer de greuance,
Et si donnons et octroions puissance,
A leglise militante passer,
A noz gaiges tous ceulx qui retourner
Vouldront a nous, mais quen pleurs et en larmes
De cueur constrict et foy sans abuser,
Loyaulx amans recongnoissez ces armes.

Besoing sera quen ayez la memoire
Du dernier iour que nous vouldrons retraire,
Dessus le val iosaphat chose est voire
Pour comdampner lancien aduersaire.
La monsterons ces armes sans nuisance:
Pour nostre gent remettre en ordonnance,
Et la vouldont souldees deliurer,
Lors coniuendra le plus hardy trembler,
Car ny vauldront espees ne guisarmes,
Mais quant orrez noz trompettes sonner,
Loyaulx amans recongnoissez ces armes.

47 *Les Faictz et Dictz de Feu de Bonne Memoire Maistre Jehan Molinet* (Paris, 1531), Sig. A.

Prince, pitie voult ce mand impetrer,
Quant il nous pleust pierre a Romme poser,
Pour recepuoir tous verteux gens darmes,
Dont se voulez en nostre regne entrer,
Loyaulx amans Recongnoissez ces armes."

A *ballade* of Alain Chartier's, "foy la premiere vertu," is likewise addressed to the deity:

"Dieu tout puissant, de qui noblesse vient
Et dont descent toute perfection,
A tout crée, tout nourrist, tout soustient
Par sa haulte digne provision;
Mais, pour tenir la terre en union,
A ordonné chascun en son office,
Ly ung seigneur, l'autre en subjection,
Pour foy garder et pour vivre en justice.

Cil qui de dieu le plus de honneur obtient
Par seigneurie et domination,
Plus est tenu et plus luy appartient
D'avoir en luy entiere affection,
Crainte et honneur, bonne devocion
Et vergoine de meffait et de vice,
Et faire tout en bonne entention,
Pour foy garder et pour vivre en justice.

Cil est noble et pour tel se maintient
Sans vantrie et sans decepcion,
Qui envers dieu obeissant se tient
Et fait le droit de sa profession;
Qui quiert noblesse en autre opinion,
Fait a dieu tort et au sang prejudice;
Car dieu forme noble condition
Pour foy garder et pour vivre en justice.

Povre et riche meurt en corruption,
Noble et commun doivent a dieu service;

Mais les nobles ont exaltation
Pour foy garder et pour vivre en justice."[48]

There are religious *ballades,* too, that treat of the ever popular seven sins. One manuscript contains seven *ballades* on the "sept pechez mortelz."

Premierement

Sur le peche dorgueil.[49]

"Sens orguilleux qui estes peruers,
Voz esperitz qui sont dorgueil couuers
Et obfusquez de ville couuerture
Descouurez les et les tenez ouuers.
Et contemplez, ie vous pry par mes vers,
Que vostre chair deuiendra pourriture.
Vous estes faictz du lymon de la terre,
Et une foys y tournerez grant erre,
Que ne voulez aduiser ne congnoistre.
Meulx vous vauldroit acquerre humilite
Que les honneurs ie vous dy verite.
Car a la fin orgeil decort son maistre.

Point ne voyez et auez les yeulx vers.
Que vng temps viendra *que* vous gyrez en vers
Viande a vers o quel griefue poincture.
Et vous voulez par voz desirs reuers,
Preemmer a tours et a trauers.

[48] K. F. Bartsch, *Chrêstomathie de l'Ancien Français* (Leipzig, 1884), p. 447.

[49] *MS. fr. 2306,* fol. 20^r–20^v, of the *Bibliothèque Nationale,* said by the librarian to be of the early sixteenth century. These *ballades* were printed also by Vérard in the volume *Les Regnars Traversant les Perilleuses Voyes des Folles Fiances du Monde* (1503) under the title "des vices et des vertus," with link pieces of octosyllabic lines not given in the MS. Cf. É. Picot, *Une Supercherie d'Antoine Vérard* (*Romania,* 1893), p. 248.

A toutes gens de quelconque stature
Vous mesprisez et menez tousiours guerre,
Aux pouures gens voulans paradis querre.
Et de vertuz leurs ames du tout paistre
Qui de leurs corps nont curiosite.
Desistez vous de celle vanite,
Car a la fin orgeil decort son maistre.

Las lucifer auecques ses comiers
Par son orgeil cruel, faulx, et diuers,
Qui jadis fut si belle creature,
De paradis fut gette es enfers.
Lequelz depuis sort estez ou yuers,
Sont ennemys de lhumaine nature.
Aussy bruyant vous estez q*ue* tonnerre.
Vanteurs, gorriers reluysans comme verre.
Ambicieux dont vous fault mes congnoistre.
Mais vous serez par vostre iniquite
De vostre espoir du tout disherite.
Car a la fin orgeil decort son maistre.

Prince, vueillez de vostre fait enquerre,
Et tout cogneu ne vouldrez point acquerre
Tous ses honneurs dont farciz voulez estre,
Mais vous laissez grant grauite
Pour euader toute perplexite,
Car a la fin orgeil decort son maistre."

Undoubtedly in the same class with the foregoing, belongs Deschamps's *ballade,* called by his editor *Allégorie Satirique des Sept Péches Capitaux:*

" N'a pas long temps qu'en une region
Vi en dormant dolereuse assemblée,
Ce fut Orgueil chevauchant le lion,
Ire emprés luy qui se fiert d'une espée,
Sur un loup siet; Envie la dervée

Dessus un chien aloit fort murmurant,
Avarice gouverne la contrée:
Onques ne vi si dolereuse gent.

Car celle avoit or, joyaulx a foison,
Et languissoit d'acquerre entalentee;
Paresce aprés dormoit une saison,
En l'an n'a pas sa quenoille filée;
Sur l'asne siet la povre escheveulée
Qui en touz lieux est toudis indigent;
Glotonnie fut sur un ours posée,
Onques ne vi si dolereuse gent.

Celle mettoit tout a destruction,
Par gourmander avoit la pence emflée;
Luxure estoit moult prés de son giron
Qui chevauchoit une truie eschaufée,
Mirant, pignant s'aloit comme une fée
Et attraioit maint homme en regardant;
Mais trop puoit sa trace et son alée,
Onques ne vi si dolereuse gent.

L'Envoy.

Princes, moult est la terre desertée
Ou telz vices sont seignour et regent;
Regne s'en pert et ame en est dampnée,
Onques ne vi si dolereuse gent."[50]

Ballades on Death

Closely allied to the religious *ballades* in tone and in general character are those in which the various aspects of death are treated. A fifteenth century *ballade*[51] representative of this class follows:

[50] Le Marquis de Queux de Saint-Hilaire, *Œuvres Complètes de Eustache Deschamps* (Paris, 1878), Vol. I, p. 319.

[51] British Museum *MS. Harley 4397*, fol. 120^{v}–121^{r}.

"Pecheur qui scez qui morir doiz,
Et que cy nest pas ton entente,
Pense a ton bien mantesfois,
A la mort qui tant test presente,
Aux mondains ne mets ton entente,
Car nas a viure deux iours ne trois,
De terre es toute puante,
Retourner cy fault vne fois.

Tous les jours a ton oeil tu vois
Nature sieuyr colle sente
Pape, prelas, princes, et roix,
Du contraire nul ne sen vante,
Et pour ce ton pechie guermente,
Et diz en toy et recongnois
Que de terre es toute puante,
Retourner cy fault vne fois.

Paradiz aras se men crois,
Ne cuide pas que je te mente.
Preng garde a ton fait aincois,
Que lame de ton corps sesuente
Il fault premier quil se repente,
Et puis que dye bien congnois
Que de terre es toute puante
Retourner cy fault vne fois.

Princes, qui pendiz en la crois,
Et morir volz de mort cruante
Pour le pecheur, ainsi le crois
Racheter de playe doulante.
Veuillez par ta digne puissante
Que dire puist de ceur courtois
Que de terre es toute puante
Retourner cy fault vne fois."

Death is the theme, too, of another *ballade*[52] in manuscript:

[52] *MS. fr. 1707*, fol. 26, of the *Bibliothèque Nationale.*

Balade de la Mort

"Moy, qui suis mort a tous humains,
Fais assavoir comme desse
Que je tieng leur vie en mes mains.
Fy de leur orgueil et richesse!
Tous fais tourner a la reuerse,
Quãt par la hault divin vouloir
ffais venir jeunesse et viellesse
En terre pourrir et manoir.

Pensent ils q*ue* mes cris soient vains?
Bien le scaront se deulx j'approche.
Ou est arthus ou est gauuains,[53]
Hector qui tant eult de proesse?
Chasteaulx villes ne forteresse
Contre moi ne leur peult valoir.
Qui que je voeul prens ou delesse
En terre pourrir et manoir.

ffuyent fort, soient pres ou loings,
Dansent, chantẽt, meñas liesse.
Voisent chasser aux cerfz aux daings,
Prennent perdris mainnẽt en lesse.
Chiens et levriers, cela n'oppresse
Ma grant vertu ne mon pouoir.
Tous fais venir par une adresse,
En terre pourrir et manoir.

Prince, cõme dame et mestresse
Autant m'est le blanc que le noir.
Au pas quant l'ame le corps lesse,
En terre pourrir et manoir."

A *Balade de la Mort*[54] is found also in Bouchet's work:

"Home aueugle des plaisirs de ce mõde,
Pense que c'est de ton estre & nature—

[53] Cf. p. 88, *The "Ubi Sunt" Ballade.*

[54] Jehan Bouchet, *XIII Rondeaulx Differens. Auec XXV Balades Differentes* (Paris, 1536), Sig. Dvii^{v}–Dviii^{r}.

Sy maintenant tu a force & faconde
Richesse, auoir, beaulte, sante, droicture—
Demain seras tresuille pouriture
Que le plus grand de tes amis fuyra;
Tres uolontiers ton corps on conduyra
Iusques en terre à son dernier conuy,
Quant ast de l'ame en ingement yra
Pour recepuoir ce que aura desseruy.

Tu es yng sac tout plain de terre imūde,
Beau par dessus dedans plain de laidure,
De toy ne vient, ne procede & redonde
Que infection qu'a grad peine on endure;
Tu ne rēdz rien de bouche & nez qu'ordure,
Tant que viuras de toy ne sortira
Que puanteur & quant departira
L'ame de toy, qui te aura bien seruy,
Par deuant dieu tous ses faictz on lyra,
Pour recepuoir ce que aura desseruy.

Le corps tousiours cōtre la raison gronde,
Et l'ame induyt à toute forfaicture,
En voluptez non en vertus se fonde,
Et ne quiert fors paresse & nourriture;
Il ne sert dieu fors par quelque aduēture,
Penser ne veult que vne fois pourrira,
Dont i'ay grand paour que au grad iour yra
Ou il sera en ame & corps rauy,
C'est deuant Dieu ou il obeyra,
Pour recepuoir ce que aura desseruy.

Prince congnoys que mourir conuiendra,
Et que ton corps charongne deuiendra
Homme n'y à qui n'y soit asseruir,
Puis deuant Dieu chascune ame viendra
Pour recepuoir ce que aura desseruy."

Three of Chastellain's poems have to do with death. The

conceptions in the second stanza of *Ballade II* are familiar yet striking:

"Lequel veulx-tu, ou vie ou mort choisir?
Choisys des deux: tu as discrétion.
Aymes-tu mieulx de ton corps le désir
Pour ton âme mettre à dampnation
Que vivre un peu en tribulation
Et qu'après mort soyt ton âme ravie
En gloire ès cieulx, qui de nul desservie
Estre ne peult en ceste vie humaine,
S'il ne laisse terre, avoir et demaine
Et père et mère et tout s'il est possible,
Et vive en paine et en labeur terrible,
En suyvant Dieu tous jours patiemment?
C'est le chemin qui conduit seurement
Après trespas l'âme à salvation;
Et qui va aultre, il va à dampnement,
Homme deffait, mis à perdition."[55]

The envoy of *Ballade III* indulges in more conventional imagery:

"Homme, arme-toy contre l'heure future
Forte et dure, car mort de la pointure
Te picquera de sa mortelle darde;
Mais sçais-tu quant? demain par aventure
Ou aujourd'huy. Pour tant donne-toy garde."[56]

In *Ballade VII,* Death with his dart figures, too, and the treatment is more pictorial:

"Pense un chacun qu'il portera son fais
Et que après mort sera ressuscité
Pour rendre à Dieu compte de ses meffais

[55] Kervyn de Lettenhove, *Œuvres de Georges Chastellain* (Brussels, 1866), Vol. VIII, p. 300.

[56] Kervyn de Lettenhove, *Opus Cit.*, Vol. VIII, p. 303.

En jugement où il sera cité:
Là luy sera tout son temps récité;
Là Dieu dira aux benoits *Venite*
Et aux mauldits *Ite*. Ceste voir ditte,
Chancun aura droit selon son mérite,
Les saulvés gloire et léesse infinite,
Et les dampnés tristesse à tousjours mais.
Las! pensons-y, car c'est chose licite:
Par ce moyen nous aurons tousjours pais.

Prince mortel, nostre vie est petite
Et nous suyt mort atout son dard subite;
Pour tant faisons des biens plus qu'onques mais,
Tant qu'après mort nostre âme ès cieux habite:
Par ce moyen nous aurons tousjours pais."[57]

In Pierre de la Vacherie's *ballade* on death, a pagan association is introduced:

"Riens il n'y plus certain que la mort
Ne moins certain quant est l'heure d'icelle;
Par quoy chascun doit avoir le remort,
Duyre son âme, de peur qu'el ne chancelle
Et que ne soit de Proserpine ancelle,
Qui tant de peine luy feroit encourir;
De penitence entrez en la nasselle,
Considerant qu'une fois fault mourir."[58]

A curious dialogue in which Death and Man parley was written possibly by Meschinot:

57 Kervyn to Lettenhove, *Opus Cit.* p. 308, third stanza and envoy.

58 Pierre de la Vacherie, *Gouvernement des Trois Estatz,* A. de Montaiglon et James de Rothschild, *Recueil de Poésies Françoises* (Paris, 1877), Vol. XII, p. 97. Stanza 3 is given. The poem was composed 1505–1512.

La mort parle a lhomme humain.

"Ren toy.
A qui
Tu le scauras.
et quay ie fait?
Greue nature.
Quen sera il?
Tu en mourras.
Quant?
Temprement.
Cest chose dure.
Las ou iray ie?
En pourriture.
Conseil me fault
Va confesser
car ie ne scay meilleur trouuer.
Se jay pechie?
Tu le diras
et sen ay peine?
Si lendure
Son ma meffait?
Tu pardonras.
Dieu & cōment?
Dentente pure.
et qui dit ce?
Saincte escripture.
Cest mon conseil, pour ce prouer
Car ie ne scay meilleur trouuer.
Ie me rendz donc.
La foy tiendras
Ce feray mon?
Tu dis droicture
Se iay laultruy?
Tu le rendras
Se iay auoir?
Tu en feras.
Aux puoures
Quoy?
Leur nourriture.
Que mangeray ie?
La pasture.
Quelle?
Que prebstre scet sacrer
Car ie ne scay meilleur trouuer.
Prince
Que veulx tu?
Ie vous iure.
Quoy?
Que je croy.
La vierge pure.
Que dieu crea pour nous sauluer
Car ie ne scay meilleur trouuer."[59]

59 *Les Lunettes des Princes auec Aulcunes Balades & Additions Nouuellement Composée par Noble Homme Iehan Meschinot Escuyer en son Vivant Grant Maistre dHotel de la Royne de France* (Paris, 1539), Sig. Qvii^{v}–Qviii^{r}.

The "Ubi sunt" Ballade[60]

Probably the most famous *ballade* ever written is Villon's "des dames du temps jadis." It is another example of how traditional literary forms and old ideas are transformed into new and glorious poetry by a great poet.[61] The "ubi sunt" formula, first used in sermons and didactic poems, was soon transferred to hymns and songs, and thence spread from Latin versions to the vernacular.[62] St. Bernard inquired:

"Dic ubi Salomon, olim tam nobilis?
Vel ubi Samson est, dux invincibilis?
Vel pulcher Absalon, vultu mirabilis?
Vel dulcis Jonathas, multum amabilis?"

And he continued his questioning for the pagans, too:

"Quo Caesar abiit, celsus imperio?
Vel Dives splendidus, totus in prandio?
Dic, ubi Tullius, clarus eloquio?
Vel Aristoteles, summus ingenio?"[63]

[60] Professor K. C. M. Sills of Bowdoin College gave me a number of references to "ubi sunt" literature.

[61] Gaston Paris, *François Villon* (Paris, 1910), p. 107: "Mais l'éscolier parisien a su faire de ce lieu commun une des perles les plus rares de la poésie de tous les temps, d'abord en n'évoquant dans son rêve que des figures des femmes, puis en les choisissant avec un art ou plutôt un instinct merveilleux."

[62–63] Sainte-Beuve, *Causeries du Lundi* (Vol. XIV), 26 Sept. 1859, pp. 297–298. Cf. C. Horstmann, *Richard Rolle of Hampole,* Library of Early English Writers (1895), Vol. II, 374; C. E. Northrop, *Ubi Sunt Heroes, Modern Language Notes* XXVIII, No. 4, p. 106; C. E. Northrop, *Like a Midsomer Rose, Modern Language Notes,* XXIV, No. 8, p. 257; Frederick Tupper, *The Ubi Sunt Formula, Modern Language Notes,* VIII, No. 8, p. 506; T. B. Bright, The *Ubi Sunt Formula, Modern Language Notes,* VIII, No. 3, p. 187.

At least three of Deschamps's poems, a *chant royal*[64] and two *ballades*, are on the "ubi sunt" theme. Their quality is suggested by the stanzas quoted:

Balade

Comment Ce Monde N'est Riens Quant a la Vie

st. 1.

"Ou est Nembroth le grant jayant,
Qui premiers obtint seigneurie
Sur Babiloine? Ou est Priant,
Hector, et toute sa lignie?
Achillès et sa compaingnie,
Troye, Carthaige et Romulus,
Athene, Alixandre, Remus,
Jullius Cesar et li sien?
Ilz sont tous cendre devenus:
Souflez, nostre vie n'est rien."[65]

But that "ubi sunt" *ballade* of his which takes for its theme the passing of "adorable jeunesse" has its share of poetic poignancy.

"Qu'est devenu printemps, Avril et May?
Ou est alé le doulx temps que j'avoie

[64] Le Marquis de Queux de Saint-Hilaire, *Œuvres Complètes de Eustache Deschamps* (Paris, 1882), Vol. III, p. 183:

"Force de corps, qu'est devenu Sanson?
Ou est Auglas, le bon practicien?
Ou est le corps du sage Salemon
Ne d'Ypocras, le bon phisicien?
Ou est Platon, le grant naturien
Ne Orpheus o sa doulce musique?
Tholomeus o son arismetique?
Ne Dedalus qui first le bel ouvrage?
Ils sont tous mors, si fu leur mort inique;
Tuit y mourront, et li fol et li saige."

[65] G. Raynaud, *Opus Cit.*, Vol. VIII, p. 149.

A .xiiii. ans, le corps plaisant et gay,
Les cheveux blons, ou temps que je cuidoie
Que l'en m'amoit pas amours que j'avoie,
Que je regnay, que je fus honnorée,
Jeune, gente, fresche et fort desirée?
Vint et cinq ans dura ma jeune flours,
Mais a trente ans fu ma colour muée.
Lasse! languir vois ou desert d'amours:

. . . .

L'Envoy

Jeunes belles, cuidez car je cuiday;
Mais avisez a la doulour que j'ay.
Prenez vo temps, car trop vault un bon jours.
Vingt et cinq ans ont tenu mon cuer gay,
Trente et le plus m'ont fait perdre toute glay
Lasse! languir vois ou desert d'amours."[66]

Sainte-Beuve makes the point that Villon's real contribution to great poetry lies not so much in the conventional questioning as in the poignant refrain, "Mais où sont les neiges d'antan?" Professor Gummere, on the other hand, has shown that these magic words are only a variant of a communal refrain.[67] The American scholar refers to a beautiful Middle English predecessor of the great *ballade*, the *Luve Ron*, in which, in response to a "maid of Christ" who asks for a love song, Thomas de Hales cites, as so many *exempla*, the miserable fates of those who gave themselves to love and recommends Christ as the only worthy lover. Quite comparable to Villon's *ballade* is this stanza:

"Hwer is paris *and* heleyne,
þat weren so bryght *and* feyre on bleo?

[66] Marquis de Queux de Saint-Hilaire, *Œuvres Complètes de Eustache Deschamps* (Paris, 1882), Vol. III, p. 373.

[67] F. B. Gummere, *The Beginnings of Poetry* (New York, 1901), p. 149.

Amadas. tristram *and* dideyne,[68]
yseude and alle þeo?
Ector wiþ his scharpe meyne,
and cesar riche of wordes feo?
Heo beþ iglyden vt of þe reyne.
so þe schef(t) is of þe cleo."[69]

These lines lack plainly the concentrated lyric sweetness of Villon's poem, the most perfect of all *ballades:*[70]

"Dictes moy ou, n'en quel pays,
Est Flora la belle Rommaine,
Archipiades[71] ne Thaïs,
Qui fut sa cousine germaine;
Echo parlant quant bruyt on maine
Dessus riviere ou sus estan,
Qui beaulté ot trop plus qu'humaine.
Mais ou sont les neiges d'antan?"

Ou est la tres sage Helloïs,
Pour qui fut chastré et puis moyne
Pierre Esbaillart a Saint Denis?
Pour son amour ot ceste essoyne.
Semblablement, ou est la royne
Qui commanda que Buridan
Fust geté en ung sac en Saine?
Mais ou sont les neiges d'antan?

La royne Blanche comme lis
Qui chantoit a voix de seraine,

68 Scribal error for *ideyne.*

69 Richard Morris, *An Old English Miscellany* (London, 1872), *Early English Text Society,* No. 49, p. 95. For further references to the treatment of the "ubi sunt" motive, see O. L. Triggs, *The Assembly of Gods by John Lydgate, Early English Text Society,* Extra Series 69, London, 1896, pp. 73–74.

70 Cf. P. Champion, *François Villon Sa Vie et Son Temps* (Paris, 1913), Vol. I, p. 145; Vol. II, pp. 186–188.

71 Alcibiades—see G. Paris, *Opus Cit.*, p. 107.

Berte au grant pié, Bietris, Alis,
Haremburgis qui tint le Maine,
Et Jehanne[72] la bonne Lorraine

[72] Cf. P. Champion, *Ballade du Sacre de Reims*, a *chant royal*. Cf. also the uninspired "ballade contre les Anglais," printed in *Romania* for 1892, p. 51, by Paul Meyer, who dates the piece 1429. For other historical *ballades* see p. 128 below.

"Ariere, Englois couez, ariere!
Vostre sort si ne resgne plus.
Pensés deu treyner vous baniere
Que bons Fransois ont rué jus
Par le voloyr dou roy Jhesus,
Et Janne, la douce pucelle,
De quoy vous estes confondus,
Dont c'est pour vous dure novelle.

De tropt orgouilleuse maniere
Longuemen vous estes tenus;
En France est vous [tre] semet[i]ere,
Dont vous estes pour foulx tenus.
Faucement y estes venus,
Mès, par bonne juste querelle,
Tourner vous en faut tous camus,
Dont c'est pour vous dure novelle.

Or esmaginés quelle chiere
Font ceulx qui vous ont soustenus
Depuis vostre emprisse premiere.
Je croy qu'i sont mort ou perdus,
Car je ne voys nulle ne nus
Qui de present de vous se mesle,
Si non chetis et maletrus,
Dont c'est pour vous dure novelle.

Pour vous gages, il est conclus,
Aiés la goute et la gravelle
Et le coul taillé rasibus,
Dont c'est pour vous dure nouvelle."

Qu'Englois brulerent a Rouan;
Ou sont ilz, ou, Vierge souvraine?
Mais ou sont les neiges d'antan?

Prince, n'enquerez de sepmaine
Ou elles sont, ne de cest an,
Que ce refrain ne vous remaine:
Mais ou sont les neiges d'antan?"[73]

Villon wrote two other *ballades* of this type, the "balade des seigneurs du temps iadis"[74] and a "balade (a ce propos en viel langage françois),"[75] neither of which is a masterpiece. A direct result also of these poems of Villon's is Gringore's pious questioning of death with its formal insistence on chastity and virtue as the prerequisites of immortality.

"Ou est Priam, ou est Agamemnon,
Et Alexandre qui eut si grant renom?
Ou la proesse des tres nobles Romains?
Qu'est devenue la puissance Sanxon,
Et la richesse du Riche Pharaon,
Qui en leur temps subjuguoient les humains?

Jean's exploits, as the *ballade* quoted shows, were not always productive of great lines. The "ballade contre les anglais" obviously belongs in the category of historical *ballades.*

73 Francois Villon, *Œuvres,* editées par un Ancien Archiviste (Paris, 1911), p. 22. J. W. Mackail, (*Springs of Helicon* London, 1909, p. 34), speaking of Pandarus's line, "Yea, farewell all the snow of ferne year," says: "The words on the lips of a later poet became the burden of the world-famous *Ballad of Dead Ladies,* but they were Chaucer's first." Cf. also H. Guy, *Histoire de la Poésie Française du XVIe Siècle* (Paris, 1910), p. 146: Octavien Saint-Gelays, one of Villon's poetic followers, had the temerity to essay twice a re-writing of the flawless *Ballade des dames du temps jadis.*

74 A. Longnon, *Œuvres Complètes de François Villon* (Paris, 1892), p. 34.

75 A. Longnon, *Opus Cit.*, p. 36.

Il sont sechéz ainsi qu'au prez les foings.
Mort en la fin les a occis, deffais,
Et qu'il soit vray, plusieurs en sont tesmoings;
Au mortel monde demeurent les bienfais."[76]

Proverbs and the Ballade

Ballades, adaptable to the sober purposes of religion and death, lent themselves easily to gnomic uses. Moreover, the proverb as a line unit frequently offered a quick solution of what might otherwise have been a difficult rime-problem. Proverbs were used singly or they were grouped to form a stanza. But the stringing together of any considerable number of proverbs was likely to produce patter rather than poetry. That proverbs should have been introduced into *ballades* was to be expected. In the early years of the existence of the *ballade,* there was, indeed, the medieval affection for sententious wisdom to account for the frequent appearance of the proverb, and in the fifteenth and sixteenth centuries, there was the obsession in favor of rhetorical ornament to explain the presence of the proverb in so many places.[77]

[76] Charles Oulmont, *Pierre Gringore* (Paris, 1911), p. 142.

[77] ''La façon dont les rhétoriqueurs concevait la morale les conduisait nécessairement à l'exprimer en proverbes. Non seulement ils ne fuyaient pas ces sentences banales et contradictoires que le dogmatisme populaire a édictées, mais il les recherchaient avec zèle en sorte que leurs livres en sont plus farcis que les discours de Sancho Pança. Des pièces entières (j'en pourrais citer plus de cent) nous offrent un proverbe à la fin de chaque strophe. Presque tous les auteurs de ce temps se sont asservis à cette mode, et le seul effort que certains—Molinet, par exemple,—aient fait pour se monstrer originaux, ç'a été de commencer quelquefois la strophe par le proverbe. Adjoutez qu'ils ne recherchent point les adages les plus significatifs ou les moins prosaïques, mais ceux qui ont le nombre de syllabes qu'il faut (dix ou huit, dix à l'ordinaire); il s'ensuit que les mêmes maximes reviennent mécaniquement, et servent flexibles et vaines, à prouver le pour et le contre.'' (H. Guy, *L'École de Rhétoriqueurs,* Paris, 1910, p. 68.)

In Deschamps's *ballades,* the proverb occurs sometimes in the body of the stanza, as in "autre balade de la complainte de grammaire," stanza 1, line 7:

"Si vielle suy et de si long temps née
Que nul ne veult plus ma doctrine entendre,
Et si fu je la premiere ordonnée,
Qui les .vii. ars fis a pluseurs aprendre,
Et les plus grans fis mainte foiz du mendre,
A rude engin, par fort continuer;
Goute d'yaue fait la pierre caver,
Si fiat aussi continuacion
De poursuir, retenir, demander:
Mais des .vi. ars voy la destruction."[78]

Or the proverb—and this fashion is more frequent—serves as the refrain. The first stanza of a "balade morale d'un paisant et son chien," shows this disposition of the material:

"Un paisant avoit un chien
De grant exploit, jeune et puissant,
Fort et hardi, si l'ama bien,
Car toute beste fut prenant,
Et si gardoit diligemment
Son hostel de jour et de nuit;
Manger lui fist de maint deduit,
Et des loups son tropiau garda.
Or devint vieulx: lors le destruit:
Quant fruit faut, desserte s'en va."[79]

This *ballade,* like many others of Deschamps's, is a fable, and of fables there is a word to be said later.

Proverbs are common in the *ballades* of Deschamps and also in those by his contemporaries, Christine de Pisan and

[78] Le Marquis de Queux de Saint-Hilaire, *Œuvres Complètes de Eustache Deschamps* (Paris, 1887), Vol. V, p. 152.

[79] Le Marquis de Queux de Saint-Hilaire, *Opus Cit.,* Vol. VI, p. 270.

Froissart.[80] The former, for instance, used a proverb as refrain in one of the *Cent Ballades,* the first stanza of which is:

> "Sage seroit qui se saroit garder
> Des faulx amans qui adès ont usage
> De dire assez pour les femmes frauder;
> Trop se plaignent de l'amoureuse rage
> Qui plus les tient que l'oisellet la cage,
> Et vont faignant qu'ilz en ont couleur fade;
> Mais quant a moy tiens de certain corage,
> Qui plus se plaint n'est pas le plus malade."[81]

Similarly, Froissart's method of availing himself of the ready made wisdom of proverbs is shown in the third and fourth lines of a *ballade* in *Méliador:*

> "Aucun dient c'amant ont trop grant painne
> Pour bien amer et loyauté tenir;
> Pour ce, s'il ont .i. bien une sepmainne,
> Encontre ce leur fault .c. maus souffrir.
> Mais a ce point ne me voel acorder,
> Car Amours poet tout ce bien amender.
> Par .i. seul eur c'on en poet recevoir,
> Couvient, il dont tout l'anoi oublier
> C'on ot onques ou puist jamais avoir."[82]

The *ballade* consisting of nothing but proverbs became popular after Villon. His "ballades des Proverbes"[83]

80 See E. Fehse, *Sprichtwort und Sentenz bei Eustache Deschamps und Dichtern Seiner Zeit* (Berlin, 1905).

81 M. Roy, *Œuvres Poétiques de Christine de Pisan* (Paris, 1886), Vol. I, p. 54.

82 A. Longnon, *Méliador par Jean Froissart* (Paris, 1895), Vol. II, p. 214.

83 Le Roux de Lincy, *Le Livre des Proverbes Français* (Paris, 1859), Vol. I, p. LVIII: "Villon connaissait bien les proverbes, non pas ces sentences pédantesques, ces mots dorés, comme on disait alors,

tempted other poets. The following stanza quoted from one of his proverbial *ballades,* in spite of its mannerisms and artifice, is extremely ingenious:

"Tant grate chievre que mal gist,
Tant va le pot a l'eau qu'il brise,
Tant chauffe on le fer qu'il rougist,
Tant le maille on qu'il se debrise,
Tant vault l'homme comme on le prise,
Tant s'eslongne il qu'il n'en souvient,
Tant mauvais est qu'on le desprise,
Tant crie l'on Noel qu'il vient."[84]

Almost identical in form and phrase is the *balade* [des Proverbes] of *Le Prisonnier Desconforté,* dating near the end of the fifteenth century. Take for example the first stanza:

"Tant ayme l'on que mal en vient,
Tant pri-on que chose est acquise,

dont Pierre Gringoire et les ennuyeux rimeurs de son école se plaisaient à orner leur écrits, mais les proverbes communs répétés à chaque moment par le peuple, et dont encore aujourd'hui il aime à faire usage.'' And p. LIX: ''Presque toutes les ballades que Villon a jointes à son Grand et à son Petit Testament se terminent ainsi, et l'on voit, d'après les exemples cités précédemment que cette manière de composer était fort répandue aux XIVe et XVe siècles.'' This *ballade* is printed in *Le Jardin de Plaisance, Société des Anciens Textes Français* (Paris, 1910), sig vi.

[84] François Villon, *Œuvres,* éd. par un Ancien Archiviste (Paris, 1911), p. 79.

The first line of Villon's poem and the refrain are recurrent in French literature. The proverb, ''Tant grate chièvre que mal gist,'' occurs twice in Le Roux de Lincy's *Chants Historiques,* in a *balade* (of 21 stanzas) by Alain Chartier (1449), at the end of stanza 8; and again at the end of stanza 11 of a *Chanson contre Hugues Aubriot* (1384). At the end of stanza 12 of the latter poem is another proverb beginning with *tant.*

Tant poursuit-on qu'on y parvient,
Tant bat-on place qu'elle est prise,
Tant plus couste plus on la prise
Tant perle-l'on qu'on se mesdit,
Tant va le pot à l'eau qu'il brise
Tant grate chievre que mal git."[85]

A *ballade* of Collerye, too, was doubtless indebted to Villon's experiments with the proverb in *ballade* form.

"Trop or et argent amasser
Sans en bien user n'est licite;
Trop son ennemy pourchasser
N'est pas tout eur, comme on recite;
Trop longue guerre mort suscite,
Au peuple mauvais peu en chault;
Trop malverser, grant mal incite;
Tant plus y a trop, et moins vault.

Trop empoigner, trop embrasser
Est ung trop assez illicite,
Trop avoir et trop tracasser
N'est pas bon, S'il n'y a poursuitte
Prisée n'est une lache fruitte,
Ne trop fin homme, ne trop cault,
Ne pareillement trop grant suitte;
Tant plus y a trop et moins vault.

Trop noiser et trop menasser
Est un trop dont on n'est pas quicte;

[85] Pierre Champion, *Le Prisonnier Desconforté du Château de Loches* (Paris, 1909), p. 13.

Two other contemporaries of Villon's are known to have composed proverb *ballades*. See P. Champion, *Vie de Charles d'Orléans* (Paris, 1911), p. 598: "La ballade des Proverbes, qu'écrivit assez tard Me Pierre Chevalier, est une bonne contribution à ce mode littéraire" . . . Bertaut de Villebresme . . . écrivit sur ce sujet une ballade dans laquelle il laissa briller toute son érudition."

Trop passer et trop rapasser
C'est un trop de sotte conduite;
Trop voit-on prudence petite
Regner sur plusieurs bas et hault
Trop voit-on mourir gens d'eslite;
Tant plus y a trop et moins vault.

Prince, ma parolle desduyte,
Puis que par trop conclure fault,
Je dis en substance bien duitte:
Tant plus y a trop et moins vault."[86]

Melin de Saint Gelais wrote two *ballades,* in one of which, a gay little plea for the right of a lover to distract himself with many beauties, he avails himself of several familiar and popular sayings:

"S'il est ainsi qu'il n'est rien si parfaict
Où il n'y ayt de l'imperfection,
Et s'il est vray qu'Amour n'ayt en effect
Nul autre object que la perfection;
Confesser faut que ceste affection,
Qui ne peut voir son object tout en une,
Se peut espandre et choisir en chacune
Ce qu'il y a plus digne d'amitié,
Ainsi l'amour dispersée et commune
Demeure entiere et n'a point de moitié.

Vertu qui tout accomplit et parfait
N'est qu'un seul bien qui a mainte action;
Beauté aussi, qui tost se deffait,
Est simple en soy; mais sa compaction,

[86] Charles d'Héricault, *Œuvres de Roger de Collerye* (Paris, 1855), p. 171. On the same page, in a foot-note, the editor says: "Cette ballade présente une tournure analogue à celle de Villon:
'Tant grate chèvre que mal gist,' etc.

Qui emplit l'œil de satisfaction,
Gist en plusieurs qui n'ont semblance aucune.
Les vices grands, comme envie ou rancune,
Dependent tous d'une seule impitié,
Ainsi amour, sous maints chois ou fortune,
Demeure entiere, et n'a point de moitié.

Qui dura donc variable, un qui fait
De divers biens prudente élection?
L'abeille prend, pour venir à son faict,
De maintes fleurs douce refection;
Tout l'univers, et la complexion
De ce grand corps qui est dessous la lune
N'est qu'un changer d'une espece à quelqu'une
D'autre accident, par sage inimitié;
Et si nature, à tous faicts opportune
Demeure entiere et n'a point de moitié.

Envoy

Soit donc fortune à moy luisante ou brune,
Me tienne au fond ou me mette à la hune,
Nul n'en doit prendre envie ne pitié;
Car mon amour, requise ou importune,
Demeure entiere et n'a point de moitié."[87]

Thoroughly sententious, too, in purpose and in expression is the "balade bien substancieuse":[88]

"Il nest dangier que de villain,
Ne orgueil que de poure enrichy,

[87] J. B. Blanchemain, *Œuvres Complètes de Melin de Saint-Gelais* (Paris, 1873), Vol. II, p. 4.

[88] British Museum *Ms. Harley 4397*, fol. 82r (written on paper in fifteenth century hand). The poem is found also with some differences in *Jardin de Plaisance, Société des Anciens Textes Français*, Sig. tii.

Ne si sceur chemin que le plain,
Ne secours que de vray amy,
Ne desespoir que jalousie,
Ne hault vouloir que damoureux,
Ne paistre quen grant seignourie,
Ne chiere que dhomme joyeulx.

Ne seruir que roy souuerain,
Ne en amour tel bien que mercy,
Ne mengier que quant on a faim,
Ne nul tel chastoy que de luy,
Ne pourete que malladie,
Ne angoisse que ceur conuoiteux,
Ne puissance ou il ny ait enuiye,
Ne chiere que dhōme joyeulx.

Et[89] nest richesse que destre sain,
Ne lait nom que dhome a honty,
Ne que de la mort plus certain,
Ne emprinse que dhōme hardy,
Ne tel tresor que preudōmie,
Ne suyr[90] que les bons et preux,
Ne la maison que bien garnie,
Ne chiere que dhōme joyeulx.

Prince, que volez que je dye,
Il nest parler que gracieux,
Ne loer gēs quaprez leur vie,
Ne chiere" [rest of refrain indicated by
abbreviation.]

The poetic tendency to moralize, which often led a writer of *ballades* to lean on proverbs, also caused him to turn to fable literature and to the fabrication of elaborate animal allegory. Deschamps wrote a number of such fable *bal-*

89 Probably should be omitted; elisions, e. g., *n'emprinse,* should be made.

90 Probably should be *suyvre* or *suivre.*

lades. He chose subjects like *Le Paysan et le Serpent,*[91] *Le Chat et les Souris*[92] and *Le Reynard et le Corbeau.*[93] The *ballade* of *Le Lion et les Fourmis*[94] is political allegory in fable guise. The ants in this case are the thrifty Flemings.

Mellin de Saint-Gelays used the fable-*ballade* in behalf of Clément Marot and against François Sagon, who had attacked Marot, by describing a kite in mid air who swoops down and fastens his talons on a sleeping cat. The inoffensive cat is Marot; the bird of prey is Sagon:

> "Mais, se voyant ainsi injustement attaqué,
> Le chat combat et au milan s'attache
> Si vivement et l'estraint si tresfort
> Que le milan, faisant tout son effort
> De s'envoler, se tint prins à la prise,
> Lors me souvint d'un qui a fait le fort,
> Qui par son mal a sa faiblesse apprise."[95]

Ballades of Courtly Love[96]

One of the favorite diversions of aristocratic society in the fifteenth century was the cultivation of courtly love.

91 Le Marquis de Queux de Saint-Hilaire, *Œuvres Complètes de Eustache Deschamps* (Paris, 1878), Vol. I, p. 120.

92 *Idem,* Vol. I, p. 151.

93 *Idem,* Vol. II, p. 61.

94 *Idem,* Vol. I, p. 287.

95 H. J. Molinier, *Mellin de Saint-Gelays* (Rodez, 1910), p. 382.

96 Cf. A. Piaget, *Un Manuscrit de la Cour Amoureuse de Charles VI, Romania* XXXI, and A. Piaget, *La Cour Amoureuse, dite de Charles VI, Romania* XX. Cf. also W. G. Dodd, *Courtly Love in Chaucer and Gower* (Boston and London, 1913). This book contains a detailed treatment of the subject and presents evidence of the almost universal presence of the doctrines of "Courtly love" in the English authors named, and in French writers after the Troubadours.

The well-born were lovers as inevitably as they were fighters. The conventions of a lover's conduct were rigidly prescribed and all well-regulated ardor was supposed to find some relief in decorous poetic devotion. The Courts of Love, which were frequently held on St. Valentine's day, or on the first of May, furnished the occasion for love *ballades* with their set phrases and shallow compliments. The *ballades* of Machaut, Deschamps,[97] Froissart, and Charles d'Orléans, are for the most part expressions of these familiar formulas of courtly love. So are the *ballade* sequences presently to be discussed; so, for that matter, are the greater number of *ballades* composed in the fifteenth and sixteenth centuries. The whole subject of the motives and modes of courtly love is involved in a study of *ballade* literature.

The allegory of these *ballades* became current with the *Roman de la Rose,* where abstractions like *Dangier, Esperance, Nonchaloir,* were popularized, and where the example of great lovers, too, first became a familiar literary resource.

Thus Charles d'Orléans accuses *Dangier:*

"C'est par Dangier, mon cruel adversaire,
Qui m'a tenu en ses mains longuement,
En tous mes faiz je le trouve contraire;
Et plus se rit quant plus me voit dolent.
Se vouloye raconter plainement
En cest escript mon ennuieux martire,
Trop long seroit: pour ce certainement
J'aymasse mieulx de bouche le vous dire."[98]

97 A. Piaget, *Un Manuscrit de la Cour Amoureuse de Charles VI, Romania,* XXXI, p. 602: The name of Eustache Deschamps appears among the *auditeurs,* one of the eight classes of members.

98 A. Champollion-Figeac, *Les Poésies du Duc Charles d'Orléans* (Paris, 1842), p. 69.

Again, the same poet basks in a St. Valentine's day sun while in the clutches of *Ennuieuse-pensée:*

"Le beau souleil, le jour Saint-Valentin,
Qui apportoit sa chandelle alumée,
N'a par longtemps, entra un bien matin
Privéement en ma chambre fermée.
Celle clarté qu'il avoit apportée
Si m'esveilla du somme de Soussy
Où j'avoye toute la nuit dormy,
Sur le dur lit d'Ennuieuse-pensée."[100]

Charles d'Orléans has a very beautiful love poem in *La Chasse et le Depart d'Amours,*[101] in which the formal element is less disturbing:

"Se dieu plaist, briefuement lannee
De ma tristesse passera,
Belle tres loyaulment amee,
Et le beau temps se monstrera.
Mais scauez vous quant ce sera?
Quant le doulx soleil gracieulx
De voltre beaulte entrera
par la fenestre de mes yeulx.

Lors la chambre de ma pensee
De grant plaisance reluyra,
Et sera de joye paree,
Adonc mon cueur sesueillera

100 A. Champollion-Figeac, *Opus Cit.*, p. 126.

101 P. Champion, *Pièces Joyeuses du XV*[e] *siècle* (vol. XXI of *Revue de Philologie Française*), p. 162: "*La Chasse et le Depart Damours* est l'une des plus étranges supercheries du libraire éditeur Antoine Vérard. Ce livre fut publié en 1509 sous le nom d'Octovien de Saint Gelais et de Blaise d'Auriol. . . . A. Piaget a montré que ce volume contenait avec quelques rajeunissements, la plupart des poésies de Charles d'Orléans démarquées, qu'il fallait y reconnaître la main d'un véritable faussaire."

Qui en dueil dormy longtemps a
plus ne dormira se maist dieux;
Quant ceste clerte le verra
par les fenestres des mes yeulx.

Helas! quant viendra la journee
Quainsi aduenir me pourra?
Ma maistresse tresdesiree,
pensez vous que brief aduiendra?
Car moncueur tousiours languira
En ennuy sans point auoir mieulx,
Juc a tant que soleil verra
Par les fenestres de mes yeulx.

De reconfort mon cueur aura
Autant que nul dessoulz les cieulx;
Belle, quant vous regardera
Par les fenestres de mes yeulx."[102]

A familiar conceit is conventionally expressed in the first stanza of one of Machaut's *ballades:*

"Tenus me sui longuement de chanter,
Mais orendroit ay loyal occoison
D'estre envoisiés et de joie mener,
Car mes cuers est gietés hors de prison
    Où il fut nus doucement.
Mais puis qu'il est mis hors delivrement,
Mener m'estuet bonne vie et joieuse,
Pris de rechief en prison amoureuse."[103]

One of the Englishmen who wrote French poetry, John Gower, shows in all his *ballades* familiarity with courtly love. Like Charles d'Orléans, who repeatedly made St. Valentine's day his point of departure, Gower includes in

[102] Blaise d'Auriol, *Depart d'Amours* (Toulouse, 1508), Sig. Biii^r.

[103] V. Chichmaref, *Guillaume de Machaut, Poésies Lyriques* (Paris, 1909), Vol. I, p. 50.

his *Cinkante Balades* two dedicated to rites of the fourteenth of February.[104] Gower, too, is fond of citing famous precedents. The refrain of *balade XIII* tells how the lover's pangs are "Plus qe Paris ne soeffrist pour Heleine."[105] The lady of one of his *balades* (XLIII) complains:

"Plus tricherous qe Jason a Medée,
A Deianire ou q'Ercules estoit,
Plus q'Eneas, q'avoit Dido lessée,
Plus qe Theseüs, q'Adriagne amoit,
Ou Demephon, quant Phillis oublioit,
Je trieus, helas, q'amer jadis soloie:
Dont chanterai desore en mon endroit,
C'est ma dolour, se fuist ainçois ma joie."[106]

Letters in *ballade* form may conveniently be considered in connection with conventional love terms. Gower's *Cinkante Balades* also contains three love letters in the usual epistolary style of *ballades*. In one case the poet concludes:

"O noble dame, a vous ce lettre irra,
Et quant dieu plest, je vous verrai apres:
Par cest escrit il vous remembrera,
Quant dolour vait, lest joies vienont pres."[107]

His other letter envoys are similar in character.[108]

Deschamps used the *ballade* as letter several times. There is a "lettre d'Eustace, en regraciant Madame d'Orliens par Balade," the first stanza of which runs:

104 G. C. Macaulay, *Complete Works of John Gower* (Oxford, 1899), Vol. I, pp. 365–366, *balades* XXXIIII and XXXV.

105 *Idem,* Vol. I, p. 349.

106 *Idem,* Vol. I, p. 371.

107 *Idem,* Vol. I, p. 339.

108 *Idem,* Vol. I, p. 340; p. 341.

"Ma treschiere et redoubtée dame,
Je vous merci tresamoureusement,
Quant pleu vous a a souvenir de l'ame,
D'Eustace, moy vostre povre servent,
Qu'om disoit mort, et si benignement
En avez fait chanter de vostre grace,
Qu'a Dieu suppli, priere ne li face
Jamais nul jour ne bien durant ma vie
Que vous n'aiez en ce vo bien et place;
De voz gens bien devez estre servie."[109]

And another letter, addressed to the "damoiselles de ma dicte Dame d'Orliens," closes with this envoy:

"Dames d'onneur, damoiselles aussi,
Eustace, d'umble cuer vous mercie
De voz biens faiz; vostres sui pour ce di,
Car je voy bien: Qui ayme, a tart oblie."[110]

In 1471, P. de Jasulhac, a French student at Toulouse, won a "dame d'argent" for the composition of the *Letra d'Amours* here given:

"Tres dossa Flor, cortes, plasen acuelh,
Nimpha plasen, del munde la plus bela;
Mantienh joyos, baselic frapan d'uelh;
Cors triumphan, ma dossa Domayzela,

[109] G. Raynaud, *Œuvres Complètes de Eustache Deschamps* (Paris, 1891), Vol. VII, p. 122.

[110] G. Raynaud, *Opus Cit.*, p. 125.

The refrain of this *ballade*, popularized by Chaucer in the *Parlement of Foules*, is found in at least two other places, as the first line of a stanza in a lyric of the *Modena MS.* (See A. Jeanroy, *Les Chansons Françaises du MS. de Modène*, Supplement of *Revue des Langues Romanes*, 1896, p. 249), and also as the refrain of *Balade XXV* in Gower's *Cinkante Balades.* (See G. C. Macaulay, *Complete Works of John Gower* (Oxford, 1899), Vol. I, p. 358.)

Mon cor soffris dolor arden, crusela,
Per vostr' amor e languis neyt e jorn,
En loc que sia trobar no pot sojorn
Tan fort vos tem e de bon' amor ama,
E se mante plus que nul a son torn
Humil, lial e secret a sa Dama.

Quant ieu regart vostras belas fayssos,
Lo gentil cors, vostra bona doctrina,
Lo bel parlar, lo regart amoros
E l bon renom qu'en vos sus tot domina,
Adone, mon cor de vos amor no fina,
Ez en re plus trobar no pot repaus,
Tant es liat en vostre' amor e claus,
Don en totz locs, desir arden l'enflama,
E tot jorn es, ses mudar son prepaus,
Humil, lial e secret a sa Dama.

Donc, rosier gay, supplic vos humilmen
Ajatz merce de ma joie simplessa,
No vulhatz pas mon dolen fenimen,
Res ieu no clam qu'amor e gentillessa:
Ieu vos crendray coma Dieu o Deesa,
En vos serven y aman de bon acort;
Vostre sera mon cors e vien e mort,
Gardan per tot vostre bon nom e fama,
Retenetz lo, quar el es ferm e fort
Humil, lial e secret a sa Dama.

Tornada

Prince tres haut, thesaur de tot deport,
Vuelhas donar a mon cor bon coffort,
En alleujan sa dolor e sa flama;
Son voler es d'esser entro la mort
Humil, lial e secret a sa Dama."

[A. F. Gatien-Arnoult, *Monumens de la Littérature Romane* (Paris-Toulouse, 1841–1849), Vol. IV, p. 239.]

Ballade Sequences

Some of the earliest *ballades* were imbedded in allegorical poems of considerable length. In the fourteenth century and in the fifteenth, too, *ballades* continued to be interspersed in narrative, though not necessarily allegorical, poems. Thus, in Froissart's *Le Livre du Trésor Amoureux,*[111] there are one hundred and twenty-eight *ballades,* arranged in three groups, two of forty-four[112] and one of forty, all of which exhibit a unity of thought and feeling in that their theme is "D'armes, d'amours et de moralité," or, in other words, chivalry. The chief interest, however, for the medieval reader lay primarily, we may suppose, in the verse into which the *ballades* were introduced, and not in the *ballades* themselves. Other poems, too, containing series of *ballades,* might be cited, such as Machaut's *Le Livre du Voir-Dit,*[113] Christine de Pisan's *Le Livre du Duc des Vrais Amans,*[114] and *Le Prisonnier Desconforté.*[115]

But at least three sequences of one hundred *ballades* and one group of fifty, unconnected with other verse or prose, were composed at the height of the enthusiasm for the form. There were the *Cinkante Balades,*[116] composed by John

111 A. Scheler, *Œuvres de Froissart* (Brussels, 1872), Vol. III, p. 54.

112 In one of these groups a *jeu-parti* occurs between the poet and a knight on the comparative merits of success in arms and success in love.

113 Guillaume de Machaut, *Le Livre du Voit-Dit,* with an introduction by P. Paris (Paris, 1885).

114 M. Roy, *Œuvres Poétiques de Christine de Pisan* (Paris, 1896), Vol. III.

115 P. Champion, *Le Prisonnier Desconforté* (Paris, 1909).

116 G. C. Macaulay, *The Complete Works of John Gower* (Oxford, 1899), Vol. I.

Gower in French verse,[117] two centuries by "Christine desolée," and a third century by Jean le Seneschal.[118] In all these the familiar situations and sentiments of courtly love figured repeatedly.

In another series by Christine de Pisan, the *Cent Ballades*,[119] the thought connection throughout is much less close than it would be in a characteristic sonnet sequence of the Elizabethans. These sonnet sequences[120] usually celebrate the matchless perfections of the beloved. The beauties of one individual, more rarely of several, secure the unity of the collection. But the *Cent Ballades*, unlike the sonnet sequences, are on a variety of subjects and seem to have been composed at long intervals.[121] For example, the first twenty *ballades* express Christine's personal loss in the death of her husband, while others treat the general

117 The rhythm is somewhat different from that of French verse on the continent. There is a noticeable conflict between the syllabic count and the accent. Gower, like the English poets who wrote *ballades* in English, did not conform wholly to the restrictions of the form. Five of his *ballades*, for example, XIII, XVI, XIV, XVII, and LI, are without refrain.

118 G. Raynaud, *Les Cent Ballades* (Paris, 1905), p. xliii: "Nous dirons donc, en combinant les données fournies par le *Livre des faits* et par le poème des *Cent Ballades* que ce dernier ouvrage, dont le cadre est l'œuvre commune de quatre auteurs, a été presque en entier versifié par le sénéchal d'Eu, aidé partiellement par Boucicault, par Crésecque et par Philippe d'Artois, dont le collaboration ne saurait être exactement définie."

119 Maurice Roy, *Œuvres Poétiques de Christine de Pisan* (Paris, 1886), Vol. I, p. 1. Roy believes the time of composition to cover the years between 1394 and 1399.

120 Cf. Sidney Lee, *Elizabethan Sonnets, An English Garner* (Westminster, 1904).

121 M. Roy, *Opus Cit.*, Vol. I, p. xxvii: "Nous pensons donc que c'est dans un intervalle d'au moins cinq ou six années qu'ont dû être composés la plupart de ces morceaux poétiques."

subject of love—vicariously, as *Balade L* would have us believe.

"Aucunes gens porroient mesjugier
Pour ce sur moy que je fais ditz d'amours;
Et diroient que l'amoureux dongier,
Je sçay trop bien compter et tous les tours,
Et que ja si vivement
N'en parlasse, sanz l'essay proprement,
Mais sauve soit la grace des diseurs,
Je m'en raport a tous sages ditteurs."[122]

Some wholly different themes, too, are found. For example, a contemporary meets ironical treatment at the hands of the lady:

"Dant chevalier, vous amez, moult beaulz ditz,
Mais je vous pri que mieulx aimiez beaulz faiz."[123]

Jealous husbands, favorite subjects for jest in the Middle Ages, come in for their share:

"Que ferons nous de ce mary jaloux?
Je pry a Dieu qu'on le puist escorchier.
Tant se prent il de près garde de nous
Que ne pouons l'un de l'autre approchier.
A male hart on le puist atachier,
L'ort vil, villain, de goute contrefait,
Qui tant de maulz et tant d'anuis nous fait!"[124]

Again, entirely different from these in tone, is *Balade XCIV*, as the closing stanza will show:

"Si devons, tous et toutes, querir voie
De parvenir avec la noble route

[122] *Idem,* Vol. I, p. 51.
[123] *Idem,* Vol. I, p. 59, *Balade LVIII.*
[124] *Idem,* Vol. I, p. 78, *Balade LXXVIII.*

Des benois sains, ou vit et regne a joye
La trés hault Dieu, en qui est bonté toute,
Qui nous donra tel salaire,
Se nous voulons repentir et bien faire,
Ou joye et paix et grant gloire est enclose.
Dieux nous y maint trestous a la parclose!"[125]

In the final *ballade* of the collection, Christine intimates that the hundred were gathered together at a friend's request:

" Cent balades ay cy escriptes,
Trestoutes de mon sentement.
Si en sont mes promesses quites
A qui m'en pria chierement.
Nommée m'i suis proprement;
Qui le vouldra savoir ou non,
En la centiesme entierement
En escrit y ay mis mon nom."[126]

Who this friend was continues to be a mystery.

The other century of *ballades* composed by Christine, the *Cent Balades d'Amant et de Dame,* was, as the first stanza of the introductory *ballade* says, composed at the behest of some gracious lady:

" Quoy que n'eusse corage ne pensée,
Quant a present, de dits amoureus faire,
Car autre part adès suis a pensée,
Par le command de personne, qui plaire
Doit bien a tous, ay empris a parfaire
D'un amoureux et sa dame ensement,
Pour obeïr a autrui et complaire,
Cent balades d'amoureux sentement."[127]

125 *Idem,* Vol. I, p. 99.
126 *Idem,* Vol. I, p. 100.
127 *Idem,* Vol. III, p. 209.

After this introduction, the lady and her servant in love proceed, in a series of *ballades,* to challenge each other. The cry of the lover is:

> "Tournez voz yeulx vers moy, doulce maitresse,"[128]

The lady's attitude is indicated by her observation:

> "Ayme qui vouldra amer,
> Quant a moy je n'en fois conte."[129]

The lover reports his lack of progress to *Amours,* and *Amours,* in a *ballade,* takes the difficult mistress to task: "Trop est folle ta vantise."[130] Finally the lady softens by degrees. First she admits, "Assez lonc temps a duré vo martires."[131] In a dialogue within a single *ballade* they then arrive at a better mutual understanding. At length, in surrender, the lady says:

> "Tienne toute
> Suis sans doubte."[132]

In the remaining *ballades* they celebrate the passionate perfection of accomplished love in terms of the courtly conventions of the day; they grieve over the inevitable estrangements and separations, and in the end, the lady, "Au lit malade couchiée," is made to say:

> "A Dieu, Amours; aprouchiée
> Suis de mort par toy; j'en sue
> Ja la sueur, et fichiée
> Suis ou pas, m'ame perdue

[128] *Idem,* Vol. III, p. 220.
[129] *Idem,* Vol. III, p. 215.
[130] *Idem,* Vol. III, p. 219.
[131] *Idem,* Vol. III, p. 235.
[132] *Idem,* Vol. III, p. 243.

9

Ne soit pas mais de Dieu eue
A Dieu, monde, a Dieu, honneurs,
J'ay yeulx troubles et voix mue,
Car ja me deffault li cueurs."[133]

Gower's *Cinkante Balades* belong approximately to the same period[134] as Christine's *Cent Balades.* Like hers, they are for the most part impersonal. The prose glosses to *Balades* V and VI show clearly that the series is in no sense autobiographical. For Gower says of the first five that they are made especially "pour ceaux q'attendont lours amours par droite mariage," and of the rest that they are "universeles a tout le monde, selonc les prophetés et les condicions des Amantz, qui sont diversement travailez en la fortune d'amour." And, moreover, five of the *balades*[135] are plainly from the feminine point of view. Various favorite *ballade* themes are treated by Gower. Love is his chief business, however, and love according to the mode of the age.

In contrast, *Les Cent Ballades* of Jean le Seneschal have considerable plot. In his own person, he begins the story: One day, when, as a young man, he is on the road between Angers and les Ponts-de-Cé, he meets a knight. This older cavalier, seeing that the young man is distracted and sad, immediately comes to the conclusion that he is in love, and, as a man of experience, he lays down certain rules of conduct in matters of love and of chivalry; he expounds the

133 M. Roy, *Opus Cit.,* Vol. III, p. 307.

134 G. C. Macaulay, *The Works of John Gower* (Oxford, 1899), Vol. I, p. lxxiii: "In any case it seems certain that some at least of the balades were composed with a view to the court of Henry IV, and the collection assumed its present shape probably in the year of his accession, 1399, for we know that either in the first or second year of Henry IV the poet became blind and ceased to write."

135 XLI–XLV, XLVI.

doctrines of love and of war and shows how real happiness in love lies in loyalty. This advice, given in the first fifty *ballades,* the pupil promises to follow. Almost six months later, he is put to the test. On the banks of the Loire, in the midst of a brilliant company, one of the ladies takes him aside and taxes him with his ideal of faith in love. She praises the charms of fickleness, and prophesies that his absurd obstinacy will in the end lead to his utter boredom. Finally, dismayed by his attitude, she suggests recourse to judges. He intimates ironically that the case is merely between treachery in love and true faith. But the lady insists that he states the question unfairly and that true happiness in love lies not in exalting constancy too highly or in condemning fickleness too vociferously. She will admit no disloyalty to any one lover in a multiplicity of lovers. The three judges by whom the debate is to be settled hold with the young man that loyalty in love brings the only true happiness, whereupon all four resolve to make a book out of this joint adventure.[136]

[136] Gaston Raynaud, *Les Cent Ballades par Jean le Seneschal* (Paris, 1905), p. xxxiv: "Le poème n'est en réalité qu'un *débat* poétique entre deux parties, dont l'une représentée par le vieux chevalier Hutin, soutient la cause de *Loyauté* en amour, et dont l'autre, sous les traits d'une jeune dame désignée sous le nom de *la Guignarde* défend au contraire les droits de *Faussetê.*" The series is thought to have been composed during a pilgrimage of the author's in the Holy Land. In regard to the date of the poems and the circumstances under which they were given publicity, Raynaud has the following to say (pp. xlviii–xlix): "En octobre 1389, les pèlerins rentrent en France... 'ils trouvèrent en leur chemin le roy, qui estoit à l'abbaye de Clugny. . . . Si les receut le roy moult joyeusement, et grand feste fit de leur venue.' Ce ne fut certainement pas durant les fêtes de Cluny que se tint le *puy* où les auteurs des *Cent Ballades* proposaient aux amateurs de poésie la question à traiter de la supériorité de l'amour loyal ou de l'amour volage. Nous savons en effet que le duc de Berry, qui prit part au concours, ne se trouvait pas à Cluny et

The give and take of the lady and her sensible cavalier are well shown in the sixteenth *Balade:*

"Or me dittes, se trouviëz
Belle dame, douce, plaisant,
Et a son maintien vëiëz
Que d'Amours vous moustrast semblant,
Vouldriëz la par convenant
Qu'amie la deussiez clamer?"
—"Nennin, car j'aim ma dame tant
Qu'autre ne quier, ne veul amer."

—"Et se priée l'aviëz
De s'amour, en lui requerant
La sienne que tant vouldriëz,
Et de ce vous fust refusant,
Dittes moi, dès la en avant
Vouldriëz vous sien demourer?"
—"Oïl, certes; je vous crëant
Qu'autre ne quier, ne veul amer."

—"Certes, fil, mestier ariëz
De bon conseil, car maintenant
Voy qu'avenir ne sariëz
Aus grans biens qu'alez desirant.
Pour ce vous pry que tant ne quant
Ne maintenez ce fol penser."

qu'il rencontra le cortège royal pour la première fois à Avignon, le 30 octobre 1389. Huit jours plus tard, le samedi 6 novembre, après de nombreuses fêtes . . . Charles VI quittait la ville, signifiant à ses deux oncles de Bourgogne et de Berry son désir de ne pas être accompagné par eux dans la suite de son voyage . . . Nous sommes donc naturellement amené à conclure que le concours poétique fait à l'occasion des *Cent Ballades,* où figure le duc de Berry, a dû se produire à Avignon pendant le séjour du roi, au nombre des fêtes . . . alors que la rupture entre le roi et le duc de Berry n'était pas encore prononcée."

—"Ne m'alez plus de ce parlant,
Qu'autre ne quier, ne veul amer."[137]

An interesting supplement to the work of Jean le Seneschal is the little series of thirteen *ballades,* the answers of as many amateurs, who undertook one side or the other of the controversy. Two of the poets support the claims of fickleness; seven champion constancy, and four take an amused, slightly skeptical tone with no reference to the real issue. Of the advocates of constancy, Guy VI de la Tremoïlle[138] may be the spokesman. The first stanza of his reply confirms the point of view of the young cavalier in *Les Cent Ballades:*

"De grant honneur amoureux enrichir
Ne peut s'il n'a Loyauté en s'aÿe,
Et pour ce fay dedens mon cuer florir
Loyal amour d'umilité garnie,
Dont doucement sans Fausseté servie
Sera la flour non pareille d'onneur,
De grant beauté, de bonté, de valeur,
Qui de mon cuer souveraine maistresse
Est et sera: s'aray dame et seignour:
En ciel un dieu, en terre une diesse."[139]

The Satirical Ballade

Satire in the centuries in which the *ballade* flourished was largely directed against the frailties of the Church and of the court, and against the sins and stupidities of women. In *ballade* literature, the clergy rarely, the aristocracy more often, and the feminine sex most often, are the objects of attack. The jargon of the lowest grades of Paris society was used by Villon and by many other poets in their gross

137 G. Raynaud, *Opus Cit.,* p. 119.
138 Born 1343.
139 G. Raynaud, *Opus Cit.,* p. 221.

attacks on gross abuses.[140] The satirical "sotte" *ballade*, nearly always expressed in terms of unspeakable indecency, assailed institutions and individuals indiscriminately. Most of these are unprintable, and because of their dialect fortunately incomprehensible to all but special students of jargon or thieves' patter.[141]

A *ballade* of Roger de Collerye here given represents the type of satire in which the restraints of decency were not felt.

" Contre les clercs de chastellet.
La Bazoche.

Dormez vous? quoy! est il vray ie men plains.
Sus, mes suppostz gectez regrectz & plains
Ou aultrement ie n'en seray contente.
Est il saison par chemins & par plains
De songer creux? non non ie me complains
Tout a part moy de vostre longe attente
Bazochiens, qu'on ne se mescontente,
Car il est dict, sans faire grant hahay
Que vous iourrez ce ioly moys de may.

Laissez courir gensdarmes & leurs train
Postes, heraulx, sil vient quilz soient contrains
De desmarcher ainsi qui le vent vente.
Que voz esbas ne soient iamais estains!

140 Marcel Schwob, *Parnasse Satyrique du XV Siècle* (Paris, 1905). Cf. also, S. Raynaud, *Ballade Addressée à Charles VII contre Arthur de Richemont, Connétable de France, Bulletin de la Société des Anciens Textes Français* (Paris, 1910), p. 45; and P. Champion, *Pièces Joyeuses des XVe Siècle, Revue de Philologie Française*, Vol. XXI, pp. 182–192, *poesim.*

141 Cf. Villon's *ballades* in jargon and *Les Contredictz de Franc Gontier;* see A. Longnon *Œuvres Complètes de François Villon* (Paris, 1892), p. 83 and P. Champion, *François Villon, sa Viet et ses Œuvres* (Paris, 1913), Vol. I, pp. 194–196.

De laschete ne fustes onc attaint
Il est tout vray i'en ay lectre patente.
Continuez, vous ares vostre rente:
Grans et petis sactendent de cueur gay
Que vous iourrez ce ioly moys de may.

Suppostz gentilz, aymes, doubtez & crains,
Empoignes moy ces tripiers a beaulx crains,
Des auiourdhuy contre eux ie me presente.
Ce sont poissars, pipereaulx, mal mondains,
Punectz, infectz & puans comme dains;
Qui ne me croit, qu'on les experimente."[142]
Du cardinal ia ne fault que i'en mente
S'il n'est papa, papelart, papegay,
Si iourrez vous ce ioly moys de may.

Prince, ie dis cōme dame et regente,
Et pour oster tout ennuy & esmay,
Veu & congneu vostre maniere gente,
Que vous iourrez ce ioly moys de may.[143]

Many of the satires against women[144] are written in the language of the gutter, but some are entrusted to the ordinary vernacular. Deschamps has a *balade* "contre les femmes" with the refrain, "Il n'est chose que femme ne conçomme."[145] Villon spares no vicious detail in the *Ballade de la Belle Hëaulmière aux Filles de Ioie.*[146] And in his

142 Of the institution of the *Bazoche*, H. Guy, *L'École des Rhétoriqueurs* (Paris, 1910), p. 56, says: "Satirique et joviale association des clercs du palais." See A. Fabre, *Les Clercs du Palais* (Lyon, 1875).

143 *Les Œuvres de Roger de Collerye* (Paris, 1536), Sig Nii^{v}.

144 An interesting account of this subject is given in T. L. Neff, *La Satire des Femmes dans la Poésie Lyrique Française du Moyen Age* (Paris, 1900).

145 Le Marquis de Queux de Saint-Hilaire, *Œuvres Complètes de Eustache Deschamps* (Paris, 1882), Vol. II, p. 36.

146 A. Longnon, *Œuvres de François Villon* (Paris, 1892), p. 42.

Ballade de Bonne Doctrine a Ceux de Mauvaise Vie,[147] his refrain is: "Tout aux tauernes & aux filles."

Bouchet, too, has his say against consuming loves. He follows the courtly lovers in searching the past for examples of affection lavished on the ladies:

Balade cõtre folles Amours.

"Tout homme, qui bien se gouuerne
Entre les mondains sagement,
Pres folles femmes ne se yuerne,
Mais fuyt d'amours l'embrasement;
Amour est vng feu vehement
Dont viennent les grandes chaleurs
Qui font a tout entendement,
Pour vng plaisir mille douleurs.

Sanson y lessa sa lanterne,
Dauid en plora longuement,
La teste y pardit Olopherne,
Troye en perist piteusement,
Philix pour aymer follement
Se pendi apres cris & pleurs,
Tarquin en eust pour paiement,
Pour vng plaisir mille douleurs.

Salomon, la clere luserne,
En mescongneust Dieu faulcement,
Et vergille au vent de galerne
Fut tout vng iour publiquement;
Aristote facillement
S'en lessa brider; quelz erreurs
Tous en eurent certainnement,
Pour vng plaisir mille douleurs.

147 A. Longnon, *Opus Cit.*, p. 93. Cf. P. Champion, *François Villon, sa Vie et ses Œuvres* (Paris, 1913), Vol. I, p. 79.

Prince, vous voyez clerement
Damours les petites valleurs,
Et qu'on y a finablement,
Pour vng plaisir mille douleurs."[148]

In Gracien du Pont's *Les Controverses des Sexes Masculin et Feminin,*[149] the masculine sex is actually moved to call on the author for aid against the "grande follie" of the ladies:

"Balade unisonne a refrain, contenant la prière et supplication du sexe masculin enuers l'autheur. En luy priant le vouloir secourir et deffendre.

Le sexe masculin.

Frere germain: humblement si te prye
Le pouure corps: qui de toy tant se fye:
Guer son affaire: le veuilles secourir
Femenin sexe: par sa grande follie
La tant blesse: de maincte villainie
Que de grand dueil: en est cuyde mourir
Par quoy te vient: de bon cueur requerir
Qua le deffendre: tu veuilles estre enclin
Guarde l'honneur: du sexe masculin.

Je scay tres bien: sans nulle flatterie
Que si tu veule: mettre ta fantasie
Facillement: la scauras mainctenir
Car mainct passaige: de la theologie
Du droict commun: et de philosophie
En trouveras: pour le bien soubstenir
Ne parmectz plus: si mal lentretenir
Je ten supplie: mon doulx frere begnin
Garde l'honneur: du sexe masculin.

148 Iehan Bouchet, *XIII Rondeaux Differens. Auec XXV Balades Differentes* (Paris, 1536). Sig. Cv^r.

149 Toulouse, 1584.

Ce nest rien plus: le droict de ma partie
Que oppinion: caquet et menterie
Pensant bon droict: en maulvais conuertir
Par ses propoz: et grande bauerie
Par ses menasses: et par sa crierie
Pense les gens: de raison diuertir
De telz abuz: je tous veule advertir
En declairant: son cauteleux engin
Garde l'honneur: du sexe masculin.

Lenuoy

Frere lequel: sans plus men enquerir
En briefz de jours: tous mes maulx peulx guerir
Et mon proces: mettre du tout affin
Garde l'honneur: du sexe masculin."

"Balade unissone a refrain et coronnee par equiuocques du sexe masculin se complaignant du sexe femenin priant lautheur derechief se vouloir secourir.

Le sexe masculin

Las je me plains: de mainctz estourdiz dictz
Qua ma partie: par faulx intenditz ditz
Contre l'honneur: de mes fleurissanz sens
Dont par le juge: des dampnez mauldítz dis
Auant desjours: si me mesconditz dir
Lauras vaincu: tes faictz si puissans sentz
Mes desirs sont: a toy addressans sens
Auoir le cueur: vers aultre quelquil soit
De motz picque: suys par mainctz fissans cens
Les bons amys: au besoing lon cognoist.

Laisse pour moy: tous les amolliz lictz
Et prens tes liures: ou par mes delictz liz
Et trouueras: des motz competens tantz

Las je trouuerez: si mal ses dediuctz duitz
Que si trouue: ieusse nulz conduitz dhuys
Leusse fouy: par long (comme entendz) temps
En brief vaincuz: ces dictz inconstans tendz
Par toy si peine: tu mectz en cest endroict
Ses arcz desprit: les plus resistans tendz
Les bons amys: au besoing lon congnoist.

Sur tous viuans: dargumens essuytz suy
Car en oyant: ce que je pour suys sueiz
De despit queuz: ouyr telz meschantz chantz
Gaigner cuydoit: dhonneur par surpris pris
Se monstrant fol: sur toutz les marchantz champs
En luy abbatras: ses faulx decepuans ventz
Tant par raison: que par le commun droict
A toy mes droictz: sans nulz reseruans vendz
Les bons amys: au besoing lon congnoist.

Enuoy

Prince puyssant: sur tous les regentz gentz
Conforte moy: si poinct faire se doibt
Car comme disent: pouures indigens gens
Les bons amys: au besoing lon congnoist."

The king and the court were naturally in a position to be treated more tenderly by the satirist. In the twenty-five *ballades* by Meschinot and Chastellain, appended to *Les Lunettes de Princes* of Meschinot, one of which is given below, Louis XI is the object of the satire:

"On ne peut mieulx pe*r*dre le nō dhōneur
Que soy trouuer desloyal & menteur,
Lasche en armes, cruel a ses amys,
A meschans gens estre large dhonneur,
sans congnoistre ceulx en qui est valeur,
Mais acquerir en tout temps ennemys;
Tel homme doit auoir mendicite,

Gaster son temps en infelicite,
Sans faire riẽs qua dieu naux hōme plaise.
Il sera plain dopprobres & diffames,
Cest cil q*ue* tous les vertueux sans blasmes
Vont mauldisant pour sa vie mauluaise.

Le peu scauant abondant sermonneur
Du nom de dieu horrible blasphemeur,
Sans rien tenir de ce quil a promis,
Qui nescoute des poures la clameur,
Mais les cōtrainct par moleste & rigeur,
Cōbien quil soit pour leur pasteur cōmis
se verra cheoir en grant perplexite,
Par son deffault & imbecillite,
se lire dieu de brief il ne repaise
Nomme sera du nombre de infames
Le malheureux: q*ue* tous seigneurs et dames
Vont mauldisant pour sa vie mauluaise.

Il naffiert pas a vng prince ou seign*eur*,
Qui de vertus doibt paroistre enseigneur,
estre inconstant ne aux vices submis,
Pour ce quil est des aultres gouuerneur;
Cest biẽ raison quil soit saige & meilleur
Que ceulx a tel estat nest permis,
Pour escheuer toute prolixite,
Comme deuant a este recite.
Ie diray vray, ou il fault que me taise,
Il nest mestier que pour sage te clames,
se celuy es que raisonnables ames
Vōt mauldisant pour sa vie mauluaise.

Georges

Prince ennemy daultruy felicite
De propre sang de propre affinite
De propre paix qui le tient a son aise
Quest il celuy fort hayneux a soymesmes

et que la voix de tous hōmes & femmes
Vont mauldisant pour sa vie mauluaise."[150]

The first stanza of a dialogue *ballade,* by Henri Baude, describes the plight of an exiled favorite of Louis XI (1466):

"Ballade Faicte Pour Mgr. de Dampmartin
Contre Messire Charles de Meslung.

Dont viens-tu, Martin?—De Melun.
—Et que dit-on? J'ai veu Charlot?
—Par ta foy? Il est tout commun,
Aussi camus comme ung rabot.
—En bon poinct? Rond comme ung sabot?
—Quelle chière fait-il? Triste et morne.
—Et que fait-il? Sans dire mot,
Il actent que le vent se tourne."[151]

And the Court itself is attacked in another *ballade* by the same author:

Ballade en Dialogue
Sur le mauvais comportement de la court.

J'allasse en court, se j'eusse de l'argent.
—A quoy faire?—Pour avoir ung office.
—Les y vent-on? Ouy, très-chièrement.
—Pourquoy est-ce?—Par faulte de police.
—Je m'en plaindroie.—Et à qui?—A justice.
—Justice dort, encor n'est esveillée.

150 *Les Lunettes des Princes avec Aulcunes Balades & Additions Nouuellement Composee par Noble Homme Iehan Meschinot Escuyer en son Viuant Grant Maistre dHotel de la Royne de France* (Paris, 1539), sig. Ivi^r–Ivii^r.

151 J. Quicherat, *Les Vers de Maître Henri Baude* (Paris, 1856), p. 26.

—Dont procède?—Le quoy?—Ceste malice.
—De nostre court qu'est mal conseillée."[152]

A *ballade* of Collerye's "contre les flatteurs de Court" begins thus:

"Pour succumber le train imbecial
Qui court en court, de flatteurs impudiques
Premeditant d'ung sens trop bestial
Villipender bons servans domestiquès,
Tympaniser par criz haulx et publiques
Et organer d'un chant vil, sans accord
Convient leurs noms; par moyens ebloiques,
De raporteurs vient tout mal et discord."[153]

Mildly satirical in tone is Sarrasin's *Balade du Pays de Cocagne:*

"Ne loüons l'Isle où Fortune jadis
Mit ses trésors, ny la plaine Elisée,
Ny de Mahom le noble Paradis;
Car chacun sçait que c'est billevesée.
Par nous plutôt Cocagne soit prisée;
C'est bons Païs; l'Almanach point ne ment,
Où l'on le voit dépeint fort dignement.
Or pour sçavoir où gît cette compagne,
Je le diray disant pays en Normand
Le Pays de Caux est le Pays de Cocagne.

Tous les Mardys sont de gras Mardys,
De ces Mardys l'Année est composée.
Cailles y vont dans le plat dix à dix,
Et perdreaux tendres comme rosée.
Le fruit y pleut, si que c'est chose aisée
De le cueillir se baissant seulement.

[152] J. Quicherat, *Opus Cit.*, p. 79, st. 1.

[153] Charles d'Héricault, *Les Œuvres de Roger de Collerye* (Paris, 1855), p. 169.

Poissons en beurre y nagent largement,
Fleuves y sont du meilleur vin d'Espagne,
Et tout cela fait dire tardement
Le pays de Caux est le Pays de Cocagne.

Pour les Beautez de ces lieux, Amadis
Eut Oriane en son temps méprisée;
Bien donnerois quatre maravedis
Si j'en avois une seule baisée.
Plus cointes sont que n'est une Epousée,
Et dans Palais s'ébattent noblement
Prés leur déduit & leur ébatement
Rien n'eut paru la Cour de Charlemagne,
Quoy que Turpin en écrive autrement
Le Pays de Caux est le Pays de Cocagne."[154]

A *ballade* in the vein of light literary satire, not wholly lacking in a kind of genuine admiration, is Sarrasin's in his *Pompe Funebre de Voiture* (1648). The poem is here printed with the introduction that precedes it in the burlesque:

"Ces Romanciers étoient suivis d'une troupe de bonnes gens, se lamentans pitoyablement: C'étaient nos vieux Poëtes que Voiture avoit remis en vogue par ses Balades, ses Triolets, & ses Rondeaux, & qui par sa mort retournoient dans leur ancien décry. Marot, qui sur tous luy étoit le plus obligé, se plaignant plus fortement que les autres & à demy desesperé, leur chantoit cette Balade.

Balade

Maître Vincent nous avoit retirez,
Par ses beaux Vers faits à notre maniere,
Des dents des Vers nos ennemis jurez,
Du long oubly, d'une sale poussiere.
Lors que jadis nous tenions cour pleniere,
Tout gentil coeur composoit un Rondeau.

[154] *Les Œuvres de M. Sarrasin* (Paris, 1694), p. 400.

Vielle Balade étoit un fruit nouveau.
Les Triolets avoient grosse pratique,
Tout nous rioit: mais tout est à vau—l'eau,
Voiture est mort, adieu la Muse antique.

Biens est raison que soyons éplorez
Quand Atropos la Parque Safraniere,
En retranchant les beaux filets dorez
Où tant se plût sa Soeur la Filandiere,
A fait tomber Voiture dans la biere.
Bien nous faut-il prendre le Chalumeau,
Et tristement, ainsi qu'au renouveau
Le Rossignol au bocage rustique,
Chacun chanter en pleurant comme un veau,
Voiture est mort, adieu la Muse antique.

Or nous serons par tout deshonorez,
L'un sera mis en cornets d'Epiciere;
L'autre exposé dans les lieux égarez
Où les Mortels d'une posture fiere
Luy tourneront par mépris le derriere.
Plusieurs seront balayez au ruisseau,
Maint au foyer traînent en maint lambeau
Sera brûlé comme un traître Héretique:
Chacun de nous aura part au gâteau,
Voiture est mort, adieu la Muse antique.

Envoy

Prince Apollon, un funeste Corbeau,
En croassant au sommet d'un Ormeau,
A dit d'une voix prophetique,
Bouqins, Bouqins, rentrez dans le tombeau,
Voiture est mort, adieu la Muse antique."[155]

The Historical Ballade

French history also finds expression in *ballades*. Both important and unimportant events, royal marriages, treaties,

[155] *Les Œuvres de M. Sarrasin* (Paris, 1694), pp. 268–270.

campaigns, and military heroes, furnished at various times the subject matter of this fixed verse form. Great historical poetry was not produced. The formal nature of the *ballade* precluded the effects of Drayton's ballad on Agincourt, or of Wolfe's *Burial of Sir John More.*

In the wealth of *ballades* furnished by Deschamps we find a *ballade* "sur la naissance de Charles VI et de Louis d'Orléans son frere,"[156] the refrain of which is, "Par ce sçara chascun ceste naissance"; another "Sur le mort de Bertrand du Guesclin" (1380),[157] with a refrain, "Plourez, plourez, flour de chevalerie"; another "sur la Trève Faite avec L'Angleterre" (1394),[158] with the refrain, "Paix n'arez jà s'ilz ne rendent Calays." The envoy of Deschamps's *ballade* "sur le mariage de Richard, roi d'Angleterre et d'Isabeau de France" is pathetic in its unconsciousness of the real outcome of the match:

L'Envoy

"Princes royaulx, de bonne affection
Querez la paix et reformacion
De voz subgiez, et vous ferez que saige,
Par le traittié d'umble conjunction.
S'estes tout un, ne doubtez, nascion:
Toute paix vint par un saint mariaige."[159]

Christine de Pisan, in 1404, wrote a *ballade* "Complainte sur le mort de Philippe Le Hardi, Duc de Bourgongne,"[160]

[156] Le Marquis de Queux de Saint-Hilaire, *Œuvres Complètes de Eustache Deschamps* (Paris, 1878), Vol. I, p. 146.

[157] *Idem,* Vol. II, p. 27. There is another on the same subject on p. 29.

[158] *Idem,* Vol. III, p. 62.

[159] *Idem,* Vol. VI, p. 134.

[160] M. Roy, *Œuvres Poétiques de Christine de Pisan* (Paris, 1886), Vol. I, p. 255.

with the refrain, "Affaire eussions du bon duc de Bourgongne."[161]

A well known historical *ballade* has for its subject "l'état de la France après la bataille d'Agincourt" (1415):

"Cy veoit-on que par piteuse adventure
Prince régnant, plein de sa voulenté,
Sang si divers qui de l'autre n'a cure,
Conseil suspect de parcialité,
Poeple destruit par prodigalité,
Feront encore tant de gens mendier
Qu'à ung chascun fauldra faire mestier.

Noblesse fait encontre sa nature;
Le clergie craint et cèle vérité;
Humble commun obéit et endure;
Faulx protecteur luy font adversité
Mais trop souffrir induit nécessité
Dont advendra, ce que jà voir ne quier,
Qu'à ung chascun fauldra faire mestier.

Foible ennemi, en grant desconfiture
Victorien et pou débilité;
Provision verbal qui petit dure,
Dont mille riens n'en est exécuté;
Le roy des cieulx meisme est persécuté!
La fin viendra, et nostre estat dernier
Qu'à ung chascun fauldra faire mestier."[162]

Fifty years later, under circumstances described in the *Mémoire de Jacques Duclercq* (liv. V, ch. XXIV),[163] the following was composed:

161 This duke of Burgundy was the father of John the Fearless, slayer of Louis d'Orléans.

162 Le Roux de Lincy, *Recueil de Chants Historiques Français* (Paris, 1844), p. 296.

163 Le Roux de Lincy, *Opus Cit.*, p. 352: "Or au mois de juillet 1465, lorsque les Bourguignons s'avançaient à la rencontre de leurs

"D'où venez vous?—D'où Voire, de la cour.
—Et qu'y faict on?—Qu'y faict on. Rien quy vaille
—A brief parler quel est bruict de la cour?
Mauvais.—Oy?—Oy certainement.—
Aurons nous pis?—Oy certainement.—
—Comment cela? On en voit l'apparence
—Quy portera ce faix entierement?
—Quy?—Voire quy?—Les trois estats de France.

Dont vient cecy? De quoy sy grief mal sourd?
—Dont voir deà? Dictes le hardiment.
—Je criens, pensant qui tient l'argent sy court.
Diray-je? Oy; dictes le baudement.
Et quy sont-ils? Je ne parle autrement.
—En ont-ils eu?—Si en ont à puissance!
—Quy leur en baille, sy très abondamment?
—Quy?—Voire quy?—Les trois estats de France.

Que dict Paris? Est-il muet et sourd?
N'ose-il parler?—Nenny, ne Parlement.
—Et le Clergié, le vous tient-on bien court?
—Par vostre foy, oy publiquement
—Noblesse, quoy?—Va moitié pirement;
Tout se périt, sans avoir espérance.
—Quy peut pourvoir à cecy bonnement?
—Quy?—Voire quy?—Les trois estats de France.

Prince, quy veult leur donner allegeance?
—A quy?—A eux? Je vous prie humblement.
—De quoy?—Que vous ayez leur règne en remembrance

alliés les Bretons, ils traversèrent Saint-Denis et vinrent, par la plaine de Clichy, jusqu'au pont de Saint-Cloud, dont ils se rendirent maîtres. Là ils firent une assez longue halte, dans l'attente que les Parisiens allaient leur ouvrir leurs portes; mais il n'en fut rien, car, au lieu de capitulation, ils ne reçurent à leur adresse, qu'un feuillet de papier òu étaient écrites les deux ballades qu'on va lire."

—Qu'y peut donner bon conseil prestement?
—Qu'y—Voire quy? Les trois estats de France."[164]

Naturally the rivalry[165] between Louis XI and Charles the Bold found *ballade* expression, too:

"Souffle, Triton, en ta bucce argentine;
Muse, en musant en ta doulce musette,
Donne louange et gloire célestine
Au dieu Phébus à la barbe roussette.
Quant du vergier où croist mainte noisette,
Où fleurs de lys yssent par millions,
Accompaigné de mes petitz lyons,
Ay combatu l'universel araigne
Qui m'a trouvée par ses rebellions
Lyon rampant en croppe de montaigne.

Le cerf vollant qui nous fait cest actine
Fut recueilly en nostre maisonnette,
Souef nourry, sans poison serpentine,
Par nous porté sa noble coronette;
Et maintenant nous point de sa cornette!
Ce sont povres rémunéracions.
Mais Dieu voyant mes opéracions.
M'a fait avoir victoire en la Champaigne,

[164] Le Roux de Lincy, *Opus Cit.*, p. 354. A text of this *ballade*, differing in a few particulars, is to be found in *MS. f. 1707*, fol. 62r in the *Bibliothèque Nationale* and in the *Jardin de Plaisance, Société des Anciens Textes Français* (Paris, 1910), sig. t ii.

[165] Le Roux de Lincy, *Opus Cit.*, p. 369: "Il [Chastelain] la [the *ballade* given] composa vers le milieu de l'année 1467, au moment où les Liégeois, pour la troisième fois depuis trois ans, venaient de se soulever contre le duc de Bourgogne, à l'instigation du roi de France. . . . *Le lyon rampant* . . . est une allusion au lion grimpant sur une montagne, qui faisait la devise du duc de Bourgogne. *Le cerf volant*, son ennemi, c'est le roi de France, qui avait pour emblème un *cerf* ailé."

Et veult que soit sur François mencions
Lyon rampant en croppe de montaigne."[166]

In the *Chroniques de Louis XII* by Jean D'Auton are several *ballades* dealing with the failure of the King's campaign in Naples (1502–1504).[167] Their general character is shown by the first stanza and envoy of *Les Tresoriers:*

Les Tresoriers

" Qui vueust soubmectre ung pays estranger
Par faictz d'armes, ou injures vanger,
Il doit avoir finences a suffire
Pour son charroy conduyre et arranger,
Et a ses gens tant donner a menger
Que nul par fain les puisse desconfire;
Ses tresoriers bons et loyaulx eslire,
Seurs, diligens, bien expertz et propices,
Promptz a payer, gardans bonnes pollices;
Convoitize ne priser deux festus,
D'Autruy avoir ne porter leurs pellices:
Avarice corrumpt toutes vertus.

. . . .

Prince, on ne peut de plus s'endommager
Que soubmectre sa chevance en danger
De ceulx qui sont par argent abbatus;
Argent fait tost meurs et propos changer,
Tesmoings mentir, arbitres mal juger:
Avarice corrumpt toutes vertus."[168]

166 Le Roux de Lincy, *Opus Cit.*, p. 371; the first two stanzas are given. Gilles des Ormes on behalf of his patron replied in a *ballade* with the refrain, "Lyon couchant au pied de la montaigne."

167 The same subject is treated by Gringore in *Les Folles Entreprises.*

168 R. de Maulde La Clavière, *Chroniques de Louis XII par Jean Auton* (Paris, 1893), Vol. III, p. 345. The circumstances referred to center about the battle of Garigliano (1503), and are thus

In 1520, the gorgeous meeting of Francis I and Henry VIII on the Field of the Cloth of Gold was celebrated in a *ballade* by Clément Marot:

"Au camp des Rois les plus beau de ce monde
Sont arrivez trois riches estendars:
Amour tient l'un de couleur blanche & munde,
Triumphe l'autre avecques ses souldars
Vivement painct de couleur celestine:
Beauté après en sa main noble, & digne
Porte le tiers tainct de vermeille sorte:
Ainsi chascun richement se comporte,
Et en tel ordre, & pompe primeraine
Sont venu veoir la Royalle cohorte
Amour, Triumphe, & Beauté souveraine.

En ces beaux lieux tost que vol d'Aronde,
Vient celle Amour des Celestines pars,
Et en apporte une vive, & claire unde,
Dont elle estainct les fureurs de Dieu Mars:
Avecques France, angleterre enlumine,
Disant, il font qu'en ce Camp je domine:
Puis à son vueil fait bon guet à la porte,
Pour empescher, que Discordre n'apporte
La pomme d'or, dont vint guerre inhumaine:
Aussi affin que seulement, en sorte
Amour, Triumphe, & Beauté souveraine

Pas ne convient, que mal plume se fonde
A rediger du triumphe les arts,
Car de si grans en hautesse profonde
N'en firent onc les belliqueurs Cesars.

described: ''Mais il ne pardonna pas de longtemps à ceux qui avaient été mêlés à ces événements. Il refusa de voir la plupart d'entre eux et les confina dans le Milanais. Il poursuivit en même temps quelques financiers qui avaient prévariqué; l'un deux fut exécuté.'' (E. Lavisse, *Histoire de France*, Paris, 1903, Vol. V, p. 66).

Que diray plus, richesses tant insigne
A tous humains bien demonstre & designe
Des deux partis la puissance très-forte.
Bref, il n'est cueur qui ne se reconforte
En ce pays, plus qu'en mer la seraine,
De veoir regner (après rencune morte)
Amour, Triumphe, & Beauté souveraine

Envoy

De la beauté des hommes ne deporte:
Et quand à celle aux Dames, je rapporte,
Qu'en ce monceau laide seroit Helaine.
Parquoy concludz, que ceste, terre porte
Amour, Triumphe, & Beauté souveraine."[169]

Cardinal Mazarin was, as might be expected, the object at times of congratulation, at times of execration in *ballade* literature. Voiture, in 1647, wrote a "ballade a Montseignieur le Cardinal Mazarin sur la prise de la Bassée." Its complimentary character is plain in the third stanza:

"Puissant esprit, qui nous fortifiez,
Et dont le soin nos ennemis réprime
Que vos succès partout soient publiés,
Que votre los en tous endroicts s'imprime,
Et que le chant dont mon âme s'imprime,
Se fasse ouïr de Paris à Maroc.
Quand je vivrois aussi longtemps qu'Enoc,
Toujours dirai de fond de ma pensée:
Seigneurs flamands, ce fut un mauvais troc,
Pour Landrecy de changer la Bassée."[170]

A bitter attack on Cardinal Mazarin is embodied in *Balade du Mazarin Grand Joueur de Hoc:*

169 *Œuvres de Clement Marot avec les ouvrages de Jean Marot son Pere ceux de Michel Marot son Fils & les Pièces du Different de Clement avec François Sagon* (A la Haye, 1741), Vol. II, p. 20.

170 A. Ubicini, *Œuvres de Voiture* (Paris, 1855), Vol. II, p. 429.

"Enfin il en aura desia le forfait clac.
Et le ieune frondeur aussi ferme qu'un roc
Sanglera la croupiere à ce joueur de hoc
Dont l'auarice a mis nostre France au bissac,
Les enquestes pour luy sont pires que le tic
Toutes ses actions s'obseruent ric à ric,
Et contre le Senat ses fourbes sont à sec
Chaque iour il fait voir qu'il n'a n'y sens ny suc
Et moins de jugement qu l'oyseau de S. Iuc,
Il ne peut ésuiter le mat dans cet eschec.

Pour le faire sortir on fait le triquetrac
Il connille, il a peur, il redoute le choc
Il franchira pourrant le pas sans brindestoc,
Et passera bien tost nos riuieres sans bac,
Il craint certain arrest plus que venire d'aspic
Il craint l'agent à croc, à crochets et à pic,
Et le coyon qu'il est, fait le salamalec
Au plus vil artisan comme il feroit au duc
Dans peu le gazetier prosnera son desjuc
Il ne peut ésuiter le mat dans cét eschec.

Il a pour son conseil gens de corde & de sac
Qui font cas de l'honneur comme huguenots d'un froc
Il vend l'espicopat et des mitres fait troc,
Car il n'en done point sans quelque miguemac
Mais il ne sera plus desormais ce traffic
L'almanach du Palais en fait le pronestic,
Et qu'on luy passera la plume par le bec,
Fust-il plus fier cent fois qu'un Flamand dans bolduc
Ou qu'vn ieune cadet du païs de Mon Iuc,
Il ne peut esuiter le mat dans cét eschec.

Envoy

Prince qui fis passer carriere au braue bec
Et qui mis l'archiduc en pitoyable affroc
Ce ministre ignorant n'a que le foy d'vn grec,

Mesme il te trahiroit pour trois plumes de coc,
Laisse la chastier & sa sequele auec
Ie suis dans l'aduenir sçauant comme vn enoc,
Il ne peut esuiter le mat dans cét eschec."[171]

The Ballade in the Drama

Sibilet, a sixteenth century critic,[172] wrote in 1548 that *ballades* and *rondeaux*[173] were to be found in *farce, sotie,* morality and mystery "comme morceaux en fricassée." His statement is richly illustrated by the *ballades* in the fifteenth and sixteenth century mysteries that have come down to us.[174] *Ballades,* like the triolets more frequently employed in the mysteries, were used as adornments of the text. They were, as the subject matter of the mysteries would suggest, for the most part prayers to the deity and supplications to Mary for her intercession. Thus, a *ballade* prayer in the *Mystère de Sainte Barbe* (fifteenth century) is spoken by Origines and three companions:

[171] *Ballade du Mazarin Grand Joueur de Hoc* (Paris, 1649); [on p. 117 of a volume of tracts in Columbia Library, 944. 033, Z1]. References to chess are common in other forms of mediaeval literature. Chess has always been a favorite source of figures with poets. Cf. Charles d'Orléans's *ballade* beginning: "J'ay aux echecs joué devant amours" (D'Héricault, Vol. I, pp. 76–77): Of this *ballade* M. Champion in his *Charles d'Orléans joueur d'échecs,* says (p. 16): "Dans cette ballade Charles d'Orléans parle en poète dans la langue du joueur. Elle résume les rapports du poète et du joueur: le poète transforme, allégorise et raffine la matière banale de son habituel passe-temps."

[172] See Chapter III.

[173] Cf. Ludwig Müller, *Das Rondel in den Französischen Mirakelspielen und Mysterien des 15 u. 16 Jahrhunderts, Ausgaben und Abhandlungen* XXIV (Marburg, 1884).

[174] M. Brandenburg, *Die Festenstrophengebilde und einige Metrische Kunsteleien des Mystère de Sainte Barbe* (Greifswald, 1907). On pp. 82–85 of this able dissertation is given a table of the *ballade* forms found in various published and unpublished French mysteries.

Origines finit.

“O dieu hault pere precieux
Et curieux
Du salut de ta creature,
Toy qui es seul victorieux
Moy vicieux,
Je te mercy[e] d’entente pure.
Pitié as tu de la laidure
Que ta facture
Enduroit par mauldit desroy,
Et as mis a desonfiture
Et confracture
Les enemys de nostre loy

Liepart

Jesus, filz du dieu vigoreux,
Non rigoureux,
Mais doulx en toute adversité,
Nous qui estions douloureux
Et langoreux
As saulvé par ton amitié.
Tu oustas de captivité
Et vilité
Les enffans d’Israel mis en foy.
Ils sont mis en mandicite,
Non respité
Les ennemys de nostre loy.

Ysacar finit

Sainct esp[e]rit qui sa bas venistes
Et si vous meistes
Es appoustres par charité,
Qui aujourduy sans noz merites
Victoire acquistes,
Je vous mercye en verité.
Nous suymes hors d’iniquité,
D’austerité,

Par vostre conduyte et arroy.
Huy sont mors et suppedité
D'audacité
Les ennemys de nostre loy.

[Envoi]

Noradin

O, Saincte unie trinité
Communité
De totalle bonté en foy,
Mect en bonne credulité
Par sainctetė
Les ennemys de nostre loy!"[175]

A *ballade* without envoy in which the stanzas are similarly distributed among several characters is to be found, too, in *Le Mystère de la Passion d'Arnoul Greban:*

Jaspar

"Je te salue, Dieu du ciel glorieux,
Dieu immortel, Dieu sur tous vertueux,
vray filz de Dieu qui creas ciel et terre;
Je te salus, rou par dessus les cieux,
monarche seul du monde et tous les lieux
que cueur humain peut penser ne enquerre.
Je congnois bien que notre char humaine
as pris ou corps de la vierge puraine
pour racheter tes amis innocens:
recoy mon don, si vray que tu le sens
offrir de cueur, et pour totalle somme
present te fais d'or, de mierre et d'encens,
toy demonstrant roy, Dieu, et mortel homme.

175 M. Brandenburg, *Opus Cit.*, pp. 65–66.

Melcior

Je te salue, chere enffant gracieux,
tres noble filz, tres saint fruit precieux,
des beaulx le chois ou plus beau ne fault querre,
Je te salue des doulx plus deliteux
le plus, des plus begnins le plus piteux,
celeste pain, vraye angulaire pierre;
Parfaicte amour par devant toy m'admaine,
recongnoissant ta puissance haultaine,
et qu'aux humains delivrer condescens,
et se je n'ay dons a toy bien decens,
excuse moy: je, qui ton serf me nomme,
present te fais d'or, de mierre et d'encens,
toy demonstrant roy, Dieu, et mortel homme.

Baltazar

Je te salue, roy du ciel plantureux,
fruit de salut, des riches plus eureux,
hors qui tresor bien ne se peust conquerre,
S'en biens mondains es me et diseteux
et dehors pers povre enffant souffeteux.
tant as en toy que nyl ne peust enquerre;
Car du plus hault de l'arche souveraine
es descendu en la vie mondaine,
juge et regent des present et absens,
et non obstant que tous biens sont recens.
en toy, saulveur, ne temps ne les consomme,
present te fais d'or, de mierre et d'encens,
toy demonstrant roy, Dieu, et mortel homme."[176]

A *ballade* addressed to the Virgin as intercessor occurs in the fourteenth century *Mystère d'une Jeune Fille qui voulut s'abandonner à peché,* where it will be seen that free stanzas alternate with those of the fixed form:

[176] Paris et Raynaud, *Le Mystère de la Passion d'Arnoul Greban* (Paris, 1878), p. 86.

Le Larron

"Ha, doulce vierge, en ce trespas
Dur repas
De mort cruëlle et douloureuse
Je te requiers: Ne me faulx,
Ton compas
Me soit conduitte glorieuse!
Ha, vierge, en ceste mort honteuse,
Langoureuse
En ce jour pour moy tres piteuse
Prens de ma pouvre ame pitié:
Par ta saincte nativité.

Le Bourreau

C'est tres bien dit en verité.
Or procede de mieulx en mieulx!
Monté tu seras herité
Ce jour au royaulme des cieulx.

Le Larron

Des cieulx requiers foys et soulas,
Las, helas,
Qui est la vraye vie heureuse.
Mon pouvre cueur dolent et las
En ces laz
Requiert ta graace precieuse.
D(e) 'oultraige fiere et haynause
. . . .
Furieusement furieuse.
Du dyable soyes preservé:
Par ta saincte nativité.

Le Bourreau

En grant ferveur de charité
Continue de bon couraige;
Mais monté par humilité
Des cieulx tu auras l'heritaige.

Le Larron

L'heritaige des cieulx tu as
Soubz tes bras.
Soit mon ame solacieuse!
Ha vierge, pense de mon cas
Maulx a tas
Ay faictz qui la rendent paoureuse
Ma vie a esté malheureuse.
Dont doubteuse
Est ma fin, Soues curieuse
De ma pouvre debilité
Par ta saincte nativité!

Ambition contencieuse
Contencion ambicieuse
M'ont de tous biens desherité.
Secours en ceste mort honteuse
Par ta saincte nativité!

Le Bourreau

C'est son cas bien solicité.
A ce monde ne pense plus.
Mais dictz pour toute auctorité
A ceste heure ton: in manus!"[177]

Occasionally the *ballade* figured as a prologue to the mystery. The prologue, whatever its form might be, was spoken by the author, by a member of the company, or by some priest not a member of the company. The purpose of such a prologue was to fix the attention of the audience, to give them some notion of the plot, or to express the author's humility.

The prologue in the fifteenth century *Le Martire de Saint Adrien* is spoken by a priest:

[177] M. Brandenburg, *Opus Cit.*, p. 74.

Preco

"En l'onneur de la Trinité,
En qui gist toute haulte puissance,
Vous prions qu'en bonne unité
Veuillez trestous fere silence,
Et vous verrés cy en presence,
S'il plaist au roy celestien
Jouer, par belle demonstrance,
Le martire saint Adrien.

Duquel la vie en verité
Vous dira, em briefve substance,
Le prescheur, par auctorité
Qu'il a de divine science.
Or luy vueilliez donc audience
Trestous prester par bon moyen,
Et escouter en reverance
Le martire saint Adrien.

Car en griefve infirmité
A mainte gens donne alegence;
Pour ce par grant sollenité
En voulons fere remembrance.
Sy vous prions par alience
Qu'en ce lieu nous faisiez ce bien
De vouloir oyr par plaisance
Le martire saint Adrien.

Prince, garde de toute oultrance
Ceulx et celles qu'entendront bien
Et mectront en leur souvenance
Le matire Saint Adrien."[178]

Another *ballade* prologue is spoken by an actor at the opening of the mystery of *Notre Dame de Puy* by Claude Doleson:[179]

178 D. H. Carnahan, *The Prologue in the Old French and Provençal Mystery* (New Haven, 1905), pp. 124–125.

179 Sixteenth century.

L'Acteur

"Puisque faict avons narration
Des faictz dignes de recordation
Ces deux jours dernierement passez,
Out fut faict l'edification
De ceste eglise de devotion,
Je croy qu'il vous en souvient assez.
Mais plus avant il nous fault proceder,
Pour ces beaulx faictz dignement recorder,
Et pour reciter, cy a brief langaige,
De toy, très-saincte Vierge Marie,
Comment fut, au Puy, sans qu'on varie,
L'advenement de ton glorieux ymaige.

Soyons trestous en consolation,
Laissons courroux et desolation,
Pensons aux biens que Dieu nous a laissez,
Regardons sa grande dilection,
En luy rendant de graces actions,
Il est raison très-bien le cognoissez.
Recognoissons aussi, sans plus tarder,
De Marie, et vueillons regarder
Et entendre de tout notre couraige.
Prestons y doulcement tous l'ouye,
Ce faisant orrons tous je vous affie.
L'advenement de ton glorieux ymaige.

Trestous nous faisons jubilation
A ton ymaige, Fille de Sion,
Et n'en voulons nullement faire ces,
Car voyons que ta representacion
Nous a donné illumination
En ce païs, Vierge, tu bien le sçais;
Et qui, en brief, nous vouldroit demander,
Qui tant de maulx nous a faict evader
Le temps jadis que nous portoient dommaige?
On diroit sans qu'on y contredire
Que l'a faict et on le certiffie;
L'advenement de ton glorieux ymaige.

Princesse, vueilles nous contregarder
De ton povoir, aussi interceder
Pour tous pecheurs envers le Juge-mage
Ainsi tenus serons-nous, quoy qu'on die,
De louer toy et en chacune partie
L'advenement de ton glorieux ymaige."[180]

Another noteworthy *ballade* prologue, a fifteenth century piece of "diablerie," the text of which is not printed, introduces *St. Martin* by André de la Vigne, and is spoken by Lucifer. The first three lines are:

"Ballade de la puissance infernalle.
Au Zodiaque du tenebreux Pluto,
Et Megera, Theziphon, Aletho,"[181]

The *Mistére de Viel Testament* alone contains seventeen *ballades.* Of considerable dramatic power is that spoken by Vesca in *Du Jugement de Salomon:*

Vesca

"Haa, mon enfant! Helas! comment?
Ne te pourray je secourir?
Je vous crie mercy humblement!
Voullez vous inhumainement
Faire ceste innoscent mourrir?
Las! ne le faictes pas perir,
Mais a ceste femme mauldicte
Le delivrez pour le nourrir;
Quant est de ma part, je luy quitte.

J'ayme mieulx qu'elle le nourrisse
Qu'il soit tué devant mes yeulx.
Helas! que mourrir je le veisse,
Mon doulx enfant? J'aymeroie mieulx

180 D. H. Carnahan, *Opus Cit.*, pp. 121–122.
181 L. Petit de Julleville, *Les Mystères* (Paris, 1880), p. 539.

Qu'on me menast ainst, m'ait Dieux,
Brusler comme femme interdicte!
Baillez luy enfant precieux;
Quant est de ma part, je luy quitte.

A Dieu, mon beau filz triumphant!
Pour toy je seuffre grant mallaise,
Mon soulas, mon bien, mon enfant!
Il est force que je te baise.
Sire! je vous prie qu'il vous plaise
Garder qu'on ne le decapite,
Et qu'el en face a son bel aise;
Quant est de ma part, je luy quitte!

Prince, saichez que ne mourray
Se sur luy on faict tel poursuyte;
A Achilla le lesseray:
Quant est de ma part, je luy quitte!"[182]

Two *ballades* of farewell and a letter *ballade* occur in *Le Mystère de Saint Louis Roi de France.* The *ballade* of farewell here reprinted is spoken by "Chevaliers de la Marche" at Louis's departure for Egypt:

Le ij^e Chevalier de la Marche

"Vray Dieu, de qui à voir est desirée
Des sainz anges ta face glorieuse,
Vois la painne rude, desmesurée,
Que nous souffrons pour ta loy gracieuse;
Confortes-nous en la painne angoisseuse
Et auz tourmens angoisseuse et divers
Que nous livre ceste gent oultrageuse
Par sa faulse mauvaistié envieuse,
Qui veut ta foy faire aler à renvers;
Tire nous amez en la gloire joyeuse,
Fais-nous victeurs contre ces gens pervers.

[182] James de Rothschild, *Le Mistère de Viel Testament* (Paris, 1891), Vol. IV, p. 327.

Le iij^e Chevalier de la Marche

Sire, qui hors la charte egipcienne
Mis hors Joseph, ton leal serviteur,
Fais nous confort contre la gent payenne;
Nous t'en prions, souverain Redempteur.
Devant nous est nostre persequteur,
Qui nous griefve par ses tiranz adverz,
Par l'ennoit du faulz deable seducteur,
Qui est leur chef, leur prince, leur ducteur.
Cely leur monstre de ta foy le renvers:
Si te prions, souverain Plasmateur,
Fais-nous victeurs contre ces gens pervers.

Le iiij^e Chevalier de la Marche

Visite-nous, souverain Roy du ciel,
Delivre-nous de ceste gente felonne.
Tu qui sauvez le prophette Daniel,
De lions fierz sa tressainte personne,
Delivre-nous, de cy, sire, et nous donne
Qu'en ton saint ciel puissent estre convers
Nos esperis, et ayent la couronne
De martire, qui tant est noble et bonne,
Et d'immortal vestement lez convers;
Et pour trouver du ciel la droite bonne,
Fais-nous victeurs contre ces gens pervers.

Le Mareschal de Cypre.

Prince du ciel, qui point ne relinquis
Ceulz qui tu as par ton saint sanc acquis,
Fais-nous du ciel les huys plaisans ouvers;
Et comme nous t'avons trestous requis,
Fais nous victeurs contre ces gens pervers."[183]

The letter *ballade* comes to Marguerite from Louis through the Seigneur de Nesle. In the text here followed, the

[183] Francisque Michel, *Le Mystère de Saint Loys, Roi de France* (Westminster, 1895), pp. 243–244.

refrain is nowhere written out and is omitted entirely after the first stanza. The whole refrain runs:

"Que pour prison ne maladie
Ne vous peut mon cueur oblier.[184]

Marguerite

"Helas! que j'en oye la lecture:
Je suis de l'ouir envieuse.

[Le seigneur de Nesle lit la cedule.]

"A ma compagne et vraye espeuse,
Marguerite, et chere amye,
Salut. Ne soyez soucieuse
De moy, dame, je vous emprie;
Car pour certain je vous affye
Qu'à vous seus sy mon cuer lier,
Que pour prise ne maladie
Ne vous peut mon cuer oblier.
Ne prenez en vous desconfort
Qui tous cueurs à pyé ralie;
Car que[elque] paine qui me lie,
Par escript vous faiz publier:
Pour prison } &c.
Ne vous peut }

Brefment je vous iray revoir,
N'en doubtez pas, ma chere amye;
Par escript le vous fais sçavoir,
Affin que plus ne vous ennuye.
Faictez joye, ne vous courcez mye,
Car je dis de cuer très-entier:
Pour prison } &c.
Ne vous peut }

Princesse, à chere très-lie
Je dis pour vous solacier:
Pour prison } &c.
Ne vous peut }

184 A. Brandenburg, *Opus Cit.*, p. 91.

Le tout vostre espoux sans nul sy,
Loys, roy françois de Poissy."[185]

A double *ballade* of the metrical variety known as "ballade fatrisée"[186] is to be found in *Sainct Didier:*

Le Bailly

"Martir de grant auctorité
Qui jadis souffris passion
Par l'inique perversité
De Croscus, plain d'infection,
Toute la congrégacion
Qui en ton service se fonde,
Préserve de la morte seconde![187]

Le Premier Bourgeoys

Préserve de la morte seconde
Les dévotz qui te font honneur,
Et s'il y a nul errabonde,
Fay que toute grâce y habonde
Pour complaire au doulx Créateur,
Tu es tousiours notre Pasteur,
Toy qui es & qui as esté
Martir de grant auctorité.

Le Second Bourgeoys

Martir de grant auctorité,
Par ta glorification,
Veul maintenir la cité
De Lengres en prospérité
Sans quelque tribulacion,
Et ceulx qui ont dévocion

185 F. Michel, *Opus Cit.*, p. 224.

186 Cf. Molinet's theory in Chapter III below.

187 A line is missing in this stanza. Whereas there are three stanzas containing the refrain of the first stanza, there are only two that have the other refrain.

Devant la châsse pure & monde
Préserve de la mort seconde!

Le Tiers Bourgeoys.

Préserve de la mort seconde
Nous qui te servons de bon cueur,
Car l'ennemy très furibonde
Tousiours est prest et sitibonde
Pour nous bouter en quelque erreur,
Garder nous peulx de cest horreur,
Toy qui est tousiours réputé,
Martir de grant auctorité!

Le Quart Bourgeoys

Martir de grant auctorité
Maintiens soubz ta protection
Ta noble confraternité,
Qui est foudée en charité,
En amour & dilection
Tous ceulx qui ont affliction
D'y laisser des biens de ce monde,
Préserve de la mort seconde!"[188]

In several of the mysteries, there are little groups of two or three *ballades* connected by various line and rime identities. In the collection of mysteries known as *Viel Testament*, for example, *De Hestre,* one of the number, contains two *ballades,* in succession, the rime of the refrain of the first being taken up by the first line of the second. The first has the added peculiarity of using the refrain as the initial line of stanzas and envoy. To indicate the effect, the envoy

[188] J. Carnandet, *La Vie et Passion de Monseigneur Sainct Didier, Martir et Evesque de Lengres p. Maistre Guillaume Flamang* (Paris, 1855), pp. 436–437. This mystery belongs to the fifteenth century. *Anciens Textes Français* (Paris, 1891), Vol. VI, p. 48.

of the first *ballade* and the first stanza of the second are given here:

"Humble de cueur, parfaicte obeissance
Assuaire roy d'Inde de valleur,
Ton ancelle te rent congru honneur,
Humble de cueur, parfaicte obeissance."[189]

"Humilité voyant en apparence
A toy, Hester, ton regart me complest,
En contraire de l'inobedience
De Vastie, qui trop si me desplaist;
Pour tant te donne cecy, car il me plaist.
Le dyadéme, couronne a humble femme,
Sur ton chef mès, et en grace parfait
Trosne d'honneur et chef de mon reame."[189]

According to Petit de Julleville, these lyric passages in the mysteries were, in general, sung, or, at any rate, were declaimed to the accompaniment of music.[190] In view of the intimate connection of the *ballade* formula with the *puy*, another circumstance in the presentation of the mysteries is here worth noting: namely, the accepted fact that, in the fourteenth century, the *Miracles de Nostre Dame* were acted at some *puy*,[191] the location of which has not been determined. The presence in these *Miracles* of the *serventoys couronnés* and *estrivés*[192] bears testimony to this situation. The *puys* had succeeded the church in the exhibition of religious drama, and, in turn, the *puys* (not all of which

[189] James de Rothschild, *Le Mistére de Viel Testament, Société des Anciens Textes Français* (Paris, 1891), vol. VI, p. 48.

[190] L. Petit de Julleville, *Les Mystères* (Paris, 1880), Vol. I, p. 290.

[191] L. Petit de Julleville, *Les Comédiens en France au Moyen Age* (Paris, 1885), p. 49.

[192] Cf. Gaston Paris and U. Robert: *Miracles de Nostre Dame par Personnages* (Paris, 1876); see also Appendix on the *serventois*.

necessarily were engaged in producing drama) were succeeded by the various "Confréries de la Passion." It is safe to assume that the religious drama of France owes to its connection with the *puy* the interpolation of the *ballade*.[193]

Conclusion

The *ballades* included in the foregoing pages range in date from the fourteenth century to the seventeenth. By far the greater number of them are insignificant as literature. They exhibit the sort of ingenuity that is inconsistent with real poetry. The tricks of the *ballade* writers, their acrostics, their word plays, made the form a kind of intellectual game. Because of this trifling, probably, there are few *ballades* that strike a modern reader as worth while. The satirical ones are remarkable for bold personalities, but such wit is not likely to appeal to a healthy sense of humor nowadays. François Villon alone in these three centuries produced *ballades,* one is tempted to say a *ballade,* of great beauty.

These poems have for us, therefore, a social rather than a literary interest. In them for three hundred years the dominant ideas of medieval society were perpetuated. The current conceptions of love, death, and religion, the hand-to-mouth wisdom of proverbs, satire mordant and mild, the chronicle of marching events, aristocratic politics, —all these subjects were accepted as within the proper

193 *Ballades* appear to be more numerous in the mysteries that survive than in other early drama. But we may take Sibilet's word for it that the form was not uncommon in farces and in *soties*. *La Basoche* at Toulouse, at the beginning of the sixteenth century, produced, for example, a *Sotise a Huit Personnaiges,* by the André de la Vigne mentioned above, in which there were two *ballades*. See E. Picot, *Recueil Général des Soties* (Paris, 1904), Vol. II, pp. 21, 102.

scope of the *ballade*. Of particular interest, too, is its presence in the religious drama. So many of the mysteries are connected with *puys* that it is not surprising to find the *ballade*, itself in part a product of the *puy*, figuring in a number of the sacred plays.[194] The *ballade* was thus considered equally appropriate for the expression of sacred or profane emotions.

The body of critical theory in regard to the *ballade*[195] reflects, as we shall see, the fluctuating esteem in which the form was held. The slighting references to it that began with du Bellay were a sure indication of its declining vogue. The *ballade* had become superannuated, too, long before the slurs of Molière's Vadius.[196] It was to be revived in the nineteenth century, but there was no attempt then made to restore to this most popular of all French artificial verse forms the importance which it had enjoyed in the Middle Ages. The French *ballade* of the present day is always, in contrast to the earlier *ballade* in the same language, a poetic trifle, rarely concerned with the solemnities of life.

194 As a matter of fact, *triolets* and *rondeaux* are quite as common as *ballades* in the sacred drama.

195 Reprinted in the following chapter.

196 The date of *Les Femmes Savantes* is 1672.

CHAPTER III

THE THEORY OF THE BALLADE FROM DESCHAMPS TO BOILEAU

The *ballade,* with all its infinite variety, came to be neglected even in France, and its decline from favor was, as we have seen, as well marked and definite as its enormous popularity had been. Naturally, the vogue of the *ballade* is reflected in the rhetorico-poetical treatises of which the poets and critics of France were so prolific in the fifteenth and sixteenth centuries. These treatises not only recorded the progress of the form and the practice of the poets who had used it, but in some cases suggested elaborate innovations or novel complications of a type already sufficiently fixed and intricate. The handbooks of poetics that multiplied in these years are very generally looked upon as a symptom of decadence. But, in the case of the *ballade,* it must be understood that the refinements and the intricacies suggested by pedants were not necessarily accepted generally by the poets. Poetasters early distorted the form in accordance with the prescriptions of theorists; but Villon, a man of some education, writing after at least four of them had appeared, produced the most beautiful *ballades* in literature.

Deschamps's *L'Art de Dictier* (1392) contains the earliest theoretical discussion of the *ballade* known to me.[1]

[1] But the Provencal *Dansa* is defined in the *Leys d'Amors,* Vol. I, pp. 341–343, and the *Leys d'Amors* was first promulgated in 1356. (See H. F. Gatien-Arnoult, *Monumens de la Littérature Romane,* Paris-Toulouse, 1841–9.) Cf. Chapter I, above.

Its neglect in France followed the invasion of ideas from Renaissance Italy. Thus Boileau's passing reference in his *Art Poétique* (1675), shows how lightly the form had come to be held at the end of the sixteenth century. The casual mention of the *ballade* by this critic indicates the verdict of the French classical age in regard to this form. The bibliography below aims to include all treatises between these two dates that dealt at all with the theory of the *ballade*. These treatises, as we have noted, not only codified usage but invented new arrangements and thereby affected current *ballade* literature, for the formal character of the *ballade* offered a tempting field to the characteristic ingenuity of the versifier of the late Middle Ages. And, whereas the poet's interest in an idea won the day in many cases, it is quite true that substance was often sacrificed to elaborate form. The complications suggested by the rhetoricians, and the *ballades* of their contemporaries embodying these strange rhetorical variations, are inextricably confused as cause and effect in the history of the French *ballade* in the fifteenth and sixteenth centuries.

I. Bibliography

Eustache Deschamps: *L'Art de Dictier,* 1392.

Jacques Legrand: *Des Rimes,* before 1405.[2]

Anonymous: *Les Règles de la Seconde Rhétorique,* 1411–1432.[3]

Baudet Herenc: *Le Doctrinal de la Seconde Rhétorique,* 1432.[4]

2 E. Langlois, *Recueil D'Arts de Seconde Rhétorique, Collection de Documents Inédits sur l'Histoire de France* (Paris, 1902), pp. 1–10. For date given, cf. p. xvi.

3 Ibid., *Opus Cit.,* pp. 11–103.

4 Ibid., *Opus Cit.,* pp. 104–198.

Anonymous: *Traité de L'Art de Rhétorique,* 1433–66.[5]
Jean Molinet: *L'Art de Rhétorique,* 1493.[6]
L'Infortuné: *L'Instructif de Seconde Rhétoricque,* about 1500.[7]

[5] E. Langlois, *Opus Cit.,* pp. 199–213.

[6] E. Langlois, *Opus Cit.,* pp. 214–252.

[7] *Le Jardin de Plaisance et Fleur de Rhetoricque* contains this treatise. *Le Jardin* was printed by Antoine Vérard twice in the first five years of the sixteenth century. (See John McFarlane, *Antoine Vérard, Illustrated Monographs,* issued by the Bibliographical Society, No. VII, London, 1900. McFarlane notes two editions by Vérard: item 141, a copy of *Le Jardin,* McFarlane places among the books printed by Vérard between 1500–1503. This edition contains a large number of cuts from Vérard's *Terence,* printed about 1500. McFarlane gives the *Bibliothèque Nationale* number of this earlier edition as Res. Ye. 168. He also records a later edition, item 165, printed by Vérard probably about 1504. A known copy of this is to be found in the British Museum, designated as C. 6. b. 8). Viollet-le-Duc in his *Catalogue des Livres Composant sa Bibliothèque Poétique,* Paris, 1843, describes the copy of *Le Jardin* belonging to him. His copy was printed "à Lyon" and is undated. He knows of another edition (p. 90) dated 1547. He comments on the manual as follows: "L'auteur de ce livre rare n'est connu que sous le nom qu'il se donne lui-même de l'Infortuné. Les auteurs que l'ont suivi, et qui l'ont souvent cité, ne lui donnent pas d'autre nom: il vivait sous Louis XI, puisqu'il parle de l'institution récente de l'Ordre de Saint-Michel (1469), et Charles VIII—" and further:

"Les bibliographes qui ont rendre compte de ce livre, peut-être sans l'avoir lu, l'ont considéré comme un recueil de plusiers pièces contenant d'abord un art poétique, et ensuite des pièces détachées, sans suite, ou plutôt sans rapport entre elles; mais ils n'ont sans doute pas remarqué que l'Infortuné en commençant sa seconde rhétorique, *Diffinito, primum Capitulum,* car tous ses titres sont en latin, après avoir indiqué qu'il va traiter des vices de la composition, de l'emploi des figures ou tropes, de la quantité des vers, de la rime, des diverses sortes de poëmes, des moralités, des mystères, des romans en vers, etc.; donne l'example en même temps que le précepte, c'est -à-dire que d'abord les règles du rondeau sont expliquées par un rondeau. Il en est de même de la ballade. . . . Il cite le nom des auteurs qui

Anonymous: *Traité de Rhétorique,*[8] 1490(?);[9] 1500(?).[10]
Pierre Fabri: *Le Grant et Vraie Art de Pleine Rhetorique,* 1521.[11]
Anonymous: *L'Art et Science de Rhétorique Vulgaire,* 1524–1525.[12]
Gratien du Pont: *Art et Science de Rhétorique Metrifiée,* 1539.
Thomas Sibilet: *Art Poëtique Françoise,* 1548.[13]

se sont distingués dans chacuns de ces genres de composition, Arnould Greban, Alain Chartier, Christine (de Pisan), etc.'' (p. 90). Viollet-le-Duc also notes the contents of the rest of the book, mentions half-a-dozen poems or more by name and calls attention to a large number of *ballades* and rondeaus. E. Stengel in *Kritische Jahresbericht über die Fortschritte der Romanischen Philologie, I,* p. 277: ''Der köngl. Bibl. in Dresden eine undatirte Ausgabe besitzt.'' In 1911, a facsimile of Vérard's first edition was issued by the *Société des Anciens Textes Français,* on p. ccvi (sig. llii) of which occurs a date: mil quatre cens cinquante neuf en auril que lon voit la fleur.

8 Langlois, *Opus Cit.,* pp. 253–264. This treatise is also printed in A. de Montaiglon's *Recueil de Poésies Françaises des XVe et XVIe Siècles* (Paris, 1855–1858), III, pp. 118 ff. Langlois says of Montaiglon's reprint, ''une reédition faite d'après la précédente [a Gothic edition printed at Lyons about 1500] avec quelques corrections sans importance mais généralment malheureuses.''

9 Marie Pellechet, *Catalogue des Incunables des Bibliothèques Publiques de France* (Paris, 1897), I, 1376, suggests the date 1490 tentatively.

10 Brunet, *Manuel du Libraire* (Paris, 1861), I, 513, notes a Gothic edition of about 1500 printed at Lyons.

11 H. Zschalig: *Die Verslehren von Fabri, du Pont und Sibilet* (Leipzig, 1884), p. 20, gives the first edition as printed at Rouen in 1521. There is a copy in the Harvard Library printed at Lyons in 1536. The latest edition is that of Héron printed at Rouen, 1889–1890, for the *Société des Bibliophiles Normands.*

12 E. Langlois, *Opus Cit.,* pp. 265–426.

13 Extensive extracts from Sibilet were printed in Charles Asselineau, *Livre des Ballades* (Paris, 1876), Appendix. Gaiffe has a reprint in preparation.

Joachim du Bellay: *Deffense et Illustration de la Langue Françoise,* 1549.[14]

Barthélemy Aneau: *Le Quintil Horatian,* 1550.[15]

Guillaume des Autelz: *Repliques aux Furieuses Defenses de Louis Meigret,* 1550.

Jacques Pelletier: *L'Art Poétique,* 1555.

Etienne Pasquier: *Recherches de la France,* 1560,[16] Bk. VII, Chap. V.

François de Pierre Delaudun Daigaliers: *L'Art Poétique,* 1598.

Vauquelin de la Fresnaye: *L'Art Poétique François,* 1605.[17]

Le Sieur de Deimier: *L'Académie de l'Art Poétique,* 1610.

Louys du Gardin: *Les Premieres Adresses du Chemin de Parnasse,* 1620.[18]

14 Ed. by Henri Chamard (Paris, 1904).

15 Brunet gives 1551 for the first edition, but there is no copy in existence. Henri Chamard, *La Date et L'Auteur du Quintil Horatian, Revue d'Histoire Littéraire de la France* (15 Jan. 1898), dates the *Quintil,* p. 58, in 1550. The *Quintil* was joined to the *Art Poëtique* of Sibilet in 1555 and was never after separated. Found in convenient form in Chamard's edition of Du Bellay's *Deffense.*

16 The Harvard Library copy was printed in Amsterdam in 1723.

17 *Jean Vauquelin de la Fresnaye, L'Art Poétique,* par F. Pelissier (Paris, 1885).

18 E. Langlois, *Opus Cit.,* and cf. Rücktäschel, *Einige Arts Poëtiques aus der Zeit Ronsard's u. Malherbes* (London, 1899). Both give extracts from du Gardin. On p. vi, note 2, Langlois says of the work: "Les exemplaires en sont très rares. J'en possède un fort beau, ayant appartenue à Viollet le-Duc, . . . c'est le seul connu de Brunet (*Manuel* II, 865); un autre, en mauvais état, se trouve à la bibliothèque de l'Arsenal (BL 736), c'est çelui qu'a connu M. Rücktäschel; un troisième appartient à la bibliothèque Pauline de Münster (cité par M. Stengel dans *Kritischer Jahresbericht über die Fortschritte der Romanischen Philologie,* I, pp. 277). Stengel in *Kritische Jahresbericht für Romanische Philologie,* I, 276, says that there is a copy

Françoise Colletet: *L'Escole des Muses*, 1652.[19]

Nicholas Boileau-Despreaux: *L'Art Poétique*, 1673.[20]

The history of the theory of the *ballade* would be incomplete, on the negative side, without the mention of certain poetical treatises of the period that with timely enthusiasm for the classical forms fail to mention the *ballade* at all.[21] Such are:

Antoine Fouquelin (or Foclin): *La Rhétorique Françoise*, 1555.

Pierre de Courcelles: *La Rhétorique*, 1557.

P. de Ronsard: *Abrégé de L'Art Poétique François*, 1565.

Claude Fauchet: *Recueil de l'Origine de la Langue et Poésie Françoise*, 1581.

Nicholas Rapin: *Vers Mesurez*, 1610.

Jules de la Mesnardiere: *La Poëtique*, 1640.

Guillaume Colletet: *L'Art Poétique*, 1658.

The theories which grew up in regard to the *ballade* and the fluctuating esteem in which it was held at various times in the course of three centuries are exemplified in the extracts here given from various works of criticism:

of Du Gardin, dated Douay 1620, in the Pauline Library at Münster. Speaking of Rückstäschel, Stengel says: "Gänzliche unbekannt ist ihm ein Abschnitt in Thevenius Bearbeitung der Ramusschen Grammatik beglieben. Es steht S 127–137 der Ausg. von 1590 unter der Überschrift: De ratione versuum in Rythmis atque metro."

19 Cf. Appendix I. Columbia Library owns a copy dated Paris, 1656.

20 A. S. Cook, *The Art of Poetry* (Boston, 1892).

21 At least three treatises that I have not been able to see may conceivably include a discussion of the *ballade*. They are:

Jean Ory: *Art Poetique* (in MS.). According to Rigoley de Juvigny, Ory flourished in Mans about 1544 as an "avocat."

Claude de Boissière: *Art Poétique*, 1554. According to Zschalig, "Keiner Pariser Bibliothek besitzt ihn."

Anonymous: *L'Introduction à la Poësie*, 1620. Mentioned by Gouget, Vol. III, p. 418.

II. Illustrative Extracts

A. Eustache Deschamps: *L'Art de Dictier*

"L'autre musique est appellée *naturele* pour ce qu'elle ne puet estre aprinse a nul, se son propre couraige naturelment ne s'i applique, et est une musique de bouche en proferant paroules metrifées, aucune foiz en *laiz,* autrefoiz en *balades,* autrefoiz in *rondeaulx cengles* et *doubles,* et en *chançons baladées,* qui sont ainsi appellées pour ce que le refrain d'une *balade* sert tousjours par maniere de rubriche a la fin de chascuns couple d'icelle, et la *chançon balladée* de trois vers doubles a tousjours, par difference des *balades,* son refrain et rubriche au commencement, que aucuns appellent du temps present *virilays.* Et ja soit ce que ceste musique naturele se face de volunté amoureuse a la louenge des dames, et en autres manieres, selon les materes et le sentement de ceuls, qui en ceste musique s'appliquent et que les faiseurs d'icelle ne saichent pas communement la musique artificiele ne donner chant par art de notes a ce qu'ilz font, toutesvoies est appellée musique ceste science naturele, pour ce que le diz et chançons par eulx faiz ou les livres metrifiez se lisent de bouche et proferent par voix non pas chantable, tant que les douces paroles ainsis faicts et recordées par vois plaisent aux escoutans qui les oyent si que au *Puy d'amours* anciennement et encores est acoustumez en pluseurs villes et citez des pais et royaumes du monde.

"Ceuls qui avoient et ont acoustumé de faire en ceste musique naturele *serventois de Nostre Dame, chançons royaulx, pastourelles, balades et rondeaulx* portoient chascun ce quel fait avoit devant le *Prince du puys,* et le recordoit par cuer, et ce recort estoit appelé *en disant,* après qu'ilz avoient chanté leur chançon devant le Prince, pour ce que neant plus que l'en pourroit proferer le chant de musique sanz la bouche ouvrir, neant plus pourroit l'en proferer ceste musique naturele sanz voix et sanz donner son et pause aux dictez qui faiz en sont.''[22]

. . . .

''Or sera dit et escript cy après la façon des Balades.

''Et premierement est assavoir que il est *balade* de huit vers, dont la rubriche est pareille en ryme au ver antesequent, et toutefois que le derrain mot du premier ver de la balade est de trois sillabes, il doit estre de .XI. piez, si comme il sera veu par exemple cy après; et se le derrenier mot du second ver n'a qu'une ou deux sillabes, ledit ver sera de dix piez; et se il ya aucun ver coppe qui soit de cinq piez,

Exemple sur ce que Dit Est.

Balade de .VIII. vers couppez.

"Je hez jours et ma vie dolente,
Et si maudis l'eure que je fu nez,
Et a la mort humblement me presente
Pour les tourmens dont je suy fortunez.
Je hez ma concepcion
Et si maudi ma constellacion
Ou Fortune me fist naistre premier,
Quant je me voy de toutz maulx prisonnier.

''Et en ceste balade *leonime,* par ce qu'en chascun ver elle emporte sillabe entiere, aussi comme *dolente* et *presente, concepcion* et *constellacion.*

Autre Balade

"De tous les biens temporelz de ce monde
Ne se doit nulz roys ne sires clamer,
Puisque telz sont que Fortune suronde
Qui par son droit les puet touldre ou embler;

[22] G. Raynaud, *Œuvres Complètes de Eustache Deschamps, Société des Anciens Textes Français* (Paris, 1891), Vol. VII, pp. 270–271.

Le plus puissant puet l'autre deserter,
Si qu'il n'est roy, duc n'empereur de Romme
Qui en terre puist vray tiltre occuper
Ne dire sien, fors que le sens de l'omme.

''Ceste balade est moitié *leonime* et moitié *sonant,* si comme il apert par *monde,* par *onde,* [ce mot ne se trouve pas à la rime dans cette pièce], par *homme* par *Romme* qui sont plaines sillabes et entieres; et les autres *sonans* tant seulement, ou il n'a point entiere sillabe, si comme *clamer* et *oster* [le not *oster* appartient au 3ᵉ couplet], ou il n'a que demie sillabe, ou si comme seroit *presentement* et *innocent.* Et ainsi es cas semblables puet estre cogneu qui est *leonime* ou *sonnant.*

Exemple de Balade de .IX. vers toute leonyme.

" Vous qui avez pour passer vostre vie
Qui chascun jour ne fait que defenir,
Vous vivez frans sanz viande ravie,
Se du vostre vous pouez maintenir.
Or vous vueilliez du serf lien tenir
Ou pluseurs par couvoitise
Ont perdu corps, esperit et franchise;
C'est de servir autrui, dont je me lasse:
Vieillesse vient, guerdon fault, temps se passe.

Exemple de Balade de dix vers de .X. et de .XI. sillabes.

''Et se doit on tousjours garder en faisant balade, qui puet, qui les vers ne soient pas de mesmes piez, mais doivent estre de .IX. our de .X., de .VII. ou de .VIII. ou de .IX., selon ce qu'il plaist au faiseur, sanz les faire touz egaulx, car la balade n'en est pas si plaisant ne de si bonne façon.''[23]

. . . .

Balade equivoque, retrograde et leonime.

[23] G. Raynaud, *Opus Cit.,* Vol. VII, p. 274–276.

"Et sont les plus fors balades qui se puissent faire, car il couvient que la derreniere sillabe de chascun ver soit reprinse au commencement du ver ensuient, en autre signification et en autre sens que la fin du ver precedent. Et pour ce sont telz mos appellez equivoques et retrogrades, car en une meisme semblance de parler et d'escripture ilz huchent et baillent significacion et entendement contraire des mos derreniers mis en la rime, si comme il apparra en ceste couple mise cy après:

Autre Balade

"Lasse, lasse maleureuse et do*lente!*
Lente me voy, fors de soupirs et *plains.*
Plains sont mes jours d'ennuy et de tour*mente!*
Mente qui veult, car mes cuer est cer*tains,*
Tains jusqu'a mort et pour celli que j'*ains;*
Ains mais ne fu dame se fort a*tainte;*
Tainte me voy quant il m'ayme le *mains*
Mains, entendez ma piteuse com*plainte.*

"Et couvient que tous le couples se finent par la maniere dessurdicte tout en equivocacion retrograde, ou autrement elle ne seroit pas dicte ne reputée pour equivoque ne retrograde, supposée ore que le derrenier mot du ver se peust reprandre a aucun entendement du ver ensuiant, se il ne reprenoit toute autre chose que le precedent."[24]

. . . .

"Item en ladicte balade a *envoy.* Et ne les souloit on point faire anciennement fors es *chançons royaulx,* qui estoient de cinq couples, chascune couple de .X., .XI. ou .XII. vers; et de tant se puelent bien faire, et non pas de plus, par droicte regle. Et doivent les envois d'icelles chançons, qui commencent par *Princes,* estre de cinq vers

[24] G. Raynaud, *Opus Cit.,* Vol. VII, p. 277–278.

entez par eulx aux rimes de la chançon sanz rebrique; c'est assavoir .II. vers premiers, et puis un pareil de la rebriche; et les .II. autres suyans les premiers, deux concluans en substance l'effecte de ladicte chançon et servens a la rebriche. Et l'envoy d'une balade de trois vers aussi, contenant sa matere et servant a la rebriche, comme il sera dit cy après.''[25]

. . . .

''Item encores puet l'en faire balades de .VII. vers, dont les deux vers sont tousjours de la rebriche, si comme il puet apparavoir cy après:

"Par fondement me doy plaindre et plourer,
Et regreter des .IX. preux la vaillance,
Car je voy bien que je ne puis durer.
Confort un fuit, Honte vers moy s'avance,
Couvoitise met en arrest sa lance
Qui me destruit mon plus noble pais.
Preux Charlemaine, se tu fusses en France,
Encore y fust Roland, ce m'est advis."[26]

B. Jacques Legrand: *Des Rimes*[27]

''Oultre plus, aucuns ditz sont nommez balades, lesquelles se font en diverses manieres; toutesfois la plus commune maniere si est de fere deux vers ed pluseurs couples, desquelz deux vers l'ung s'appelle l'ouvert et l'autre le clos; et

25 G. Raynaud, *Opus Cit.*, Vol. VII, p. 278.

26 G. Raynaud, *Opus Cit.*, Vol. VII, p. 279.

27 E. Langlois, *Opus Cit.*, pp. 1–10. *Des Rimes* was included in the *Archiloge Sophie* of which there are four MSS. in the *Bibliothèque Nationale.* The longer work has never been printed as a whole. Legrand, the author, was born in the third quarter of the fourteenth century and died about 1425. He was probably not a poet himself; his theory represents an earlier poetic practice. (See E. Langlois, *Opus Cit.*, p. xiv.)

puis après on doit fere ung ver nommé oultre passe, lequel doit tenir sa ryme des deux premiers, ou du refrain, ou de tous deux, qui peult. Et finablement on doit fere ung refrain, lequel doit estre appartenant et declairé par les vers devant ditz. Et semblablement on doit tousjours après proceder, en tendant tousjours a une fin; c'est assavoir a prouver et demonstrer son refrain, et a parler pertinamment a luy, aultrement la ballade n'est pas bien composée.''[28]

C. *Les Règles de la Seconde Rhétorique*[29]

''Item, la taille des balades tumbans et en figure de petiz lais, comme il s'ensuit.

" Dire ne vous saroie
N'escripre ne porroie
N'en vision songier,
Pour nouvelles que j'oye,
Le bien, l'onneur, la joye
Qu'amans ont sans dangier
El gracieux bergier
Ou Amours seur avoye,
Le bon temps que j'avoye
Quant j'estoie bergier.[30]

[28] E. Langlois, *Opus Cit.*, pp. 7–8. In order to understand Legrand's formula for the *ballade* it is necessary to remember that the word *vers* should be taken to mean ''group of verses,'' *pluseurs* to mean ''two,'' and *couples* to mean those lines that rime together. (See Langlois, *Opus Cit.*, p. 5, notes 5, 6, and 7.)

[29] The author of *Les Règles de la Seconde Rhétorique* is not known and the work is undated, but its compiler quotes Deschamps, who died in 1404, and Jean Froissart, who died in 1411. On the other hand, Langlois shows that in 1432 Baudet Herenc used *Les Règles* in his own *Doctrinal*. The MS. of this anonymous manual of poetics is in the *Bibliothèque Nationale.* (See Langlois, *Opus Cit.*, p. xix, ff.)

[30] Langlois, *Opus Cit.*, p. 58: ''L'autheur compte la dernière syllabe du vers féminin.''

"Il est a noter que on puet fere sa balade tumbant de tout mettre puiz le nombre de sept sillabes jusques a[u] nombre de .xj.

"*Item, autres tailles de doubles croisies en balladant.*

Balade

J'ay esperé long temps don de mercy,
Maiz il ne vuet venir sans reculer.
Ce sait Dangier, point ne l'en remercy,
Car clers voyans font semblant d'avuler,
Nulz fors les sours ne vuet oyr parler.
Fortune m'a ceste oeuvre pourpensée,
Si en escrips, plus ne le puiz celer,
De plours, de sang et de triste pensée."[31]

. . . .

"*Item, autres tailles de balades estranges en soties selonc les .v. voieulx.*

Pour moy parer hier me vestis de — nate
Et affulay chaperon sans cor — nette
Comme celui qui a amer s'e — nate
Sote cornant qui n'est pas de corps — nette
Lors dame Amours en guise de pen — nite
Se traist vers moy et me dist espa — nite
A Sote amer qui a nom Vince — note
Car [moult] bien scet de truande le — note
Et des marans sur toutes est cong — nute
Je responder, dont j'eus une hor — nute
Non feray voir, point ne l'aray je."[32]

. . . .

"*Cy s'ensuit une taille plainne laie balladant.*

Jeune, joyeux, gallant, frique, joly,
Gay et poly, plain d'amoureux espoir,
Et main et soir seray, quar enbelly,

[31] Langlois, *Opus Cit.*, pp. 58–59.
[32] Langlois, *Opus Cit.*, p. 65.

Sans nul faulx sy meu a loyal vouloir,
Dont, sans mouvoir mon cueur de beau manoir
Ou esmouvoir l'a voulu bonne amour,
Par grant doulçour, prennent en moy sejour
Paiz et Honnour, Loyauté et Leese.
Se ne chesse d'eus loer en cest jour,
Cest pour l'amour de ma dame et maistresse."[33]

* * * * * * * * * * *

" *Cy s'ensuit ballade laye.*

Helas! Amours, regardés e n pité,
Par vostre gré,
La grant durté qui nuit et jour m'esprent
Si durement que je pers ma santé,
Car agripé
Et attrapé m'a douloureusement
Triste tourment par quoy n'ay sentement
Nesunement
N'alegement qui me puist conforter.
Ainsi finer Me faut piteusement
Et tristrement
Pour loyaument vous servir et amer.

" *Cy s'ensuit ballades a .iij. manieres.*

*B*ien doit amant que vuet amours servir
*J*oyeusement par maniere ordonnée.
*A*u temps plaisant avoir doulz souvenir
*V*ray sentement faut qu'il ait c'est l'entrée
*T*enir en soy largesce et courtoisie
*E*t esbanoy si convient sans boidie
*C*ar bien dire os se il vuet remanoir
*L*a ou enclos par amoureux vouloir
A sens bonté son cuer comme soubgis
*R*ens par compos. en la fin puet avoir.

[Two other stanzas given.]

*R*imes en mos Princes sans non chaloir
*Y*cy enté sens bien en vous a mis

33 Langlois, *Opus Cit.*, p. 97.

Sont dont je los chil qui puet esmouvoir."

P. de Compiengne.[34]

D. Baudet Herenc: *Le Doctrinal de la Seconde Rhétorique*[35]

"Cy s'ensuit une balade, et de matiere que l'on doibt tenir en puy d'escole, laquelle est de .xj. lignes en chascun couplet, pour ce que le reffrain et de .xj. sillabes.

"Cil qui des fais d'Amour n'a congnoissance
Et desire savoir trouver maniere
De rendre a luy loyale obeïssance,
Pour parvenir a sa grace planiere
Et a l'amour de dame doulce et gente,
Viengne servir en sa court excellente;
La trouvera tourment delicieux,
Confort dolant, ennuy solacieux,
Doulceur amere, esjoy[e] tristresse,
Guerre amoureuse; et si domine en eulx
Haultain plaisir, qui cueur tient en destresse.

[Two other stanzas given.]

Prince d'Amours, pour estre plus eureux
Ou service d'Amours, tenés l'adresse
D'avoir en vous, comme amant cremeteux,
Haultain plaisir, qui cueur tient en destresse.

"Aultre taille de balade que on doibt faire ou dict puy d'escolle laquelle ne doibt contenir que dix lignes, pour ce que le reffrain ne contient que dix sillabes.

[34] Langlois, *Opus Cit.*, pp. 100–101.

[35] The *Doctrinal* gives evidence that its author knew the preceding treatise. Langlois (*Opus Cit.*, p. xxxvii) says that Herenc's innovations and his reorganization of material are always in the direction of greater system and more logical arrangement. Both treatises are written in the dialect of Picardy.

Je me suis mis ou plus joieux dangier
Qu'onque[s] amant se mist pour grace attraire
De celle a qui j'ay requis que logier
Voeulle mon cueur ou sien, sans le retraire;
Et loyalment, sans aler au contraire,
A le servir je mettray mon entente;
Car j'espoire, quoy que vive en attente
D'avoir mercy, qu'en bien me partira.
Donques, affin que ceste doulceur sente,
Jamais mon cueur qu'elle me ch[o]isira.

[Two other stanzas given.]

Prince d'Amours, pour la beaulté trés gente
De ma chiere maistresse, ou se mira
Mon vray desir par plaisance evidente,
Jamais mon cueur qu'elle ne choisira.

"Aultre taille de balade d'escolle, l'une de huit lignes, pour ce que le reffrain contient .viij. sillabes et l'aultre de .ix. lignes, pour ce que le reffrain contient .ix. sillabes.

"Le monde va en amendant,
Car Orgueil, Ire et Gloutonnie
Ne si moustrent plus maintenant,
Paresse, Luxure ne Envye,
N'Avarice que Dieu mauldie!
On a huy du mal d'aultruy doeul;
Misericorde est exaulchie.
Se je dis vray, crevés moy l'oeul.

[Two other stanzas given.]

Prince, ma femme est vien m'amie
Car pour faire de que je voeul
Elle est toudis appareillie.
Se je dis vray, crevés moy l'oeul.

"Ballade contenant .ix. lignes, pour ce que le reffrain est de .ix. sillabes, comme dit est.

Un compaignon d'entendement
Et une femme de raison
Entroïs n'a mye gramment,
S'oys que celle au compaignon
Disoit: 'Il me faut presenter
Poulain, pour mon car atteler,
Car je voeul aler ou voyage
Ou on peult souvent encontrer
Les broudes visaige a visaige.'

C'il respondi centainement:
'Dame, j'ay poulain de fason,
Fouet a deux noux, dont souvent
Le chasseray, mais que ou moilon
Des limons le voeullés mener.'
Adonc vis le dame lever
Les limons comme il est d'usaige,
Disant: 'Hastés vous de trouver
Les broudes visaige a visaige.'

[The third stanza is given.]

Prince, pour en paix demourer,
Home que est en mariaige,
Il luy fault souvent adjuster
Les broudes visaige a visaige.

"Aultre forme de balade, que ne doibt comprendre que .vij. lignes, pour ce que le mettre ne doibt estre que [de] .vij. sillabes le masculin, et le feminin de .viij. sillabes; et s'appelle balade baladant.

"Ung homme, provre d'avoir,
Au lit mortel disoit hier,
En plourant: 'Bon doit avoir
Dieu de moy contrarier,
Que tant de biens envoier

En ce monde me soloit,
Et sie ne m'en souvenoit.

[Two other stanzas given.]

Prince, maint an a entier
Qu'on m'a volu enseigner
Tous les poins que cil disoit,
Et si ne m'en souvenoit."

Cy s'ensuivent aultres balades nouvelle faittes a plaisance.

Balade Faitte A La Volenté De L'Ouvrier.

"Je vous mercye, Amours,
De trés loyal vouloir
De voz plaisans doulçours
Que me faittes avoir;
En vo service gent
Vostre suis ligement;
Car par rians regars,
A mon cueur contenté
Celle qui les deux pars
De son cueur m'a donné.

[Another stanza given.]

Prince, des joyaulx dars
D'Amour m'a assené
Celle qui les deux pars
De son cueur m'a donné.

Balade Layée

"Belle, en vous servant m'est venue
Desplaisance en lieu de lïesse,
Qui piece a vous ay esleüe
Pour ma souv[e]raine maistresse
Et desse;

Et vous m'avés habandonné
Et donné.
Reffus, qui foy vous ai promis,
Comme amis.
C'est par envye venimeuse
Et doubteuse,
Qui grevé m'a vers vous a tort:
Jamais n'aray vie joieuse,
Ains array paine doloureuse
San confort.

[Two other stanzas given.]

Aultre Balade De Court Mett[r]e

" Chiere maistresse,
A vous me plains
De la destresse
Dont je suis plains
Par Bel Accoeil,
Dont je recoil
Angoisse dure,
Qui trop me dure,
Car mes solas
Troeuve en decours,
Criant: 'Helas !
Mort ou secours!'

[Another stanza given.]

Princesse pure,
De humble figure,
N'oubliés pas
Moy en doulours,
Criant: 'Helas!
Mort ou secours!' "[36]

[36] Langlois, *Opus Cit.*, pp. 179–189.

E. *Traité de L'Art de Rhétorique*[37]

"Item, on doit sçavoir que communement rondelz ne balades n'ont point de nombre de silabes en leurs bastons."[38]

. . . .

"*Cy s'ensuit le tractié des balades de toute fourmes.*

La balade ait .iij. clause et une demey clause; et doit avoir au moin .vij. bastons en chascune plainne clause; et en demey clause lemoin que on puet mettre se le scens puet estre bon.

"En une chascune balade doit estre ung reffrain d'un baston, et ce reffrain doit estre mis en la fin de chascun vers ou de chascune clause et demi clause d'une balade, comme il appert bien evidemment au balades faictes. Et doit estre le scens rapportés et refferez de chascune clause a celui reffrain, comme il appert az autres balades. Et pour ceu que on ne doit point redire une chose, on doit panre nouvel propos ou nouvel moz en la fin de chascune clause qui soient rapportez au bastons de celle ballade, tant que le scens soit bons et passable devant tous.

"Item, la maniere de rimer balades est de plusiers manieres, mais en une chacune clause doit estre une croisiée de rime au commancement, comme cy appert en l'example de cest balade la. On puet pranre fourme et maniere de faire balades autrez sus la forme de cest cy:

> "Je croy que Dieu trestout crea:
> Le ciel [et] le terre et la mer,
> Et en après qu'il procrea
> Adam et Eve sans doubter;

[37] Langlois, *Opus Cit.*, p. xliv: The next authority whom we consult for the theory of the *ballade* is the unknown author of the *Traité de l'Art de Rhétorique.* This essay is preserved in the *Bibliothèque Nationale* in a manuscript apparently of the second third of the fifteenth century. The only forms of poetry for which rules are given are the *ballade* and the *rondeau.*

[38] Langlois, *Opus Cit.*, p. 203.

Puis par la pomme hors bouter
Lez fist du paradis terrestre,
Et pour nous de painne getter
Il volt de mere vierge nestre.

"Item, aussi on puet faire balades de plus de bastons et de plux clauses, mais, pour cause de briefté, je lasse ceste chose et la mès en la bonne diligence d'un chascun, etc."[39]

F. Jean Molinet: *L'Art de Rhétorique Vulgaire*[40]

"Autre taille de rimes se nomme enchayennée, pour ce que la fin d'un metre est pareil en voix au commencement de l'autre, et est diverse en signification. Et se puet ceste taille causer en balades, vers huitains. . . .

Exemple[41]

"Trop durement mon cuer souspire,
Pire mal sent que desconfort;

39 Langlois, *Opus Cit.*, pp. 205–206, *passim:* Here, *baston* means line; *demey clause*, envoy; and *vers*, a strophe or stanza. When the author says that a stanza should have at least seven lines he probably does not count the refrain.

40 This treatise, long attributed to Henri de Croy, is known in an edition of 1493, published by Antoine Vérard at Paris. It is more lucid than any of its predecessors or than any of its successors in the field. Just what Molinet's obligations to former works are it is difficult to say. He seems to have been the kind of person who would have worked into his scheme everything that was suitable, and so he probably gathered a distinction here, or a classification there, from the rhetoricians who preceeded him. L'Infortuné, Fabri, and the authors of the two other anonymous treatises, published by Langlois in the *Recueil*, in their turn, levied contributions on Molinet. These obligations are, however, not so plain, if we base our comparison only on the *ballade*. (See Langlois, *De Artibus Rhetoricae Rhythmicae*, Paris, 1890, pp. 51 ff.)

41 The same tortured variety is called by Deschamps, *Ballade equivoque retrograde et leonine.*

Confort le fait, plus n'a riens fort.
Fort se plaint, ne scet qu'il doit dire.[42]

"Balade commune doit avoir refrain et trois couplès et l'envoy. Le refrain et la derreniere ligne desdis couplès et de l'envoy, auquel refrain se tire toute la sustance de la balade, ainsi que la sayette au signe du bersail. Et doit chascun couplet, par rigour d'examen, avoir autant de lignes que le refrain contient de sillabes. Se le refrain a .viij. sillabes et la derrieniere est parfaitte, la balade doit tenir forme de vers huytains; se le refrain a .ix. sillabes, les couplès seront de .ix. lignes, dont les quatre premieres se croisent; la .v^{e}., .vj^{e} et .viij^{e}. sont de pareille termination, different, aux premieres, et la .vij^{e}. et .ixe. lignes pareilles en consonance et distinctes a toutes autres. Se la refrain a .x. sillabes, les couples de la balade sont de .x. lignes, dont les .iiij. premieres se croisent; la .v^{e}. pareille a la .iiij^{e}., la .vij^{e}. et la .ix^{e}. de pareille termination, et la .viij^{e}. et .x^{e}. egales en consonnance. Se le refrain a .xj. sillabes, les couples avront .xj. lignes, les .iiij. premieres se croisent la .v^{e}., et .vj^{e}. pareilles en rimes, la .vij^{e}., .viij^{e}. et .x^{e}. egales en consonance et la .ixe. et .xj^{e}. de pareille termination. Et est a noter que tout envoy lequel a la fois recommence par Prince, a son refrain comme les autres couplès, mais il ne contient que .v. lignes au plus et prent ses terminations et rimes selon les derrenieres lignes des dessusdis couplès.

Exemple de Balade Commune[43]

"Des Mirmidons la hardiesse emprendre,
Pour envayr le trés puissant Athlas,
De Medea les cauteles aprendre,
Pour inpugner les ars dame Palas,

[42] Three other similar quartrains are given. See Langlois, *Recueil*, pp. 224–225.

[43] Found also in Molinet's *Faictz et Dictz*, f. 74.

Faire trambler de monde la machine,
Fourdroier Mars, qui contre nous machine,
Fouder chasteaux sus le mont Pernasus
Voler en air ainsi que Pegasus,
Endormir gens au flagol de Mercure
N'est il besoing pour parvenir lassus:
Il fait assez qui son salut procure.

[Two other stanzas given.]

Prince du puy, le grant dieu Saturnus,
Demogorgon, Pheton, Phebé, Phebus
Ne demandent grant labour ne grant cure,
Mais que le corps soit bien entretenus
Il fait assez qui son salut procure.

"Balade balladant tient les termes de ballade commune, si non que les couplès sont comme vers septains. Autres dient qu'elle est de dix et de .xj. sillabes, et est batelée a la .iiij^e^. sillabe en certaines lignes; car en toutes lignes de dix ou de .xj. sillabes, soit en balade ou autre taille, tousjours la quarte sillabe on piét doit estre de mot complet, et doit on illec reposer en la pronunçant.

Exemple[44]

" Juïs ont dit que nostre redempteur
Fut enchanteur pas art dyabolique
Fol seducteur, faulx prevaricateur,
Menteur, vanteur facteur de voie oblique;
Mais sainct Jehan dist qu'il nous inspira,
Qu'il nous crea et si bien nous ama
Qu'il nous forma a son divin semblant.
Il fut enfant du pere triumphant,
Soleil luisant, sente on nul ne devie,
Fleur flourissant, vraie messie naissant,
Dieu tout puissant, verité, voie et vie.

[Two more stanzas; then comes the envoy.]

[44] Also printed in Molinet's *Faictz et Dictz,* f. 1.

Prince du puy, si estes obeïssant
A son command, en sa gloire infinie
Laseus regnant le verrez dominant,
Dieu tout puissant, verité, voie et vie.

"Balade fatrisée ou jumelle sont deux ballades communes telement annexéez ensemble que le commencement de l'une donne refrain a l'autre. C'est couleur de rhethorique est decente a faire regrez, comme il appert en l'Ystoire de sainct Quentin, ou l'escuier trouva sainct Maurice mutilé sur les champs.

Exemple[45]

"Maurice, le beau chevalier,
Tu es mort! Ellas! que feray je?
Je ne te puis vie baillier,
Ne susciter, ne conseillier!
Tu as paié mortel treuage.
Quel perte! quel dueil! quel dommage!
Quel criminel occision!
O terrible prodition!

O terrible prodition!
Faulx empereur de Rommenie,
Maudite generation,
Pute enge, pute nation,
Pute gent, pute progenie,
Vous avez par grant tyrannie
Mis a mort et fait exillier
Maurice, le beau chevalier!

Maurice, le beau chevalier,
Noble duc de hardy corage,
Tu estois venus bataillier,
Pour le bien publique habillier

45 The reference to the *Sainct Quentin* and the presence of the following *ballade* here and in the Mystery, led Langlois to attribute the Mystery to Molinet. See *Romania,* XXII, p. 552.

De paix et de hautain parage,
Mais les traytres plains de rage
Ont failly de promission.
O terrible prodition!

O terrible prodition!
Faulz tirans, plains de dyablerie,
Destruite avez la legion
De la thebée region,
Et sa noble chevalerie.
Entre lesquelz la fleur flourie
Estoit pour tous cuers resveillier,
Maurice, le beau chevalier!

Maurice, le beau chevalier
Que dira ton hault parentage,
Si tost qu'il porra soutillier
Comment on t'a fait detaillier
Et murdrir en fleur de ton age?
Quel desconfort! quel grief outrage!
Quel pleur! quel lamentation!
O terrible prodition!

O terrible prodition!
As tu fait ceste villonnie!
Tu ev avra pugnition
Et horrible dampnation
Avec l'enfernale maisnie.
La terre est couverte et honnie
Du sang du bon duc famillier,
Maurice, le beau chevalier!

Prince, vous avez pas envie
Assomé et fait traveillier
Maurice, le beau chevalier."[46]

[46] Langlois, *Opus Cit.*, pp. 235–241.

G. L'Infortuné: *L'Instructif de Seconde Rhetoricque*[47]

Sig. b iii verso

De nona specie

"Les balades communement
Par telz formes sont composees
Reprendre on doit premierement
Les premieres lignes croisees
Au quart et quint lieu apposees
Troys coupletz egaulx au renger
Ainsi doiuent estre posees

Refrain pareil sans riens changer
Auec troys coupletz mesmement
Desgales lignes proposees
Vng prince y soit pareillement
De la moitie des exposees
Coupletz qui seront imposees
Sans aucun vice y calanger
Si non par na aux disposees
Refrains pareil sans riens changer.

Les coupletz soient signament
Dautant de lignes compassees
Comme le refrain proprement
A de sillabes proposees
Et ces reigles presupposees
Lon peult les balades forger
En forme bien auctorisees
Refrain pareil sans riens changer

[47] *L'Instructif de Seconde Rhetoricque,* printed in *Le Jardin de Plaisance,* was written by an author who signed himself L'Infortuné. He may have been a certain Jourdain or Joannes Caletenses. The treatise is in rime and the various forms of poetry described are exemplified in the statement of the rules that present in themselves the very type of verse they are explaining. See G. Pellissier, *De Sexti Decimi Saeculi in Francia Artibus Poeticis* (Paris, 1882).

Le prince soit tant seulement
De la moitie pour abregier
Des coupletz et non autrement
Refrain pareil sans riens changer

Notabile

Doppinion sōt aucūs cōe puis entēdre
Que balade ait refrain et trois coupletz semblables
Et le prince sās les vers point reprēdre
Lesquelles croisent desgales lignes sortables"

Sig. b. iiij. recto

Balada retrograda

"Constellation nous produit
Refection dhumain engin
Jeunesse ne quiert que deduit
Chascun doit craĩdre mal engin
Sans corde file ne engin
Notēt et preignēt sans leuriers
Ces prouerbes les manouuriers
Soit de colericque ou sanguin
Plus sont de maistres que douuriers

A rimer maint cueur se reduit
Tant sur coefe que sur beguin
Ou sur mot ou sens mieulx se duit
Sur clerc sur lourt ou sur bourdin[48]

. . . .

Doultrecuidez se meslent dautres mestiers
Puis lors que dit lon dung badin
Plus sont de maistres que douuriers
La science sabatardit
De rethoricque sans latin
Quant de rimer chascun en dit

48 Two lines missing.

A plaisir: soit soir ou matin
Lon rime chien contre matin
Chascun sen mesle en tous quartiers
Dieux que de nouueaulx charpentiers
De rimer chascun tatin
Plus sont de maistres que douuiers."

Balada per dyalogum

"Ha maistre alain quoy qui mapelle
Cest moy: tu qui: cest linfortune: las
Que te fault il: las lon rue a la pelle
Rethoricque: voire dis tu: helas
Oy qui fait ce: Aucune diceulx ia las
Ou ne scauent. Est il vray tu te gales
Mais en quel lieu ou en festes ou en gales
Est il certain: oy benedicite
Vous perdres bruit pour telz cimbales
Boute chouque si est ressuscite.

Reuit il dieux: oy. Quelle vielle
Comment: ne scay. tais toy cu songes las
Sauf vostre honneur. Non dea quel kirielle
Mais ou en galans saillans en voz las
Puis en font ilz de bons biens: cest solas
Quoy nettemēt cōme vng autre en brimbales
Dis tu: sans voz couleurs rethoricales
Voir est ce tout. Nest ce pas bien dicte
Pour le commun: quen tiēs tu. quen tregales
Boute chouque si est ressuscite.

Cest vng grant cas: si est ce grant nouuelle
Comme rime il: en beaux termes tous plas
Cest rigole contrepaye est telle
Ou se fait el. tant sur potz que sur plas
En beau goret, oncques mieulx nacouplas
Aumoins pieca bon nota de cancales

Donnez leur: quoy pour loyer deux escales
Ou masure pour leur habilite
Dea sanf farcer pourquoy car en gringales
Boute chouque si est ressuscite.

Prince notez. quoy: ce present libelle
De qui de quoy de iourdain qui la belle
Pour ses deux blans gardez diuersite
A quoy faire pour cause telle quelle
Boute chouque si est ressuscite."

H. *Traité de Rhétorique*[49]

Vers Septains

" Pluseurs vers qui sont septains
Sont a le fois pour chanssons
Que chantent les gens mondains,
Et se font de telz fassons.
Or regardons se sont bons
Pour resconforter malades
Souvent on en fait balades.

Vers Witains Et Coppés.

" On dit couplet
Ou vers witain
Quant il est fait
De bone main
Et qu'il est plain

[49] The author of the *Traité de Rhétorique* (1490?; 1500?), like L'Infortuné, defines a form by means of the form itself. It is impossible, since the exact date of neither is known, to say who originated the method. The *Traité* is not a complete *seconde rhetorique,* but is intended only to instruct some friend of the author who wished to poetize. The treatise gives isolated *ballade* stanzas but says nothing about the structure of the whole *ballade.* Much of the stuff is pure doggerel.

De rime sade.
S'il a refrain
Il est ballade."[50]

. . . .

Vers Dizains de .x. Piés et De .x. Lignes

"Vers de .x. piés de .x. lignes rimés
Sont vers dizains, deroisiés en ce point.
Es balades sont il souvent trouvés,
Quant le refrain leur est donné a point.
Mais touteffois oublier ne fault point
A faire arrest et poser au quart piét,
Car aultrement il seroit reprochiét
C'est balade quant il porte refrain,
Et a le fois enlachiét et croisiét,
Ne plus ne mains que s'il fut vers douzain."[51]

Nota

"On treuve balade souvant
De .v. piés, de .vj. et de sept,
De .viij., de dix communement,
De .ix., ne .xij., nul n'en scet.

. . . .

Pluseurs balades baladans
Virlais, fatras d'aultre fachon
Ont en leur ait les biens rimans,
Dont point je ne fais mension.
Se j'en dis mon entention,
Pardonnés moy se j'ay failly;
Je n'ay faict ce traictiét se non
Pour aprendre ung mien amy."[52]

[50] Langlois, *Opus Cit.*, p. 257.
[51] Ibid., *Opus Cit.*, p. 261.
[52] Ibid., *Opus Cit.*, p. 264.

I. Pierre Fabri: *Le Grand et Vrai Art de Pleine Rhetorique*

"Ballades se font de huyt lignes pour clause et huyt syllabes en masculin pour ligne. Et doibuent estre trois clauses de semblable lisiere ou rithme et semblable reffrain pour derniere ligne, lequel doibt estre masculin avec demye clause de semblable ou aultre lisiere au quattre dernieres lignes, qui s'appelle l'enuoy, ou le prince, pource que, en tenant le puy de ballades, voluntiers ledict enuoy se adrece ou enuoye au prince. Et disent aulcuns qu'il n'est point necessaire, ne aussi l'enuoy d'vng champ royal, veu que l'en y peult changer lisiere. Mais la coustume plus commune c'est qui sont de l'essence de ballade et de champ royal, et doibuent en puy estre de semblable lisiere, et se, par eulx a redicte, ilz sont a reffuser. Aulcuns font ballades et lignes de dix syllabes en masculin, et les aultres prennent deux lignes pour reffrain et se peuent layer, retrograder en tant de manieres que l'acteur trouuera de suauité en son ordonnance; mais s'il excede huyt lignes et huyt syllabes, ce n'est plus ballade, et ceulx de dix syllabes s'appellent bastars de champ royal ou demy champ royal, ballade quant ilz changent lisiere en la cinquiesime ou sixiesme ligne, comme sont les XXV ballades de Meschinot enuoyees a George l'Auanturier, et celles de maistre Alain que sont au *Breuiaire des nobles.* Et differe ballade a reffrain branlant, pource que en ballade les IIII et V lignes sont de semblabe lisiere et terminaison, et le reffrain branlant change, et si a VI ou VIII couplectz sans prince, et ne sont point les clauses de semblable lisiere."[53]

. . . .

[53] A. Héron, *Le Grand et Vrai Art de Pleine Rhetorique de Pierre Fabri* (*Rouen, 1890*), *Second Livre,* pp. 87–88. Fabri quotes here L'Infortuné's verse definition of the *ballade.*

"Frere Oliuier Maillart:
Seigneurs, qui les grans biens auez
Pour seruir la chose publique,
Prelatz et clercs les droitz sçauez,
Gens qui menez vie lubrique,
De voz pechez et voye oblique
Vous rendrez conte et reliqua,
Ou serez dampnez sans replique,
M'arme, il n'y a ne sy ne qua.

Gorgyas basteurs de pauez,
Bourgoys, marchans, gens de practique,
Femmes qui vos faces lauez
Et pour intention inique
Fringuez bien en forme autentique,
Le diable qui vous prouoqua
En fin pour vous auoir s'applique.
M'arme, il n'y a, etc.

Tricherres qui l'autruy debuez,
Gens, nobles, gens d'art mecanique,
Leuez tous les testes, leuez,
Vous vous dampnez, raison l'explique.
Vous yrez au Dieu pacifique
Qui oncques pecheur ne mocqua,
Ou au logis diabolique.
M'arme, il n'y a ne sy ne qua.

Enuoy

Prince, redempteur magnifique
Qui d'enfer Adam reuoqua,
Se par toy n'auons pais vnique,
M'arme, il n'y a ne sy ne qua."[54]

"Septains different a ballade, pource qu'ilz sont sept lignes, et ballade est de huyt. . . . Les Picars apprennent les ballades que sont d'autant de lignes qu'il y a de syllabes au

[54] A. Héron, *Opus Cit.*, pp. 89–90.

pallinode; mais, se il passe huyt en masculin et neuf en feminin, ce n'est plus ballade.

"Item, ilz font difference entre commune et ballade balladant' qu'ilz appellent batelee en la quarte syllabe, c'est a dire que toute ligne de dix ou de vnze doibt auoir couppe en mot complet et masculin, comme il est dict de champ royal.

Ballade antique de dix syllabes en masculin:

"Quant vous verrez les princes reculler
Et les riches estre en division;
Quant vous verrez les sages acculler
Pour soustenir police et vnion;
Quant les flatteurs par leur sedition
Informeront les seigneurs au contraire;
Quant en croirta des folz l'oppinion,
Tenez vous seurs qu'aurez beaucoup a faire.

[Two other stanzas given.]

Prince, pour Dieu ayez affection
D'entretenir la iustice ordinaire,
Ou aultrement et pour conclusion
Tenez vous seurs, etc."

L'en faict aussi des ballades a paige ou layees, Comme cy:

"Fleur de beaulté gracieuse,
    Precieuse,
Gente d'honneur excellente,
Viue face sumpteuse,
    Verteuse,
Blanche dame et nouvelle ente."[55]

J. *L'Art et Science de Rhétorique Vulgaire*

Autre Reigle

"Encores autre taille de dix lignes se treuvent, la quelle est bonne a faire ballades de dix mettres, selon le refrain de

[55] A. Héron, *Opus Cit.*, pp. 91–93.

dix sillabes, comme icy appert par ung article d'une double ballade de feu maistre Jehan Le Mayre:

Exemple

"Cent ans a creu; tout se paye en une heure.
Il est escript par ung noble chapitre:
Qui feu nourrit pour mectre en autruy feurre,
Finer par feu doibt tel pervers ministre.
De trahison tous enfans de trahistre
Sont entachez, soit en taille ou en fonte.
Tel fut Enée et Anthenor en compte;
Telz estes vous leurs successeurs encore.
Mais le bon droit la malice surmonte.
Or est Priam bien vengé de Anthenor.[56]

"Autre maniere de ryme se treuve de onze lignes, de la quelle communement on fait ballades ou chantz royaulx, selon et en ensuyvant le refrain qui est feminin et de onze sillabes, comme il appert:

Exemple[57]

"Artaxersès, plein de gloyre et facunde,
Jadis monstrant ses triumphes royaulx,
Fit ung convy d'opulence fecunde
Aux princes siens, gentz et subjects loyaulx.
Vasty la royne, habondante en richesses,
Tint court planiere aux dames et duchesses
Adoncq el roy, pour plus fort s'esjouyr,
Voult que a luy vint, mais il n'en sceut jouyr;
Lors couronna Hester, vierge opportune,
Puys decreta et fit par tout ouyr
La loy de mort condempnant tous fors une.[58]

[56] Langlois, *Opus Cit.*, p. 277, says that this is the second stanza of a double *ballade* in the *Légende de Vénitiens* of Jean Lemaire.

[57] The first stanza of a *chant royal* given later in the same treatise.

[58] Langlois, *Opus Cit.*, pp. 277–278.

"*Sensuyvent Les Reigles de Balades et Chantz Royaux.*

Ballade commune doibt avoir refrain et troys cupletz, et l'envoy; dont le refrain tire la substance de la ballade. Et doibt chascun couplet par rigueur d'examen avoir autant de lignes que le refrain contient de sillabes.

De huyt sillabes.

"Se le refrain a huyt sillabes et la derreniere est parfaicte et masculine, la ballade doibt tenir forme de vers huytains.

De neuf sillabes.

"Se le refrain a neuf sillabes et la derreniere est feminine et imparfaicte, les coupletz doibvent avoir neuf lignes, dont les quartres premieres se croysent, et la .v^{e}., .vj^{e}. et .viij^{e}., sont de pareilles terminations et ryme differente aux quatre premieres lignes croysées et la septiesme et neuvfiesme consonantes en ryme et differantes de toutes les autres.

De Dix sillabes.

"Se le reffrain a dix sillabes, les coupletz de la ballade sont de dix lignes; mais il fault que la derreniere sillabe de la ligne dudit refrain soit en ryme masculine et parfaicte; des quelles dix lignes les quatres premieres se croysent, la .v^{e}. pareille a la .iiij^{e}., la .vi^{e}., .vij^{e}. et .ix^{e}. de pareille termination differante a celle de la croysure, et la .viij^{e}. et .x^{e}. egalles en ryme et consonance distinctes de toutes les autres.

De Onze sillabes.

"Se le refrain a onze sillabes, dont la derreniere est feminine et imparfaicte, les coupletz auront onze lignes, des quelles les quatre premieres se croysent, la .v^{e}. et .vj^{e}. pareilles et d'autre ryme; la .vij^{e}., .viij^{e}., et .x^{e}. egalles en consonance et differante aux premieres; et la .ix^{e}. et .xj^{e}.

aussi de pareille termination et differante a toutes les autres.

De L'Envoy

"Il est a noter que tout envoy, qui se commance par Prince, a les mesme refrain des coupletz; mais il ne contient que cinq lignes tout au plus es coupletz de dix et onze sillabes, et prend ses terminations et rymes sur les cinq derrenieres lignes desditz coupletz; et se ilz n'ont que huyt ou neuf lignes, les rymes de l'envoy se feront sur le quatres derrenieres lignes d'iceulx coupletz.

"Exemple de huyt lignes les coupletz et de huyt sillabes le refrain se monstrera en une double ballade cy après ensuyvant, qui se commance ainsi:

Le roy Francois chevaleureux, etc.

Exemple de neuf sillabes

"Suys je pas le plus malheureux
Qui soit vivant dessus la terre,
De veoir Ennuy de douloureux,
Accourir sus moy si grand erre?
Helas! ce cas dur et amer
Est seullement pour trop aymer
Une trés belle et jeune dame;
Dont voy qu'il est a presumer
Par amour on reçoit maint blasme.

[Two other stanzas given.]

Prince, on me debvroit assommer,
Puys que j'ay fait moy mesme infame,
Car je voy pour me consommer
Par amour on reçoit maint blasme.

Exemple de dix sillabes

[None given.]

"Exemple de onze lignes les coupletz et onze sillabes le refrain se verra en ung chant royal cy après ensuyvant et commençant:

Artaxersès, plain de gloire et faconde, etc.[59]

"Et n'y a autre difference, sinon que le chant royal est fait de cinq coupletz et l'envoy, et la ballade n'en a que troys et l'envoy.

"En vers alexandrins se peult aussi faire ballade, les coupletz de douze lignes, et le refrain de douze sillabes, combien que n'en aye encores veu.

Exemple

"Si jadis le dieu Mars eut des filz belliqueux
Es granctz et noble Grecz, es Troyans fortz et preux;
Et es prudents Rommains, puissans d'antiquité,
Au temps present en Gaulle en est de vertueux.
Adextres et hardiz, si qu' en faictz sumptueux,
Aulcun d'eulx, pour mourir, n'a les armes quicté.
On en voit toute France ennoblie et trés seure
Par le nombre alié des princes qui l'asseure,
Dont l'eslite et perle est un ung prince françoys,
Franc, begnin, saige et jeune et de belle stature,
Qui tousjours a le cueur, de vertus nourriture,
Le myeulx aymé de tous et l'espoir de Françoys.

[Two other stanzas given.]

Prince, faiz nous ce bien que jusque a cent ans dure
Ce riche et beau joyau, pur et nect, sans laidure,
Qui, comme hoir, garde et tient, de mont et de val, loix;
Garde le, s'il te plaist, d'infortune trop dure,
Car seul nous le tenons, et, s'il luy plaist, l'endure
Le myeulx aymé de tous et l'espoir de Françoys.[60]

59 See p. 187 above.

60 By the author of the treatise.

''Ballade balladant tient termes de ballade, commune, fors qu'elle est bastellée a la quatriesme et cinquiesme sillabes en certaines lignes de la quadrure; car en toutes lignes de dix ou de onze sillabes, soit en ballade, rondeau ou autre taille, tousjours la quatriesme sillabe en masculin ou la cinquiesme en feminin et singulier nombre, qui fait la quadrure, doibt estre de mettre complet, et avoir sentence entiere, et fault illecq reposer en pronunçant. Et autant es vers alexandrins s'en doibt faire en la sixiesme sillabe masculine et en la septiesme feminine, qui fait la quadrure, comme plus a plain, et declairé et par exemple monstré au commancement de cest oeuvre, en la dilucidation et exposition du parfaict ou masculin et le l'imparfaict ou feminin. Toutesvoyes encore, ainsi que dit est, le coupletz de ceste forme de ballade doib[vent] contenir autant de lignes comme le refrain a de sillabes.

Exemple

"Juïfz ont dit que nostre redemption."[61]

. . . .

''Ballade fatrisée ou gemelle sont deux ballades communes tellement ordonnées et entrelacées ensemble que le commancement de l'une donne refrain a l'autre. Et se peuent faire et composer de quelque quantité et nombre de sillabes que l'acteur vouldra, en y observant les reigle, dessus dictes en forme de ballades.

Exemple

"Le roy François, chevaleureux,
Doué de tous dons de nature,
Est a pied et cheval heureux,
Franc, fort, de vertus désireux,

[61] Langlois, *Opus Cit.*, pp. 294–298. This same *ballade* is given in Molinet's treatise.

Moult aymant justice et droicture;
Par quoy sus toute creature
Gloire il a, car par ses haultz faictz
Ses ennemys sont tous deffaitz.

Ses ennemys sont tous deffaitz
Et est leur puissance abolie;
Bien ont congneu par vilz effectz
Les lasches tours qu'ilz avoient faitz ;
Car sont puniz de leur folie,
Lors n'eurent que melencolie,
Quant si près virent entour eulx
Le roy François, chevaleureux.

[Four other stanzas given.]

Prince entretiens tousjours l'armeure
De prudence, par bon art meure,
Au roy, puys que publier faiz;
Ses ennemeys sont tous deffaiz."[62]

K. Gracien du Pont: *Art et Science de Rhetorique Metrifiée.*

fol. 49–50[63]

Quést ce que Ballades

"Nous auōs souuēt dessus parle, des Ballades et des Chāps royaulx. Toutesfoys nauōs encores declaire quést ce que Ballade, & quést ce que Chāp royal.

Premieremēt debuez noter q ballade nést aultre chose, q̄ troys coupletz à ung mesme reffrain, avec Lēuoy qui porte pareil reffrain que lesd coupletz. Et pour biē entendre quest ce q Enuoy, ce n'ést que vng sommaire de fin & cōclusion quant au sens, qui ne doibt estre en nōbre & mesure de

[62] Langlois, *Opus Cit.*, pp. 300–301.

[63] The references are to the edition printed in 1539 at Toulouse.

lignes, que le moytie de lung desd troys coupletz. Et ce debuez entendre de la derniere moytie dudict couplet, nō de la premiere. Laq̄lle moytie se prend apres la premiers clause parfaicte faisant couplet parfaict, cōe auons dessus dict. Cést à scauoir en Rithme platte, ou croysee, despuys les quatre premieres lignes, & en rithme riche despuys les six dictes. Apres lesqlles pouez chāger de croyseure & facōs en mainctes sortes pour faire couplet double. Cōe verrez en mains lieux dessoubz alleguez composez p*ar* diuers Autheurs. Et notez que de riguer dudict art / chascū couplet doibt auoir aultant de lignes, hors mys ledict Enuoy, q̄ le reffrain a de syllabes. Toutesfoys, nest telle rigeur obseruee, & gardee, ains se practique au plaisir de cōposeur, cōe voyez toutz les iours par exēples. Pourueu que en mesure, ny quātitez de lignes ne soit excede le nōbre de douz lignes cōe avons dict. Et sachez aussi que les coupletz des Ballades ne doibuent estre hors mys ledict Enuoy, de moins de lignes, que de sept, cōpris ledict reffrain, de moins ne seroyt Ballade ains coupletz à reffrain, ne meritanz porter le nom de Ballades. Et pose quilz portēt nōbre competent, selon nostre aduys, si tous lesdictz coupletz ne sont vnissones, aussi ne merite estre dicte Ballade. Combien quē soyent plusiers au cōtraire. Vous trouuerez de Ballades en forme deue en maīctz & duiers lieux. Et audict liure des Cōtrouerses, toutes sont vnissones. Et premieremēt, au fueillet .ij. tournè, vne a .ix. lignes. Vne aultre au fueillet .iij. tournè à .x. lignes, corōnee. Au feuillet .vj. tournè, vne enchaisnee, a .viij. lignes, au fueillet .xj. vne coronnee à dix lignes, au fueillet .xlix. tourné, vne batellee à .x. lignes, au fueillet .liiij. vne emperiere, à .viij. lignes, au fueillet tournè, vne aultre emperiere, par enquiuocs mariez à .viij. lig. au fueillet .lv. vne coronnee & batellee à sēblables corōnes à .vij. lignes, au fueillet .lix. vne batellee à .viij. lignes, au fueillet .lx. tourné vne p*ar* equiuocques à .x. lignes, au fueillet

.lxvij. tourné, vne latinisee à .x. lignes, au fueillet .lxxviij. vne à .x. lignes, au fueillet .lxxviij. vne à .x. lignes, au fueillet .lxxxij. tourné, Vne par equiuocqs à .x. lignes, au fueillet .cxix. vne batelle à .xij. lignes. Itē aulx fueilletz .cxxvij. & .cxx. .vij. troys suyuãtes à double sens à .viij. lignes au fueillet .clxxviij. tourné, vne coronee, & batellee à .viij. lignes.

Notez que despuys le nõbre de .vij. lig. inclusivement, jusq̄ à douze, se peuēt faire Ballades. Et quant aulx coupletz, il ny en doibt auoir que troys, & Lēuoy. Aultremēt me seroyt Ballade ains chãp royal."

Fol. lii verso

"Des mesdisans des rithmes graues, & subtilles de termes. . . . Mays quelq̄ chose quilz saichent dire, quant elles sont bien faictes, soit en Ballade vnisonne. Et mesmement corõnee par equiuocques, Emperiere, ou aultre, est plus riche, & digne destre mieulx prisee, que cēt, ne mille desdictz aultres bas stilles. Et auront lesdictz grossiers ignorantz, plustost faictes cent, voyre mille Ballades de leurs maternelz patoys, & principes dapprentys, que vne bõne Ballade desdictz haultz stilles, qui ne se laissent digerer en lestomac de toutes gens."

"Il fault presuppose, que ceulx qui font vne bonne ballade des dictz haultz stilles peneux & subtilz, quilz en ferõt bien vne planiere & grossiere. Vng hõme qui scait lyre le Pater noster, & toutes aultres escriptures, tant de main que de Impression scauroit bien lyre le A, B, C. Et scait bien espeler & assembler les lettres en syllabes, & dictions. Nous ne voullons poinct soubstenir q̄ quant vne desdicts especes graues ne seroyt de bõne mesure, de bon sens, & seroit viceuse, fust plus estimee que vne bonne Ballade simple à bon sens & termes sans aulcũ vice."

The varieties of *ballades* that appear in du Pont's *Controverses* are given below:

Ballade unissone à IX lignes et dix syllabes.

Ballade dyaloguée à VIII syllabes et X lignes.

Ballade unissone par dizains.

Ballade unisonne batellée à X syllabes.

Ballade unissone léonine et batellée à II terminaisons tant seullement a dizains.

Ballade unissone par termes scabreulx et latinisez à dizaine.

Ballade unissone et batellée à XII lignes.

Ballade unissone par equivocques à dix syllabes et X lignes.

Ballade unissone à doubles equivocques.

Ballade unissone coronnée par equivocques à dizains.

Ballade unissone par vers enchaisnez equivocquez.

Ballade unissone coronnée par equivocques mariez en la premiere terminaison ou sont accordez deux contraires cest le plurier avec le singulier et le masculin avec le feminin: car la teste est masculin et pluriere et la coronne feminine et singuliere à dizains.

Ballade unissone coronnée par equivoques et batellée par coronez equivocquez.

Ballade unissone batellée et coronnée par double coronne equivocquee chascune ligne portant son equivocque aultrement dicte emperière.

Ballade unissone batellée par termes déonismes riches hors mys le refrain et son subject coronnée à deux coronnes par coronnez mariez dicte emperière par equivocques tante le masculin que le feminin.

Ballade unissone coronnée par equivocques et batellée par semblables coronnes equivocquees, autrement dicte coronnée par equivocques redoublez en laquelle est coronne le refrain.

Ballade unissone à double sens retrogradée en diverses

façons dont en lysant toute la ligne dit mal des femmes aussy en la lysant au rebours mot à mot. Et ne lysant que une moytié de chascun quartier que vous vouldrez dit bien desdites femmes tant le lysant en hault que en bas.

Ballade unissone à double sens et de mesme sorte que la dessus quant à lestille, mays contraire à lautre devant car en lysant toute la ligne dit bien des femmes et les moytiez en disent mal.

Ballade unissone de mesme stille que les dessus dictes, sauf que en lysant toute la ligne dit bien des femmes et de moytiez lune dit mal et lautre bien desdictes femmes parainсy toutes les troys susdictes ballades sont differentes l'une de l'autre, combien que soyent d'ung mesme stille et de retrogradent d'une sorte.[64]

L. Thomas Sibilet: *Art Poëtique François*

"La Balade est Poëme plus graue que nul des precedens [Sonnet and Rondeau], pour ce que de son origine s'adressoit aux Princesses et ne traitoit que materes graves et dignes de l'aureille d'vn roi. Auec le temps empireur de toutes choses, les Poëtes Françoys l'ont adaptée à matières plus legeres et facecieuses, en sorte qu'auiourd' huy la matiere de la Balade est toute telle qu'il plaist à celuy qui en est autheur. Si est elle neantmoins moins propre à facecies et legeretez.

"Sa forme est telle qu'elle contient trois coupletz entiers, et vn epilogue communement appellé Enuoy. Les trois coupletz doyuent auoir tous autant de vers les vns comme les autres, et unisones en ryme: car s'ilz sont de different son, ia la bonne part de la grace que doit la Balade, est esgarée. Le nombre des vers en chasque couplet est huittain ou dizain, par foys septain ou vnzain. . . . L'enuoy ou

64 Gracien du Pont, *Les Controverses des Sexes Masculin et Feminin*, Tholoze, 1534.

epilogue mesure le nombre de ses vers à la forme du couplet: car si le couplet est huictain, l'Enuoy sera quatrain. Se le couplet ha dis vers, l'epilogue en aura cinq plus communément: aulcuns foys sept. S'il est vnzain, l'Enuoy sera icy de cinq, là de six, ailleurs de sept vers. Et si le couplet a douze vers, comme tu en trouueras, en aucunes Balades de Marot, l'Enuoy en doit auoit sept pour legitime proposition. Voyla quant au nombre des vers: mais quant à la ryme, tu entens assez dans mon auertissement, qu'à raison de l'analogie, les vers de l'Enuoy, en quelque nombre qu'ils soyent, doyuent resembler en son, autant des derniers du couplet, qu'ilz sont en leur nombre: comme si l'epilogue a cinq vers, ces cinq doyuent estre vnisones aux cinq derniers de chasque couplet precedent, et ainsi en plus grand nombre. Mais sur tout fault que tu auises au dernier vers du premier couplet, qu'on appelle Refrain, pource qu'il repete entier en la fin de chasque couplet, et de l'Enuoy de mesme. Repete di-ie, non comme au Rondeau simple ou double, auquel la repetition du vers ou hemistiche est abondante, c'est à dire qu'elle ne diminue point le nombre des vers autrement requis au couplet, ains est supernumeraire. Mais en la Balade le refrain repeté est conté pour vn des vers constituans le couplet, comme tu peuz voir en ceste Balade de Marot:

[Here Sibilet prints Marot's *ballade,* the refrain of which is: "Le beau Dauphin, tant desiré en France."]

"Tu trouueras d'autres Balades à double refrain, l'vn repeté au mylieu du couplet, et l'autre à la fin: comme en la Balade de Marot à Frere Lubin:[65] et ceste maniere de refrain double, est autant rare que plaisante. La Balade au demourant se fait de vers de huit et dix syllabes mieux et plus communément. Mais tiens tousiours en memoire ceste regle generalle, qui le vers de huit syllabes est né

[65] See Chapter V, below, p. 319, and the present chapter, p. 206.

seulement pour les choses legeres et plaisantes. Note conséquemment quant au fait de la Balade, que sa premier vertu et perfection est, quand le refrain n'est point tiré par les cheveux pour rentrer en fin de couplet: mais y est repeté de mesme grace et connexion que je t'ay dit au chaptire precedent estre requise à la reprise du Rondeau.

"L'Enuoy commence quasi tousiours par ce mot, Prince si la Balade dresse à homme; & par Princesse, si à femme, d'où tu peuz cognoistre la maiesté et pris d'elle. Cela toutesfois n'est tant necessaire que tu ne trouues en beaucoup d'Enuoys ces mots laissez pour autres mieulx à propos qui ayent pareille ou meilleure harmonie."[66]

M. Joachim du Bellay: *La Deffence et Illustration de Langue Françoyse*

"Ly doncques, et rely premierement, (ò Poëte futur) fueillette de main nocturne et journelle les exemplaires grecz et latins: puis me laisse toutes ces vielles poësies françoyses aux Jeux Floraux de Thoulouze et au Puy de Rouan:[67] comme rondeaux, ballades, vyrelaiz, chantz, royaux, chansons, et autres telles episseries, qui corrompent legoust de nostre langue et ne servent si non à porter temoignage de notre ignorance."[68]

N. Barthélemy Aneau: *Le Quintil Horatian*

"Trop dedaigneuse est ceste exportation de laisser les vieilles poësies aux Floraux de Tholose et au Puytz de Rouan. Par laquelle trop superbe dehortation sont indignement et trop arrogament deprisées deux tresnobles choses.

66 Charles Asselineau: *Livre des Ballades* (Paris, 1876), pp. 171–174

67 See Chapter I.

68 H. Chamard, *Joachim du Bellay, La Deffence et Illustration de la Langue Francoyse* (Paris, 1904), p. 201.

D'ont l'une est l'institution ancienne en deux tresbonnes villes de France de l'honneur attribué au mieux faisans, pour l'entretien eternal de la poësie françoise, jouxte le proverbe: *l'honneur nourrit les ars.* Tel que jadis fut en Grece és Olynpiques, et à Rome és jeux publiques. L'autre est l'excellence et noblesse de noz poëmes les plus beaux et les plus artificielz, comme rondeaux, balades, chans royaux, virlais, lesquelz tu nommes, par terrible translation, espicerie corrumpant le goust: qui toutefois en toute perfection d'art et d'invention excedent tes beaux sonnetz et odes (que tu nommes ainsi) desquelz plus amplement cy apres je parleray. Et en cest endroit, tu ne cognois, ou ne veux cognoistre, que ces nobles poëmes sont propres et peculiers à langue françoise, et de la sienne et propre et antique invention. Sinon que par adventure on les vousist rapporter a d'aucunes formes hebraïques et gréques és Prophetes et en Isocrat, et quelques latines en Ciceron et oraisons et en Vergile és vers intercalaires. Ce que mesmes les noms de ces poëmes donnent à entendre. Car rondeau est periode, balade est nom Grec, chant royal est carme heroïque, par principale denomination, virlay est lyrique ou laïque, c'est à dire populaire. Ce que ne pensant pas, tu les rejettes, mesmement les virlais, et à la fin ordonnes les vers lyriques, qui sont tout un et une mesme chose. Mais ce que te fais les depriser, à mon avis que c'est la difficulté d'iceux poëmes, qui ne sortent jamais de povre esprit, et d'autant sont plus beaux que de difficile facture, selon le proverbe grec τὰ χαλεπὰ καλα, les *choses difficules sont belles.* Tout ainsi comme en grec et latin les vers exametres, cheminans a deux piedz seulement, sont plus nobles et plus beaux que les trochaïques ou iambiques ou comiques, qui recoivent plusieurs piedz indifferement et plus à l'aise. Pource ne blasme point ce que tant est louable, et ne defendz aux autres ce que tu desperes povoir parfaire. Et ne dy point que telz poëmes ne serve sinon à porter tesmoignage de nostre ignorance. Car au contraire par excellence de vers et ligatures, nombreuse multiplicité de cadences unisonnantes, et argute rentrée, refrains et reprinses avec la majesté de la chose traitée, et epilogue des envoys, tesmoignent la magnificence et richesse de nostre langue, et la noblesse et la felicité des espritz françois, en cela excedans toute les poësies vulgares. Mais pour le difficile artifice et élabourée beauté d'iceux anciens poëmes, tu les veux estre laisséz.''[69]

. . . .

''Sonnez luy l'antiquaille. Tu nouz as bien induit à laisser le blanc pour le bis, les balades, rondeaux, virlaiz et chans royaux pour les sonnetz, invention (comme tu dis) italienne. Dequoy (si à Dieu plait) ils sont beaucop plus à priser. Et certes ils sont d'une merveilleuse invention (à bien les consyderer) et tresdificile, comme d'un huitain bien libre, à deux ou trois cadences [rimes], et un sizain, à autant d'unisonances ou croisées, ou entreposées si abondonnéement et deregléement, qu le plus souvent en cinq vers sont trois rymes diverses et la ryme du premier renduë finalement au cinquieme, tellement que en oyant le dernier, on a desja perdu le son et la memoire de son premier unisonant, qui est desja à cinq lieuës de là. Vela une brave poësie, pour en mepriser et dedaigner toutes les autres excellentes françoises, si conjointes en leurs croisures qu'elles ne laissent jamais perdre et loing voller le son de leur compagne, encore demourant en l'oreille, et en l'*e* fenit[70] plus d'un ver, ou deux au plus, et ce en double croysure et entreposée quaternaire. Outre ce au lieu de defendre et

[69] H. Chamard, *Joachim du Bellay, La Deffence et Illustration de la Langue Francoyse* (Paris, 1904), pp. 203–204.

[70] A corrupt passage. Chamard says: ''Le sens est bien peu clair.'' This remark applies to the unemended text.

illustrer nostre langue (comme tu le promets), tu nous fais grand deshonneur, de nous renvoyer à l'italien, qui a prins la forme de sa poësie des Francois, et en laquelle il est si licentieux, qu'il use de motz et couppes, divisions et contractions à l'estriviere.''[71]

. . . .

''Comme tu as jeté les plus belles formes de la poësie françoise, ainsi maintenant rejectes tu la plus exquise sorte de ryme que nous ayons, moyenant qu'elle ne soit affectée et cerchée trop curieusement. Et en cecy tu blasmes taisiblement Meschinot, Molinet, Cretin et Marot, tels personnages que chacun les coignoit. Mais comme j'ay dit des chants royaux, balades, rondeaux et virlais, la difficulté des equivoques, qui ne te viennent pas tousjours à propos, les te fait rejecter.[72]

O. Guillaume des Autelz: *Repliques aux Furieuses Defenses de Louis Meigret*

''Au reste, encores, ne tiens je si peu de conte de noz anciens François, que je mesprise tant leurs propres inventions que ceux qui les appellent espisseries, qui ne servent d'autre chose que de porter temoignage de nostre ignorance. Pourquoy est plus à mespriser l'elaboree ballade françoise que la superstitieuse sextine italiene? Ou y trouvez vous si grande ineptie? Est ce en la palynodie? mais elle nous est commune avecques les Grecs et Latins. Est ce en la difficulte? mais tant plus en est elle louable, pourveu qu'elle n'en apparoisse ny moins ornee ny plus contrainte. Est ce en l'abus de ceux qui escrivent mal? mais nous pourrions ainsi universellement condemner toute la poësie. Et tant

71 H. Chamard, *Opus Cit.*, p. 222.
72 *Ibid.*, p. 264.

s'en faut que pour sa difficulté je l'estime incapable des ornemens poëtiques que je n'en forclus pas le chant royal, beaucoup plus difficile et ingenieux: d'autant qu'il est plus long et doit contenir une perpetuelle allegorie jusques à l'epilogue, qui la doit ouvrir et declairer. Et quant ce ne seroit qu'un exercice pour nous preparer à plus grans œuvres, pource ne devrions nous vituperer l'eglantine tholosane, ou lon ne defend pas de proposer d'autres poëmes. Cecy n'est pas dit pour soutenir la façon de nostre vieille poësie: mais je pense que ce temps luy peult donner ce que le passé luy ha refusé, et qu'elle n'est inhabible à le recevoir. Ce que j'ay dit de la ballade, je l'estens jusques au lay, que noz predecesseurs prenoient pour l'ode: et pource je ne me soucie pas qu'on rejette le nom, pourveu qu'on retienne la chose et que lon l'agence mieux.''[73]

P. Jacques Pelletier: *L'Art Poetique*

''Combien de tans à etè notre langue languissante an barbarie pövrete et contannemènt! . . . Combien longuemant a ele sofistiquè an Balades, Rondeaus, Lez, Virelez, Triolez, e s'il i an à de téz.[74]

Q. Etienne Pasquier: *Recherches de la France*

''Quant à la Ballade, c'estoit un chant Royal racourci au petit pied, auquel toutes les reigles de l'autre s'observoient et en la suite continuelle de la rime, et en la closture du vers, et au Renvoy, mais ils se passoient par trois ou quatre dizains, ou huitains, et encores en vers de sept, huit on dix syllabes à la discretion du fatiste, et en tel argument qu'il vouloir choisir.''

. . . .

[73] *Ibid.*, p. 204.

[74] H. Chamard, *De Jacobi Peletarii Cenomanensis Arte Poetica* (*Insulis*, 1900), p. 57.

"Si ces trois especes de Poësie estoient encores en usage, je ne les vous eusse icy representées, comme sur un tableau: vous les recevrez de moi comme d'une antiquiaille. Toute mon intention estoit, et est, de vous monstrer dont provenoit, que combien que les chant Royaux et Ballades ne parlassent en aucune façon des Princes, toutesfois leurs conclusions aboutissent seulement en eux."

. . . .

"Il n'est pas qu'en ma jeunesse és disputes qui se faisoient entre nous dedans nos classes, celuy qui avoit mal respondu, estoit par nous appellé *Reus,* comme si on luy eust faict son procez. Il en prit autrement à nos vieux Poëtes. Car comme ainsi fust qu'ils eussent certain jeux de prix en leur Poësies, ils ne condamnoient point celuy qui faisoit le plus mal, mais bien honoroient du nom tantost de Roy, tantost le Prince, celuy qui avoit le mieux fait."

. . . .

"Tous ces chants [chants Royaux Ballades], comme j'ay dit, estoient dediez à l'honneur, et celebration des Festes les plus celebres, comme de la Nativité de nostre Seigneur, de sa Passion, de la Conception de nostre Dame, et ainsi des autres: La fin estoit un couplet de cinq, ou sex vers que l'on addressoit à un Prince, duquel on n'avoit faict aucune mention par tout le discours du chant. Chose qui peut apprester à penser à celuy qui ne sçaura ceste ancienneté. La verité donques est (que j'ay apprise du vieux Art Poëtique François par moy cy-dessus allegué [Dolet]) que l'on celebroit en plusieurs endroits de, la France des jeux Floraux, où celuy qui avoit rapporté l'honneur de mieux escrire, estant appellé tantost Roy, tantost Prince, quand il falloit renouveler les jeux, donnoit ordinairement des ces Chants à faire, qui furent pour ceste cause appellez Royaux, d'autant que de toute leur Poësie, cestuy estoit le plus riche sujet qui estoit donné par le Roy, lequel donnoit aussi des Ballades à faire qui estoient comme demy chants Royaux. Ces jeunes fatistes ayans composé ce qui leur estoit enjoinct, reblandissoient à la fin de leurs Chants Royaux et Ballades leur Prince, afin que l'honorant ils fussent aussi par luy gratifiez, et lors il distribuoit Chapeaux et Couronnes de fleurs, uns et autres, selon le plus ou le moins qu'ils avoient bien-faict. Chose qui s'observe encores dans Tholose, où l'on baille l'Englentine à celuy qui a gaigné le dessus, au second la Soulcie, et quelques autres fleurs par ordre, le tout toutesfois d'argent, et port encores cet honneste exercise, le nom de jeux Floraux, tout ainsi qu'anciennement.

Ces chants Royaux, Ballades, Rondeaux et Pastorales, commencerent d'avoir cours vers le regne de Charles cinquiesme.[74]

R. François de Pierre Delaudun Daigaliers: *L'Art Poétique*

De la Ballade

Chap. V

"Avtrefois la ballade a esté en telle vogue, qu'elle ne seruoit qu' à choses grādes & dignes d'estre presentees à vn Roy ou Prince: mais auiourd'huy outre ce que l'on ne s'en sert plus, encores ceux qui s'en seruent ne l'employēt qu'à risée, & n'estoit, *le puy de la Conception des Carmes de Roüan,* qui se tient vne fois l'an, ie croy que desja la memoire en seroit perdue. La Ballade est appellée ainsi, pource qu'elle seruoit au Bal, & contient quatre parties, sçauoir trois couplets entiers & vn enuoy, qui sert d'epilogue. Les couplets ont autant de vers les vns que les autres, & sont vnisones en rime. I'ay dict que c'estoit

75 E. Pasquier, *Les Recherches de la France* (Amsterdam, 1723), Book VII, Ch. V.

à dire, qu'ils sont semblables & fraternisans. L'on y met des vers selon le plaisir du Poëte. Les plus communs sont de huict, sept, dix & vnze, l'enuoy n'a que la moitié des carmes d'vn couplet, comme si le couplet est de huict ou de sept, l'enuoy en aura quatre s'il est de dix ou de sept, l'enuoy en aura quatre s'il est de dix ou de vnze, l'enuoy aura cinq & quelquesfois sept, pourueu qu'il soit vnzain, si le couplet a douze vers l'ēuoy en a sept, & les vers de l'enuoy doiuent estre vnisones aux derniers du couplet. Le refrain de la Ballade est le vers qui se repete tousiours à la fin du couplet & de l'enuoy; lequel est compté pour vn des vers du couplet, & n'est pas superflus, comme le refrain ou repetitiō du Rondeau. I'en mets icy vne qui est prise de mes Meslāges pour n'en trouuer en Ronsard, Desportes, & autres bon autheurs.''

"Pour bien dormir la matinée,
Iusqu'à midy ou bien plus tard,
Pour enployer mal sa iournée,
Bien le fera maistre Mordart,
Car s'il ne se leuoit si tard,
Ce seroit chose salutaire:
Et de faire un acte gaillard,
Maistre Mordart ne le peut faire.

Pour caqueter l'apres-disnee,
Au coing d'vn feu comme vn cagnard,
Et pour faire chose mal née,
Bien le fera Maistre Mordart,
Mais si par vne fois d'hazard
Il eust pensé de vous complaire:
Pour aller chez maistre Richard,
Maistre Mordart le peut bien faire.

Pour bien aller à l'haquenée
Dessus vn beau cheual bayart,
Se pourmener la matinée

Bien le faira Maistre Mordart,
Et puis venant de ceste part,
Comme vn braue soldat de guerre:
De prendre son repos bien tart,
Maistre Mordart ne le peut faire.

Enuoy

Pour faire l'acte d'vn cagnart,
Bien le fera Maistre Mordart.
Mais si c'est chose salutaire,
Maistre Mordart ne le peut faire."[76]

"Ceste Ballade est appellée à double refrain l'vn au milieu du couplet, & l'autre à la fin, mais és Ballades dont j'ay parlé cy dessus, il n'est pas requis de mettre que celuy de la fin. La Ballade de huict syllabes n'est pour que risée, mais celle de dix est pour choses graues, & faut que le premier mot de l'enuoy se commence par le tiltre d'honneur de celuy à qui elle s'adresse."[77]

S. Vauquelin de la Fresnaye: *L'Art Poétique François*

"Et des vieux chants Royaux décharge le fardeau,
Oste moy Ballade, oste moy le Rondeau.
Les Sonnets amoureux des Tançons Prouençalles,
Succederent depuis aux marches inegalles
Dont marche l'Elegie; alors des Troubadors
Fut la Rime trouee en chantant leurs amours:
Et quand leur vers Rimez ils mirent en estime
Il sonnoient, il chantoient, ils balloient sous leur Rime.
Du Son se fist Sonnet, du Chant se fist chanson,
Et du Bal la Ballade, en diverse façon:

[76] Cf. the refrain of *Frère Lubin* by Clément Marot: "Frère Lubin ne le peult faire."

[77] Francois de Pierre Delaudun Daigaliers, *L'Art Poétique* (Paris, 1598), pp. 56–59.

Ces Trouuerres alloient par toutes les Prouinces
Sonner, chanter, danser leurs Rimes chez les Princes."[78]

T. Le Sieur de Deimier: *L'Académie de l'Art Poétique*

. . . "la Poësie Françoise est traictee en trente-deux sortes de Poëmes, qui sont nommez ainsi, et en premier lieu comme le plus excellent de tous: le Poëme Heroïque, Discours, Hymne, Confession, Priere, Auanture, Elegie, Stances, Ode, Sonnet, Madrigal, Plainte, Chansō, Prosopopee, Lamentations ou Regrets, Epigrāme, Cartel, Echo, Satyre, Eglogue, Epithalame, Tragedie Tragi-comedie, Chant Royal, Epitaphe, Moralité, Farce, Rondeau, Balade, Vire-lay & Triolet. Lesquels a mon auis, sont, ou comprennent toutes les formes et manieres dont les Poetes ont d'escrit, ou peuuent d'escrire leurs imaginations. Aussi les six derniers de ces Poëmes ont esté fort pratiquez entre les anciens Poëtes François, mais à present on n'en plus d'estat."[79]

U. Francois Colletet: *L'Escole des Muses*

"La Balade autrefois ne s'adressoit qu'aux Princes, et ne traittoit que matieres graues et serieuses: depuis, les Poëtes s'en sont seruis en toutes sortes de matieres: Elle contient trois couplets et vn enuoy ou epilogue: les couplets doiuent auoir autant de vers les vns comme les autres, et les rimes doiuent estre vnisonnes, c'est à dire, que les rimes qui sont au premier, doiuent estre semblables de son à celles du second et troisiéme.

"La disposition des rimes des couplets est semblable à celle de l'Epigramme: les Vers communs sont communément employez en sa composition.

[78] Vauquelin de la Fresnaye, *L'Art Poétique François* (Paris, 1885), Livre I, ll. 545–556.

[79] Le Sieur de Deimier, *L'Académie de l'Art Poétique* (Paris, 1610), pp. 19–20.

"Le nombre des Vers de chaque couplet est à l'arbitre du Poëte; toutefois les plus reguliers sont de huit, dix, sept ou vnze, et quelque fois de douze Vers.

"L'enuoy ou epilogue mesure le nombre de ses Vers à celuy des couplets: car si les couplets ont huit Vers, l'enuoy en aura quatre; s'il en a dix, l'epilogue en aura cinq plus communement, quelque fois sept; si'il est d'vnze, l'enuoy sera de cinq, six ou sept; si le couplet en a douze, l'enuoy sera de sept; les Vers de l'enuoy doiuent auoir les mesmes rimes que les derniers Vers du couplet.

"Le dernier Vers de chacun des trois couplets de l'enuoy, doit estre le mesme, et on l'appelle le refrain de la Balade, lequel ne doit estre compté pour vn des Vers constituans le couplet comme il se pourra voir en cette Balade de Marot, laquelle, quoy que son style ne soit pas à imiter, nous pourra toutesfois servir pour voir la disposition de ce Poëme.

"Il faut bien prendre garde que le refrain ne soit tiré par les cheueux."[80]

V. Boileau: *L'Art Poëtique*

"Tout poëme est brillant de sa propre beauté:
Le rondeau, né gaulois, à la naïveté;
La ballade, asservie à ses vieilles maximes,
Souvent doit tout son lustre au caprice des rimes."[80]

III. Summary

The theories in regard to the *ballade* in the selections given above are concerned with the structure of the stanzas and of the line units; with the rime-scheme, the refrain, and the envoy. The rhetoricians, from the beginning, were keenly interested in devising embellishment and

[80] Francois Colletet, *L'Escole des Muses* (Paris, 1656), pp. 48–50.

[81] Nicolas Boileau-Despréaux, *L'Art Poëtique*, ll. 139–142 reprinted in A. S. Cook, *The Art of Poetry* (Boston, 1892), p. 180.

multiplying variations. Their distinctive contributions practically ceased with the work of Sibilet, after whose treatise the *ballade* was no longer of importance in the handbooks of poetics. Sibilet himself was indebted to his predecessors, Deschamps, Molinet, L'Infortuné, Fabri, and du Pont.

The first of the writers on the *ballade*, Deschamps, discriminated between music and poetry in his effort to show that in the *puy*, where the *ballade* was presented before the *prince* of the *puy*, the poet recited his poem and did not sing it. In his text and in the examples (not all of which are given above), he speaks of nine varieties of the *ballade*. They are:

(1) The stanza of 7 lines.
(2) The stanza of 8 lines (8 syllables); a b a b b c b c, with envoy a c a c.
(3) The stanza of 8 lines (10 syllables); a b a b b c b c.
(4) The stanza of 8 lines with 7 lines of 10 syllables and the fifth line of 7 syllables; a b a b c c d d.
(5) The stanza of 8 lines (10 syllables) with a two line refrain; a b a b b c b c.
(6) The stanza of 9 lines with 8 lines of 10 syllables and the sixth line of seven; a b a b c c d d.
(7) The stanza of 10 lines (8 syllables); a b a b b c c d c d.
(8) The stanza of 10 lines (10 syllables); a b a b b c c d c d.
(9) The stanza of 11 lines with 10 lines of 10 syllables and the fifth line of 7 syllables; a b a b c c d d e d e; envoy, d d e d d e.

The envoy according to Deschamps was attached formerly only to the *chant royal*. In connection with the rime of the *ballade* he explains the nature of *leonine* and *sonant*. By the former he means what is called in English feminine rime, and by the latter what we call masculine rime. A *ballade equivoque* and *retrograde* is peculiar in taking the last one or two syllables of the preceding line for the first word of the following line and employing this last in an entirely different sense from that in which it had first appeared.

Legrand, unlike Deschamps, reflects an earlier stage of the *ballade*. In his short treatise he takes up the interior structure of the *ballade* stanza, and what he says of it is applicable to the commonest *ballade* scheme. By *l'ouvert* and *le clos* he must mean the crossed rimes a b a b; *l'outrepasse* must then be those lines intervening between the cross-riming lines and the refrain. It is therefore impossible for the latter not to contain the rime of the refrain. Legrand's statement is not explained by the evidence of fifteenth century *ballades,* though he means perhaps that the *oultre passe* may contain rimes, especially in the case of the longer *ballade* stanzas, that are found also either in the first four lines or in the refrain.[92]

82 E. Stengel, reviewing Langlois' *Recueil,* pointed out that Legrand's theory was based on the usage of the fourteenth, even perhaps of the thirteenth century. To illustrate, he referred to the Oxford collection of *baletes* in *MS. Douce 308* as furnishing specimens built on the rules of the *ballade* set down by Legrand. He says "Sehen wir uns den Bau der *baletes* in der Oxforder Sammlung an, so finden sich allerdings nur zwei darunter deren Strophenabschluss jede Reimverbindung mit dem Refrain vermissen lässt, nämlich No. 163 und 69.

"In 163 steht überdies der zweite und in 69 der einzige Reim des Strophenabschlusses auch selbstständig denen der Stollen gegenüber. Nach Legrands Vorschrift sollte eine solche völlige Reimselbständigkeit eigentlich ausgeschlossen sein. Ähnliche Fälle einzelner selbständiger Reime des Strophenabschlusses kommen in unserer Sammlung auch noch sehr selten vor (z. B. No. 57). Dagegen reimt in allen übrigen Balladen der Strophenabschluss entweder nur mit dem Refrain oder sowohl mit dem Refrain wie mit den Stollen. Dass Legrand ferner das *envoi* der Ballade verschweigt, deutet wohl auch eher

The author of *Les Règles de la Seconde Rhétorique* mentions six varieties of the *ballade:*

(1) The stanza of 9 lines (10 syllables); a b a b c c d c d, with envoy c c d c d. (An unquotable *sote balade.*)[83]

(2) The stanza of 10 lines (7 syllables); a a b a a b b a a b.

(3) The stanza of 8 lines (10 syllables); a b a b b c b c.

(4) The stanza of 11 lines (10 syllables); a b a b c c d d e d e. The vowels in the end rimes follow the order of vowels in the alphabet.

(5) The stanza of 10 lines (first half line of 4 syllables; second half line of six syllables; constructed to read like 7 below); a b a b b c c d c d.

(6) The stanza of 12 lines (the first, third, fourth, sixth, seventh, ninth, tenth, and twelfth of 10 syllables, with a break after the third syllable; the second, fifth, eighth, and eleventh lines of 4 syllables); a a b a a b b b c b b c.

(7) The stanza of ten lines (the lines divided into two parts, the first half line having 4 syllables, the second half, 6 syllables); a b a b c c d d e d, with envoy d e d. All three stanzas and envoy of this *ballade* are given. There is no refrain. The first letters of all the lines present the acrostic *Biauté, Clarté, Honneur, Richesse* and *Pris.* The *ballade* may read in three ways: (*a*) only the first half-lines; (*b*) only the second half-lines; (*c*)

darauf, dass er die alte Baleteform im Auge halte, als dass er 'ne s'est pas bien rendu compte de ce qu'il écrivait'; denn Deschamps (S 278) bemerkt betreffs der *Envois* ausdrücklich: '*Et ne les souloit on point faire anciennement, fors es Chançons royaulx.*' '' See Stengel, in *Zeit. f. Rom. Phil.*, XXVIII, p. 369.

[83] E. Langlois, *Opus Cit.*, p. 38.

both the first half and the second half of the line together. Read in the last way, the *ballade* shows internal rime.

The specimen stanza given of a *balade en figure de poetiz lais,* and the *plaine laie balladant cited,* are both referred to the *lai,* because in the fifteenth century that kind of poem employed either short lines only or long and short lines mixed.

In the work of Herenc, who knew *Les Règles,* we have the first mention of a relationship between the number of lines in the stanza and the number of syllables in the refrain, an eleven-line stanza having an eleven-syllable refrain (and so other lines of eleven syllables), the same arrangement making ten-line, nine-line, and eight-line stanzas. The *ballade* varieties in Herenc's book on poetics are:

(1) The stanza of 11 lines (11 syllables); a b a b c c d d e d e, with an envoy d e d e.

(2) The stanza of 10 lines (10 syllables); a b a b b c c d c d, with an envoy c d c d.

(3) The stanza of 8 lines (8 syllables); a b a b b c b c, with an envoy b c b c.

(4) The stanza of 9 lines (9 syllables); a b a b c c d c d, with an envoy c d c d.

(5) The stanza of 7 lines (7 syllables); a b a b b c c, with an envoy b b c c.

(6) The stanza of ten lines (6 syllables); a b a b c c d e d e, with an envoy d e d e.

(7) The stanza of 15 lines (the first, second, third, fourth, sixth, eighth, tenth, twelfth, thirteenth, fourteenth lines of 8 syllables; the fifth, seventh, ninth, eleventh and fifteenth lines of three syllables); a b a b b c c d d e e f e e f.

(8) The stanza of 12 lines (4 syllables); a b a b c c d d e f e f, with an envoy d d e f e f. The refrain is composed of two lines.

One of the *ballades* quoted above contains the familiar catalogue of the Seven Deadly Sins, a matter not wholly uncongenial to this form of poetry.[84] Another quoted by Herenc shows the use of the *ballade* for purposes of dialogue.[85]

The *Traité de l'Art de Rhétorique* gives rules for the *ballade* and the *rondeau* only, among the fixed forms, "car en cest art y falt mettre moult l'usaige." Forms like the *chant royal,* the *serventois,* etc., had come to be considered purely academic exercises even at the time of Deschamps. At the end of the treatise, as a sort of appendix, the author transcribes a number of *ballades* (not printed by Langlois) some of which have the same refrain. They were undoubtedly composed in competition at some *puy*. One of the series is always labeled *le pris*. The author of the *Traité* says in one place that the *ballade* stanza may be of any number of lines, but later on he prescribes at least seven lines, probably not including the refrain. He recommends crossed rimes for every stanza. Legrand, it will be noticed, anticipates this author in emphasizing the relation of the refrain to the rest of the stanza.

Molinet, like Deschamps, was a prolific poet as well as a theorizer, and he draws his examples from his own works. He repeats the direction that the lines of the stanza should equal the number of syllables in the refrain. He distinguishes:

(1) The stanza of 8 lines (8 syllables).

(2) The stanza of 9 lines (9 syllables); a b a b c c d c d.

(3) The stanza of 10 lines (10 syllables); a b a b b c c d c d.

[84] See Chapter II. Cf. MS. *Français 2306* in the *Bibliothèque Nationale.*

[85] E. Langlois, *Opus Cit.*, p. xlv.

(4) The stanza of 11 lines (11 syllables); a b a b c c d d e d e, with an envoy d d e d e.

(5) The stanza of 11 lines (the first and fifth lines are of 10 syllables unbroken; the other lines are of 11 syllables, broken after the fourth syllable); a b a b c c d d e d e, with an envoy d e d e.

(6) The stanza of 8 lines (8 syllables); the first, third, fifth stanzas riming a b a a b b c c; the second, fourth and sixth riming c d c c d d a a, with an envoy d a a. The first, third, and fifth stanzas taken together form a *ballade,* as do the second, fourth, and sixth stanzas. A further complication is the fact that in both cases the refrain of a stanza serves as the first line of the next stanza.

The *ballade balladant* (see 5 above) was defined by Herenc as composed of seven seven-syllable line stanzas. What Molinet calls a *ballade balladant* was described under the title *Taille Pleine Laie Balladant* in the first anonymous treatise we examined. Langlois explains Molinet's use of the word *balladant* by supposing Molinet's familiarity with that treatise just referred to, where the title *Taille Plaine Balladant* occurs. Langlois believes that *balladant* in the title means simply *pour ballade.* He thinks it possible that Molinet misapprehended the title, hence his double and unusual definition of the *ballade balladant.*

L'Infortuné adds nothing new to the theory of the subject. He reiterates in verse the two well-known formulas that the *ballade* stanza must begin with crossed rimes and that the number of syllables in the refrain must correspond to the number of lines in the stanza. He uses in the *Instructif* proper three types:

(1) The stanza of 8 lines (8 syllables); a b a b b c b c, with an envoy a c a c. Appropriately enough he employs this type for the definition of the form.

(2) The stanza of 9 lines (9 syllables); a b a b b c c b c.

(3) The stanza of 10 lines (10 syllables); a b a b b c c d c d, with an envoy a a d a d. This form shows the *ballade* with dialogue carried on within the line unit.

The *Traité de Rhétorique* covers only a small part of the field of poetics and is plainly amateur in scope. It suggests for use in the *ballade:*

(1) The stanza of 7 lines (7 syllables); a b a b b c c.

(2) The stanza of 8 lines (4 syllables); a b a b b c b c.

(3) The stanza of 10 lines (10 syllables); a b a b b c c d c d.

Fabri's *Pleine Rhétorique* is based on L'Infortuné and on Molinet. He quotes from both, especially from L'Infortuné, who appears on practically on every page of that part of the *Pleine Rhétorique* that deals with poetry. Fabri's work is especially interesting as the work of a man who was one of the early participators in the "Concours du Puy de la Conception" at Rouen. He says at the beginning of the *Rhétorique en Rithme* that he has composed his handbook of rime "a celle fin que les deuotz facteurs de champ royal du Puy de l'Immaculee Conception de la Vierge ayent plus ardant desir de composer, de tant qu'ilz en congnoissent la maniere, par laquelle leur deuotion croistra, et affin que noz treshonnorez seigneurs et maistres, les princes et poetes laurez d'iceluy Puy, ayent aulcune recreation."[86] Fabri follows Molinet in the theory of the *ballade,* as his reference to the "Picars" implies. His first example is L'Infortuné's *ballade* on the *ballade.* The *ballade layée* is taken from Molinet; Molinet was more elaborate, it will be remembered in his explanation of the *ballade balladant.* Fabri's examples embrace these varieties:

[86] A. Héron, *Opus Cit.,* Pt. II, p. 2.

(1) The stanza of 8 lines (8 syllables); a b a b b c b c, with an envoy a c a c.

(2) The stanza of 8 lines (8 syllables); a b a b b c b c, with an envoy b c b c.

(3) The stanza of 8 lines (10 syllables); a b a b b c b c, with an envoy b c b c.

Another treatise based largely on Molinet is *L'Art et Science de Rhétorique Vulgaire.* It is a reproduction of Molinet with some additions, the chief of which is the recommendation relative to the alternation of masculine and feminine rimes. With the new restriction in view, Molinet's examples are several times revised at the expense of their meaning.[87] The following are recommended for the *ballade:*

(1) The stanza of 10 lines (10 syllables); a b a b b c c d c d.

(2) The stanza of 11 lines (11 syllables); a b a b c c d d e d e.

(3) The stanza of 8 lines (8 syllables); a b a a b b c c.

(4) The stanza of 9 lines (9 syllables); a b a b c c d c d, with an envoy c d c d.

(5) The stanza of 12 lines (alexandrines); a a b a a b c c d c c d, with an envoy c c d c c d.

(6) See stanza form (5) of Molinet.

(7) See stanza form (6) of Molinet.

In general, du Pont bases his rules on Fabri, who in turn, as we have seen, derives from Molinet and L'Infortuné. Du Pont, it is plain, was familiar, too, with the manual of Deschamps. The *ballade,* according to du Pont, must have at least seven lines and no more than twelve lines. He speaks specifically of

(1) The stanza of 7 lines *couronnée* and *batelée* in which the last syllable of the line was to be twice repeated, and in which the last word of the line was

[87] Langlois, *Opus Cit.,* p. lxvii.

to rime with the cesura of the following line. This last variation is illustrated also in *Les Règles de la Seconde Rhetorique* in the *taille plaine laie balladant.*

(2) The stanza of 8 lines.
(3) The stanza of 9 lines.
(4) The stanza of 8 lines, *emperière* when the sound was to be repeated three times at the end of each line.
(5) The stanza of 8 lines *equivoque.*
(6) The stanza of 8 lines *batelée.*
(7) The stanza of 10 lines *batelée.*
(8) The stanza of 10 lines, *couronnée.* The term *couronnée* is open to two interpretations in connection with the *ballade. Rime couronée* means ordinarily rime which demands the repetition of the last syllable in the line. The *ballade couronée* may mean a *ballade* composed of 2 stanzas of 10 lines (4 syllables); a b a b b c c d c d, followed by 2 stanzas of 10 lines (6 syllables), with another refrain riming e f e f f g g h g h, followed, in turn, by two stanzas, one of which conforms to the first type, the other of which to the second type. This kind of *ballade* is completed by an envoy of 6 lines (with the refrain of the second group of stanzas), riming h h g g h h.

The *Controverses* referred to as du Pont's work is his *Controverses des sexes masculin et feminin, en trois livres, suivi de la Requête du sexe masculin contre le feminin* (Toulouse, 1534), a collection of *ballades,* rondeaux, lais, and virelais, the main purpose of which is made plain by its title. But its subsidiary purpose is,

"Pareillement aussi pour inciter
(Dont grandement y peuuent proufiter)
Les ieunes gens, qui desirent apprendre

De composer et rhetorique entendre.
Ilz y uerront des Rythmes bien subtiles
Aux apprentiz de tel art fort utiles."[88]

Sibilet's *Art Poëtique François* was notably the first of the manuals to show humanistic tendencies, yet his inclusion in his body of poetical theory of the earlier poetic formulas showed him to be only partly under the spell of classical antiquity.

Sibilet, strangely enough, makes the address to the prince in the envoy an excuse for believing that the *ballade* was originally adapted, because of its connection with royalty, only to subjects of dignity and weight. The rest of Sibilet's statements about the *ballade* present no great variation from those of other authorities. His use of the word epilogue for envoy is an evidence of classical influence. He fixes the numerical relation between the number of lines in the stanza and the number of lines in the envoy as follows:

Stanza	*Envoy*	*Stanza*	*Envoy*
8	4	11	5
10	5	11	6
10	7	12	7

He concludes that lines of 8 syllables or of 10 syllables are most commonly used in the *ballade.*

Only a year after Sibilet's work, appeared the better known *Deffense et Illustration de la Langue Françoise,* which, depending as it does almost wholly on the works of Sperone Speroni and Tolomeio, marked Du Bellay as a Renaissance man, vowed to the building up of a native style formed by classically educated taste. Against the *ballade* he inveighs as an evidence of the ignorance of his predecessors. His reference to the *Floureaux de Tholose* and the *Puy de Rouan* are evidently depreciatory.

88 H. Zschalig, *Die Verslehren von Fabri, du Pont und Sibilet* (Leipsig, 1884), p. 58.

Aneau's *Le Quintil Horation* was strangely reactionary, attacking Du Bellay's contemptuous references to the contests at Toulouse and to the *puy* at Rouen, and deprecating du Bellay's treatment of the older forms of French poetry. Inconsistently, Aneau bases his defence on the precedents of Greece and Rome. He meets Du Bellay on his own ground and justifies the native types of verse by their classical (?) analogues.

In the same year that Aneau was writing (1550), Guillaume des Autelz in his *Repliques aux Furieuses Defenses de Louis Meigret* took much the same ground. He is even more indignant than Aneau at the intrusion of the antique form.

But Pelletier, whose *L'Art Poétique* appeared five years later, was a follower of Du Bellay's. Although, as we shall see, there are books on poetics published even after Aneau that take the trouble to do more than name the *ballade,* really Du Bellay marks a boundary line between the old and the new French poets. Delaudun writes of it as a curiosity, whereas Pasquier and Francois Collette, being literary historians, are highly particular and definite in their handling of the form. Vauquelin de la Fresnaye, Le Sieur de Deimier, and Boileau only name the *ballade not* to praise it, while Pelletier, imitating Du Bellay's method, treats it with contempt.

The very title of Etienne Pasquier's *Recherches de la France* (1560) shows it to be different in scope from the narrower handbooks that we have been examining. It aims, in truth, to give an historically accurate account of the political and cultural progress of France. Pasquier, in the spirit of the antiquary, devotes some space to the *ballade,* which he derives from the *chant royal.* It is noteworthy, on the other hand, that Colletet seems to have lost sight of the connection of the *puy* with the origin of the *ballade.*

Before Boileau, the classical despot, disposes of the *ballade* as a form that owes its popularity chiefly to tricks of rime, Molière in *Les Femmes Savantes,* played the year before Boileau's set of rules appeared, embodies in Trissotin's fatal phrase the timely verdict of the seventeenth-century man of letters in regard to the *ballade.* Vadius and Trissotin are bandying compliments:[89]

Trissotin

"Rien qui soit plus charmant que vos petits rondeaux?

Vadius

Rien de si plein d'esprit que tous vos madrigaux?

Trissotin

Au ballades surtout vous êtes admirable.

Vadius

Et dans les bouts-rimés je vous trouve adorable."

They continue to outdo each other; then:

Vadius

"On verroit le public vous dressez de statues.
Hom! c'est une ballade, et je veux que tout net
Vous m'en . . .

Trissotin

Avez-vous vue certain petit sonnet
Sur la fièvre qui tient la princesse Uranie?"

Vadius admits having heard the sonnet, but declares it to be trash of the worst kind. At this they fall to quarrelling. Vadius tries to propitiate Trissotin in order that the *ballade* may be read aloud:

Vadius

"Il fant qu'en écoutant j'aie eu l'esprit distrait,
Ou bien que le lecteur m'ait gâté le sonnet,
Mais laissons ce discours, et voyons ma ballade.

89 Molière, *Les Femmes Savantes,* Act III, Sc. 5.

Trissotin

La ballade, à mon goût, est une chose fade;
Ce n'en est plus la mode, elle sent son vieux temps.

Vadius

La ballade pourtant charme beaucoup de gens.

. . . .

Trissotin

Elle a pour les pédans de merveilleux appas."

Trissotin is speaking for his age when he says: "La ballade à mon goût est une chose fade."

CHAPTER IV

THE MIDDLE ENGLISH BALLADE

In all probability, it will never be explained to our entire satisfaction why the *ballade,* which had met with so much favor in France and which won its way with the greatest Middle English poet, did not achieve greater popularity with Chaucer's contemporaries and successors. In England, the fifteenth century man of letters seems to have been susceptible to a variety of French conventions, but only occasionally did he feel impelled to use the form that in France had become a favorite means of literary expression. France, indeed, had seen the production of *ballades* by the thousands, whereas England saw an output that could be counted by the hundreds. A complete bibliography of the Middle English *ballade* might contain only some two hundred and twenty items, but even this list would certainly include questionable specimens of the type. To Chaucer himself are attributed with considerable certainty sixteen genuine *ballades.* Lydgate introduced the form into *The Temple of Glas, The Legend of Seynt Margaret,* and *The Fall of Princes.* He also wrote *ballades* independent of his longer poems. Hoccleve seems never to have composed a true *ballade,* although the character of his seven-line and eight-line stanza shows how familiar he must have been with the form.[1] Two Middle

[1] See F. J. Furnivall, *Hoccleve's Minor Poems, Early English Text Society* (London, 1892), Extra Series 61, p. 63, in which is found *Balade to my Maister Carpenter,* of three stanzas and a fourth stanza used as a kind of envoy with no common rimes and no refrain.

English collections of *ballades* are known, namely, the series that, for many years, went under the name of Charles d'Orléans, and the translation by one Quixley of John Gower's *Traitié pour Essempler les Amants Marietz.* A small number of *ballades* in print have, at various times, been attributed to Chaucer, or to one or another of his followers. Other *ballades,* anonymous, still unprinted, are probably to be unearthed in English and in Scotch libraries.[2]

In Middle English the rigor of the French form is relaxed. The *ballade* is found occasionally, it is true, cast in the mould most commonly used in France. For example, Lydgate's *Flour of Courtesye,* with its three similar stanzas and envoy of fewer lines than the stanzas, its rime-scheme and refrain, is in form like hundreds of French *ballades.* Many of the Middle English poems are three-stanza *ballades* without envoys, like some of Deschamps's and Machaut's, but with common rimes and a refrain in all three stanzas. A few Middle English lyrics we must call *ballades,* because the refrain is constant even though the rimes change. Such *ballades* are seen in *The Ile of Ladies* and in *The Court of Sapience.* A three-stanza poem, with different rime in every stanza, and with no refrain, called

[2] F. M. Padelford, *The Cambridge History of English Literature* (New York, 1908), Vol. II, Chap. XVI, pp. 442–443: "Of all forms of French amatory verse, the ballade enjoyed the greatest popularity in England. It was the form in which the gallant most often essayed to ease his bosom of the torments of love. Every phase of the conventional love complaint, every chapter in the cycle of the lover's history, is treated in these ballades precisely as in the corresponding verse in France." There seems to be no evidence to bear out this general statement of the case. As the succeeding pages show, the number of *ballades* written in England in the fifteenth century was inconsiderable; such as were written showed little variety in theme, and with certain notable exceptions, were ineffectual imitations of the form as adapted by Chaucer from that in vogue in France.

in the manuscript a *balade,* served as a kind of preface to *The Chaunce of the Dyse.*[3] This three-stanza form was undoubtedly written under the influence of the French, but it certainly cannot be accounted a true *ballade* any more than Hoccleve's envoy to the *Regement of Princes,*[4] or certain other three-stanza poems in the same manuscript, to be mentioned later. The envoy in the French *ballade* is composed, as we have seen, of lines whose number bears some relation to the number of lines in the stanza. But the envoy in the English *ballade* may, as is the case in the *Fall of Princes,* be composed of as many lines as the stanza that it follows. We shall hold those Middle English poems to be *ballades* which are composed of three stanzas with refrain. We may allow the name *ballade* to such poems even when new rimes are introduced in every stanza, although even in Middle English the best *ballades* carry the rimes of the first stanza throughout the poem. The *ballade* in Middle English, as in French, may or may not have an envoy. The envoy may be of fewer lines than the stanza or of the same number. In the French *ballade* it is clear that there is a considerable variety in line structure, as the number of syllables in the line employed vary widely, and in certain cases condition the number of lines in the stanzas. In Middle English, on the contrary, the almost invariable line is the five stress line, used according to the pleasure of the individual poet. It is the aim of the following pages to record the use of the word *balade* or *ballade* and to consider the *ballades* of Chaucer, Lydgate, and the lesser Middle English versifiers.

[3] Bodleian *MS. Fairfax 16.*

[4] F. J. Furnivall, *Hoccleve's Regement of Princes, Early English Text Society* (London, 1897), Extra Series 72, p. 196.

I. Nomenclature

According to Middle English nomenclature, a *balade* might be a narrative poem of purely popular origin,[5] or the lyric of special artificial character, with its various modifications, in which we are interested, or a stanzaic lyric of indefinite length.[6] Chaucer, referring, of course, to the seven-line stanza *ballade* without envoy, in the *Prologue* B. F. of the *Legend of Good Women* makes Love speak of "'Hyd, Absolon, thy tresses in *balade*." The other Chaucerian *ballades* are of seven-line, eight-line, or nine-line stanzas, some with envoys some without.[7] At the end of the fourteenth century, Gower too, was using the title *Cinkante Balades* to describe the conventional French form of either seven-line or eight-line stanzas with envoy. Lydgate, on the other hand, extends the word to mean stanzas of sevens, with or without the same rimes as the others, as he implies in:

> "I took a penne and wroot in myn maneer
> The said *balladys* as they stonden heere."[8]

Again Lydgate, alluding to seven-line stanzas, writes in *Bycorne and Chichevache* (about 1430), in a kind of gloss, "An ymage in Poete wise, seyeng these iij *balades*."

A glance at the latest[9] Lydgate bibliography will con-

[5] British Museum *MS. Harley 372*, fol. 113.

[6] In Bodleian *MS. Fairfax 16*, *The Compleynt of the Dethe of Pity* is headed *balade* (fol. 187).

[7] In British Museum *MS. Add. 34360*, *Womanly Noblesse*, labeled *Balade that Chauncier made*, is composed of nine-line stanzas, riming a a b a a b b a b, with the same rimes in all three stanzas but without refrain. The envoy is of six lines riming a c a c a a.

[8] *The Fifteen Joys of Our Lady*, quoted in H. N. MacCracken, *King James' Claim to Rhyme Royal*, *Modern Language Notes*, XXIV, p. 32.

[9] H. N. MacCracken, *The Lydgate Canon*, *Transactions of the Philological Society*, Pt. I for 1907, London, 1908.

vince one that the scribes of this poet used the term *balade* most frequently to mark the stanzaic lyric of indefinite length,[10] although, as we have seen, the poet himself produced *ballades* in the stricter sense of the word as well. Particularly in the *Fall of Princes* are there *ballades* of seven-line and eight-line stanzas, with and without envoys. James Shirley, the scribe, writing about 1430, included in a manuscript[11] the three following titles:

Balade Ryal de saine counsylle.
Balade moult Bon et Ryal.
Balade Ryal made by oure laureate poete of Albyon.

MacCracken, who calls attention to these three items,[12] says of them: "These poems, two of them French and one English, show the Chaucerian use of the term *ballade.* But the same scribe uses the term *balade ryal* of poems transcribed twenty years later in *MS. Bodley Ashmole 59,* where the stanzas do not have the same rimes but merely a common refrain." The same Shirley, in another manuscript,[13] uses *balade* as a descriptive title for a six-line stanza riming a b a b c c,[14] and for a seven-line stanza riming a b a b b c c.[15]

10 For example, at the end of *A Sayenge of the Nyghtyngale,* a poem of fifty-four stanzas of sevens, Shirley wrote:

"Of this *Balade* Dan Iohn̄
Lydgate made nomore."

(Otto Glauning, *The Two Nightingale Poems,* London, 1900, *Early English Text Society,* Extra Series 80, p. 28.)

11 Trinity College, Cambridge *MS. R. 3. 20.*

12 H. N. MacCracken, *King James' Claim to Rhyme Royal, Modern Language Notes,* XXIV, p. 32.

13 British Museum *MS. Harley 7333.*

14 "The worlde so wyde," E. Flügel, *Anglia,* XIV, p. 463.

15 "Þhe more I goo," E. Flügel, *Anglia,* XIV, p. 463. Shirley's heading runs, "Halsam Squiere made these ij *balades.*" These stanzas were popular enough to appear in several MSS. See also E. P. Hammond, *Two British Museum MSS., Anglia,* XXVIII, p. 4.

Ballade was used by Lydgate himself to describe seven-line stanzas in the *Fifteen Joys and Sorrows of Mary:*

> "Off ech of them the noum*b*re was Fifteene,
> Bothe of hir Ioyes and her adversitees,
> Ech after othir, and to that hevenlie queene
> I sauh Oon kneele deuoutly on his knees;
> A Pater-noster and ten tyme Auees
> In ordre he sayde [at thende] o f ech *ballade*
> Cessyd nat, tyl he an eende made."[16]

Another early illustration of the use of the word is seen in John Hardyng's *Chronicle* (about 1440), in which he writes: "Into *balade* I wyll it now translate," and means thereby the seven-line, a b a b b c c stanza:

> "Yet wyll I vse the symple witte I haue
> To your plesaunce and consolacion,
> Most noble lorde and prince, so God me saue,
> That in chronycles hath delectacion.
> Though it be farre above myne estimacion,
> Into *balade* I wyll it now translate,
> Ryght in this form with all myne estymate."[17]

The use of the word in Sir Richard Ros's translation of *La Belle Dame sans Merci*, made about 1460,[18] is not definite, but merely goes to show the conventional association between lovers and *ballades*. The conjunction of *balades* and "songes" makes it probable that the short French lyric is here referred to:

> "Thes seke louers, I leue *þat* to hem longes,
> Whiche led þair lyfe in hope of allegeaunce,

[16] H. N. MacCracken, *The Minor Poems of John Lydgate, Early English Text Society* (London, 1911), Extra Series, 107, p. 269.

[17] John Hardyng, *Chronicle,* ed. Henry Ellis (London, 1812), p. 16.

[18] F. J. Furnivall, *Political and Religious Poems, Early English Text Society,* Vol. 15 (London, 1866), p. 54.

þat is to say, to make *balade* or songes,
 Eu*er*yche of hem as þei fele her grevaunce,
ffor sche þ*at* wasse my joy *and* my plesaunce,—
 Whos soule, I pray God of his m*er*cy saue,—
Sche hath myn wyle, my hertës ordeynaunce,
 which lithe w*ith* her vnder her toumbe in graue."[19]

Before 1500, too, we have Ashby writing in his *Active Policy of the Prince:*

"Maisters Gower, Chaucer & Lydgate,
 Primier poetes of this nacion,
Embelysshing oure englisshe tendure algate,
 Firste finders to oure consolacion̄
Off fresshe, douce englisshe and formacion̄
 Of newe *balades,* not vsed before,
By whome we all may haue lernying and lore."[20]

The presence of Master Gower's name in the first line of this stanza makes it seem probable that Ashby had in mind a *ballade* in the special sense. Gower, so far as we know, wrote no English *ballades,* yet Ashby seems to dwell on the function of the three poets in beautifying and enriching the poetic forms of their mother tongue. It is quite possible that Ashby, without examining facts too closely, associated the exotic fixed form, French or English, with all three poets. All three certainly were known as the authors of *ballades* in the most technical interpretation of the word.

Quixley (1502?) says of Gower's *Traitié:*

"Gower it made in frensh with gret studie
 In *ballades ryal.*"[21]

19 F. J. Furnivall, *Opus Cit.,* p. 82.

20 M. Bateson, *George Ashby's Poems, Early English Text Society,* Extra Series 76 (London, 1899), p. 13.

21 The use of the word ''royal'' in this connection may be traced, in England as in France, to the usages of the *puy.* The statutes of a London *puy,* as a matter of fact, give evidence earlier in date than any similar French records of the use of the word *reale* as applied to a *chanson* in the *puy.* Cf. Chapter I, and Appendix on *Chant Royal.*

Quixley's *ballades* are, indeed, of the three-stanza, seven-line variety, without envoy, riming a b a b b c c, with the same rimes in all stanzas and a common refrain.

In the fourteenth chapter of Stephen Hawes's *Pastime of Pleasure,* dated by Wynkyn de Worde 1505–6, in a commendation of Lydgate, we read:

> "O Mayster Lydgate, the most dulcet sprynge
> Of famous rethoryke, with *balade ryall,*
> The chefe orygynal of my lerning,
> What vaylethe it on you for to call
> Me for to ayde, now in especiall;
> Sythen your body is now wrapte in chest,
> I pray God to gyve your soule good rest.
> . . . .
> But many a one is ryghte well experte
> In this connyng, but upon auctoryte,
> They fayne no fables pleasaunt & covert,
> But spende theyr time in vaynful vanyte
> Makynge *balades* of fervent amyte.
> As gestes and tryfles wythout frutefulnes;
> Thus al in vayne they spend their besynes."[22]

In this passage, Hawes seems to be contrasting the substantial Lydgate poems of many seven-line stanzas with the courtly poetry of the new century. "Amyte" is presumably used to describe the relation between a gallant and his *amie.* As a matter of fact, however, the courtly *ballades* of the early sixteenth century have survived apparently in only modified form. Three or four years later, in 1509, Barclay, in translating Brandt's *Narrenschiff,* modestly begins his arraignment of the wicked ladies of history with,

> "My *balade* bare of frute and eloquence."[23]

[22] Stephen Howes, *The Pastime of Pleasur* (London, 1845), p. 55.
[23] Barclay's *Ship of Fools* (London, 1874), Vol. II, p. 2.

Here the word *balade* is applied to one division of the translation, called "Of the yre immoderate, the wrath and great lewdness of wymen," and composed of a number of eight-line stanzas, riming a b a b b c b c, concluding with an envoy of two stanzas in which the translator allows himself to speak, and addresses himself directly to "Ye wrathfull wymen by vyce lesynge your name." *Balade* appears again in the same sense in another stanza of the division:

"Cornelia prudent
Chaste and discrete and of beauty souerayne
Shall not my *Balade* rede."[24]

It seems probable, from the context, that Spenser, in the third book of the *Faerie Queene* had in mind the *ballade* of fixed form, when he catalogued Paridell's efforts to win Hellenore:

"And otherwhyles with amorous delights
And pleasing toyes he would her entertaine;
Now singing sweetly to surprize her sprights,
Now making layes of love and lovers paine,
Bransles, *Ballads,* virelays and verses vaine;
Oft purposes, oft riddles he devysd,
And thousands like which flowed in his braine,
With which he fed her fancy, and entysd
To take to his new love, and leave her old despysd."[25]

[24] *Opus Cit.*, Vol. II, p. 2. Compare with this sentiment the stanza that occurs in Bk. I of the *Fall of Princes,* at the end of Ch. XX (On the Malice of Women):

"Though Ihon Bochas, in his opinion
Agaynst women lyst a processe make,
They that ben good of condicion
Shoulde ayenst it no maner quarel take
But lightly, I passe and their sleues shake:
For againe good be nothinge made
Who can conceyue th effect of this *balade.*"

[25] *The Faerie Queene* (1590), Book III, Canto X, stanza VIII.

By *Ballads* Spenser may have meant the fixed verse form; if he did, it was a piece of conscious archaizing or perhaps only a recognition of the former overwhelming popularity of the *ballade* in courtly circles.

The *ballade* proper was, then, no longer in current use in England in the last three quarters of the sixteenth century, nor was it destined to reappear in English poetry until the lapse of four hundred years. In France, as we have seen, its peculiarities engaged students of poetic theory for at least two centuries; in England, however, in consequence of its short and comparatively obscure career, it is referred to in its fixed form by only two Elizabethan critics, George Gascoigne and James VI of Scotland. Gascoigne evidently is thinking of an entirely different "kinde" when he explains:

> "There is also another kinde, called *Ballade,* and thereof are sundrie sortes: for a man may write *ballade* in a staffe of six lines, every line conteyning eighte or sixe sillables, whereof the firste and third, second and fourth do rime acrosse, and the fifth and sixth do rime togither in conclusion. You may write also your *ballad* of tenne syllables, rimying as before is declared, but these two were wont to be most comonly used in *ballade,* which propre name was (I thinke) derived of this worde in Italian *Ballare,* whiche signifieth to daunce, and indeed, those kinds of rimes serve beste for daunces and light matters."[26]

James VI of Scotland, however, in his *Essayes of a Prentise in the Divine Art of Poesie,* gives the name *Ballat*

[26] Later in conclusion he says: "Ballades are beste of matters of love." Tradition still associated the *ballade* with love, but its three stanzas, refrain, and envoy had come to be neglected and a different stanzaic form associated with the name. Even the country of its provenience was ignored (George Gascoigne, *Certain Notes of Instruction,* 1575). Cf. on Halsam, p. 226, above.

Royal to the stanzas most popular in the writing of *ballades,* namely to the a b a b b c b c stanza. His conception of the uses of the stanza is far removed from the French fixed form, but may be reminiscent of the recommendations of certain French authorities that the *Chant Royal* be dedicated to graver purposes than the *ballade.*[27] His directions are as follows:

"For any heich and graue subiectis, specially drawin out of learnit authouris, vse this kynde of verse following, callit *Ballat Royal,* as

> That nicht he ceist, and vvent to bed, bot greind
> Zit fast for day, and thocht the nicht to lang:
> At last Diana doun her head recleind,
> Into the sea. Then Lucifer vpsprang,
> Aurora's post, vvhome sho did send amang
> The Ieittie cludds, for to foretell ane hour,
> Before sho stay her tears, quhilk Ouide sang
> Fell for her loue, quhilk turnit in a flour."[28]

Finally, if we turn to Cotgrave's dictionary, so useful for word meanings of the early seventeenth century,[29] we see that for Cotgrave's contemporaries *balade* has become merely a synonym for the ballet. *Ballade* or *balade* cease to figure as poetic terms till the eighteenth century revival of interest in Middle English, and the form itself is not again attempted in English till the last thirty years of the nineteenth century.

[27] See Chapter III.

[28] *Revlis and Cautelis, Essays of a Prentise in the Divine Art of Poesie* (Edinburgh, 1585).

[29] Randle Cotgrave, *A Dictionarie of the French and English Tongues* (London, 1611).

II. Chaucer

In the Prologue to the *Fall of Princes,* Lydgate wrote:

> "This sayd Poete my master in his dayes
> Made and compiled ful many a fresh dittie
> Complants, *ballades,* roūdels, vyrelayes
> Full delectable to heare and to se:
> For whiche men should of ryght and equitie,
> Syth he in englysh in making was the best,
> Pray vnto God to geue his soule good rest."

And with lyrics, wrought in the French fashion, in honor of Love, Alcestis credits Chaucer in both prologues to the *Legend of Good Women.*

> "And many an ympne for your halydayes,
> That highten *Balades,* Roundels, Virelayes."[30]

The "Virelayes" have vanished, the "Roundels" survive in four specimens only,[31] but the *Balades* are still extant in sufficient numbers to bear witness to the fact that this kind of poem when handled delicately and withal precisely may be worth writing. In the Oxford Chaucer canon, there are in all twelve of these *ballades.*[32] In addition, there is a

30 Prologue A G to the *Legend of Good Women,* ll. 410–411.

31 Namely, the Roundel in the *Parlement of Foules* and the three examples in *Merciles Beaute.*

32 W. W. Skeat, *The Complete Works of Geoffrey Chaucer* (Oxford, 1894). These *ballades* are found in Volume I on the following pages:

Fortune (3 *ballades*), p. 383.
To Rosamounde, p. 389.
Truth, p. 390.
Gentilesse, p. 392.
Lak of Stedfastnesse, p. 394.
The Compleynt of Venus (three *ballades*), p. 400.
The Compleint of Chaucer to his Empty Purse, p. 405.
Against Women Inconstant, p. 409.
A Balade of Compleynt, p. 415.

ballade in both versions of the Prologue of the *Legend of Good Women.*[33]

Furthermore, of this list, two are compound *ballades,* if we may use the term, namely, *Fortune* and *The Compleynt of Venus.* The former comprises really three *ballades:* first, that known as *Le Pleintif countre Fortune,* second, *La Respounse de Fortune au Pleintif,* third, *La Respounse du Pleintif countre Fortune* (the last two stanzas of the same *balade* are headed *La Respounse de Fortune countre le Pleintif*), and finally, *Lenvoy de Fortune.*[34] Each of the *ballades* has three stanzas of eight lines each, with the rime-scheme a b a b b c b c, and the rimes are identical in each of the three stanzas. The envoy is a stanza of seven lines, riming a b a b b c b. The seventh line shows no similarity to any one of the three refrains. The envoy applies to the group as a whole rather than to the final *ballade* to which it is attached. Conventionally the first line invokes

The last two are printed in the Appendix under these words: "The following poems are also probably genuine, but are placed here for lack of external evidence." Miss E. P. Hammond [*Chaucer, A. Bibliographical Manual* (New York, 1908), pp. 440–441], following Furnivall in the Chaucer Society Prints, calls *Against Women Inconstant, Newfanglenesse,* and finds no mark of authorship in any of the manuscripts. Nor, according to the authority of Miss Hammond, is there any mark of authorship in the manuscripts in the case of *A Balade of Compleynt.* This *ballade,* however, need not concern us further, since it is merely a three stanza form, written in rime royal; the rimes in every stanza differ and there is no refrain or envoy.

33 Prologue A, ll. 203–223; Prologue B, ll. 249–269.

34 Bodleian *MSS. Fairfax 16, Bodley 633,* and Univ. Lib. Camb. *MS. Ii, iii,* 21, head this triple *ballade* "*Balade (s) de vilage saunz peynture.* Cf. E. P. Hammond, *Chaucer, A Bibliographical Manual* (New York, 1908), p. 369. Bradshaw, basing his emendation on Boethius, "This like Fortune hath departed and uncovered to thee both the certain *visages,* and eke the doutous *visages* of thyne felawes," [Cf. F. J. Furnivall, *Trial-Forewords,* London, 1871, p. 8, note.] Changed *vilage* to *visage.*

"Princes," but the royalty addressed is probably literary, not literal. The fourth line runs: "at my requeste, as three of you or tweyne," specifying the number called upon. Skeat says: "If the reference is to the Dukes of Lancaster, York, and Gloucester, then the 'beste frend' must be the king himself."[35] The nicety of metrical structure is here no obstacle to the poet. The most striking features of the poem are rather its insistence on the adequacy of the individual to cope with things; the challenge contained in the line, "for fynally, Fortune, I thee defye"; and the boast that, " he that hath himself hath suffisaunce."

One's first instinct is to search old records and accounts to discover whether Chaucer did "unlock his heart" here with a *ballade*-key. Furnivall, indeed, once speculated:[36] "I suppose Chaucer wrote his *Fortune* when he was himself 'ensample trewe and newe,' of the Goddess's caprice, fit to be added to his 'ensamples trewe and olde' of his Monk's Tale. When sued by Mrs. Buckholt in Easter Term, 1398, and getting Letters of Protection against her and other enemies at law in that year's May, Chaucer might well change his note from the Daisy and Lady of the *Legende*, to the False Dissembler who had left him in the lurch, and who later, on July 24 and 31, 1398, reduced him to borrow 6s. 8d. each day from the Exchequer. But Chaucer is cheery still. He has not so fallen that 'there is no remedye to bring him out of his adversitie.' He seems to recur to his *Truth's* 'Suffise þyn owen þing, þei it be smal,' and says 'his suffysaunce shall be his socour,' he has the mastery

35 W. W. Skeat, *Opus Cit.*, Vol. I, p. 547. According to the same authority, the line of the envoy quoted occurs only in Cambridge University Library *MS. Ii, 3. 21*, but is probably due to the author's revision.

36 F. J. Furnivall, *A Parallel-Text Edition of Chaucer's Minor Poems* (London, no date), Part III, p. 439.

over himself, and knows that 'no man is wrechyd but hymself yt wene,' and that he has yet his best friend alive. No lucky side-note tells who his friend then was, though we know that Henry Bolingbroke, Blanche's son, with her sweet soft speech, provd the poet's helper."

In view of the conventional treatment of Lady Fortune in Dante,[37] in the *Consolation of Philosophy* of Boethius.[38] in the *Roman de la Rose,*[39] it is impossible to insist strongly on the autobiographical revelation in *Fortune.* It was customary all through the Middle Ages to write of Fortune's Wheel in a highly figurative way.[40] Plainly, in this triple *ballade,* Chaucer was making use of a popular French verse form; he was using it, moreover, to incorporate ideas derived from the *Roman de la Rose,*[41] and from the *Consolation of Philosophy.*[42] Yet, granted that the form is fixed[43] and that the ideas in the main are commonplace, is Chaucer's dramatic assertion of his valiancy in the face of disaster any less effective?

Chaucer's other triple *ballade,* the *Compleynt of Venus,*

[37] J. S. P. Tatlock, *Chaucer and Dante, Modern Philology,* III, p. 369.

[38] G. W. Prothero, *A Memoir of Henry Bradshaw* (London, 1880), p. 212.

[39] E. Koeppel, *Chauceriana, Anglia,* XIV, p. 248.

[40] Cf. *Carmina Burana,* Poem I and Provençal lyrics *passim.*

[41] English version (attributed to Chaucer), ll. 5403–5584.

[42] W. W. Skeat, *The Complete Works of Geoffrey Chaucer* (Oxford, 1894), Vol. I, p. 543, says that Boethius' *De Consolatione,* Bk. II, prose 1, 2, 3, 4, 5, 8, and metre 1, is the foundation.

[43] F. J. Furnivall, *A Parallel-Text Selection of Chaucer's Minor Poems* (London), Part III, p. 439, note: "Tho Shirley says this Fortune was 'translated out of Frenshe into English,' yet no French original has yet been found for it; and if ever one turns up, I believe it'll prove an original after the manner of the Boece, Metre V, Book 2, for the *Former Age,* and *O intemerata* for the *Mother of God* rather than one like De Guileville's Virgin poem for the *A B C.*"

differs somewhat in form from *Fortune*. Each of the *ballades* in the *Compleynt of Venus* is made up of eight-line stanzas, too, but in this case they rime a b a b b c c b. The rimes are, of course, identical within each of the three *ballades*. The envoy has ten lines riming a a b a a b b a a b independent of the three preceding *ballades*. Only the envoy is original. The MSS. vary between *Princesse* and *Princes*[44] in the first line of the envoy. A note of Shirley's in one of the manuscripts[45] reads: "Hit is sayde that Graunsone made this last *balade* for Venus, resembled to my Lady of York; answering the complaynt of Mars." Piaget, in his articles on Granson,[46] discusses Shirley's note in the light of those *ballades* of Granson's that served as Chaucer's original, and comes to the conclusion[47] that Gran-

[44] W. W. Skeat, *Complete Works of Geoffrey Chaucer* (Oxford, 1894), Vol. I, p. 404, foot-notes; p. 561.

[45] Trinity College, Cambridge *MS. R. 3. 20.*

[46] A. Piaget, *Oton de Granson et ses Poésies, Romania*, XIX, 237–259; 403–448.

[47] The steps which led to these conclusions may be summarized as follows: According to Shirley, the *Compleynt of Mars* was composed by Chaucer for Isabelle, Duchess of York, daughter of Don Pedro of Castille. This princess was designated in the poem under the name of Venus, and Mars represented John Holland, Count of Huntingdon, later Duke of Exeter, "frère utérin de Richard II." At the end of the *Compleynt of Venus*, in MS. T of the works of Chaucer (Trinity College, Cambridge, *R. 3. 20*), Shirley put the following note: "Hit is sayde that Graunsone made this last *balade* for Venus, resembled to my lady of York; answering the complaynt of Mars." If this were true, it would mean that Granson, having read the *Compleynt of Mars* during one of his visits in England, had responded with a *Compleynt of Venus* also addressed to the Duchess of York. And this great lady, who in this case would be the Venus of both complaints, must have begged Chaucer to translate into English Granson's little poem. Skeat, relying on Shirley's notes, puts the date of the *Compleynt of Mars* at about 1374 and as the date for the composition and trans-

son never wrote a poem or poems called the *Compleynt of Venus,* but that he *had,* in his youth—in 1393 he was over fifty—composed *ballades* on the occasion of an unhappy love, that Chaucer chose three of them, translated them, and combined them as one poem. In this form, according to Piaget, there is no question of either Venus or Mars; and it must be admitted that the title of *Compleynt of Venus* is not Chaucer's but Shirley's. Piaget points out that the lady, who in the complaint praises the cavalier, her friend, speaks in terms very inappropriate to Venus. Why should Venus say:

> "But certes, Love, I sey nat in such wyse
> That for tescape out of your lace I mente."

He holds that Shirley was mistaken; that the so-called *Compleynt of Venus* has really nothing to do with the *Compleynt of Mars,* but that nothing prevents our assuming that Chaucer translated, as one may conclude from Shirley's note, the three *ballades* of Granson at the demand of the Duchess of York.

Piaget calls attention, too, to the extremely significant change of viewpoint in Chaucer's translation or adaptation. In the original it is the man praising his mistress; in the Middle English version it is the woman eulogizing her lover. The conclusions of Piaget are generally accepted.

These three *ballades,* close as they are to Granson's, exhibit much original dramatic ability on Chaucer's part.

lation of the *Compleynt of Venus* about 1393, just at the time when Granson, compromised by the death of Comte Rouge, fled his country and secured a pension in England from Richard II.

The different tone in the complaints might have cast some doubt on the affirmations of Shirley. Much good will is necessary to make one see in Granson's three *ballades* an answer to an English poem, filled with astronomical allusions.

He seems to have understood and expressed a mental attitude highly characteristic of one type of woman, and a type, indeed, probably most acceptable to the modern as well as to the mediaeval man, namely:

> "Thus oghte I blesse well myn aventure,
> Sith that him list me serven and honoure."

To Rosemounde[48] (a title given by Skeat) is a single *ballade*. Although it appears with the unquestioned poems in the Oxford edition edition of Chaucer's works, its position there is guaranteed rather by the character of the poem itself than by external evidence.[49] There are three stanzas of the common rime-scheme a b a b b c b c and no envoy. The refrain runs, "Thogh ye to me ne do no daliaunce," and refers to the aloofness of Rosemounde. The *ballade* is *vers de société* in the gayest vein with mock heroic touches:

> "Nas never pyk walwed in galauntyne
> As I in love am walwed and y-wounde;
> For which ful ofte I of my-self divyne
> That I am trewe Tristam the secounde."[50]

48 W. W. Skeat, *Complete Works of Geoffrey Chaucer* (Oxford, 1894), Vol. I, p. 389.

49 E. P. Hammond, *Chaucer, A Bibliographical Manual* (New York, 1908), p. 460: "The MS. which also contains the Troilus, writes below the poem 'Tregentil. Chaucer,' the two names 'a considerable distant apart,' Oxford Chaucer I: 81. This poem appears on the flyleaf of the MS., and the Troilus has, according to Skeat, the same two names written, one just before, the other just after, the colophon. Skeat considers that by 'Tregentil' is meant the scribe. Accepted by Koch as genuine, p. 41 of Chronology."

50 E. P. Hammond, *Opus Cit.*, p. 461: Koch places this poem about 1380–84.

Truth, or the *Balade de Bon Conseyl,*[51] has three seven-line stanzas, riming a b a b b c c, and an envoy of seven lines riming similarly. The title of the *ballade* is variously given as *Balade de bon conseyl,*[52] *La bon Counseil de le Auctour,*[53] *Moral balade of Chaucyre.*[54] In one of the manuscripts,[55] Shirley calls it a "*Balade* that Chaucier made on his deeth-bedde."[56]

Again, as in the case of *Fortune,* the main source of the poem seems to be Boethius.[57] Indeed, in lines 8 and 9,

> "Tempest thee noght al croked to redresse,
> In trust of hir that turneth as a bal,"

we have another reference to the medieval conception of Fortune's wheel. The refrain,

> "And trouthe shal delivere, hit is no drede,"

was no doubt suggested by, "The truth shall make you free" (*John,* VIII, 32).

51 W. W. Skeat, *Complete Works of Geoffrey Chaucer* (Oxford, 1894), Vol. I, p. 390. Cf. p. 82: The envoy occurs only in British Museum *MS. Additional 10340.* According to Skeat, the envoy "may have been suppressed owing to a misunderstanding of the word *vache* (cow), the true sense of which is a little obscure. The reference is to Boethius, bk. V, met. 5, where it is explained that quadrupeds *look down* upon the earth, whilst man alone *looks up* toward heaven." Cf., however, Edith Rickert, *Thou Vache, Modern Philology,* XI, p. 209. In this article, *Vache* is shown to refer to Sir Phillip la Vache or de la Vache, a contemporary of Chaucer's.

52 Cambridge University Library *Ms. Gg. 4. 27.*

53 British Museum *Ms. Lansdowne 699.*

54 British Museum *Ms. Harley 7333.*

55 Trinity College, Cambridge *Ms. R. 3. 20.*

56 W. W. Skeat, *Complete Works of Geoffrey Chaucer* (Oxford, 1894), Vol. I, p. 82. Skeat characterizes this statement as "probably a mere bad guess." F. J. Furnivall, *Trial Forewords* (London, 1871), pp. 8–9, gives date as 1386 or 1388.

57 Bk. III, met. 11; bk. I, pr. 5; etc.

The tone of the *Balade de Bon Conseyl* contrasts strongly with the tone in *Fortune.*

> "That thee is sent, receyve in buxumnesse,
> The wrastling for this worlde axeth a fal,"

is the expression of failure and discouragement; it is not the cry of one who would say,

> "I was ever a fighter, so—one fight more,
> The best and the last!"

Gentilesse,[58] a *Moral Balade of Chaucier,*[59] is a poem of three seven-line stanzas, riming a b a b b c c, with no envoy. The refrain, "Al were he mytre, croune, or diademe," is repeated without variation at the close of every stanza. Both Furnivall[60] and Koch[61] place the date of composition after 1390. The ideas in *Gentilesse,* as in the case notably of *Fortune,* presented themselves to Chaucer's mind from the *Consolation of Philosophy*[62] and from the *Roman de la Rose.*[62] Chaucer took his theory of *Gentilesse* from con-

58 W. W. Skeat, *Complete Works of Geoffrey Chaucer* (Oxford, 1894), Vol. I, p. 392.

59 British Museum *Ms. 7333.*

60 F. J. Furnivall, *Trial-Forewords* (London, 1871), p. 12; p. 17.

61 John Koch, *Chronology of Chaucer's Writings* (London, 1890), p. 79.

62 E. P. Hammond, *Chaucer: A Bibliographical Manual* (New York, 1908), p. 372. "Skeat I: 553 gives as groundwork Boethius bk. III, prose 6; cp. *Roman de la Rose,* 18807 ff.; see W.B. Tale 253 ff., Dante, *Purgatorio* 7: 121, Convito IV canzone 3. These refs. were pointed out by F. J. Child in Athen. 1870 II: 721, with mention also of Gower, Conf. Amantis IV: 2200 ff., —— *A Dis de Gentilesse* is in the Works of de Condé III: 97." [This last poem proves on examination to have nothing in common with Chaucer's *ballade.*] H. M. Ayres of Columbia University holds that "the discussion of the nature of true nobility . . . which Tyrwhitt credits Boethius with having set abroad in the Middle Ages, proves to contain much that antedates the

temporary standards, yet his application of the theory is his own.

In *Lak of Stedfastnesse*[63] Chaucer used the French form with an animus different from that found in his other *ballades.* In *Fortune,* in *Truth,* and in *Gentilesse* he uses the *ballade* seriously, it is true, but in *Lak of Stedfastnesse* he makes it a means of expressing the social confusion and the unrest of his day. This *ballade* contains three[64] seven-line stanzas, riming a b a b b c c, and an envoy stanza, riming in the same way. The refrain, "That al is lost for lak of stedfastnesse," occurs at the end of all the stanzas, but appears as, "And wed thy folk again to stedfastnesse," at the end of the envoy. According to one manuscript,[65] "This *balade* made Geffrey Chaunciers the Laurealle Poete of Albion and sente it to his souerain lorde kynge Richarde the secounde þane being / in his Castell of Windesore."[66] On the date of this *ballade,* Furnivall enumerating says: "Then the *Lack of Steadfastness*—evidently written in the later years of Richard II's reign, and probably in 1397, when the king had his uncle the Duke of Gloucester seized and murdered, also seized the Earl of Warwick and Arundel, and got his Parliament (who doubtless hoped he'd mend his ways) to do all he wisht."[67] If the poem was dispatched to the king at this epoch in his activities, the sentiments of the envoy are certainly timely. Chaucer, as has often been remarked, only occasionally reflects the social discontents

Consolations of Philosophy, and provides an excellent example of a literary commonplace of which Classical Antiquity, the Middle Ages, and the Renaissance alike made abundant use."

63 W. W. Skeat, *Complete Works of Geoffrey Chaucer* (Oxford, 1894), Vol. I, p. 394.

64 *Bannatyne MS. 1568* inserts a spurious fourth stanza.

65 British Museum *MS. Harley 7333.*

66 E. P. Hammond, *Chaucer, A Biographical Manual* (New York, 1908), p. 394.

67 F. J. Furnivall, *Trial Fore-Words* (London, 1871), p. 8.

of his day; his outlook on life is plainly not that of a professional reformer, but certainly in this *ballade* he pauses to analyse the source of evil in his age. If the *general* idea of the *ballade* be taken from Boethius, Bk. II, met. 8, one can only say that the old philosopher's reflections merely furnished Chaucer with a point of departure.

The Compleynt of Chaucer to his Empty Purse[68] is also composed of three seven-line stanzas. Again, as usual, the rimes are identical in all three stanzas; the scheme is a b a b b c c. There is an envoy of five lines riming a a b b a.[69] The refrain of the three stanzas is not used in the envoy. There are, however, two other forms in which the poem is found, namely, in three seven-line stanzas without an envoy,[70] and also without the envoy but with a series of seven-line stanzas on imprisonment following.[71] The envoy[72] is usually considered the last piece of writing done by Chaucer, for it contains a direct appeal to Henry IV, who was accepted by Parliament September 30, 1399; as a result of the poet's appeal, he was in all probability granted an additional forty marks yearly on October third or thirteenth of the same year.[73]

Skeat suggests that a similar complaint was addressed to the French king, John II, by Guillaume de Machaut in 1351–6, in short rimed lines, but adds, "the real model which Chaucer had in view was, in my opinion, the Ballade . . . by

68 W. W. Skeat, *Complete Works of Geoffrey Chaucer* (Oxford, 1894), Vol. I, p. 404.

69 Bodleian *MS. Fairfax 16.*

70 British Museum *MS. Additional 22139.*

71 British Museum *MSS. Harley 2251* and *Additional 34360.* See E. P. Hammond, *Lament of a Prisoner against Fortune, Anglia,* XXXII, p. 481, ff.

72 In British Museum *MS. Harley 7333, Purse* is headed "A supplicacion to Kyng Richard by Chaucier."

73 W. W. Skeat, *Complete Works of Chaucer* (Oxford, 1894), Vol. I, p. 562. Cf. also E. Flügel, *Chauceriana Minora, Anglia,* XXI, p. 245.

Eustache Deschamps, . . . written on a similar occasion, viz. after the death of Charles V of France, and the accession of Charles VI, who had promised Deschamps a pension but had not paid it.''[74] Apparently both Deschamps[75] and Chaucer were prompted to write by similar circumstances, and both poets, like ordinary men who are impoverished, cherished similar sentiments. But Chaucer may quite easily have written his complaint without having been familiar with Deschamps's cheerless *ballade*. The French and the English poems show little similarity in metrical structure. The former has three eight-line stanzas, riming a b a b b c b c, and a six-line envoy riming b b c b c b; the latter, as we have noticed, three seven-line stanzas (a b a b b c c), and a five-line envoy (a a b b a). In subject matter, even, the poems show only accidental and factitious similarities. Chaucer apostrophizes his purse as his ''ladye dere''; he supplicates her to be his ''queene of comfort''; he appeals to her ''curtyse.'' His refrain is ever,

"Beth hevy ageyn, or elles mot I dye."

It is only in the envoy that the appeal to a royal patron comes. On the contrary, in Deschamps's *ballade,* there are throughout the stanzas repeated references to pensions and kingly bounties in the past and repeated plaints of neglect. It is a whining, not a whimsical kind of poverty that the Frenchman sings of, with a somewhat sordidly worded refrain:

"Mais du paier n'y sçay voie ne tour."

The claims of Machaut's *Complainte,*[76] addressed to John

[74] W. W. Skeat, *Complete Works of Geoffrey Chaucer* (Oxford, 1894), Vol. I, pp. 562–563.

[75] Le Marquis de Queux de Saint-Hilaire, *Œuvres Complètes de Eustache Deschamps* (Paris, 1880), Vol. II, p. 81.

[76] V. Chichmaref, *Guillaume de Machaut, Poésies Lyriques,* (Paris, 1909), Vol. I, p. 262.

II of France, to be considered as a source of *The Compleynt of Chaucer to his Empty Purse* are unimportant. It is to be noted in this connection again that there are certain conventions that have always been well recognized in a state of society where poetry flourished under patronage, and these conventions are common alike to Chaucer's complaint and the poems of Deschamps and Machaut. Machaut's detailed account of his own infirmities and very definite appeal for amount denied do not suggest Chaucer's lyric vein at all.

Against Women Inconstant,[77] as Stow[78] named it, or *Newfanglenesse,* as it is called by Furnivall,[79] employs the seven-line stanza riming a b a b b c c, has three stanzas and no envoy. The refrain, "In stede of blew, thus may ye were al grene," is an adaptation of Machaut's, "Qu'en lieu de bleu, Dame, vous vestez vert."[80] Beside this similarity, the French and the English *ballade* are alike in stanza form and in the absence of an envoy. But they are dissimilar in tone. Chaucer grimly arraigns a lady in the wholesouled fashion so popular in the Middle Ages, when satire alternated with adulation, whereas Machaut's reproaches are without spirit in comparison, and his theme is the havoc wrought in his constitution by the fickleness of his dame.[81]

77 W. W. Skeat, *Complete Works of Geoffrey Chaucer* (Oxford, 1894), Vol. I, p. 409.

78 E. P. Hammond, *Chaucer, A Bibliographical Manual* (New York, 1908), p. 441.

79 In Chaucer Society Print.

80 V. Chichmaref, *Guillaume de Machaut, Poésies Lyriques* (Paris, 1909), Vol I, p. 218.

81 The letter that follows is what "she said" on the receipt of Machaut's *ballade.* Agnes of Navarre (?) wrote her lover: "Montrès doulz cuer, man très chier et doulz ami,—Je ai vue une balade en laquelle il ha: en lieu de blan, Dame, vous vestés vert. Et se ne

In 1894 Skeat issued what is generally accepted[82] as a genuine Chaucerian *ballade, Womanly Noblesse.*[83] It has three nine-line stanzas, riming a a b a a b b a b, and an envoy riming a c a c a a. The envoy and each of the three stanzas end differently. If this *ballade* is Chaucer's, he certainly departs widely from his usual custom of following closely the fixed French form. There is no such thing as transcending form if the artistic problem is to restrain the development of the theme by the exigencies of a certain fixed type. Chaucer, if it be Chaucer, certainly gained nothing by the looseness of construction in his poem. To a fifteenth century reader it must have been annoying to be disappointed of a refrain at the end of every stanza. Koch's doubts of the authenticity of the poem do not rest, however, on the looseness of the *ballade.*[84]

say pour qui vous le feystes. Car se ce fu pour moi, vous avez tort. Car, foy que je doi à vous que j'aime de tout mon cuer, unques puisque, vous meystes et envelopastes mon cuer en fin azur et l'enfermates au trésor dont vous avez la clef, il ne fut changiés ne sera toute ma vie. Car si je volois bien ne le porrois je faire sans vous; car moi ne autre n'en porte la clef que vous. Si en poés estre à seur, comme se vous le teniez en vostre main. Mon chier ami je vous pri que vous me veuillez renvoier pas ce message le commencement de vostre livre cellui que je vous renvoiai piece ha, car je n'en retins point de copie et l'ai trop grant fain de veoir. Et si les lettres sont mal escriptes si le me pardonnés, car je ne trouve mie notaire tousjours à ma volenté. Escript le Xe jour d'octembre. Vostre très loiale amie."

[P. Tarbé, *Œuvres de Guilaume de Machault* (Paris, 1849), p. 151; *blan* is probably a misreading for *bleu* in some form.]

82 Kittredge in *Nation,* 1895, p. 240. W. W. Skeat, *Chaucer Canon* (Oxford, 1900), p. 147. Koch, *Englische Studien,* XXVII, p. 60; XXX, p. 450.

83 W. W. Skeat, *Complete Works of Geoffrey Chaucer* (Oxford, 1900), Vol. IV, p. xxv.

84 J. Koch, *Englische Studien,* XXVII, p. 60, says: "'*Balade that Chaucier made*' . . . metrisch (z. b. v. 5 und 25) und inhaltlich zu dürftig ist, als dass wir der überschrift glauben schenken könnten."

The two verses that Koch selects for special reprobation are rough specimens: l. 5, "So wel me lyketh your womanly contenaunce"; l. 24, "In ful rebating of my hevinesse." But better evidence of the spuriousness of the poem, to my mind, is the fact that in his other *ballades* Chaucer shows a stronger artistic consciousness of the restrictions of the French type.

In the *Prologue* to the *Legend of Good Women*[85] occurs what is probably the best known of Chaucer's *ballades.* The version in the A Text differs in some minor ways from that in the B Text, but the two differ radically in the refrain. Both versions of the *ballade* are made up of three seven-line stanzas riming a b a b b c c. There is no envoy. In the A version, the refrain runs, "Alceste is here, that al that may desteyne"; in the B version, "My Lady cometh, that al this may disteyne." The most striking feature of the poem is its use of proper names. The French *ballade* writers conventionally introduced these lists, which were in reality a medieval device for throwing a glamour of romance about the subject. The following lines in a *ballade* printed among *Les Pièces Attribuables à Deschamps*[86] will illustrate the convention:

"Hester, Judith, Penelopé, Helaine,
Sarra, Tisbé, Rebeque et Sarry,
Lucresce, Yseult, Genevre, chastellaine,
La trés loyal nommée de Vergy,
Rachel aussi, la dame de Fayel
Onc ne furent sy precieux jouel
D'onneur, bonté, senz, beauté et valour
Con est ma trés doulce dame d'onnour.

Se d'Absalon la grant beauté humaine," etc.

85 W. W. Skeat, *Complete Works of Geoffrey Chaucer* (Oxford, 1894), Vol. III, p. 83.

86 G. Raynaud, *Œuvres Complètes de Eustache Deschamps* (Paris, 1901), Vol. X, p. xlix.

The resemblance between these nine lines of a *ballade* attributed to Deschamps and Chaucer's *ballade* in the *Legend of Good Women* has been noted by Skeat.[87] He does not pretend to say whether the French writer or Chaucer originated this particular catalogue of famous beauties who were, according to both poets, inferior to the particular lady of their praise. In innumerable other poems of the period, chiefly French, but occasionally English, the author enumerates individuals whom the subject of the poem either equals or surpasses. For purposes of illustration take Deschamps's *Rondel:*[88]

"Dame a Judith et Hester comparée,
A Eccuba et Rebecque autrecy,

De loyaulté a Sarre equipolée,
Dame a Judith et Hester comparée,

De bonne meurs a Seneque parée,
Mon cuer vous donne; aiez de moy mercy,
Dame a Judith et Hester comparée,
A Eccuba et Rebecque autrecy;"

or the *ballade* of Deschamps in which a lady praises her *ami:*

"A Salomon puet estre comparez
Pour son savoir; de beauté ensement
A Absalon; et de force parez
Au roy Hector et Sanson proprement;
A Seneques de meurs, d'enseignement;
Et a Paris, qui bien d'amours joy;
Mais d'eulz trestous est nul le parlement,
Aux grans vertus de mon loyal amy."[89]

87 W. W. Skeat, *Complete Works of Geoffrey Chaucer* (Oxford, 1894), Vol. III, p. 298.

88 G. Raynaud, *Œuvres Complètes de Eustache Deschamps* (Paris, 1884), Vol. IV, p. 110.

89 Le Marquis de Queux de Saint-Hilaire, *Œuvres Complètes de Eustache Deschamps* (Paris, 1882), vol. III, p. 239.

Far more striking than any of these resemblances, however, is the similarity between this *ballade* of Chaucer's and that one of Machaut's which begins with a reference to Absalon. Even the refrains suggest each other:

"Ne quier veoir la biauté d'Absalon
Ne d'Ulixès le sens et la faconde,
Ne esprouver la force de Sanson,
Ne regarder que Dalida le tonde,
    Ne cure n'ay par nul tour
Des yeux Argus, ne de joie gringnour,
Car pour plaisance et sans aÿde d'ame
Je voy assez, puis que je voy ma dame.

De l'ymage que fist Pymalion
Elle n'avoit pareille ne seconde;
Mais la belle qui m'a en sa prison
Cent mille fois est plus bele et plus monde:
    C'est uns drois fluns de douçour
Qui puet et scet garir toute dolour;
Dont cilz a tort que de dire me blame:
Je voy assez, puis que je voy ma dame.

Si ne me chaut dou sens de Salemon,
Ne que Phebus en termine ou responde,
Ne que Venus s'en mesle ne Mennon
Que Jupiter fist muer en aronde,
    Car je di, quant je l'aour,
Aim et desir, ser et crieng et honnour,
Et que s'amour seur toute rien m'enflame,
Je voy assez, puis que je voy ma dame."[90]

Moreover, as J. L. Lowes has brilliantly demonstrated,[91]

[90] Chichmaref, *Opus Cit.*, Vol. II, p. 560.

[91] J. L. Lowes, *The Prologue to the Legend of Good Women as Related to the French Marguerite Poems, Publications of Modern Language Association*, XIX, pp. 655–6: "That [*ballade*] of the *Paradys* is sung by the poet himself of his lady, whose name is Mar-

the *ballade* in the *Prologue* to the *Legend of Good Women* much resembles in substance, function, and treatment, the *ballade* that begins at line 1627 of Froissart's *Paradys D'Amours.* Mr. Lowes considers the "happy transfer of the *ballade* in A from the poet to the attendant ladies, by virtue of which it becomes an integral part of the action,"[92] evidence for the priority of the B version.

The recent possible additions to the Chaucer canon have included only two *ballades,* "either or both of which may well have been written by the author of some of the Canterbury Tales."[93 and 94] The first of these[95] has the regula-

guerite, and files a bead-roll of the other flowers, which, despite their merits, the marguerite surpasses. . . . The *balade* in the B. version of the Prologue is also sung, not as in A. by the attendant ladies, but as in the *Paradys* by the poet himself, though the direct movement of the poem is thereby sharply interrupted and the time changed from past to present. It is likewise distinctly asserted that it is sung of his lady, who has just been identified with the daisy. Since, however, in the Prologue the praises of the daisy have been already sung—in part in the phraseology of this very *balade*—the *balade* of B. instead of keeping the allegory of rival flowers, names directly rather than symbolically the rival bearers of his lady's qualities."

92 J. L. Lowes, *Opus Cit.,* p. 681. "If the *balade* in B was suggested by the *balade* of the *Paradys,* the setting in the latter, where it is sung by a poet in his own person, would naturally be carried over too. Its looseness of connection would then be quite of a piece with the other instances in B, already pointed out, of rapid and spontaneous adaptation of French originals." Its context in A "may once more be readily explained by the absence of the direct suggestion of the original, in whose place was now uppermost the instinct of the maturer artist."

93 F. J. Furnivall, *Tyl of Brentford's Testament,* etc. (London, 1871), p. 34.

94 E. P. Hammond, *Omissions from the Editions of Chaucer, Mod. Lang. Notes,* Vol. XIX, pp. 35–38. Both are found in a Shirley Manuscript, British Museum *MS. Additional* 16165.

95 E. P. Hammond, *Opus Cit.,* p. 37: "Fol. 244^{b} is headed 'Balade by Chaucer' in the hand of Shirley. This page contains the second

tion seven-line stanza, riming a b a b b c c, the last two lines of each stanza serving as a refrain:

> "Ageyns þe hill Tpruk in Tpruk out I calle
> ffor of my ploughe þe best stott is balle."

This poem is probably an example of the *ballade's* occasional use for purposes of *double entendre*.[96] The second of these *ballades* has three seven-line stanzas, riming a b a b b c c, with a constant refrain in all three stanzas and no envoy. The poem is as coarse as several of the *Canterbury Tales*, but unlike them has nothing in it but its coarseness.

There are thus only sixteen *ballades* that may be attributed to Chaucer with any degree of certainty. These we must still assume to be the earliest English examples of that verse form, although the temptation is strong to suspect the genial members of the English *puy* of having composed *ballades* antedating Chaucer's. As has been stated, he knew the poetic practice of his famous French contemporaries. This familiarity is evidenced not only by his own use of the form, but more often by his imitation of French *ballades* in his other poems.[97] He wrote his *ballades* with conscious

and third stanzas of a poem, which began on folio 244[r] and was there marked simply 'Balade'; below this on 244[b] is another 'Balade' also thus marked, which runs over on to leaf 245[a]. The running title of 244[b] might therefore be interpreted as belonging to either of the short poems, parts of which appear on that page; but as it is Shirley's usual custom to make his running title fit the poem which begins on the page below, I have considered that the ballad meant is probably the second.'' The *ballade* copied on fol. 244[v] and 245[r] has only two stanzas, but there is space enough for another stanza before the next number follows and there is no *explicit*.

96 The French musical *ballade* on fol. 258 of British Museum *MS. Lansdowne 380* is an illustration of the same perversion.

97 See also note at end of this chapter.

artifice, although he heeded the form of the French models with infinitely less care than a later generation of Englishmen who followed the prescriptions of the Pléiade. English, indeed, does not lend itself to the word-tricks and rime-juggling that the French poets and poetasters practiced in the *ballade.* Chaucer plainly was not sufficiently attracted to the form to do more than trifle with it. *Ballades* by the thousand were not for him. His bent was quite obviously toward narrative rather than lyric poetry, and his predilection may have helped to cut short the English career of the *ballade.*[99]

III. Lydgate

The *ballade* in the hands of Chaucer's successors never rose above mediocrity. The most telling influence of the French *ballade,* indeed, from the time of Chaucer, was on the structure of the English stanza. The popularity of the seven-line stanza, riming a b a b b c c, and of the eight-line stanza, riming a b a b b c b c, in both England and Scotland is due to the repeated use of these stanzaic forms by the French *ballade* writers, to Chaucer's interest in these stanzas, to his metrical experiments, and to the fidelity of his imitators. Lydgate's *ballades*[99] outnumber Chaucer's,

[98] In recent years, some notable work has been done by scholars in investigating the literary relations between Chaucer and contemporary writers in French. Cf. E. Koeppel, *Gower's Franz, Balladen u. Chaucer, Eng. Studien* XX; G. L. Kittredge, *Chaucer and Some of his Friends, Modern Philology,* I; J. L. Lowes, *The Prologue to the Legend of Good Women As Related to the French Marguerite Poems and the Filostrato, Publications of Modern Language Association,* XIX; J. L. Lowes, *The Chaucerian 'Merciles Beaute' and Three Poems of Deschamps, Modern Language Review,* V.

[99] In Lydgate ascriptions, I follow the *Lydgate Canon* given in H. N. MacCracken, *The Minor Poems of John Lydgate, Early English Text Society,* Extra Series, 107 (London, 1911), p. v.

but he is even less bound than Chaucer by the French formulas. Lydgate used the *ballade,* as Chaucer is not known to have done, as the conclusion or envoy of longer poems. *Ballades* appear thus in the *Fall of Princes,* and are found fulfilling the same function at the conclusion of the *Flour of Courtesye,* at the end of the *Serpent of Division,* and again after the *Legend of St. Margarete.* In the *Temple of Glas* the *ballade* is a part of the story as in the *Prologue* to the *Legend of Good Women.* The *ballade* beginning, "Who will been holle and kepe him frō sekenesse," is differently placed in different MSS. Lydgate's other *ballades* occur as separate lyrics.

A typical *ballade* in the French form is that found at the close of the *Flour of Courtesye,* a poem devoted to the description of an ideal woman of the same general characteristics as the Alcestis of Chaucer. The poem as a whole is reprinted because of its evident conformity, unusual in English, to the *ballade* type. It has three seven-line stanzas, riming a b a b b c c, a refrain repeated with some modifications at the end of the stanzas, and an envoy riming a c a c, beginning with the familiar "Princesse."

Balade simple

"'With al my mightë and my beste entente,
With al the faith that mighty God of kynde
Me yaf, sith he me soule and knowing sente,
I chese, and to this bonde ever I me bynde,
To love you best, whyl I have lyf and mynde':—
Thus herde I foules in the dawëninge
Upon the day of saint Valentyne singe.

'Yet chese I, at the ginning, in this entente,
To love you, though I no mercy fynde;
And if you list I dyed, I wolde assente,
As ever twinne I quik out of this lynde!

Suffyseth me to seen your fetheres ynde':
Thus herde I foules in the morweninge
Upon the day of saint Valentyne singe.

'And over this myn hertes luste to-bente,
In honour only of the wodëbynde,
Hoolly I yeve, never to repente
In joye or wo, wher so that I wynde
Tofore Cupyde, with his eyën blynde':—
The foules alle, when Tytan did springe,
With devout herte, me thoughte I herde singe!

Lenvoy

Princesse of beautee, to you I represente
This simple dytè, rude as in makinge,
Of herte and wel faithful in myn entente,
Lyk as, this day [the] foules herde I singe."[100]

The reference to Saint Valentine's day may very easily be an echo of the significance of that feast in the *Parlement of Foules.* Or Lydgate may simply be drawing from the large fund of St. Valentine lore then current. After 1449, Charles d'Orléans had retired to Blois, where he celebrated annually the day of Saint Valentine in connection with his *cour d'amour.* Almost every year a *ballade, chançon,* or *rondeau* was composed for this festival by this poet and patron of letters. His interest in the day has been attributed to the fact that his mother's name was Valentine.[101]

The envoy that closes Lydgate's *Seynt Margarete* has, itself, no envoy, but is composed of three seven-line stanzas riming a b a b b c c. The refrain, like that in the *Flour of Courtesye balade,* is, as may be seen, practically double

[100] W. W. Skeat, *Chaucerian and Other Pieces* (Oxford, 1897), Vol. VII, p. 273.

[101] Aimé Champollion-Figeac, *Louis et Charles ducs d'Orléans* (Paris, 1844), p. 355.

in the first two stanzas, but in the third stanza is curiously inverted. The address to "Noble princesses" comes, as it frequently does in Lydgate, in the first line of a stanza other than the envoy:

"Noble princesses and ladyes of estate,
And gentilwomen louer of degre,
Lefte vp your hertes, calle to your aduocate
Seynt Margarete, gemme of chastite;
And alle wy*m*men that haue neccessite,
Praye this mayde ageyn syknesse and dissese,
In trayvalynge for to do yow ese!

And folkes alle that be disconsolat,
In your myschief and grete adue*r*site,
And alle that stonde of helpe desolate,
With devout hert and with humylite
Of ful trust, knelyng on your kne,
Pray this mayde in trouble and all dissese
You to releue and to do yow ese!

Now, blissed virgyne, in heuene hy exaltat,
With other martirs in the celestialle se,
Styntith werre, the dreadfulle fel debat
That vs assaileth of oure enemyes thre,
From whos assaute impossible is to fle;
But, chaste gemme, thi servauntes sette at ese
And be her shelde in myschief and dissese!"[102]

The *ballade* envoy of the *Serpent of Division* has three eight-line stanzas riming a b a b b c b c, with an identical refrain in all three. Like the envoy of *St. Margarete* and the envoys in the *Fall of Princes,* it merely tediously repeats the theme of what has preceded:

102 H. N. MacCracken, *The Minor Poems of John Lydgate, Early English Text Society* (London, 1911), Extra Series, 107, p. 192.

"This litill prose declarith in figure
The grete damage and distruccion,
That whilome fill, bi fatell auenture,
Vnto Rome, þe myȝti riall towne,
Caused only bi false devision
Amonge hem selfe, þe storie tellith þis.
Thorowe covetise and veyne Ambicion
Of Pompey and Cesar Iulius.

Criste hymselfe recordith in scripture
That euery londe and euery region
Whiche is divided may no while endure,
But turne in haste to desolacion;
For whiche ȝe lords and prynces of renowne,
So wyse, so manly, and so vertuous,
Maketh a merowre toforne in youre resoun
Of Pompey and Cesar Iulius.

Harme don bi deþe no man may recure,
A ȝeins whose stroke is no redempcion,
Hit is full hard in fortune to assure,
Here whele so ofte turnth vp and downe.
And for tescheue stryf and dissencion
Within yowreself beth not contrarious,
Remembring ay in yowre discrecion
Of Pompey and Cesar Iulius."[103]

Here again it is much more probable that the reference to the familiar wheel of fortune[104] occurred independently to Lydgate than that he had in mind Chaucerian passages of a similar character.

To Humphrey of Gloucester's taste we owe the envoys that occur at the end of nearly all the chapters in the *Fall of Princes.* Among these tail-pieces are found thirty-one

[103] H. N. MacCracken, *The Serpent of Division by John Lydgate* (Oxford, 1910), p. 66.

[104] See p. 258 below, and p. 236 above.

ballades, whose purpose is to enforce the lesson of the harrowing narratives that they conclude. Their sledge-hammer morality does not harmonize with the peculiarity vivacious art-form of the *ballade,* so that the result in every case is depressing. There are ten three-stanza *ballades* and twenty-one with three stanzas and an envoy. In the former class, we find five with an address to "noble princes" at the beginning of the third stanza and five without that characteristic. The stanza in all these is the seven-line stanza riming a b a b b c c. Of course, it must be said that, in view of the subject matter of this translation from Boccaccio, an appeal to royalty in the "envoys" is to be expected. So, in the *ballade* here quoted, we see the appeal made at the beginning of the second stanza:

"O folkes al that this tragedies rede,
Haueth to mekenes amonge youre aduertence
Of proude Nembroth also taketh hede,
How that he fel from his magnificence,
Onely for he by sturdy violence,
List of malice the mighty lorde assayle.
But in such case what myght his pride auayle.

Noble princes which this world do possede,
Ye that be famous of wysdome and science,
And haue so many subiectes that you drede,
In gouernaunce vnder your excellence:
Let your power with mekenes so dispence,
That false pride oppresse not the poreyle,
Which to your nobles so much may auayle.

Pride of Nembroth dyd the brydel lede,
Which him conuayed with great insolence:
Pride apertayneth nothynge to manhede,
Saue in armes to shewe this presence:
Wherefore honour, laude, and reuerence

Be to mekenes, that hath the gouernaile
Of al vertues, which man may most auayle."[105]

The next *ballade*, a second illustration of the three-stanza type in the *Fall of Princes*, both because of its form, and incidentally to call attention to a statement of the customary medieval conception of tragedy, is quoted:

"O what estate may him selfe assure,
For to conserue his life in sikernes?
What worldly ioy may here long endure?
Or where shall men finde now stablenes,
Sithe kinges & princes frō their high nobles
(Record of Cadmus) been sodēly brought low
And from the whele of fortune ouerthrow?

Who may susteyne the pyteous aduenture
Of this tragedy, by writyng to expresse?
It is like to the chaunteplure
All worldly blisse is meinte with bitternes
Beginning with ioy, endyng in wretchednes.
The sodayn chaūg thereof may no man know
For who sytteth highest is sonest ouerthrow.

Was in this world yet neuer creature,
(Reken by princes for all their hygh noblesse)
But fortune coulde enclyne them to her lure;
And them enperishe through her frowardnes.
Wherefore ye lordes w^t all your great riches,
Beware afore or ye daunce in the rowe,
Of such as fortune hath frō her whele throw."[106]

[105] *A Treatise Excellent and Compendious Shewing and Declaring in Maner of Tragedye the Falles of Sondry Most Notable Princes, etc., by Dan John Lidgate Monke of Burye*, Bk. 1, Lenuoye of Chap. III. (This copy is in the Columbia Library. A note in pencil on the fly leaf reads, "See Lowndes—this appears to be the edition printed by John Wayland 1558.")

[106] Book I, Lenuoye of Ch. VII. See p. 256 above.

The three-stanza form with the appeal to "noble princes" is shown in Lydgate's fling at "surquedy" and the bloody tragedies growing out of that vice common to all ages but censured with special effectiveness in Middle English:

"Whan surquedy oppressed hath pitie,
And mekenes is w^{t} tyranny bore doun
Agayne all ryght, then hasty crueltie
To be vengeable maketh no delation,
What foloweth thereof by good aspection,
Se an example how Pyrus in his tene
Of hateful yre slough yong Pollicene.

Kynge Eolus to outragious was parde,
And to vengeable in his intencion:
Agaynst his children, Machaire, & Canace,
So importable was his punicion,
Of haste proceadyng their destruction.
Worse in his eyre as it was well sene,
Than cruell Pyrus whiche slewe Policene.

Noble princes, prudent and attempre,
Deferre vengeaunce of high discrecion:
Tyll your yre sumwhat aswaged be,
Do neuer of doome none execusion.
For hate and rancour perturben the reason
Of hasty iudges, more of entent vnclene,
Than cruell Pyrrus whych slewe Policene."[107]

Lydgate, in the *ballades* in the *Fall of Princes,* did not adhere to the common practice of making the envoy of fewer lines than the stanzas. In fact, he himself does not use the word "envoy" at all to describe the fourth stanza with its direct appeal. All the envoy stanzas in these *ballades* are of exactly the same number of lines as the other stanzas, as witness the following:

[107] Book I, Lenuoye of Ch. XXV.

"Prynces, pricesses cōsider how in euery age
Folkes ben diuers of their condicion:
To ply & turne and chaunge in their courage,
Yet there is none to mine opinion,
So dreadfull chaunge ne transmutation,
As chaunge of prynces, to geue iugement,
Or hasty credence without auisement.

It is well founde a passyng great domage,
Knowen and expert in euery region,
Though a tale haue a fayre vysage,
It may enclude full great deception,
Hide vnder sugar galle and fell poyson,
With a freshe face of double entendement,
Yet geue no credence without suisement.

Let folkes beware of their langage,
Kepe their tonges from oblocution:
To hynder or hurte by no maner outrage,
Preserue their lyppes fron all detraction,
From champarty and contradiction,
Lest that fraude were found in their entent,
Ne geue no credence without auisement.

Prynces, princesses of noble and high parage,
Whiche haue lordshyp and domination,
Voyde them asyde that can flatter and fage:
Fro tonges that haue a terrage of treason
Stoppe your eares, from their bitter soun,
Be circumspect, not hastye but prudent,
And geue no credence without auisement."[108]

Five of the *ballades* in the *Fall of Princes* are written in octaves. The sententious commentary on the sad life of Charles of Jerusalem is one of these. The rime-scheme in the three stanzas and envoy is the usual a b a b b c b c:

108 Bk. I, Lenuoy of Ch. XIII. The last three stanzas of this envoy are found by themselves in British Museum *MS. Arundel 26*, fol. 31r.

"Lyke as Phebus in some freshe morninge
After Aurora the day doth clarifye,
Falleth oft that his bryght shining
Is derked with some cloudy skye,
A lykenes shewed in this tragedye:
Expert in Charles the story doth well preue
Youth and age rekened truely
The fayre day men do prayse at eue.

The noble fame of his fresh gynning
To Saint Lowes he was nygh of alye,
Ryght wyse, manly, & vertuous of liuyng,
Called of knighthod flour of chiualry.
Tyll maintenaunce of anoutry
Came in to hys courte to hurte hys name and greue
His life, his deth, put in ieoparty
The fayre day men do prayse at eue.

Lyke desertes mē haue theyr guerdoning,
Vertuous lyfe doth princes magnify,
The contrary to them is great hyndring
Folke experte the trouth may not denye,
Serche out the rewarde of cursed lechery
Where it is vsed the household may not preue,
In this matter to Charles haue an eye
The fayre day to prayse towarde eue.

Noble princes al vyces eschewing
Your hyghe corage let reason gye,
With draw your hand fro riotous watchyng,
Flye fleshly lustes and vicious companye:
Oppresse no man, do no tiranny
Socour the nedy, pore folke do releue,
Let men report the prudent policye,
Of your last age whan it draweth to eue."[109]

The envoys mentioned in the *Fall of Princes* conform, with the exception noted, to the French laws for the *bal-*

[109] Bk. IX, Lenuoye of Ch. XXVIII.

lade; but Lydgate, like Chaucer, modified the type. Two of Lydgate's religious poems are written in a loose *ballade* form. The first of these, "My fader above beholdyng thy mekenesse," is the most poetic piece ascribed to the Monk of Bury.[110] It is a *ballade* in the sense that it has three seven-line stanzas with a refrain, varying in the last stanza, but the rimes in all three stanzas differ. In the second of these religious poems, "Heyl hooly Sitha, Maide of gret vertu," the rimes differ in all three of the eight-line stanzas and the refrain is modified in three different ways.[111] Both are certainly poor specimens of the *ballade* kind, but written, I believe, with reference, however remote, to the French fashion. The comparison of the Virgin, in the first of the poems, to a flower, and the homage paid her in this character, illustrate a custom, frequent with medieval writers of religious lyrics, of borrowing the apparatus of the secular courtly poem and converting it to the uses of piety. A third short religious poem, called a *Prayer to Mary,* attributed to Lydgate, is in the restricted form of the *ballade,* with three eight-line stanzas riming a b a b b c b c, the same rimes occurring in all stanzas, with an identical refrain.[112]

Another three-stanza poem of Lydgate's is prefixed to a *Dietary* in one of the manuscripts.[113] Although these three stanzas are found in a great variety of combinations in the

[110] British Museum *MS. Harley 2251,* fol. 79. Also printed in H. N. MacCracken, *The Minor Poems of John Lydgate, Early English Text Society* (London, 1911), Extra Series, 107, p. 235.

[111] H. N. MacCracken, *Opus Cit.,* p. 137.

[112] H. N. MacCracken, *Opus Cit.,* p. 296.

Lydgate's *A Prayer Upon the Cross* (MacCracken, *Opus Cit.,* p. 252), in spite of its five stanzas, may well be classified as a *ballade.* The same rimes and refrain persist in all the stanzas and the last two constitute a kind of double envoy.

[113] British Museum *MS. Lansdowne 699.*

manuscripts,[114] I venture to think that they were originally conceived as a *ballade,* and were translated very possibly from the French *ballade*[115] one stanza of which is given below in connection with an English version:

"Who will been holle / & kepe hym frō sekenesse
And resiste / the strok of pestilence
lat hȳ be glad / & voide al hevynesse
fflee wikkyd heires / eschew the presence
Off infect placys / causyng the violence
Drȳk a good wyn*e* / and holsom meetis take
Smelle swote thyng̅ / & for his deffence
Walk in cleene heir*e* / eschew mystis blake.

With voide stomak / outward the nat dresse
Risyng erly / with fyr*e* have assistence
Delite in gardeyns / for ther gret swetnesse
to be weele clad / do thy dilygence
Keep welle thi silf / from incontynence
In stawes Battis / no soiour that thou make.
Opnyng of humours / this doth gret offence
Walk in clene heir*e* / eschew mystis blake.

Ete nat gret flesshe / for no greedynesse
And fro fruties / hold thyn abstynence
Poletys & chekenys / for ther tendirnesse
Ete hē with sauce / & spare not for dispence
Various / vynegre / & thynfluence
Of holsom spices / dar*e* undirtake
the morwe sleep / callid gyldene in sentence
Gretly helpith / ayeen the mystis blake."[116]

114 E. P. Hammond, *Two British Museum MSS., Anglia,* XXVIII, p. 7; p. 143. See also Sir Egerton Brydge, *Censura Literaria* (London, 1815), pp. 137–138; and F. N. Robinson, *On Two MMS. of Lydgate's Guy of Warwick, Harvard Studies, V* (Boston, 1896).

115 Trinity College, Cambridge *MS. R. 3. 20.*

116 British Museum *MS. Lansdowne 699,* fol. 85ᵛ.

"Vesty vn hounourable balade francoys du regymente du corps.

Qui veult son corps en sante maintenir
Et resister contre lespidemie
Doit joye anoie et tristesse fouir
Laisser lieu ou est la maladie
Et frequanter joyeuse compayngnye
Boir bone vin nette viande vsser
Port bone odour contre la punnesie
Et ne va hors si ne fait bel & cler"[117]

The well-known *ballade*[118] in the same poet's *Temple of Glas* presents no unusual features. It is made up of the three seven-line stanzas riming a b a b b c c, and has a refrain that is substantially the same in all three places where it occurs. It is sung by the choirs of Venus to celebrate the understanding between the two lovers, and its pleasant noise arouses the poet from his vision.

Lydgate's *ballades* add nothing to his reputation as a poet. In only one of them, as we have seen, does he follow the form with comparative fidelity, namely, in the envoy of the *Flour of Curtesye,* and in only one of them, the *ballade* to the Virgin, have we verse of any beauty. The *ballades* that serve as envoys are merely dull and repetitious; while that in the *Temple of Glas* is smooth but conventional. A study of Lydgate's *ballades* merely emphasizes the conclusion before stated that the *ballade* never ceased to be an exotic in middle English literature, and that it owes its chief importance to its effect on the English stanza.

IV. Quixley

Probably the earliest *ballade* sequence in Middle English is the northern translation of Gower's *Un Traitié selonc les*

117 Trinity College, Cambridge *MS. R. 3. 20,* fol. 52.

118 *Lydgate's Temple of Glas,* ed. by J. Schick, *Early English Text Society* (London, 1891), Extra Series, 40, p. 55.

auctours pour essampler les amantz marietz.[119] Gower's eighteen *ballades* are in this version[120] expanded by means of an introductory stanza of the translator, who says, among other things,

"Gower it made in frenshe with gret studie
In *balades* ryal whos sentence here
Translated hath Quixley in his manere;"

and they are also expanded by two stanzas at the end prefixed to Gower's little envoy addressed to the, "université de tout le monde." Quixley's collection thus contains nineteen of the *balades ryale*. This use of this latter term antedates, of course, its use in connection with the *Kingis Quair*. It may be well to repeat at this point that the combination in English of *royal* with *ballade* is likely to have been due to the influence of the English *puy* enforced by contemporaneous French usage in the phrase *chant royal*. Professor MacCracken conjectures that the translation was made by a certain John Quixley of Quixley (modern Whixley) as a present to his daughter Alice, preparations for whose wedding were in progress in 1402. His hypothesis is based on external evidence afforded by the manuscript and by contemporary records, and on the internal evidence of certain northern forms. He accounts for the presence of the Gower *Traitié* in York by the supposition that the neighboring family of Gowers situated at Stitenham procured from London the latest work of John Gower, who is not known to have been related to them.

Gower's *ballades* in the *Traitié* are made up, as we remember, of three seven-line stanzas, riming a b a b b c c,

119 See Chapter I.

120 Found in British Museum *MS. Stowe 451* and printed by H. N. MacCracken, *Quixley's Ballades Royal, Yorkshire Archaeological Journal,* XX, pp. 33–50, 1908.

with refrains and no envoy save the general one at the end. His translator follows the form of the original exactly; in the matter of line structure, however, ten-syllable lines are occasionally represented by lines of nine syllables.[121] MacCracken calls attention to the fact that "Quixley was totally ignorant of the syllabic value of the final *-e*, as it appears, for example, in Gower's English poetry." The French rimes are closely followed. As a matter of fact, only in the eighteenth *ballade* is there an absolute departure from the rimes of the original. The translation is very close; in many instances the sense is transferred line by line.

The Middle English version is considerably rougher in line structure than the French, as a result, probably, of the translator's occasional following of the laws of French metrics. The translation, like the original *ballades* on adultery, is an uninspired performance. This Middle English rendering of the *ballades* on so promising a theme as,

> That all her lyfe stant, without dep*ar*ting,"[122]
>
> " Trewe loue is betwix twoo þe holy bonde

is, to tell the truth, a tedious affair.

V. Anonymous Ballades

The authorship of the Middle English *ballades* that remain to be considered has in no case been surely determined. This last group includes the translated *ballades* printed by G. Watson Taylor in 1827, four in Volume VII of Skeat's Oxford edition of Chaucer, those in the *Ile of Ladies* and the *Court of Sapience,* some recently printed,[123] and certain others still in manuscript. The ascription of almost all of

[121] H. N. MacCracken, *Opus Cit.,* pp. 35–36. MacCracken gives a complete analysis of the metrical structure of the poems.

[122] H. N. MacCracken, *Opus Cit.,* p. 49.

[123] From Bodleian *MS. Fairfax 16.*

these *ballades* to some fifteenth century poet or other has from time to time been attempted, but these attributions, while occasionally ingenious, are nevertheless conjectural.

The most imposing collection of Middle English *ballades* is the series of translations of the poems of Charles d'Orléans and of certain other French poets[124] that were printed for the Roxburghe Club in 1827 under the editorship of Watson Taylor, as the *English Poems of Charles d'Orléans.* The editor declared that these English versions of Charles d'Orléans were by the great Frenchman himself, and, further, showed himself to be ignorant of the fact that a number of the translations were of poems not by Charles d'Orléans at all. In the same year, an anonymous critic, reviewing the Roxburghe Club publication in the *Retrospective Review,*[125] amicably remarked: "We have done what we do not believe that gentleman [Watson Taylor] or the person he employed ever took the trouble to do —carefully examined a MS. of selections from Orléans's work in the British Museum [*MS. Reg. 16. F. ij*], among which are three original 'Roundels' in English; but they are so decidedly inferior to the translations in the manuscript printed by Mr. Watson Taylor that it is scarcely possible the duke could have been the translator of his own writings." Critical opinion on the subject of the authorship of these *ballades* had not advanced beyond the critic of the *Retrospective Review* until quite recently, when MacCracken assigned these translations to William de la Pole, first Duke of Suffolk (1396–1450). MacCracken has put his conclusions[126] in regard to the authorship of these translations and of a group of poems in an Oxford manu-

124 In British Museum *MS. Harley 682.*

125 Second Series, Vol. I, p. 148.

126 *An English Friend of Charles of Orleans, Publications of Modern Language Association,* XXVI, pp. 142–180.

script[127] at the disposal of scholars to be tested and confirmed. And Pierre Champion, the eminent French authority on the manuscripts of Charles d'Orléans, is known to be studying the evidences offered by French manuscripts that contain English poems ascribed to the Duke.

In Watson Taylor's volume there are seventy-nine *ballades* translated from the French of Charles d'Orléans. As translations, they are less literal than the Quixley *ballades;* as poetry they are incomparably superior. It is only fair, however, to remember the dull muse of Gower's *Traitié* and the lyric inspiration of the original from which the Harley translator worked. A critical edition of these poems must shortly be forthcoming.[128]

The line of eight syllables common to the *ballades* in French is represented in English by the ten-beat line, but in stanza form and in rime-scheme, the translated *ballades* follow the French closely, varying from seven-line to eleven-line stanzas with refrains. Characteristic stanza forms used in the Middle English versions rime thus:

Bl.	*Stanza.*	*Envoy*	*Taylor*	*C. F.*
IV.	a b a b b c c	b c b c (none in Fr.)	p. 12	p. 18
XXIII.	a b a b b c b c	b b c b c	p. 37	p. 71
XXVII.	a b a b b c c b	b b c c b	p. 41	p. 75
XVIII.	a b a b b c d c d	c d c d	p. 30	p. 66
V.	a b a b b b c b c	b c b c (none in Fr.)	p. 13	p. 19
XXI.	a b a b b c c d c d	c d c d (none in Fr.)	p. 34	p. 69
XXII.	a b a b b c c b c b	c b c b	p. 36	p. 70
III.	a b a b b a a c a c	a a c a c	p. 11	p. 17
XXIX.	a b a b b c c d e d e	c c d e d e	p. 45	p. 77

[127] Bodleian *MS. Fairfax 16.*

[128] As I have had only limited opportunity of comparing *MS. Harley 682* with the 1827 print, my references will be to the imperfect text furnished by Watson Taylor; but the *ballades* are printed direct from the MS. The references to the French versions are to the text in A. Champollion-Figeac, *Poésies du Duc Charles d'Orléans* (Paris, 1842).

But such variations of rime-scheme occur as in *Balade III,* where the English envoy rimes a a c a c and the French one, c c d c d, and the stanzas of the French form of the *Balade* rime a b a b b c c c d c d. In *Balade XXII* also the French stanza differs from the English in riming a b a b b c c d c d, and the two envoys rime thus, the English c b c b, the French c d c d. The two envoys in the case of *Balade XXVI* (p. 44 in Taylor; p. 74 in C. F.) differ too, the English riming b b c a a c, the French b b c d d c. The second stanza of *Balade XIII* (p. 24 in Taylor; p. 61 in C. F.), unlike the original, rimes a b a b b b b c, and the first stanza rimes a b a b b c b c. The rime words in general, however, correspond closely.[129]

129 Examples *passim:*

Balade IV

p. 12	*E.*	*p. 18 F.*
l. 6	allyaunce	aliance
l. 7	pusshaunce	puissance
l. 13	Gouvenaunce	gouvernance
l. 20	vttraunce	oultrance

Balade XIII

p. 24		*p. 61*
l. 4	curtsey	courtoisie
l. 5	company	compagnie
l. 13	cry	crye
l. 20	foly	folie
l. 28	party	partie

Balade XXIII

p. 37		*p. 71*
l. 5	plesaunce	Plaisance
l. 7	fraũce	France
l. 8	parte	party
l. 10	penaũce	penance
l. 12	esperaunce	Espéraunce
l. 15	reken aunce	recouvrance

It will be seen that certain words like *France, plaisance, aliance, maistresse, espérance,* in the original appear inevi-

l. 18	puysshaunce	puissance
l. 20	allyaunce	aliance
l. 21	grevaunce	grevance
l. 23	vttraunce	oultrance
l. 26	fyaunce	france

Balade XXV

p. 40		*p. 73*
l. 6	mastres	maistresse
l. 14	promes	promesse
l. 22	humbles	humblesse

Balade XXVII

p. 41		*p. 75*
l. 1	baner	bannière
l. 3	fronter	frontière
l. 6	prisonere	prisonnière
l. 7	straungere	estrangière
l. 9	chere	chière
l. 10	company	compaignie
l. 11	manere	manière
l. 20	party	partie
l. 23	counselere	conseillière
l. 25	maystre	maistrie
l. 29	bere	bière
l. 28	prayere	prière

Balade XIX

p. 32		*p. 67*
l. 3	distres	destresse
l. 11	maystres	maistresse
l. 17	rewdenes	rudesse

Balade XVIII

p. 30		*p. 66*
l. 4	plesaunce	plaisance
l. 5	recoueraunce	recouvrance
l. 6	conquere	conquester

tably in the translation. But, it is also true that *Balades* II, XXIV, XVI, XVII, XI, VIII, VI, XXI, III and XXII have no rimes in common with their originals.[130]

Rimes like the following find place in the Harley translation: *pressen* and *seson* (in *Balade II*, p. 10 of Taylor); *mastres* and *promys* (in *Balade XV*, p. 26 of Taylor); *dye*

l. 11	fraunce	France
l. 14	esperaunce	espérance
l. 20	penaunce	penance
l. 22	affyaunce	fiance

Balade XII

p. 22		*p. 60*
l. 1	maystres	maistresse
l. 2	ay	ay
l. 8	esperaunce	Espérance
l. 10	displesaunce	desplaisance
l. 12	assay	essay
l. 13	larges	largesse
l. 14	say	sçay
l. 18	penaunce	penance
l. 21	princesse	princesse

Balade XXIX

p. 45		*p. 77*
l. 2	reconfort	Reconfort
l. 5	port	port
l. 8	fraunce	France
l. 9	maystres	maistresse
l. 13	report	report
l. 19	plesaunce	plaisance
l. 20	fortres	fotresse
l. 30	aqueyntaunce	acointance
l. 31	pryncesse	princesse
l. 36	allyaunce	aliance
l. 37	rewdenes	rudesse

130 See pp. 16, 72, 64, 65, 59, 22, 20, 21, 69, 17 and 70 in Champollion-Figeac, and pp. 10, 38, 28, 29, 21, 27, 15, 16, 34, 11 and 36 in Taylor.

and *foly* (in *Balade III*, p. 11 of Taylor); *habound* and *stounde, se* and *mercy* (in *Balade XXII*. p. 36 of Taylor).

In envoys, the English *ballades* are better supplied than the French. At least ten of the English versions show envoys not in the text of the corresponding French poems.[131] It may be, of course, that the translations were made from a French text different from the one we now possess. My own impression of these envoys is that they harmonize perfectly, in every case, with the *ballade* to which they are attached and that they are on the same poetic level with the other stanzas of the poem.

Three of the *ballades* bear on Chaucer. The first of these (*Balade XXXII*, p. 49 of Taylor; p. 80 of C. F.) refers in its third stanza to the popular idea exploited in *Newfanglenesse* of connecting the color blue with constancy. This reference, it will be seen, is inserted by the translator:

"O come to me sum gladsum tidyng newe
My faynty hert to comfort in distres
Say me how farith the goodly fayre and trewe
Herdist thou hir speke of me oft moch or lesse
Me callyng loue of hir gret gentilesse
Hath she forgete O nay bi God aboue
I trust as that she made me of promys
When she me gafe this name as loo my loue.

131

Balade	*Taylor*	*C. F.*
Balade XVI	p. 28	p. 64
Balade IV	p. 12	p. 18
Balade I	p. 9	p. 15
Balade XX	p. 33	p. 68
Balade XI	p. 21	p. 59
Balade V	p. 13	p. 19
Balade XXVIII	p. 42	p. 76
Balade VI	p. 15	p. 20
Balade XII	p. 22	p. 60
Balade XXI	p. 34	p. 69

Though absence hold me fro my service dewe
And dowte of daunger doth me heuynes
So moche goodnes knowe y hir doth pursewe
That y kan neuyr this bithynke dowtles
But she will holde the verry trewe prynces
The p*ro*mys which was made to my bihoue
Knyttyng so oure hondis to witnes
When she me gafe this name as loo my loue.

Me thynkith gret pite were hit by ihū
If that a lady of so gret nobles
Shulde do hir silf refuse the coloure blew
Which hewe in loue is called stedfastnes
She may perceyue bi good avisynes
Whi y so rudely out my wordis shoue
And als what loue vs causid swere y gesse
When she me gafe this name as lo my loue.

Go belle for trouthe ensewre þou my maystres
That y am hiris in all maner prove
As she comaundid me to my gladnes
When she me gafe this name as lo my loue."[132]

The second of these *ballades* (*Balade VIII,* p. 17 in Taylor; p. 22 in C. F.) refers directly to Chaucer, and this direct reference, too, is inserted by the translator:

"When y am leyd to slepe as for a stound
To haue my rest y kan in no manere

[132] British Museum *MS. Harley 682* f. 22. The third stanza in French is (p. 81 of C. F.):

"Pitié seroit se dame telle
Qui doit tout houneur desirer,
Failloit de tenir la querelle
De bien et loyaument amer,
Son sens lui scet bien remonstrer
Toutes les choses que je dy,
Et ce qu'Amour nous fist jurer
Quant me donna le nom d'amy."

19

ffor all the nyght myn hert aredith round
As in the romaunce of plesaunt pancer
Me praiyng so as him to hark and here
And y ne dar his love disobay
In dowtyng so to do him displesere
This is my slepe y falle into decay.

In this book which he redde is write & bound
As alle dedis of my lady dere
Which doth myn hert in laught*er* oft abound
When he hit rett or tellith the matere
Which gretly is to prayse without were
For y mysilf delite it here mafay
Which if thei hered so wolde esche straungers
This is my slepe y falle into decay.

As with myn eyen a respit to be found
As for an howre y axe not for a yere
ffor which dispite wehnygh he doth confoūde
That they ne kan fulfille my desere
For which to rage and sighe as in a gere
He farith so that even as well y may
As make him stynt likke out a cole of fyre
This is my slepe y falle as in decay.

Thus may y loo more sonner wyn my bere
Then make my froward hert to me obay
ffor wt myn hurt he doth him silf achere
This is my slepe y falle into decay."[133]

[133] British Museum *MS. Harley 682*, f. 8. This *ballade* was transcribed from MS. after the rest of the chapter was completed. The last word of line four is found to be *pancer* and not *chaucer*. Watson Taylor or his scribe was in error. Stanza 1 of the French is:

"Quant je suy couchié en mon lit,
Je ne puis en pais reposer:
Car, toute la nuit mon cueur lit
On roumant de Plaisant-penser
Et me prie de l'escouter.
Si ne l'ose désobéir,
Pour doubte de le courroucer:
Ainsi je laisse le dormir."

In a third *ballade* there is a stanza written in the "ubi sunt" vein. In this stanza of *Balade LXII* (p. 97 in Taylor; *Harley 682,* f. 42; p. 120 in C. F.), there occurs a list of ladies, splendid in their day, whom death laid low:

"In tyme a past ther ran gret renomaunce	"On vieil temps, quant renom couroit
Of dido cresseid Alcest and Eleyne	De Criséis, de Yseud et Elaine
And many moo as fynde we in romaunce	Et maintes autres qu'on nommoit
That were of bewte huge and welbesayne	Parfaites en beaulté haultaine
But in the ende allas to thynke agayne	Mais au derrain, en son domaine
How deth hem slew and sleth moo day bi day	La Mort les prist piteusement
Hit doth me wel aduert this may y say	Par quoy puis véoir clerement:
That this world nys but even a thyng in vayne."	Ce monde n'est que chose vaine."

It is worth noting that the translator, remembering, perhaps, the *Prologue* to the *Legend of Good Women,* has substituted *Alcest* for *Yseud,* and has added *Dido,* the heroine of one of the Legends. True, *Isoude* appears in the *ballade* of the *Prologue,* but certainly *Alcest* is more especially Chaucerian in association than the Irish princess.

There are some forty other *ballades* in Watson Taylor's volume, translations, too, presumably, but not of poems by Orléans.[134] One of these is a translation of a poem by Christine de Pisan and illustrates in English a device, over frequent in France, of repeating the same word at the

[134] Cf. Georg Bullrich, *Über Charles d'Orleans und die ihm Zugeschriebene Englische Übersetzungen seiner Gedichte* (Berlin, 1893), pp. 18–20.

beginning of every line.[135] The translation is here given for purposes of comparison.[136]

"Alone am y and wille to be alone
Alone withouten plesere or gladnes
Alone in care to sighe and grone
Alone to wayle the deth of my maystres
Alone which sorow will me neuyr cesse
Alone y curse the lyf y do endure
Alone this fayntith me my gret distres
Alone y lyue an ofcast creature.

Alone am y most wofullest bigoon
Alone forlost in paynful wildirnes
Alone withouten whom to make my mone
Alone my wrechid case forto redresse
Alone thus wandir y in heuynes
Alone so wo worth myn aventure
Alone to rage this thynkith me swetnes
Alone y lyue an ofcast creature.

Alone deth com take me here anoon
Alone that dost me dure so moche distres
Alone y lyue, my frendis alle ad foon
Alone to die thus in my lustynes
Alone most welcome deth to thi rudenes
Alone that worst kan pete lo mesure
Alone come on, y bide but thee dowtles
Alone y lyue an ofcast creature.

Alone of woo y haue take such excesse
Alone that phisik nys ther me to cure
Alone y lyue that willith it were lesse
Alone y lyue an of cast creature."

[*U. S. Harley 682,* f. 40]

135 On p. 261 of the same collection is another *ballade* that employs the same device.

136 K. Bartsch, *Chréstomathie de l'Ancien Français* (Leipzig, 1884), p. 439.

In Skeat's collection of pseudo-Chaucerian pieces, there are four orthodox *ballades,* not counting the Lydgate *Flour of Courtesye* example. They are a triple *ballade*[137] and the *Envoy to Alison.*[138] The latter has three seven-line stanzas riming a b a b b c c, and a six-line envoy riming a b a b c c. The acrostic in the envoy was first pointed out by Lidell.[139] The refrain is the same in all three stanzas:

"For of al goode she is the best livinge,"

And this refrain is substantially the same in the envoy, where "Now" is substituted, for obvious reasons, for the initial "For." Poetically it is very poor stuff.[140] In 1801, Wordsworth modernized this *ballade,* first called the *Envoy to Alison* by Skeat, in connection with his rendering of the *Cuckoo and the Nightingale.* Part of it is as follows:

"Unlearned Book and rude, as well I know,
For beauty thou hast none, nor eloquence,
Who did on thee the hardinesse bestow

137 W. W. Skeat, *Chaucerian and Other Pieces* (Oxford, 1897), Vol. VII, p. 405. Printed by Thynne as "A goodly balade of Chaucer."

138 W. W. Skeat, *Opus Cit.,* Vol. VI, p. 358. In Bodleian *MS. Fairfax 16,* the *Envoy to Alison* follows the *Book of the Duchess* without a break; in Bodleian *MS. Tanner 346,* the *Alison* follows the *Cuckoo and the Nightingale.*

139 "A urore of gladnesse, and day of lustinesse,
L ucerne a-night, with hevenly influence
I llumined, rote of beautee and goodnesse,
S uspiries which I effunde in silence,
O f grace I beseche, alegge let your wrytinge,
N ow of al goode sith ye be best livinge."

Cf. *Academy,* 1896, II, p. 116.

140 W. W. Skeat, *Opus Cit.,* Vol. VII, p. lxii: "My chief object in reprinting it is to shew how unworthy it is of Clanvowe, not to mention Chaucer. We have no right even to assign it to Lydgate. And its date may be later than 1450."

To appear before my Lady? but a sense
Thou surely hast of her benevolence,
Whereof her hourly bearing proof doth give;
For of all good she is the best alive."

. . . .

L'Envoy

"Pleasure's Aurora, Day of gladsomeness!
Luna by night, with heavenly influence
Illumined! root of beauty and goodness,
Write, and allay, by your beneficence,
My sighs breathed forth in silence,—comfort give!
Since of all good, you are the best alive."[141]

Wordsworth's rendering of the envoy is certainly an improvement on the original, but the poem, whether in fifteenth century or nineteenth century guise, is wordy and lacks the grace characteristic of the *ballade* at its best.

Skeat prints as "manifestly Lydgate's" the triple *ballade* which Professor MacCracken does not include in the latest Lydgate Canon. This "goodly balade" resembles Chaucer's *Fortune* and his *Compleynt of Venus* in form. The first poem of the trio is made up of three seven-line stanzas riming a b a b b c c, with a refrain at the end of the stanzas. The second obviously is short one stanza, as it must have been in the manuscript from which Thynne printed. The two seven-line stanzas rime a b a b b c c. The refrain of the first stanza is, "Than closen ye, my lyves lady dere!"; of the secand stanza, "Disclose and sprede my lyves lady dere!" The third *ballade* has three seven-line stanzas riming a b a b b c c, with a refrain. Each of the three has its own system of rimes and at the end there is an envoy of eight lines, riming b d b d d e d e, that serves as general envoy.

141 *Complete Poetical Works of William Wordsworth* (London, 1899), p. 165.

This triple *ballade* addresses itself to a Margaret, and exhibits characteristics of that daisy cult practised first in France and later in England. To quote Lounsbury: "It reads like a translation from the French."[142] Skeat believes that the sixth stanza probably began with the letter D; in this case the initial letters of the stanzas would be M, M, M; D, D, D; J, C, Q. "And as it was evidently addressed to a lady named Margaret, we seem to see here, Margaret, Dame Jacques."[143]

The poem called by Speght in his 1598 edition *Chaucer's Dreame* and in his 1602 print *The Ile of Ladies*[144] has for its envoy four stanzas, the first of which is unconnected with what follows. The last three are seven-line stanzas riming a b a b b c c, with different rimes in every stanza and with a refrain. The poet of the *Ile of Ladies* must have been familiar with the French and the Middle English custom of using the *ballade* as an envoy to a longer poem, but he is following the custom here without adhering to the strict form of the *ballade.* In subject matter, as may be seen, this envoy departs in no way from the conventional presentation of the period.

> "Ffayrest of fayer, and goodleste on lyve,
> all my secre to you I playne *and* shreve,
> requiringe grace and of all my complainte,
> to be heled or martered as a saynt,
> Ffor by my trothe I swere, and by this booke,
> Ye may bothe hele and slaye me w*i*th a looke.

142 T. R. Lounsbury, *Studies in Chaucer* (New York, 1892), Vol. I, p. 479.

143 W. W. Skeat, *Chaucerian and Other Pieces* (Oxford, 1894), Vol. VII, p. xxi.

144 The *Ile of Ladies* is found in two MSS.: in British Museum *MS. Additional 10303* and in *MS. Longleat 256*, the latter in the library of the Marquis of Bath. In the reprint of the envoy *ballade,* I reproduce the text given in J. B. Sherzer's *The Ile of Ladies* (Berlin, 1903), p. 116.

Go forthe myn owne trew harte innocent,
and withe humblesse do thine obseruaunce,
And to thi lady on thi knes present
thi seruice new, and thinke how great pleasaunce
hit is to lyve vnder the obeysaunce
of her that may withe her[e] lookes softe
geve the the blisse that thou desyers ofte.

Be diligent, awacke, obye, and dread,
and not to wilde of thi countenaunce,
but meke and glade, and thi nature fead,
to do eche thinge that may here plesaunce,
when you shall slepe, haue ay in remembraunce
the image of her whiche may withe lookes softe
geve the the the blysse that thou desyers ofte.

And yf so be that thou her name fynde
writton in booke, or else vppon *a* wall,
looke that thou do, as servaunte trew *and* kynde,
thyne obeysaunce, as she were there withe all.
ffayninge in love is breading of a fall
from the grace of her, whose lookes softe
may geve the the blisse that thou desyers ofte.

Finis

Ye that this balad red shall,
I pray you kepe you from the fall."

The following envoy at the end of the *Court of Sapience,* spoken by Dame Clennesse and her friends, is like that in the *Ile of Ladies* in being a loose form of the *ballade* which performs a function usually fulfilled by the stricter form. Here too the rimes differ in every stanza. The lines at the close of each stanza are close enough in sense and in diction to be regarded as refrains.

"It better is to trowe in god aboue
Than in mankynde or in many other thynge

Who troweth in hym / for he can kepe and loue
Theyr lust fulfyll / & graunt them theyr askynge
And in his gospell eke a worthy kynge
He sayd hymselfe in me / who lust byleue
Though he be deed ywys yet shall he leue.

O cursed folke with your ydolatrye
Whiche in false goddes setten your delyte
Blynde dome / and deef is all your mametrye
Of stocke and stone / men may suche karue & thwyte
Leue them for false with sour and despyte
In our one god cast anker and byleue
Though ye were deed / he can make you leue.

He is all lyfe* whan your goddes be dede
They haue a tyme / and he is sempyterne
They are but erthe / and brought lowe as lede
He regneth god aboue the heuen superne
Blyssed be he / for he no grace wyll werne
To them that wyll in him beset theyr byleue
And though they dye ywys yet shall they lyue."[145]

A three-stanza poem with envoy occurs in the manuscript with the *Pricke of Conscience.*[146] The stanzas have a refrain, "Mesure is best of all*e* thynge," but no rimes in common. The envoy does not show the refrain. The poem as it stands here, however, seems to have been written with some reference, at least, to the *ballade* form. The stanzas rime a b a b b c b c, and the four-line envoy rimes across,

* The top line of the page has been partly cut off.

145 *The Courte of Sapyence* (printed by Winkyn de Worde in 1510), p. giii.

146 Printed in W. H. Hulme, The *Middle English Harrowing of Hell and Gospel of Nicodemus, Early English Text Society* (London, 1907), Extra Series 100, pp. xxx–xxxi. The editor says of *MS. Addit. 32578:* "There is no valid reason why we should not accept 1405 as the date of the *Pricke of Conscience* part of the MS. and the other portion cannot be much later." The poem in question closes the MS.

This poem, with the addition of the envoy, resembles the *ballade* as practised by the writers of the *Ile of Ladies* and the *Court of Sapience,* and all three show the gradations by which the *ballade* as a fixed form passed out of the artistic consciousness of the Middle English poet.

Side by side in the same manuscript[147] we have the *ballade* with refrain (and in two cases no common rimes running through the stanza), and the three-stanza poem with no token of the *ballade* about it except its three stanzas and the presence of certain ideas usually associated with the *ballade.* This group of poems[148] has recently been conjecturally identified as the work of the Duke of Suffolk, and a corollary to this identification has been the attribution of a little group of eleven English poems, hitherto unquestionably assigned to Charles d'Orléans, also to the Duke of Suffolk. This second identification came about through the presence in both the Bodleian *MS. Fairfax 16* and the *Bibliothèque Nationale MS. fr. 25485* of a *ballade* beginning, "O thou Fortune, whyche hast the gouernaunce." This *ballade* has a refrain and a fourth stanza of equal length (seven lines) with others, that serves as an envoy. The rimes are different in all four stanzas, and each one rimes a b a b b c c. The refrain reads, "Why wyltow not wythstand myn heuynesse?" Two other *ballades* occur in the same portion of the Oxford manuscript. The first of these has three seven-line stanzas, each with a separate system of rimes (a b a b b c c), and a refrain.[149]

The second of these *ballades,*[150] called in the MS. "A Compleynt," resembles in form the one just mentioned in hav-

[147] Bodleian *MS. Fairfax 16,* ff. 318–329.

[148] H. N. MacCracken, *An English Friend of Charles of Orléans, Publications of Modern Language Association,* XXVI, p. 142.

[149] H. N. MacCracken, *Opus Cit.,* p. 155.

[150] H. N. MacCracken, *Opus Cit.,* p. 166.

ing three stanzas, a refrain, and no envoy, but conforms to the strict *ballade* form in maintaining throughout its three eight-line stanzas a common rime-scheme (a b a b b c b c). The refrain, "Thus to endure yt is a wondir thyng," is repeated without modifications. The most significant feature of this *balade compleynt* is the reference in the third stanza to the color blue as the color of steadfastness, an association of ideas that we have found in *ballades* by Machaut, by Chaucer, and by the translator of the Charles d'Orléans poems. The stanza tells how after having consorted in "a goodly playn" with "othir fair peple," in an effort to gain relief from love, the lover gives up the quest and returns home:

> " And vpon thys I t*ur*nyd hom agayn,
> Vn-to myn hert wyth visage pale of hewe.
> ' I trow,' q*u*od he, ' thy labour ys in vayn:'
> And I answerd that I non othir knewe,—
> ' Lo, yit,' ' quod he, ' my colour shal be blewe,
> That folke may know of my stedfast lyuying.'
> But for to thynke how my sorous renewe,
> Thus to endure yt is a wondir thyng."[151]

In the same series of poems attributed to the Duke of Suffolk are seven three-stanza and three four-stanza poems that were plainly written as modified *ballades*.[152] The three four-stanza poems have no rime-scheme common to their stanzas and no refrain, and their fourth stanza is in the nature of an envoy. In one of them the fourth stanza quoted below gives confirmation to our theory that the implied (or as in this case expressed) intention of the poet

151 H. N. MacCracken, *Opus Cit.*, p. 166.

152 Two of these loose *ballades* are cast in the letter form used by Gower occasionally in his *Cinkante Balades* and by numerous French writers. They are printed by H. N. MacCracken, *Opus Cit.*, p. 165; p. 167.

guides us in the classification of the Middle English lyric:[153, 154 and 155]

> "Go forth, balade, and I shall give yow wage;
> To her that ys my lady and maistresse
> Be not a-ferde, but sey her thy message,
> Me recomaundyng to her hye noblesse,
> Lettyng her wyt, in verey sothfastnesse,
> I wyl be truly hers in eu*er*y place
> Besechyng her accept me to her grace."

MacCracken also printed as a poem "in Suffolk's manner," a *ballade*[156] presenting a new system of rimes in every stanza (a b a b b c c), but running a two-line refrain through all three stanzas:

> "Then torne thy whele, and be my frend agayn,
> And sende me Ioy wher*e* I am now in payn."

It is thus one of the many prayers to Fortune entrusted to the *ballade* form and contains one of the countless references to the Lady's indispensable wheel.[157]

As a prefix to the *Chaunce of the Dyse,* there occurs a three-stanza poem which the rubrics pronounce a *balade.* Here again the *intention* of the author is to be taken into consideration, for the poem is *ballade*-like only in the number of stanzas, the metrical scheme of each individual stanza, and in being used where the regular form would be employed. Earlier bibliographies[158] gave the *Chaunce of the*

[153, 154 and 155] H. N. MacCracken, *Opus Cit.,* p. 162.

[156] H. N. MacCracken, *Opus Cit.,* p. 180.

[157] A Fortune poem in British Museum *MS. Harley 682,* printed in Watson Taylor's edition on pp. 208 ff., contains another such reference. Cf. notes above on Chaucer's *Fortune.*

[158] Tanner, *Bibliotheca* (ed. 1748), pp. 489–493. *The Chaunce of the Dyse* is found in Bodleian *MS. Fairfax 16*; the three stanza poem referred to is on fol. 148^r.

Dyse to Lydgate, but its authorship still remains uncertain. This little prologue is printed as another telling piece of evidence of how easily the Middle English poet slipped out of the fixed form:

Balade vpon the chaunse of the dyse.

"First myn vnkunnynge and my rudenesse
Vnto yow alle that lysten knowe her chaunce
By caste of dyse in your hertys inpresse
And by goode wille to doon folles plesaunce
All be I haue of wytte no suffisaunce
This worldes course I haue herd sey ful ryve
Ys that alle folle shal not at ones thryve.

I pray to god that eu*er*y wight may caste
Vpon three dyse ryght as is in hys herte
Whether he be rechlesse or stedfaste
So moote he laughen outher elles smerte
He that is gilty his lyfe to converte
They that in trouthe haue suffred many a throwe
Moote ther chaunce fal as they moote be knowe.

Syth fortune of alle thynge gou*er*naunce
How euer ys happe excused holdeth me
ffor neyther am I worthy to bere penaunce
Ne thanke truly in no maner degre
But natheles this wol I say for me
She that yow beste may helpen in this nede
Ryght wel to caste I pre fortune yow spede"

Explicit Balade vpon the chaunce of the dyse.[159]

In a sixteenth century manuscript occurs a *ballade* of the early fifteenth century.[160] The inclusion of a *ballade*

159 Bodleian *MS. Fairfax 16,* fol. 148r.

160 In British Museum *MS. Arundel 26.* Printed also by H. N. MacCracken in *An English Friend of Charles of Orleans,* and referred by him also to the Duke of Suffolk.

in a sixteenth century manuscript testifies to the fact that, although *ballades* had ceased to be written, their kind was still of a sufficient interest to be included in a miscellaneous volume[161] belonging to that antiquary of Henry VIII's time, Sir William Dethek. This *ballade,* with three eight-line stanzas riming a b a b b c b c, a refrain, and an envoy riming b c b c, is a satisfactory fifteenth century specimen of the form. Its honor roll of great ladies recalls inevitably similar poems by Deschamps, by Chaucer, and by their followers.

Balade coulourd and Reuersid

"hounour and beaute vertue and gentilnesse
noblesse and bounte of grete valure
ffygure playsant wt coulour and fresshenesse
witnesse prudent wt cōn̄yng and norture
humblesse wt contynance demure
plente of this haue ye lo souuerayn
expresse soo youe formyd hath nature
pyte savyng ye want no thyng certayne

Creature nōōn hath more goodlynesse
goodenesse grete so wred yow hath vre
ffeture and shap of faire lucresse
mekenesse of Tesbe as wide of all rigure
ffrendelynesse of mede port of geynure
pennolope of hestis true and playne
Alcesse of Bounte lo thus ar ye sure
pite savyng ye want no thyng certayn.

Endure me dothe lo payne and hevynesse
distresse and thought wt trouble and langour
vnsure stondyng of socour or relesse
maistres and lady trustyng you of cure

161 British Museum *MS. Arundel 26.* Transcribed by me before the appearance of MacCracken's version.

witnesse of God I gre myn auenture
parde is fall me what joy or payne
gladnesse or woo thus I you ensure
pyte savyng ye want no thyng certeyn

Prince I you beseche this rude meture
ye not disdayne behold wt them tweyn
witnesse thowe I doo in this scripture
pite savyng ye want no thyng certeyne."[162]

In two fifteenth century manuscripts,[163] is found what seems to be a triple *ballade,* with, in the case of the Cambridge MS., two stanzas lost, and in the case of the Oxford MS., only one gone. The seven stanzas in the Cambridge MS. were numbered from one to seven by Henry Bradshawe, who considered them one poem. The first three stanzas and the last four and envoy from the Cambridge MS. with the fifth stanza supplied from the Oxford MS., are given below. The stanza omitted in both MSS. should end with the refrain, "Of my desire that I may se ryghte noghte."

In what seems to have been a triple *ballade,* the first two stanzas are bound together by a refrain; the next three are grouped together by a common refrain, and so are the last three. The other structural features are plain:

" for lac of sight grete cause I haue to pleyn̄
longe absense so sore me werieyth
The thinge to se I may nought attayn̄
Which that myn hert most inwardely obeyth
And thus my spirite in my body dyeth
So am I dulleth by constreynt of my thoght
ffortunes whele so felly wyth me pleyt
Of my desires that I may se ryghte noghte

162 British Museum *MS. Arundel 26,* fol. 32^{v}.

163 Cambridge University Library *MS. Ff. 1. 6,* fol. 13^{a}–13^{b}, and Bodleian *MS. Tanner 346,* fol. 74^{v}–75^{r}.

I se castels I se eke high towres
Walles of stone crestyd and bataylled
Medes welles river sote flourys
And many paleys fressh aparayled
De vises new vn couthly entayled
Butte whyle I haue loked long and soghte
Disdeyn so thik his haburion hath mayled
Of my desires that I may se ryghte[164] noghte[165]

I see huntynge I se hornes blow
Houndes renne the dere drawe a doun
And atte her triste bowes set a row
Now in August this lusti fressh seson
The hert I chasyd the bere and the lion
Butte all this myrth vnto myn entent
May do non ese vnto myn opynyon̄
ffor cause onely my lady is absent

I here also the attricable sownes
of instrumentis in her armone
lusty trumpetes and lyght clarionne
harpes lutes make melody
ffleytes shalle that so loude crye
Almoste atteynynge to the firmament
But to my ese all this no remedye
Be cause onely my lady is absent

I here folkis talke of stories
Of princes noble and worthy conquer*our*s,
Of cheualrye of conquest of victories
Songes dites y made of p*ar*am*our*s
Som of somer som of wintrie showres
Som of Cupide how his bow hath bent
Butte to my sore all doth no socour*e*s
By cause my lady is absente

164 MS. ryth.
165 MS. nowthe.

I taste sugar I taste hony sote
I drynke wynes of Gascoyne and fraũnce
I take my parts of many holsom rote
Of fine spices full gret habundaunce
butte in all this I fynde no pleasaunc*e*
like as I wold to myn herte lyghte
ffor cause onely hertely suffisaunce
My souereyn lady so fer ys owte of sighte

I se sōme lagh for gladnesse
And also sōme joy and myrthe mak
And sōme sighen and wepp*e*n in distresse
Euen and morow for her lady sake
And all the nyght in compleynynge wake
Venus on hem hath made so f elle a feyghte
Amonges which I am caght and take
My lady is so fer oute of my sight

And somme I se wounded to the hert
Wt loues darte and dar not be a knowe
And othir eke felyn ful grete smerte
Cupike eke hem hath so merked wt his bow
That for distresse they courve wondir low
They be so feble for to stand uprighte
Amonge whiche I may goon on the row
My soueryn lady is so fer oute of my sighte

Princes of beaute myrrour of godely hede
When so be fall this dite that ye se
Disdeyneth not but of godeley hede
Haueth ther on mercy and pite."

A *ballade,* interesting because of its remotely possible reference to Katherine of Valois, wife of Henry V, is found in a fifteenth century manuscript. It is headed, "Balade fet de la Reygne Katerine Russell." On the last fly-leaf of the manuscript is a large drawing of a circular horse-mill and below it in very large letters the name Russell. It seems, therefore, quite likely that in one of the two places the scribe interchanged "R" and "B." I can see no reason for attaching the name "Russell" to Katherine of Valois; it seems more likely that the "Russell" or "Bussell" is the name either of the owner of the manuscript or of the author of the *ballade.* Some flourishes show faintly between "Katerine" and "Russell" which may stand for "par." Queen Katherine died in 1437; John Russell, author of the *Book of Nurture,* usher in chamber and marshal in hall to Humphrey, Duke of Gloucester, who flourished about 1450, may conceivably have written the *ballade.*[166, 167 and 168] The only other queen Katherine to whom the *ballade* might refer is Katherine of Aragon, but she could hardly be designated as of French descent. Henry VIII's first Katherine was an auburn haired Spaniard, however, to whom the adjective "russel," referring to coloring, might be appropriate.[169] There is a third possibility; it is not wholly improbable that a lady is here addressed who was a temporary queen on the occasion of some festival.

Balade fet de la Reygne Katerine Russell

Slombrying ryhgt choncefull ful of vnykyndenes
That now haþe reyne &| dominacyun
Me thought y saw bunte & gentillesse
Ordene solempnely a conuocacion
Of the most noble of al ther nacion
Causys rygt notable to avyse & se
Weche lamantyng sayde in ther concluoon
Adew the curt rygt gentyl large & fre

166, 167 and 168 *Dictionary of National Biography.*

169 Godefroy does not give the word in this sense.

Ryhgt gentyl we may wel sey and expresse
ffor theyr strangers hadde consolacyun
ffurst of here that wasse sovereyn maystresse
And after of here everyche in comune
Wurchyp gode rule trowthe prudense & renoun
Supportyt thys curt weche sey now asse we
Euer sey & wiht whi owht afeccyon
Adew the cort ryhgt large gentyl & fre

Large in exspense hytt wasse dowhteles
for ther wasse neuer yet desolacyon
Scheuyd to astat neþ*er* more ne lasse
But al the gentylnese that myhgt be don
Al so largely they hedde ther gerdoun
That thedur senyd for answere or decre
Adew the curt ryhgt gentyl large gentyl & fre

ffre to furþ*er* euery man with fayrenes
Euer wasse thys curt the weche by owre reson
We calle Katheryne the exelent pryncesse
Quene of Engelond by generacyon
Of kyngys of fraunse dyssendyt down
Whos hey nobeles in euery cuntrey
Adew the curt right gentyl large & fre.[170]

Two other manuscripts have been noted by former writers as being rich in *ballades.* Gleeson White in a popular introduction to his delightful collection of *Ballades and Rondeaus,* stated that "John Shirley, who lived about 1440, made a collection of *Ballades, Roundels, Virelais* and *Tragedies* in MSS., which are still extant in the Ashmolean Museum at Oxford."[171] There is only one Ashmole MS. written by Shirley, and in it occurs:

170 Trinity College, Cambridge *MS. R. 14. 51,* fol. 95. Note the French trick of having some word in the last line of a stanza appear in the first line of the following stanza.

171 Gleeson White, *Ballades and Rondeaus* (London, 1887), p. xxiv.

"Here begynne þe [þe] boke cleped þe Abstracte Brevyayre compyled of divers *balades,* roundels, virilayes, tragedyes, envoyes, compleynts, moralities, storyes, practysed and eke devysed and ymagyned, as it shewe þe here folowyig."[172]

This heading was plainly responsible for Gleeson White's belief that this *Ashmole MS.* is full of *ballades.* There are in reality no *ballades* at all in it.[173] Of the nineteen items called *balades* or spoken of as being written in '*balade wyse,*' one shows a six-line stanza, nine a seven-line stanza, and nine an eight-line stanza.

Another exaggeration of the wealth of *ballade* material still in manuscript is found in the *Cambridge History of English Literature,* where Padelford, who has just been discussing the use of this French verse form in Middle English, remarks in a footnote, "*MS. Rawlinson C 813* contains a large number of the *ballades.*" But Padelford's own work on this manuscript[174] confirmed the results of my examination, which revealed no *ballades.* A later student of the same manuscript says:

"Die Form der Ballade findet sich nirgends streng befolgt; bei manchen (44, 45, 48), die der Gebrauch des Refrains noch deutlich hierherstellt, ist nur ein teil der Strophen durch die Wiederannahme des Reims verbunden."[175]

The life of the *ballade* in Middle English is probably less than one hundred years, extending as it does from the last twenty years of the fourteenth century, when Chaucer was

172 Fol. 13.

173 E. P. Hammond, *Ashmole 59 and Other Shirley Manuscripts, Anglia,* XXX, p. 320.

174 F. M. Padelford, *The Songs in MS. Rawlinson, C 813, Anglia,* XXXI, p. 309.

175 Wilhelm Bolle, *Zu Lyrik der Rawlinson MS. C 813, Anglia,* XXXIV, p. 281.

making first trials, to not later than the seventies of the following century. The courtly makers of the reigns of the Early Tudors were not *ballade* writers. Wyatt had the *rondeau*[176] to his credit but not a *ballade*. The following poem of his by virtue of its three-stanza form and its refrain suggests what is most natural, however, that he was familiar with the *ballade* form:

"The restfull place, revyver of my smarte;
the labor's salve, incressyng my sorrow;
the body's ese, and trobler off my hart;
quieter of mynd, and my vnquyet foe;
fforgetter of payn, remembryng my woo;
the place of slepe, wherein I do but wake;
be sprent *with* ter*es*, my bed, I the forsake.

The frost, the snow, may not redresse my hete,
nor yet no heate abate my fervent cold;
I know nothyng to ese my payn*es* mete.
Eche care cawsythe increse by XXty fold,
revyvyng carys vpon my sorrows old.
Suche overthwart affect*es* they do me make,
by sprent *with* terys, my bed for to forsake.

Yet helpythe yt not: I fynd no better ese
in bed, or owt. Thys moste cawsythe my payn:
where most I seke how beste that I may plese,
my lost labor, alas! ys all in vayn;
yet that I gave, I cannot call a gayn.
No place fro me my greffe away can take;
Wher for *with* terys, my bed, I the forsake."[177]

Probably the last vestige of specific *ballade* influence is seen in the work of Gascoigne who professes,

"Yn barreyne verse, to doe the best I can
Lyke *Chaucers* boye, and Petrarks journeyman,"

176 F. M. Padelford, *Early Sixteenth Century Lyrics* (New York, 1907), p. xliv.

177 F. M. Padelford, *Opus Cit.*, p. 19.

and further proclaims,

> "But is some Englische woorde herein seme sweet,
> Let *Chaucers* name exalted be therefore."[178]

As a preface to the *Grief of Joy* (1576) Gascoigne uses the following poem that certainly is reminiscent of the *ballade* form. Its stanza is constructed in conformity to the formula given in the same author's *Notes of Instruction:*

The Preface.

"Mount mynd & muze, you come before a *Queene*
before a *Queene,* whose Bewtye skornes compare /
for yett on earth hath selde (or nott) bene seene,
A *Queene* so fraught with gyfts & graces rare
then (that your words her worthy wyll may pearce)
mount mynd and muze, the *Queene* shall reade yr verse.

And in your verse, be bolld to tell her playne,
that in my lyfe (one onely Joye except)
I never fownd delight that could remayne,
styll permanent / nor free from dole be kept
A thousand Joyes, my Jollye youth hath tryed
Yett none but one, could styll with me abyde.

One sweete ther ys, which never yett seemd sowre
one Joye of Joyes, whom never gryef disgraste,
one worlde of myrth, withowt one mowrnfull howre
one happy thoughte, which (yett) no dowbt defast
what is ytt? speake! (my mynde & muze) be bolld
ytt is butt this: my *Queene* for to behold.

L'Envoie

Queene by your leave, hath bene (yn olden dayes)
A pretye playe / whereyn the prynce gave chardge,
(So that the pale, were styll kept hole allwayes)
to take the best, and leave the rest att large. /

178 F. M. Padelford, *Opus Cit.,* p. 19.

Queene by your leave: my muze the best hath fownde,
And yett I hope, the pale ys safe and sownde. / "[179]

Two other poems of Gascoigne's show his consciousness of the *ballade* form. In *Hearbes* we find, "In that other ende of his sayde close walks were written these toyes in ryme." The "toyes in ryme" are three six-line stanzas with refrain (but no rimes in common).[180] The third of the five six-line stanzas of *The Shield of Love*[181] (each one riming a b a b c c), suggests certainly the *ballade* stock of ideas.

> "In colder cares are my conceipts consumd,
> Than *Dido* felt when false *Æneas* fled;
> In farre more heat, than trusty Troylus fumde,
> When craftie Cressyde dwelt with *Diomed:*
> My hope such frost, my hot desire such flame
> That I both fryse and smoulder in the same."

VI. The Ballade in Scotland

That there were a number of *ballades* composed in Middle Scots seems likely,[182] although only three examples of the form in that dialect seem to have been printed. And of the three, only one, *The Ballad of Good Counsel*, exhibits the conventional structure. Skeat has devised this title because the Scots poem "is an obvious imitation of the 'Ballad of Good Counsel' by Chaucer which begins, 'Fle fro the presse and dwel with sothfastnesse.' "[183] Both of these consist of three seven-line stanzas.

179 J. W. Cunliffe, *The Glasse of Government and Other Works* (Cambridge, 1910), p. 516.

180 J. W. Cunliffe, *Gascoigne's The Posies* (Cambridge, 1907), p. 353.

181 J. W. Cunliffe, *Opus Cit.*, p. 340.

182 The present author looks forward to investigating the manuscript collections in the various Scottish libraries.

183 W. W. Skeat, *Kingis Quair* (London, 1884), p. 94.

"Sen throw Vertew incressis dignitie,
And vertew is flour and rute of Noblesse ay,
Of ony wit, or quhat estait thow be,
His steppis follow, and dreid for none effray:
Eject vice, and follow treuth alway:
Lufe maist thy God that first thy lufe began,
And for ilk inche he will the quyte ane span.

Be not ouir proude in thy prosperitie,
For as it cummis, sa will it pas away;
The tyme to compt is schort, thow may weill se,
For of grene gress sone cummis wallowit hay.
Labour in treuth, quhilk suith is of thy fay;
Traist maist in God, for he best gyde the can,
And for ilk inche he will the quyte ane span.

Sen word is thrall, and thocht is only fre,
Thou dant thy toung, that power hes and may,
Thou steik thy ene fra warldis vanitie:
Refraine thy lust and harkin quhat I say:
Graip or thow slyde, and keip furth the hie way,
Thow hald the fast upon thy God and man,
And for ilk inche he will the quyte ane span."[184]

The three stanza poem in the *Palice of Honour* was, as its refrain implies, probably intended by Douglas for a *ballade.* The *is* rime appears in both the second and third stanzas.

"And not but caus my spreitis wer abaisit
All solitair in that desert arraisit.
Allace I said in name vther remeid.
Cruell Fortoun quhy hes thow me betraisit?
Quhy hes thow thus my fatall end compassit?
Allace, allace sall I thus sone be deid
In this desert, and wait nane vther reid.
Bot be deuoirit with sum beest Rauenous
I weip, I waill, I plene, I cry, I pleid
Inconstant world and quheill contrarious.

184 W. W. Skeat, *Opus Cit.*, p. 54.

Thy transitorie plesance quhat auaillis?
Now thair, now heir, now hie and now deuaillis
Now to, now fra, now law, now Magnifyis
Now hait, now cald, now lauchis, now beuaillis
Now seik, now haill, now werie, now not aillis,
Now gude, now euill, now weitis, and now dryis
Now thow promittis, and richt now thow denyis
Now wo, now weill, now firme, now friuolous,
Now gam, now gram, now lowis, now defyis,
Inconstant world and quheill contrarious

Ha quha suld have affyance in thy blis?
Ha quha suld have firme esperance in this?
Quhilk is allace se freuch and variant.
Certes nane, sum hes, no wicht? surelie ʒis
Than hes my self bene gyltie: ʒe: I wis
Thairfoir allace sall danger thus me dant?
Quhidder is becum sa sone this duillie hant?
And Ver translait in winter furious?
Thus I beuaill my faites repugnant.
Inconstant world and quheill contrarious."[185]

Another poem, the author of which is unknown, suggests by reason of its three stanzas and refrain the French fixed verse form:

"When Flora had o'erfret the firth,
In May of every moneth queen;
When merle and mavis sings with mirth,
Sweet melling in the schawës sheen;
When all lovers rejoicéd been
And most desirous of their prey;
I heard a lusty lover mene:—
'I love but I dare nocht assay.'

'Strong are the pains I daily prove,
But yet with patience I sustene

185 Gawyn Douglas, *The Palice of Honour* (Edinburgh, 1827), pp. 2–3.

I am so fettered with the love
Only of my lady sheen,
Whilk for her beauty might be queen
Nature so craftily alway
Has done depaint that sweet serene!—
Whom I love I dare nocht assay.

'She is so bright of hyd and hue
I love but her alone, I ween;
Is none her love that may eschew,
That blinkis of that dulce amene;
So comely clear are her twa een,
That she mae lovers does affrae
Than ever of Greece did fair Helene!—
Whom I love I dare nocht assay.' "[186]

Conclusion

The chronology of the *ballade* in Middle English literature is difficult to determine. There were probably experiments with the form before Chaucer. And it may well have been in use also at the very end of the fifteenth and the beginning of the sixteenth century. There are few names connected with its history: with Chaucer, Lydgate, and Quixley the tale is told. Chaucer's *ballades* stand out as superior to all in poetic quality, though even their merit is uneven. Lydgate's adaptation of the form to the purposes of religion did not produce a *ballade* worthy to be compared to Villon's prayer. As for the translations from the French of Charles d'Orléans, they retain only in a measure whatever glamour is possessed by the originals.

That a student of fifteenth century writers finds much

[186] W. E. Henley, *English Lyrics* (London, 1897), p. 25. Henley said of the poem (*Opus Cit.*, p. 376): "Preserved in the *Bannatyne Ms.* (Pt. V. no. cxcii in the Hunterian Club's impression), it was transcribed by Ramsay for *The Ever Green* and there may well have given Burns a hint for the metrical structure of *Mary Morrison.*"

that is curious rather than beautiful has long been a commonplace of literary criticism. The *ballade* of that century is no exception; it, too, is for the most part curious rather than beautiful. The discursiveness of the age, the tendency then prevalent to compose prolonged verse narratives, the scarcity of rime words in Middle English,—all these circumstances were obstacles to the further development of the *ballade*. Though it is probably true that the stanzaic structure of both English and Scottish poetry was modified by the various types of French *ballade* stanzas, the form itself languished in England for about three hundred years. After Chaucer, for that matter, the *ballade* was not conspicuously successful until the days of Swinburne, Andrew Lang, Austin Dobson, and Edmund Gosse.

CHAPTER V

THE BALLADE IN THE NINETEENTH CENTURY

The *ballade,* neglected in France for a hundred and fifty years or more, was revived there in the late fifties of the last century. Shortly afterward, in England and in America, the same verse form was widely adopted both by poets and by poetasters. Its reappearance in English literature, after the lapse of four centuries, was due obviously to the close intellectual relations existing between France and England during the past century. At its second coming to England, it found a much more general recognition than it had in the age of Chaucer. In fact, a group of mid-Victorian poets produced such successful examples of the form that their contemporaries were also moved to write *ballades.* And in this way English letters came again into this charming legacy from medieval France.

The revival of the *ballade* is a phase of the so-called Romanticism which expressed itself variously in nineteenth century French literature.[1] The poetic sons of Victor Hugo, far from slavishly following his type of revolt, appear to have prided themselves generally on the "dissidence of their dissent." Sainte-Beuve is generally credited with having reintroduced the *ballade* into France.[2]

[1] Théophile Gautier, in *Les Grotesques,* devotes some pages to Villon; Villon's place in *Les Grotesques* undoubtedly foreshadows the revival of the *ballade.* (In the article in the *Encyclopædia Britannica* on Gautier, the date of the first edition of *Les Grotesques* is given as 1844.)

[2] E. Gosse, *A Plea for Certain Exotic Forms of Verse, Cornhill Magazine* (1877), p. 67.

Two stanzas indeed of a *Ballade du Vieux Temps* are included in his collected poems:

> "A qui mettait tout dans l'amour,
> Quand l'amour lui-même décline,
> Il est une lente ruine,
> Un deuil amer et sans retour,
> L'automne traînant s'achemine;
> Chaque hiver s'allonge d'un tour;
> En vain le printemps s'illumine;
> Sa lumière n'est plus divine
> A qui mettait tout dans l'amour!
>
> En vain la Beauté sur sa tour,
> Où fleurit en bas l'aubépine,
> Moulte avec l'aurore et fascine
> Le regard qui rôde à l'entour.
> En vain sur l'écume marine
> De jour encore sourit Cyprine:
> Ah! quand ce n'est plus que de jour,
> Sa grâce elle-même est chagrine
> A qui mettait tout dans l'amour!"[3]

It was, in particular, Théodore de Banville (1820–1891), who, in his conscious desire to introduce unusual and intricate rime combinations into French poetry once more, returned to the native fixed forms and especially to the *ballade*. A survey of the generation which revived the *ballade* leads to the conclusion that Banville is by far the most significant figure so far as this form goes. Glatigny, Coppée, Rollinat, Jean Richepin, Rostand, Bergerat, Tailhade, and others,[4] followed his direction; but his work was admittedly the most influential.

[3] C. Sainte-Beuve, *Poésies Complètes* (Paris, 1879), p. 350.

[4] Other nineteenth century Frenchmen who have used the *ballade* are Raoul Ponchon, Paul Verlaine, Maurice Boucher. It is not, of course, the purpose of the present writer to discuss *all* the *ballades* written at any given time in either France or England.

In the *dizain,* addressed to the reader, which is prefixed to Banville's *Trente-six Ballades Joyeuses,* he refers to Villon:

> "Comme Villon qui polit sa Ballade
> Au temps jadis, pour charmer ton souci
> J'ai façonné la mienne, et la voici";

and again, at the close of the same collection, there occurs an enthusiastic defense of the poet vagabond. If, ingeniously writes Banville, Villon is to be classed with thieves, he must rank at least, because of the nature of his theft, with Prometheus, who filched divine fire. As this prologue and epilogue indicate, it was clearly Villon from whom Banville learned the gracious art of the *ballade.* Similarly, the English poets, once they became interested in the old French form, studied Villon.

Whatever the source of Banville's inspiration, his technique became remarkably effective. It is his technique to which critics call our attention with favorable or unfavorable comment. Dowden said of him, some years ago, that he "taught modern poets to unite lyrical impulse with the most delicate technical skill."[5] On the other hand, one of the latest historians of French literature takes pleasure in recalling the epithet by which a French critic distinguished Banville, "cuisinier poétique,"[6] and adds that Banville was the author of "poetry in which the Romanticist's fondness for rhyme has become the writer's chief cult, so that he is always endeavoring to surmount some obstacle of verse, and the effect is often that produced by an acrobat who has

[5] E. Dowden, *On Some French Writers of Verse, Cornhill Magazine* (1877), p. 294.

[6] C. H. C. Wright, *A History of French Literature* (New York and London, 1912), p. 791.

just performed a difficult task.''[7] Andrew Lang, less severe, said of him in general, ''he is careful of form rather than abundant in manner.''[8] But of the *Trente-six Ballades Joyeuses*,[9] Lang wrote, ''There is scarcely a more delightful little volume in the French language than this collection of verses in the most difficult of forms, which pour forth with absolute ease and fluency, notes of mirth, banter, joy in the spring, in letters, art, and good fellowship.

'L'oiselet retourne aux forêts;
Je suis un poëte lyrique,—'

he cries with a note like a bird's song.''[10]

And Stevenson, with equal enthusiasm, declared, '' When De Banville revives a forgotten form of verse—and he has already had the honor of reviving the ballade—he does it in the spirit of the workman choosing a good tool wherever he can find one, and not at all in that of the dilettante, who seeks to renew bygone forms of thought and make historic forgeries. . . . De Banville's poems are full of color; they smack racily of modern life.''[11]

Banville's *ballades* justify these generous appreciations, whatever charge of poetic trickery may be lodged against his other verse. His early *Ballade des Célébrités du Temps*

[7] *Ibid.* Cf. also Jules Lemaître, *Les Contemporains* (Paris, 1890), p. 7: ''M. Théodore de Banville est un poète lyrique hypnotisé par la rime, le dernier venu, le plus amusé et dans ses bon jours le plus amusant des romantiques, un clown en poésie qui a eu dans sa vie plusieurs idées, dont la plus persistante a été de n'exprimer aucune idée dans ses vers.''

[8] Andrew Lang, *Théodore de Banville, Essays in Little* (New York, 1891), p. 65.

[9] Composed between 1861 and 1869.

[10] Andrew Lang, *Opus Cit.*, p. 65.

[11] R. L. Stevenson, *Charles of Orleans, Familiar Studies of Men and Books* (New York, 1900), p. 273.

Jadis,[12] a parody of Villon's masterpiece, is a satire concerned with the literati of the day. Banville says in his notes, "J'ai conservé tel qu'il est le célèbre refrain de Villon: *Mais où sont les neiges d'antan!* et j'ai tâché de mettre mon art à amener ce refrain par un jeu de rimes tout différent de celui que le maître avait employé."[13] Of the same year, and included, too, in the *Odes Funambulesques,* is the *Ballade des Travers de ce Temps,*[14] which deals, also in a satirical vein, with the literary notables of the day. His *Ballade de la Vraie Sagesse*[15] begins thus:

> "Mon bon ami, poëte aux longs cheveux,
> Joueur de flûte à l'humeur vagabonde,
> Pour l'an qui vient je t'addresse mes vœux:
> Enivre-toi, dans une paix profonde,
> Du vin sanglant et de la beauté blonde.
> Comme à Noël, pour faire réveillon
> Près du foyer en flamme, où le grillon
> Chant à mi-voix pour charmer ta paresse,
> Toi, vieux Gaulois et fils du bon Villon,
> Vide ton verre et baise ta maîtresse."

Of the *Trente-six Ballades Joyeuses,*[16] at least twelve are similar in tone. These seem for the most part to have been undertaken to show how certain conventional themes might be shaped in the newly revived form. There is, for example, a *Ballade des Belles Châlonnaises,* the first stanza of which runs:

> "Pour boire j'aime un compagnon,
> J'aime une franche gaillardise,

[12] Théodore de Banville, *Odes Funambulesques* (Paris, no date), p. 254. The *ballades* in this collection are dated 1856.

[13] *Ibid.,* p. 380.

[14] *Ibid.,* p. 260.

[15] *Ibid.,* p. 284.

[16] Cf. A. T. Strong, *The Ballades of Théodore de Banville* (London, 1913).

J'aime un broc de vin bourguignon,
J'aime de l'or dans ma valise,
Jaime un verre fait à Venise,
J'aime parfois les violons,
Et sourtout, pour faire à ma guise,
J'aime les filles de Châlons."[17]

Then, there is the *Ballade pour les Parisiennes,* in which throughout "la femme" is confidently stated to be "un article de Paris."[18] A more formal style is indicated by the refrain, "Le plus subtil ouvrier, c'est Amour."[19] *Pour la Servante du Cabaret,*[20] with its refrain, "Vive Margot, avec sa jupe rouge," is reminiscent in its abandon of several of the more reckless of Villon's *ballades.*

Six of the collection refer to Banville's notions about poets and poetry. He expresses regret for the men of 1830,[21] and addresses "Victor Hugo, père de tous les rimeurs."[22] He says in one of this group, "Pourquoi je vis? Pour l'amour du laurier."[23] In still another *ballade,* he apostrophizes himself:

"Assembleur de rimes, Banville,
C'est bien que les chardonnerets
Chantent dans les bois de Chaville;
Mais veux-tu chez les Turcarets
Emplir ton coffre et tes coffrets?
Plante là ton rêve féerique

[17] Théodore de Banville, *Trente-six Ballades Joyeuses* (Paris, 1890), p. 199.

[18] *Ibid.,* p. 238. Cf. Villon's refrain, "Il n'est bon bec que de Paris."

[19] *Ibid.,* p. 251.

[20] *Ibid.,* p. 221.

[21] *Ibid.,* p. 197.

[22] *Ibid.,* p. 255.

[23] *Ibid.,* p. 207.

C'est bien dit, mais je ne saurais,
Je suis un poëte lyrique."[24]

And the envoy of the same poem is an interesting example of literary self-portraiture:

"Prince, voilà tous mes secrets,
Je ne m'intends qu'à la métrique;
Fils du dieu qui lance des traits,
Je suis un poëte lyrique."[25]

The *Ballade à la Sainte Vierge* is confessedly an echo of Villon, as the first stanza testifies:

"Vierge Marie! Après ce bon rimeur
François Villon, qui sut prier et croire,
Et qui jadis, malgré sa folle humeur,
Fit sa ballade immortelle à ta gloire,
Je chanterai ton règne et ta victoire.
Ton diadème éclate avec fierté
Et sur ton front il rayonne, enchanté.
Milles astres d'or frissonnent sur tes voiles.
Tu resplendis, ô Lys de pureté,
Dame des Cieux, dans l'azur plein d'étoiles."[26]

Banville's little play *Gringoire*[27] introduces two *ballades*. The hero, Pierre Gringoire,[28] is plainly modeled on the lines of Banville's predecessor, Villon. Banville makes his poet hero compose for King Louis a *Ballade des Pendus* as well as a *Ballade des Pauvres Gens*. The title of the former suggests Villon's well known epitaph, but is in reality very different, as the third stanza and envoy demonstrate:

24 *Ibid.*, p. 249.
25 *Ibid.*, p. 250.
26 *Ibid.*, p. 267.
27 Written 1866.
28 The spelling Gringore seems now to be preferred.

"Ces pendus, au diable entendus,
Appellent des pendus encore.
Tandis qu'aux cieux, d'azur tendus,
Où semble luire météore,
La rosée en l'air s'évapore,
Un essaim d'oiseaux réjouis
Par-dessus leur tête picore,
C'est le verger du roi Louis.

Envoi

Prince, il est un bois que décore
Un tas de pendus enfouis
Dans le doux feuillage sonore,
C'est le verger du roi Louis."[29]

Indeed, the spirit of Villon is more evident in the first stanza of the "ballade des pauvres gens":

"Rois, qui serez jugés à votre tour,
Songez à ceux qui n'ont ni sou ni maille,
Ayez pitié du peuple tout amour,
Bon pour fouiller le sol, bon pour la taille
Et la charrue, et bon pour la bataille.
Les malheureux sont damnés—c'est ainsi!—
Et leur fardeau n'est jamais adouci,
Les moins meurtris n'ont pas le nécessaire.
Le froid, la pluie et le soleil aussi,
Aux pauvres gens tout est peine et misère."[30]

As earlier writers of *ballades* had done, Banville published a treatise on poetics. In his *Petit Traitié de Poésie Française,*[31] he gives a whole chapter to "les poëmes traditionnels à forme fixe." According to his rules for the *ballade,* the line unit must consist invariably either of eight or

[29] Théodore de Banville, *Gringoire* (Paris, 1877), p. 53.
[30] Théodore de Banville, *Opus Cit.*, p. 53.
[31] First published in 1872.

of ten syllables and may be either a masculine or a feminine line. Banville decrees that the three stanzas must be composed of ten ten-syllable lines or of eight eight-syllable lines.[32] He makes no attempt to codify the numerous departures from this procedure in earlier French literature. Banville also describes the double *ballade*[33] with its six stanzas, a form which he used twice in his own *Trente-six Ballades Joyeuses.* In all his theoretical talk he makes it plain that it was interest in form that led to his revival of the *ballade* and similar pieces. It must have been his fondness for elaborate rime-schemes that made him see poetic possibilities in these types of old French verse.[34]

A pleasant interchange of *ballades* took place between François Coppée (1843–1908) and Banville. The *Ballade de François Coppée à son Maitre Théodore de Banville sur leur Commun Amour de la Poésie,* is in the vein of a disciple, as the envoy testifies:

> "O maître! ô toi que la Muse éternelle
> Sur le Parnasse a mis en sentinelle
> Et pour son preux entre tous sut choisir,
> Notre œuvre est bonne et nous croyons en elle:
> Faisons des vers pour rien, pour le plaisir!"[35]

And Banville responded cordially:

> "Aimons la Muse, en dépit des revers,
> Comme Rubens les déesses d'Anvers

32 Théodore de Banville, *Petit Traité de Poésie Française* (Paris, 1909), pp. 188–192.

33 Théodore de Banville, *Opus Cit.*, pp. 193–194.

34 Jules Lemaître, *Les Contemporains* (Paris, 1890), p. 16: "Du moment qu'il était né ou qu'il s'était fait servant de la rime et son homme-lige, il était inévitable qu'il nous rendît ces bagatelles compliquées d'une symétrie difficile, minutieuse et quelque peu enfantine et barbare, où la rime est en effet reine, maîtresse et génétrice."

35 François Coppée, *Poésies,* 1864–1887 (Paris, no date), p. 406.

Ou bien Néron sa maîtresse Poppée.
Pour elle encore j'ai la tête à l'envers,
Car tu dis bien, maître François Coppée!"[36]

Coppée's other *ballade, Pour Deux Dames Qui Sont Amies*,[37] is dedicated to two ladies whose charms bewildered the poet. It expresses in *ballade* form the amatory sentiment so characteristic of Coppée's other verse.

Albert Glatigny (1839–1873), Laurent Tailhade (1857–), and Emile Bergerat (1845–) have followed Banville. Glatigny has been described as "a travelling actor and extraordinary improvisor in the moods of Théodore de Banville,"[38] Tailhade as "a poet with some of the virtuosity of Banville combined with Gascon exuberance,"[39] and Bergerat labelled as "Banvillesque."[40] Both in France and in England Banville was beyond doubt the one man responsible for the renewed vogue of the *ballade*.

Glatigny, the vagabond poet of the nineteenth century, contributed to *Le Parnasse Contemporain*,[41] a *Ballade des Enfants Sans Souci*,[42] which is conceived in the same pathetic spirit in which Villon wrote of the life he led:

"Ils vont pieds nus, le plus souvent, l'hiver
Met à leurs doigts des mitaines d'onglée.
Le soir, hélas! ils soupent de grand air,
Et sur leurs fronts la bise echevelée
Gronde, pareille au bruit d'une mêlée.
A peine un peu leur sort est adouci

36 François Coppée, *Opus Cit.*, p. 407.

37 François Coppée, *Opus Cit.*, p. 421.

38 C. H. C. Wright, *A History of French Literature* (New York and London, 1912), p. 796.

39 *Ibid.*, p. 879.

40 *Ibid.*, p. 848.

41 1866.

42 Job-Lazare, *Albert Glatigny Sa Vie Son Œuvre* (Paris, 1878), p. 147.

Quand Avril fait la terre consolée.
Ayez pitié des Enfants sans souci.

Ils n'ont sur eux que le manteau du ver,
Quand les frissons de la voûte étoilée,
Font tressaillir et briller leur œil clair.
Par la montagne abrupte et la vallée,
Ils vont, ils vont! à leur troupe affolée
Chacun répond: 'Vous n'êtes pas d'ici,
Prenez ailleurs, oiseaux, votre volée.'
Ayez pitié des Enfants sans souci.

Un froid de mort fait dans leur pauvre chair
Glacer le sang, et leur veine est gelée.
Les cœurs pour eux se cuirassent de fer.
Le trépas vient. Ils vont sans mausolée
Pourrir au coin d'un champ ou d'une allée,
Et les corbeaux mangent leur corps transi
Que lavera la froide giboulée.
Ayez pitié des Enfants sans souci.

Envoi

Pour cette vie effroyable, filée
De mal, de peine, ils te disent: merci!
Muse, comme eux, avec eux exilée,
Ayez pitié des Enfants sans souci."

Laurent Tailhade's *Douze Ballades Familières pour Exaspérer le Mufle*[43] employ the form for ferocious satire.[44]

[43] Laurent Tailhade, *Au Pays du Mufle*, Preface d'Armand Silvestre (Paris, 1891).

[44] Cf. Silvestre (ibid., p. 11): "les ballades . . . sont parmi les plus parfaites que j'aie vues écrites, et dans le sentiment le plus raffiné d'un rythme, essentiellement française. Elles sont d'ailleurs d'une gaieté également féroce avec le cinglement en plus, à l'oreille, des assonances répétés. . . . Dans toutes le rire déchire la lèvre. On n'a jamais rien écrit de moins bon enfant. Autant de sang que de fiel, cependant, dans ces indignations,—il semble que, de ce stylet sans pitié qui déchire un peu à l'aventure peut-être, le poète se soit lui-même souvent égratigné."

Because of their coarseness, Rabelaisian in quality, they are unsuitable for quotation. Such titles as *De la Génération Artificielle,*[45] *Touchant L'Ignominie de la Classe Moyenne,*[46] *Confraternelle pour Servir à L'Histoire des Lettres Françaises,*[47] suggest, too mildly perhaps, some victims of the "stylet sans pitié." The last-named *ballade* contains a series of vicious attacks on contemporary French writers; happily Banville is not named.

A more urbane follower of Banville, Émile Bergerat, acknowledges his master in his *Ballade à Banville:*

> "Je te le dis, tel le pécheur au prêtre:
> Si j'étais riche,—et je sais pourquoi
> Point ne le suis, tant j'en vois d'autres l'être
> Qui ne l'ont point mérité plus que moi,—
> De tout le jour je ne ferais emploi,
> Habile ou non, bien portant ou malade,
> Qu'au jeu charmant dont tu fixes la loi;
> Il n'est plaisir qu'à baller la ballade.
>
> Travail français, dont Villon est le maître,
> Fait à la main en ces siècles de foi
> Où l'on prenait ou mot, voire à la lettre,
> L'honneur du verbe et la faveur du roi.
> Y triompher c'était vaincre au tournoi:
> Mais aujourd'hui quelle dégringolade!
> Ouvrer les vers c'est se parer pour soi;
> Il n'est plaisir qu'à baller la ballade.
>
> Dans notre état, heroïque peut-être,
> Rien ne se paie au prix de bon aloi;
> L'argent comptant est en boutons de guêtre
> Et nul, vivant, n'y gagne son convoi.
> Pour la critique, ô muses, c'est l'octroi

45 L. Tailhade, *Opus Cit.*, p. 17.
46 L. Tailhade, *Opus Cit.*, p. 19.
47 L. Tailhade, *Opus Cit.*, p. 37.

Qui juge au poids et juge à l'accolade
Et la sagesse est de se tenir coi.
Il n'est plaisir qu'à baller la ballade.

Envoi

Prince, et chez nous, Théodore, c'est toi,
Nous buvons tous l'encre à la régalade,
Le mal d'écrire en a tué l'effroi,
Il n'est plaisir qu'à baller la ballade."[48]

Bergerat is one of the most prolific of modern *ballade* writers. His themes are chiefly those of familiar verse. Possibly the most interesting from the standpoint of literary history is the *Ballade Cambogienne*, printed anonymously by *Comœdia*, which challenged its readers to guess the author. The first stanza reads thus:

"D'un gave—j'emprunte à Nisard
Ses périphrases gangrenées
De lieux communs—en saut d'isard.
Un bruit de rimes égrenées
Qui semblent du zéphyre nées
Sur le vent de l'arc qu'Eros tend
Nous arrive des Pyrénées:
C'est l'atelier d'Edmond Rostand."[49]

On the following day, Rostand himself sent to the same journal his solution, *Ballade sur une Ballade Anonyme*, the second stanza of which proclaims:

"Aussi vrai que d'Hermès naquit
Sa lyre, et de Pan la syringe,
Que le Hongrois boit du raki,

[48] Emile Bergerat, *Ballades et Sonnets* (Paris, 1910), p. 11. This *ballade* is one of three "en honneur de la bonne ballade française." This volume contains in all forty-four *ballades*.

[49] Émile Bergerat, *Opus Cit.*, p. 141.

Que le Chinois tresse la ginge,
Qu'il était en écus de singe
Le trésor qu'une Humbert géra,
Et que Mergy tua Comminge,
La ballade est de Bergerat."[50]

Another member of this second generation of Romanticists followed Banville in writing *ballades.* The decadent author of *Les Névroses,* Maurice Rollinat (1846–1903), includes twelve among this "wild collection of poems on disease and corruption." These twelve are in truth not unwholesome in tone. Only the *Ballade du Cadavre,* with its refrain, "La pourriture lente et l'ennui du squelette,"[51] is strikingly unpleasant. The *Ballade de l'Arc-en-ciel* has for its ingenious refrain the line, "Bleu, rouge, indigo, vert, violet, jaune, orange."[52] *De la Reine des Fourmis et du Roi des Cigales*[53] is a kind of allegory, not indeed as Deschamps used the *ballade* for conveying a fable, but in the same spirit as Brieux used the title *Hannetons* for a play in which the lovers treat each other with a cruelty comparable to that of their insect prototypes. The relations between the queen of the ants and the king of the grasshoppers are described by Rollinat in such a way as to suggest an idyllic human love. *De la Petite Rose et du Petit Bluet*[54] is a similarly conceived symbol of idyllic sentiment. In several of the other *ballades,* notably *Des Lézards Verts,* with its refrain, "Leurs petits flancs peureux qui tremblent au soleil,"[55] and *Du Chataignier Rond,* with its refrain, "Sous le chataignier rond dressé comme un fan-

[50] Émile Bergerat, *Opus Cit.,* p. 144.
[52] *Ibid.,* p. 128.
[51] Maurice Rollinat, *Les Névroses* (Paris, 1907), p. 377.
[53] *Ibid.,* p. 156.
[54] *Ibid.,* p. 178.
[55] *Ibid.,* p. 198.

tôme,''[56] Rollinat shows a less generalized and more intimate observation of nature. Wholly unlike his other *ballades* is *La Dame en Cire,* a distressing cry to a lay figure in wax to come to life:

> " O toi qui m'as si souvent visité,
> Satan! vieux roi de la perversité,
> Fais-moi la grâce, ô sulfureux Messire,
> Par un minuit lugubrement tinté,
> De voir entrer chez moi la dame en cire!"[57]

Rollinat generally used the *ballade* to express a reflective mood and once or twice to convey queer trifling. His *ballades,* if considered apart from his other poetry, would never impress one as the products of decadence. In form, they follow Banville's models closely. Rollinat could not, however, from his very nature, have made his *ballades* the delicious lighthearted lyrics that Banville's were.

Rostand's (1868–) three *ballades,* included in *Les Musardises,*[58] are the lightest of poetic trifles. There is the guileless *Ballade au Petit Bébé,* one stanza of which will show that the art of the author of *Cyrano* is not adapted, as was that of Blake and Christina Rossetti, to the interpretation of child life:

> " Après quoi, longuement, il bave.
> Et comme un objet inconnu
> Il contemple, rêveur et grave,
> Son pied dans ses deux mains tenu.
> Et, pris du désir saugrenu
> De sucer son bout de chausette
> Auquel il n'est pas parvenu,
> Le petit bébé fait risette."[59]

[56] *Ibid.,* p. 226.
[57] *Ibid.,* p. 329.
[58] Written 1887–1893.
[59] Edmond Rostand, *Les Musardises* (Paris, 1911), p. 85.

The *Ballade de la Nouvelle Année* is a half-serious appeal to the New Year to endow everyone with his particular heart's desire:

"Donne un papillon aux touffes de thym
Et des goélands au cap de la Hève;
Le touriste Anglais au Napolitain;
Au duc de Nemours Madame de Clève;
Au vieillard un songe, au jeune homme un rêve;
Donne un livre au sage, un tambour au fou,
Un élève au maître, un maître a l'élève . . .
Il faut à chacun donner son joujou."[60]

The *Ballade des Vers Qu'on ne Finit Jamais* is delicately expressed but perfectly superficial in emotion. The sentiment of the whole poem is plain from the envoy:

"Lecteur, je suis navré. Ces vers que je te livre
—Dont, peut-être on vendre le papier à la livre,—
Ne sont pas, il s'en faut, hélas! ceux que j'aimais.
Car les meilleurs, comment les mettre dans un livre?
Les meilleurs, sont les vers qu'on ne finit jamais."[61]

Jean Richepin's (1849–) *Ballade de Bonne Recompense* recalls the more sordid of Villon's genius:

"A qui, civil ou militaire,
A pied, même en aérostat,
Trouverait le mot du mystère
Par où mon être s'enchanta,
A qui m'appellerait bêta
De pleurer encor quand j'y pense,
A celui-là j'offre recta
Quarante sous de récompense.

A qui de Montmatre à Cythère,
Trouverait, pour qu'il l'attestât,

60 E. Rostand, *Opus Cit.*, p. 96.
61 E. Rostand, *Opus Cit.*, p. 121.

Fille de gueux ou de notaire
Plus belle d'un seul iota
Que la maîtresse qui fit à
Mon coeur le grand trou que je panse,
A qui de ses yeux s'abrita,
Quarante sous de récompense.

A qui rapporterait de terre
Ou du ciel que mon vol tenta,
Mon dernier espoir, solitaire
Loin de celle qui me quitta,
Las! dans n'importe quel état,
Je lui garnirais bien la panse,
Pourvu qu'il me le rapportât.
Quarante sous de récompense.

Envoi

O toi qui commis l'attentat,
Femme, voici pour la dépense
De la croix de mon Golgotha,
Quarante soux de récompense."[62]

In the last part of the decade between 1870 and 1880, about twenty years after Banville's beginnings, the revival of the English *ballade* took place. In England, the form was in favor with Dobson, Gosse, Lang, Swinburne, and Henley. In America it has recommended itself to Brander Matthews, Frank Dempster Sherman, Clinton Scollard, and others. In both countries, the *ballade* continues to be written for the daily papers and for the magazines. This return of the *ballade* to English literature was effected by a revival of interest in such older poets as Charles d'Orléans and François Villon, and by the impression made in England by the work of Théodore de Banville. Very significant, too, in the history of the *ballade*, are

[62] Jean Richepin, *Les Caresses* (Paris, 1898), p. 240.

the articles published in the *Cornhill Magazine* in 1876 and in 1877.[63] In the first of these years appeared Stevenson's sympathetic study of *Charles of Orleans,* and in the following year, the same author's brilliant *François Villon, Student, Poet and Housebreaker,* Dowden's *On Some French Verse Writers, 1830–1877*, and Gosse's *A Plea for Certain Exotic Forms of Verse.* In this last essay, Gosse advocated a poetic policy which he has since constantly followed in his criticism. He wrote then: "We acknowledge that the severity of the plan and the rich and copious recurrence of the rhyme serve the double end of repelling the incompetent workman and stimulating the competent. This being so, why should we not proceed to the cultivation of other [than the sonnet] fixed forms of verse, which flourished in the earliest days of modern poetic literature, and of which the sonnet, if the finest, is at least but one?

"In point of fact, the movement I advocate has begun on all sides, with the spontaneity of an idea obviously ready to be born. I myself, without suggestion from any acquaintance, but merely in consequence of reading the early French poets, determined to attempt the introduction of the *balade* and the *rondeau.* But, to my surprise, I found that I had no right to claim the first invention of the idea. First on one hand, then on another, I discovered that several young writers, previously unknown to me and to one another, had determined on the same innovation. For some time the idea was confined to conversation and private discussion. But these forms are now being adopted by a still wider circle, and the movement seems so general that the

[63] In 1868 had been published Walter Besant's *Studies in Early French Poetry.* This work, among other things, contained an account of Villon, quotations from his work, and a prose translation of his *Epitaph in the Form of a Ballad.*

time has come to define a little more exactly what seems to be desirable in this matter and what not.''[64]

In 1911, in a letter to the present writer, Mr. Gosse said in answer to some inquiries about the revival of the *ballade:* ''But you should note that 1876 is the date of the re-introduction of the ballade into English literature, Rossetti's translation from Villon being accidental, in the sense that he was attracted to the beauty of the old French poem without having perceived, or having attempted to retain, the character of the form. The reason for the simultaneous adoption of this beautiful form by a number of poets is difficult to trace. But I think it was connected with the circulation in London of certain copies of Banville's 'Trente-six ballades joyeuses.' This was certainly the case with Swinburne, Lang and myself, and I believe with Dobson and Henley. But a desire for the support of a more rigid and disciplined metre was in the air, and we all independently and simultaneously seized upon the French forms of which Banville gave the precise rules in his 'Petit Traité.' I cannot find the book, but I believe that a new edition of the Petit Traité was issued in 1876. I know that I wrote at that time a letter of adoring inquiry, and received in return a long letter of sympathy and advice from Théodore de Banville. But do not suppose that any of this interest in the 'forms,' as we used to call them, dates back earlier than 1870 in England. Rossetti never sympathized with it all.''

Andrew Lang, replying to a question similar to that addressed to Mr. Gosse, answered thus: ''I happened to try to translate a ballade of Villon in 1870 and later found Austin Dobson and Gosse sporting with these toys. Prob-

[64] E. Gosse, *A Plea for Certain Exotic Forms of Verse, Cornhill Magazine* (1877), p. 56.

ably Rossetti and Swinburne first drew my attention to Villon & Co."

Mr. Austin Dobson, explaining his preoccupation with the *ballade,* wrote me as follows: "I was attracted to the French forms because I was seeking to give a novel turn to the lighter kinds of verse which I had then been writing. Some time between 1873 and 1877, I chanced on the *Odes Funambulesques* of Théodore de Banville, whose essays in this kind gave me the hint I wanted. I tried most of the forms in the *Proverbs in Porcelain* of 1877."

It was not until 1876, then, that the first pure *ballades* appeared in modern English. In May of that year was printed Austin Dobson's *Ballad of the Prodigals,* and Swinburne's *Ballad of Dreamland* came out in September. There had, it is true, been translations of *ballades* of Alain Chartier, of Charles d'Orléans, and of Villon, in Louisa Costello's *Specimens of Early Poetry of France,* published in 1835; but Miss Costello showed no consciousness at all of the rime features of the old French form. Four years before (1831), Longfellow had incorporated in his paper on the *Origin and Progress of the French Language*[65] his version of Clément Marot's *Le Frère Lubin.*[66] Longfellow, like Miss Costello, ignored the peculiar rime system of the original. Rossetti's rendering of Villon's greatest *ballade,* also earlier than Mr. Dobson's *Ballad of the Prodigals,* was, as Gosse wrote, "accidental"; Rossetti did not attempt to preserve the character of the form and never sympathized, to quote Gosse again, with the group who were experiment-

65 T. W. Higginson, *Henry Wadsworth Longfellow* (Boston & New York, 1902), p. 58.

66 H. W. Longfellow, *Complete Poetical Works* (Boston & New York, 1893), p. 632. Bryant is also said to have made an early translation of this poem. Andrew Lang was the first to translate *Frêre Lubin* into the original measure of *ballad à double refrain.* See *Ballades and Verses Vain* (New York, 1884), p. 23.

ing with it. Austin Dobson, the genius of familiar verse, and the first to print his experiment, found in the *ballade* one of many metrical expedients for varying the treatment of light and tender themes.[67] The latest collection of his poetry contains fourteen *ballades.* Their range of subject is not wide. There is *The Prodigals,* the first in point of time, with its touching burden, "Give us—ah! give us—but yesterday."[68] Then there is a rollicking historical *Ballad to Queen Elizabeth,* ending thus:

> " Gloriana! the Don may attack us
> Whenever his stomach be fain;
> He must reach us before he can rack us,
> And where are the galleons of Spain?"[69]

The Horation imitation, *O Navis,*[70] is a new use for the form. The *Ballad of the Bore,*[71] too, is reminiscent of Horace. Austin Dobson's other *ballades* are in the quaint lively vein of his familiar verse. There is a special fillip of humor in the *Ballad of Imitation,* with its fling at all critics who charge plagiarism, in the words, "the man who plants cabbages imitates, too!"[72] A *chant royal* on the *Dance of Death*[73] (*after Holbein*) is this poet's only adaptation of a French verse form to the grim aspects of life.

[67] Cf. G. Rabache, *Austin Dobson, Poète, Revue Germanique* (1913), p. 523: "Toujours apparaît son désir de suppléer à l'unité coordinatrice d'une pensée forte par l'enchaînement ingénieux des rimes. A un tel souci répondaient admirablement les vielles formes françaises. . . . Dobson revendique l'honneur de les avoir, le premier à notre époque, employées en Angleterre. C'est sa réussite, en effet, qui lui suscita de nombreux imitateurs."

[68] Austin Dobson, *Collected Poems* (London, 1909), p. 486.

[69] *Ibid.,* p. 491.

[70] *Ibid.,* p. 502.

[71] *Ibid.,* p. 524.

[72] *Ibid.,* p. 498.

[73] *Ibid.,* p. 504.

In 1878, Austin Dobson contributed to a volume[74] containing *ballades* of his own, of Edmund Gosse's and of John Payne's, a preface on *Some Foreign Forms of Verse,* in which he gave rules for the making of a *ballade.* His conception of the restrictions imposed by a fixed rime-scheme are interesting: "The rhymes play so important a part in the foregoing rules, that a few words on this head may not unfitly close these notes, especially as those who write the forms do not appear to be wholly agreed in the matter. On the one hand, it is advanced that the forms are sufficiently difficult in French, and that to transfer them to our tongue without at the same time adopting the French system of rhyming is to hamper them with superfluous difficulties. By the French system of rhyming is meant the license used by French writers to rhyme words of exactly similar sound and spelling so long as they have different meanings. This is not held to be admissible in English, although cases might be cited. Milton, for example, has 'Ruth' and 'ruth' in one of his sonnets. On the other hand, it is contended that if we import these forms, we must, to make them really English, adopt them with all their native difficulties, and add our own as well."[75]

In the same preface, Dobson set down what may serve as a final word on his own use of the *ballade:* "What is modestly advanced for some of them (by the present writer at least), is that they may add a new charm of buoyancy,—a lyric freshness,—to amatory and familiar verse already too much condemned to faded measures and outworn cadences. Further, upon assumption that merely graceful or tuneful trifles may be sometimes written (and even read), that they are admirable vehicles for the expression of trifles or *jeux d'esprit.*"[76]

[74] W. Davenport Adams, *Latter Day Lyrics* (London, 1878).

[75] W. D. Adams, *Opus Cit.,* p. 348.

[76] W. D. Adams, *Opus Cit.,* p. 335.

Whatever of Andrew Lang's lives or dies, it is safe to say that his *ballades* will not be forgotten. He is the author of at least thirty-six. The translations from Villon, Froissart, Marot, La Fontaine, and from Banville, together with his own words in the letter sent to the present writer in 1911, point to the influences that lead to his adoption of the poem. Lang's translations from Villon include *Of Good Counsel,*[77] *Arbor Amoris,*[78] *Ballad of the Gibbet,*[79] and the *Ballade of Dead Ladies,* which follows:

"Nay, tell me now in what strange air
The Roman Flora dwells to-day.
Where Archippiada hides, and where
Beautiful Thais has passed away?
Whence answers Echo, afield, astray,
By mere or stream,—around, below?
Lovelier she than a woman of clay;
Nay, but where is the last year's snow?

Where is wise Héloïse, that care
Brought on Abeilard, and dismay?
All for her love he found a snare,
A maimed poor monk in orders grey;
And where's the Queen who willed to slay
Buridan, that in a sack must go
Afloat down Seine,—a perilous way—
Nay, but where is the last year's snow?

Where's that White Queen, a lily rare,
With her sweet song, the Siren's lay?
Where's Bertha Broadfoot, Beatrice fair?
Alys and Ermengarde, where are they?
Good Joan, whom English did betray,

[77] A. Lang, *Ballades and Verses Vain* (New York, 1884), pp. 65–66.

[78] A. Lang, *Ballades and Lyrics of Old France* (Portland, 1898), pp. 4–5; not included in either of Longnon's editions of Villon.

[79] A. Lang, *Opus Cit.,* pp. 11–13; also translated by Payne and Swinburne.

In Rouen town, and burned her? No,
Maiden and Queen, no man may say;
Nay, but where is the last year's snow?

Envoy

Prince, all this week thou needst not pray,
Nor yet this year the thing to know.
One burden answers, ever and aye,
'Nay, but where is the last year's snow?' "[80]

For purposes of comparison, four other translations of the same poem are given, first, an anonymous version, possibly by Cary:

" Tell me where, or in what clime,
Is that mistress of the prime,
Roman Flora? she of Greece,
Thais? or that maid so fond,
That, an ye shout o'er stream or pond,
Answering holdeth not her peace?
—Where are they?—Tell me, if ye know;
What is become of last year's snow?

Where is Heloise the wise,
For whom Abelard was fain,
Mangled in such cruel wise,
To turn monk instead of man?
Where the Queen, who into Seine
Bade them cast poor Buridan?
—Where are they?—Tell me, if ye know;
What is come of last year's snow?

The Queen that was as lily fair,
Whose songs were sweet as linnets' are,
Bertha, or she who govern'd Maine?
Alice, Beatrix, or Joan,
That good damsel of Lorraine,

80 A. Lang, *Ballades in Blue China* (London, 1888), p. 57.

Whom the English burnt at Roan?
—Where are they?—Tell me, if ye know;
What is come of last year's snow?

Prince, question by the month or year;
The burden of my song is here:
—Where are they?—Tell me, if ye know;
What is come of last year's snow?"[81]

Miss Costello's simple and incomplete version is as follows:

"Tell me to what region flown
Is Flora the fair Roman gone?
Where lovely Thaïs' hiding-place,
Her sister in each charm and grace?
Echo—let thy voice awake,
Over river, stream, and lake:
Answer, where does beauty go?
Where is fled the south wind's snow?

Where is Eloïse the wise,
For whose two bewitching eyes
Hapless Abeillard was doom'd,
In his cell to live entomb'd?
Where the Queen, her love who gave,
Cast in Seine a watery grave?
Where each lovely cause of woe?
Where is fled the south wind's snow?

Where thy voice, oh regal fair,
Sweet as is the lark's in air?

81 *London Magazine* (October, 1823), p. 437. My attention was first called to this version by *François Villon en Angleterre* par H. Vigier (*Revue Germanique,* Paris, July–August, 1913), in which this translation is given to Cary of Dante fame. I am, therefore, indebted to Vigier for my knowledge of the *ballade* printed above. although the present chapter had been completed in every other respect before his article appeared.

Where is Bertha? Alix?—she
Who le Mayne held gallantly?
Where is Joan, whom English flame
Gave, at Rouen, death and fame?
Where are all?—does any know?
Where is fled the south wind's snow?"[82]

Here is Payne's labored and literal translation:

"Tell me where, in what land of shade,
  Bides fair Flora of Rome, and where
Are Thaïs and Archipiade,
  Cousins-german of beauty rare,
  And Echo, more than mortal fair,
That, when one calls by river-flow
  Or marish, answers out of the air?
But what is become of last year's snow?

Where did the learn'd Heloïsa vade,
  For whose sake Abelard might not spare
(Such dole for love on him was laid)
  Manhood to lose and a cowl to wear?
  And where is the queen who willed whilere
That Buridan, tied in a sack should go
  Floating down Seine from the turret-stair?
But what is become of last year's snow?

Blanche, too, the lily-white queen, that made
  Sweet music as if she a siren were;
Broad-foot Bertha; and Joan the maid,
  The good Lorrainer, the English bare
  Captive to Rouen and burned her there;
Beatrix, Eremburge, Alys—lo!
  Where are they, Virgin debonair?
But what is become of last year's snow?

[82] Louisa S. Costello, *Specimens of the Early Poetry of France* (London, 1835), p. 161.

Envoi

Prince, you may question how they fare
This week, or liefer this year, I trow;
Still shall the answer this burden bear,
But what is become of last year's snow?"[83]

Finally there is the inspired poem by Rossetti, which, albeit at the expense of the form, makes the spirit of the original live again:

"Tell me now in what hidden way is
Lady Flora the lovely Roman?
Where's Hipparchia, and where is Thais,
Neither of them the fairer woman?
Where is Echo, beheld of no man,
Only heard on river and mere,—
She whose beauty was more than human? . . .
But where are the snows of yester-year?

Where's Héloïse, the learned nun,
For whose sake Abeillard, I ween,
Lost manhood and put priesthood on?
(From love he won such dule and teen!)
And where, I pray you, is the Queen
Who willed that Buridan should steer
Sewed in a sack's mouth down the Seine? . . .
But where are the snows of yester-year?

White Queen Blanche, like a queen of lilies,
With a voice like any mermaiden,—
Bertha Broadfoot, Beatrice, Alice,
And Ermengarde the Lady of Maine,—
And that good Joan whom Englishmen
At Rouen doomed and burnt her there,—
Mother of God, where are they then? . . .
But where are the snows of yester-year?

[83] John Payne, *The Poems of Master François Villon of Paris* (London, 1892), p. 33.

Nay, never ask this week, fair lord,
Where they are gone, nor yet this year,
Except with this for an overword,—
But where are the snows of yester-year?"[84]

Lang translated, also, Villon's *Ballad of the Gibbet,* as did both Swinburne and Payne too. The third stanza of Villon's *ballade,* the hardest of the three to translate and therefore the best test of the poetic quality of the translator, is here given, reprinted from all these versions:

"We are whiles scoured and soddened of the rain
And whiles burnt up and blackened of the sun:
Corbies and pyets have our eyes out-ta'en
And plucked our beards and hair out, one by one.
Whether by night or day, rest have we none:
Now here, now there, as the wind shifts its stead,
We swing and creak and rattle overhead,
No thimble dented like our bird-pecked face.
Brothers, have heed and shun the life we led:
The rather pray, God grant us of His grace!"[85]

"The rain has washed and laundered us all five,
And the sun dried and blackened; yea, perdie,
Ravens and pies with beaks that rend and rive
Have dug our eyes out, and plucked off for fee
Our beards and eyebrows; never are we free,
Not once, to rest; but here and there still speed,
Drive at its wild will by the wind's change led,
More pecked of birds than fruits on garden-wall;
Men, for God's love, let no gibe here be said,
But pray to God that he forgive us all."[86]

[84] D. G. Rossetti, *Poetical Work* (Boston, 1899), Vol. I, p. 237. Cf. *The Poems of François Villon.* Translated by H. De Vere Stacpoole (London, 1913), p. 20.

[85] John Payne, *The Poems of Master François Villon of Paris* (London, 1892), p. 115.

[86] A. C. Swinburne, *Poems* (Philadelphia, no date), p. 266. Besant's prose version of this same *ballade* has been referred to earlier in this chapter.

"The rain out of heaven has washed us clean,
The sun has scorched us black and bare,
Ravens and rooks have pecked at our eyne,
And feathered their nests with our beards and hair.
Round are we tossed and here and there,
This way and that, at the wild wind's will,
Never a moment my body is still;
Birds they are busy about my face.
Live not as we, nor fare as we fare;
Pray God pardon us out of His grace."[87]

Payne's lines are marked by archaisms, by difficult figures, and by a very perceptible roughness of metre. Swinburne's rendering lacks force. But Lang's comes nearest to the despair and sweetness, to the grim music of the French. Lang, to make no further mention of his other translations, chose to translate three of Banville's *ballades: Sur les Hôtes Mystérieux de la Forêt,*[88] *Aux Enfants Perdus*[89] and *Ballade des Pendus* from *Gringoire.*[90] His essay on *Théodore de Banville* sums up the case for French fixed forms in English poetry: "It may be worth while to quote his [Banville's] testimony as to the merit of these modes of expression. 'This cluster of forms is one of our most precious treasures, for each of them forms a rhythmic whole, complete and perfect, while at the same time they all possess the fresh and unconscious grace which marks the productions of primitive times.' Now there is some truth in his criticism; for it is a mark of man's early ingenuity, in many arts, to seek complexity (when you would expect simplicity), and yet to lend to that complexity an infantine naturalness. One can see this phenomenon in early decora-

[87] A. Lang, *Ballads and Lyrics of Old France* (Portland, 1898), p. 6. Cf. H. De Vere Stacpoole, *Opus Cit.*, p. 18.

[88] A. Lang, *Ballades in Blue China* (London, 1888), p. 24.

[89] A. Lang, *Opus Cit.*, p. 31.

[90] Gleeson White, *Ballades and Rondeaus* (London, 1887), p. 24.

tive art, and in early law and custom, and even in the complicated structure of primitive languages. Now, just as early, and even savage, races are our masters in the decorative use of color and of carving, so the nameless master-singers of ancient France may be our teachers in decorative poetry, the poetry some call *vers de société*. Whether it is possible to go beyond this, and adapt the old French forms to serious modern poetry, it is not for anyone but time to decide. In this matter, as in greater affairs, *securus judicat orbis terrarum!* For my own part I scarcely believe that the revival would serve the nobler ends of English poetry.''[91]

Lang's *ballades,* the untranslated, original ones, are, as his theories would lead one to suppose, light in theme and conventional. There is a *Valentine in Form of Ballade,*[92] like so many of the fifteenth century French poems; there is the *Ballade of Queen Anne,*[93] a strange mingling of medieval verse form and Augustan manners. More up-to-date is the subject matter of the gay *Ballade of the Girton Girl.*[94] In the *Ballade of Old Plays,*[95] dedicated appropriately to Brander Matthews, the first of the three stanzas represents *Le Cour,* the second, *La Comédie,* and the third, *La Ville;* this *ballade* was called forth by an edition of Molière published in Paris in 1667. The ''ubi sunt'' motif appears in the *Ballade of Literary Fame*[96] and also in the *Ballade of Dead Cities.* This last, dedicated to E. W. Gosse, was an answer to that writer's *Ballad of Dead Cities* written the year before (1879). Both *ballades* show clever manipulation of proper names and ingenuity of rime-scheme. The first stanzas and envoys of both are quoted. Andrew Lang's is:

91 A. Lang, *Essays in Little* (New York, 1891), p. 74.

92 A. Lang, *Ballades in Blue China* (London, 1888), p. 63.

93 A. Lang, *Opus Cit.,* p. 77.

94 A. Lang, *Rhymes à La Mode* (London, 1887), p. 43.

95 A. Lang, *Ballades and Verses Vain* (New York, 1884), p. 19.

96 A. Lang, *Rhymes à La Mode* (London, 1887), p. 85.

"The dust of Carthage and the dust
Of Babel on the desert wold,
The loves of Corinth, and the lust,
Orchomenos increased with gold;
The tower of Jason, over-bold,
And Cherson, smitten in her prime—
What are they but a dream half-told?
Where are the cities of old time?

. . . .

Envoy

Prince, all thy towns and cities must
Decay as these, till all their crime,
And mirth, and wealth, and toil, are thrust
Where are the cities of old time";[97]

and Gosse's, that apparently provoked the contest:

"Where are the cities of the plain?
And where the shrines of rapt Bethel?
And Calah built of Tubal-Cain?
And Shinar whence King Amraphel
Came out in arms, and fought, and fell,
Decoyed into the pits of slime
By Sidim, and sent sheer to hell;
Where are the cities of old time?

. . . .

Envoy

Prince, with a dolorous, ceaseless knell
Above their wasted toil and crime
The waters of oblivion swell:
Where are the cities of old time?"[98]

Edmund Gosse, in the article on the *Ballade* in the eleventh edition of the *Encyclopædia Britannica*, says of

[97] A. Lang, *Ballades in Blue China* (London, 1888), p. 40.
[98] E. W. Gosse, *New Poems* (London, 1879), p. 164.

the possibilities of the form: "With the exception of the sonnet, the ballade is the noblest of the artificial forms of verse cultivated in English literature. It lends itself equally well to pathos and to mockery, and in the hands of a competent poet produces an effect which is rich in melody without seeming fantastic or artificial."

Alfred Noyes, writing recently[99] of Gosse's own poetry, says that the school to which Gosse belongs, which experimented with the French forms, "permanently raised the standard of technique in English verse." Of the influences that moulded this school Gosse himself has written: "It is in Théophile Gautier and Théodore de Banville that our English Parnassians found something of the same æsthetic stimulus that their predecessors of the fourteenth century found in Guillaume de Machault and Eustache Deschamps."[100]

Gosse's beautiful *ballade* tribute "for the funeral of the last of the Joyous Poets," contains much valid literary criticism, as the first stanza and envoy show:

"One ballade more before we say good-night,
O dying Muse, one mournful ballade more!
Then let the new men fall to their delight,
The Impressionist, the Decadent, a score
Of other fresh fanatics, who adore
Quaint demons, and disdain thy golden shrine;
Ah! faded goddess, thou wert held divine
When we were young! But now each laurelled head
Has fallen, and fallen the ancient glorious line;
The last is gone, since Banville too is dead.

. . . .

99 Alfred Noyes, *The Poems of Edmund Gosse, Fortnightly Review*, August, 1912.

100 E. Gosse, *French Profiles* (New York, 1905), p. 362.

Envoi

Prince-Jeweller, whose facet-rhymes combine
All hues that glow, all rays that shift and shine,
Farewell! thy song is sung, thy splendour fled!
No bards to Aganippe's wave incline;
The last is gone, since Banville too is dead."[101]

Swinburne also wrote two poems in memory of the genius of the nineteenth century *ballade*, Théodore de Banville. In the French lines *Au Tombeau de Banville* occurs the phrase, "poete à la bouche de miel,"[102] by which the English poet described the author of the *Trente-six Ballades Joyeuses.* Banville is celebrated again by Swinburne in the *Ballad of Melicertes,* where he is addressed as,

"Prince of song more sweet than honey, lyric lord,
Not thy France here only mourns a light adored,
One whose love-lit fame the world inheriteth.
Strangers, too, now brethren, hail with heart's accord
Life so sweet as this that dies and casts off death."[103]

The same poet has a *ballade* to Villon, also with a refrain, "Villon, our sad bad glad mad brother's name,"[104] suggestive of Browning's familiar combination of adjectives. Swinburne turned eight of Villon's *ballades* into English.[105] The same luscious quality that characterizes Swinburne's

101 E. W. Gosse, *In Russet and Silver* (London, 1894), p. 93.

102 A. C. Swinburne, *Poems* (Philadelphia, no date), p. 623.

103 A. C. Swinburne, *Opus Cit.*, p. 623.

104 A. C. Swinburne, *Opus Cit.*, p. 245.

105 One has been mentioned above. The other seven, found on the following pages of the edition noted above, 261, 262, 262, 263, 263, 264, 265, are: *A Double Ballad of Good Counsel, Ballad of the Lords of Old Time, Ballad of the Women of Paris, Ballad Written for a Bridegroom, Ballad Against the Enemies of France, The Dispute of the Heart and Body of François Villon,* and *Epistle in Form of a Ballad to his Friends.*

other poetry likewise pervades his *ballades.* The music of the first stanza and envoy of *A Ballad of Dreamland* is unique in English *ballade* literature:

"I hid my heart in a nest of roses,
Out of the sun's way, hidden apart;
In a softer bed than the soft white snow's is,
Under the roses I hid my heart.
Why would it sleep not, why should it start,
When never a leaf of the rose-tree stirred?
What made sleep flutter his wings and part?
Only the song of a secret bird.

. . . .

Envoi

In the world of dreams I have chosen my part.
To sleep for a season and have no word
Of true love's truth or of light love's art,
Only the song of a secret bird."[106]

The use of anapæsts is especially fine in these verses; but in the *Ballad at Parting,* in which the line is much longer, there is that sterner kind of music which the two-syllable foot alone is capable of producing in English:

"Sea to sea that clasps and fosters England, uttering evermore
Song eterne and praise immortal of the indomitable shore,
Lifts aloud her constant heart up, south to north and east to west,
Here in speech that shames all music, there in thunder-throated roar,
Chiming concord out of discord, waking rapture out of rest.
All her ways are lovely, all her works and symbols are divine,
Yet shall man love best what first bade leap his heart and bend his knee;
Yet where first his whole soul worshipped shall his soul set up his shrine:

[106] A. C. Swinburne, *Opus Cit.*, p. 245.

Nor may love not know the lovelier, fair as both beheld may be,
Here the limitless north-eastern, there the strait south-western sea."[107]

Another *ballade* contains Swinburne's appeal to Christina Rossetti to continue her writing:

"Blithe verse made all the dim sense clear
That smiles of babbling babes conceal:
Prayer's perfect heart spake here: and here
Rose notes of blameless woe and weal,
More soft than this poor song's appeal.
Where orchards bask, where cornfields wave,
They dropped like rains that cleanse and lave,
And scattered all the year along,
Like dewfall on an April grave,
Sweet water from the well of song.

Ballad, go bear our prayer, and crave
Pardon, because thy lowlier stave
Can do this plea no right but wrong.
Ask naught beside thy pardon, save
Sweet water from the well of song."[108]

Henley belongs with Dobson, Gosse, Lang, and Swinburne in the history of the *ballade*. He, too, believed in the form, and experimented not only with the simple *ballade*, but with the double *ballade* and with the *ballade* of two refrains. His *Ballade of Truisms* is comparable to the old French type of sententious *ballade:*

"Gold or silver every day,
Dies to grey.
There are knots in every skein.
Hours of work and hours of play
Fade away

[107] A. C. Swinburne, *Opus Cit.*, p. 570.
[108] A. C. Swinburne, *Opus Cit.*, p. 558.

Into one immense Inane.
Shadow and substance, chaff and grain,
Are as vain
As the foam or as the spray.
Life goes crooning, faint and fair—
One refrain—
'If it could be always May.'"[109]

He has also tried his hand at the "ubi sunt" theme in the *Ballade of Dead Actors:*

"Where are the passions they essayed,
And where the tears they made to flow?
Where the wild humours they portrayed
For laughing worlds to see and know?
Othello's wrath and Juliet's woe?
Sir Peter's whims and Timon's gall?
And Millamant and Romeo?
Into the night go one and all.

. . . .

Envoy

Prince, in one common overthrow
The Hero tumbles with the Thrall:
As dust that drives, as straws that blow,
Into the night go one and all."[110]

109 W. E. Henley, *London Voluntaries and Other Poems* (Portland, 1910), p. 45.

110 W. E. Henley, *Opus Cit.*, p. 37. As A. M. Moore's burlesque has it:

"In *Ballades* things always contrive to get lost,
And Echo is constantly asking where
Are last year's roses and last year's frost?
And where are the fashions we used to wear?
And what is a 'gentleman,' what is a 'player?'
Irrelevant questions I like to ask:
Can you reap the *tret* as well as the *tare?*
And who was the Man in the Iron Mask?

In America, Brander Matthews, both by his writings on the theory of versification and by his own experiments, has done much to develop the *ballade* and to cultivate a taste for this special form. In his best vein is the *Ballade of Adaptation:*

" The native drama's sick and dying,
So say the cynic critic crew:
The native dramatist is crying—
'Bring me the paste! Bring me the glue!
Bring me the pen, and scissors, too!
Bring me the works of E. Augier!
Bring me the works of V. Sardou!
I am the man to write a play!'

What has become of the ring I tossed
In the lap of my mistress, false and fair?
Her grave is green and her tombstone mossed;
But who is to be the next Lord Mayor,
And where is King William of Leicester Square?
And who has emptied my hunting flask?
And who is possessed of Stella's hair?
And who was the Man in the Iron Mask?

And what has become of the knee I crossed,
And the rod, and the child they would not spare?
And what will a dozen herring cost
When herring are sold at threehalfpence a pair—
And what in the world is the Golden Stair?
Did Diogenes die in a tub or a cask,
Like Clarence for love of liquor there?
And who was the Man in the Iron Mask?

Envoy

Poets, your readers have much to bear,
For *Ballade*-making is no great task.
If you do not remember, I don't much care
Who was the Man in the Iron Mask."

(Gleeson White, *Ballades and Roundeaus,* London, 1887, p. 289.)

For want of plays the stage is sighing,
　　Such is the song the wide world through:
The native dramatist is crying—
　　'Behold the comedies I brew!
　　Behold my dramas not a few!
On German farces I can prey,
　　And English novels I can hew:
I am the man to write a play!'

There is, indeed, no use denying
　　That fashion's turned from old to new:
The native dramatist is crying—
　　'Molière, good-bye! Shakespeare adieu!
　　I do not think so much of you.
Although not bad, you've had your day,
　　And for the present you won't do.
I am the man to write a play!'

Envoi

Prince of the stage, don't miss the cue,
　　A native dramatist, I say
To every cynic critic, 'Pooh!
　　I am the man to write a play!' "[111]

Frank Dempster Sherman's *To Austin Dobson* shows a charmingly facile use of the form:

"From the sunny climes of France,
　Flying to the west,
Came a flock of birds by chance,
　There to sing and rest:
Of some secrets deep in quest,—
　Justice for their wrongs,—
Seeking one to shield their heart,
　One to write their songs.

111 Gleeson White, *Ballades and Rondeaus* (London, 1887), p. 38.

Melodies of old romance,
  Joy and gentle jest,
Note that made the dull heart dance
  With a merry zest;—
Maids in matchless beauty drest,
  Youths in happy throngs;—
There they sang to tempt and test
  One to write their songs.

In old London's wide expanse
  Built each feathered guest,—
Man's small pleasure to enhance,
  Singing him to rest,—
Came, and tenderly confessed,
  Perched on leafy prongs,
Life were sweet if they possessed
  One to write their songs.

Envoy

Austin, it was you they blest:
  Fame to you belongs!
Time has proven you're the best
  One to write their songs!"[112]

Scarcely a week passes without the publication of *ballades* in both English and American newspapers. These journalistic *ballades,* often topical in character, are usually of no real poetic value. The bad sonnets that are written are likely to be either sentimental or lugubrious in tone; the inferior *ballade,* on the other hand, is frequently either clownish or banal, though, of course, there are still published occasionally in magazines and collections new *ballades* of genuine poetic worth.

If Villon were to revisit Paris for the purpose of scanning the literature produced by the French in the century

[112] F. D. Sherman, *Madrigals and Catches* (New York, 1887), p. 138.

just past, he would find comparatively few specimens of his favorite form, and these only after the year 1856. Not only would he perceive that the custom of writing *ballades* had decayed, but he would, if he were sufficiently interested in the matter, discover that contemporary French writers on poetic theory give no more than passing mention to the *ballade*. He would, doubtless, recognize in Albert Glatigny a boon companion, and he would commend Théodore de Banville for reviving a golden tradition. Should Villon, drawn by the homage given him in England and in America, turn his attention to the *ballade* among English speaking peoples, he might admire the intellectual subtlety and the grace of form of the *ballade* written in English in the nineteenth century, but he would be likely to display some indignation at its lack of sincerity and its indifference to the very substance of great poetry, deep human emotion.

APPENDIX I

POETRY COMPOSED IN THE PUY

A. *MS. DOUCE 379*

Manuscript *Douce 379* contains a collection of poems presented to "Maistre Guillaume Challenge, chanoyne de Rouen, prince du Puy," upon the celebration of the festival of the Conception of the Virgin Mary at Rouen, 14 December, 1511. The prologue begins: "Le dimenche quatoriesme jour de decembre, lan mil cinq cens et unz a Rouen, en leglise paroisialle de sainct Jehan, maistre Guillaume Challenge, chanoyne de Rouen et conseiller du roy en sa cour de le Sehignier comme prince tint le puy." Beside *champs royaux* and *rondeaulz,* the MS. contains "les ballades damours pretendans au prix du disner du lendemain dudit Puy, sus ce reffrain. 'Vielx amoureux faictes ung Sault.' Christien a eu le prix (fol. 86)." From the collection the following are given:

f. 186r

Gentilz gallans faictes armee
Pour assailir tous faulx viellars
Lesquelz ont obtins mainte annee
Le prix damours par leurs vieulx ars
Dictes hardiment qu'ilz sont ars
Et leur liurez cruel assault
Escrivez en voz estandars
Vieulx amoureux faictes vng sault.

Ilz ont la braye(?) toute vsee
Et nont espieu lance ne dardz
Ilz ne sauvront prendre visee

Ne tyrer vng bon coup droit de arcz
Ilz sont cassez, Ils sont couardz
Chacun le cognoit sans deffault
Tant quon leur dit en toutes pars
Vieulx amoureux faictes vng sault.

Ilz ont bien en mainte assemblee
Aucune ffois de bons hazardz
Mais quoy cest de myct et demble
Et si font bien souvent des ars
Puis il me souvient de buzars
Quant ilz lievent ces veulx en hault
Et quon crye apres telz musars
Vieulx amoureux faictes vng sault.

Gentilz amoureux et gaillardz
A quy jamais le cueur ne fault
Criez tous apres ces paillars
Vieulx amoureux faictes vng sault.[1]

fol. 92^r

Les dames ont veu la Requeste
Quont faict sur lamoureuse enqueste
Puis vng peu noz mygnons de court
En tant que touche la conqueste
En bien du proces l'enqueste
Il est dist par arrest de court
Bref tous ceulx que viellesse oppresse
Plus n'auront dame ne maistresse
Quy damours les prengne en sursault
Ce que deffend la loy expresse
Vieulx amoureux faictes vng sault.

[1] For help in deciphering this *ballade* and the one following, I am indebted to Professor Raymond Weeks of Columbia University, and through him to Professor John M. Burnam of the University of Cincinnati.

Or se vng viellard a blanche teste
Enfant les groingz ou sen tempeste
Il en sera tenu plus lourd
Et quy pys est pour vne beste
Raison car soubz grise barbeste
En amours peu de plaisir sourd
Pour tant luy fault faire le sourd
Car vng jeune homme a hardiesse
Cueur joyaux passe temps lyesse
Dont en amours tremble et tressault
Vng corquis plein de jeunesse
Et toutesfoys qua vous jeunesse
Vieulx amoureux faictes un sault.

A une dame ou femme honneste
Par droit vraye amour admonneste
Damour en chambre salle ou court
Vng Rustre quy du tout sappreste
Puis que ses biens luy donne ou preste
Destre a son gre tenu de court
Et viel quy viel art en court
Soubz bourgoisie et gentillesse
Desormais fault quun gentil laisse
Faire le petit soubressault
Dont homme caduc na laddresse
Veu donc le mestier quon vous dresse
Vieulx amoureux faictes vng sault.

Prince pourtant que le bas blesse
A tel quy crolle de foiblesse
Et veult prendre femme dassaut
Quy est a luy trop grant simplesse
Pour monstrer vng tour de soupplesse
Vieulx amoureux faictes vng sault.

B. *BALADE LATINE*

Tota pulchra es amica
Per trinum numen celicum

Virgo mater & unica /
Virus non gerens antiquum /
Hoc sacrum refert canticum /
Quod macula non est in te
Dicta per os angelicum
Flos producens fructum vite.

Virga fortis mosaica /
Fontem donans salutificum
Regna celebrant celica /
Cuum conceptum pudicum;
Per quem agmen propheticum
Jucunda cecinit mente
Tu das rorem vivisicum.
Flos producens fructum vite.

O flos stirpe Judaica
Per spiritum davidicum
Arte conteris bellica
Aspidem et basilicum /
Tu leonem inimicum
Et drachonem unicis tute
Morsum tegis veneficum /
Flos producens fructum vite.

O levamen deificum
Confer opem cum salute /
Serva horum monasticum
Flos producens fructum vite.[4]
Dom Nicolle Lescarre[5]

4 *Palinods Présentés au Puy de Rouen, Recueil de Pierre Vidoue* (Precédé d'une Introduction par E. de Robillard de Beaurepaire), Rouen, 1897, feuillet LXVI–LXVII of reprint of Vidoue.

5 *Opus Cit.*, p. xix: ''La reputation de Nicolle Lescarre était d'ailleurs si bien établie que Pierre Fabri a tenu lui-même à la reconnaître en citant dans son Grand Art de Rhétorique, à titre d'exemple deux de ses compositions: un chant royal et une ballade.''

C. *BALLADE*

Donée au Prince

L'argument est pris de Valerius Flaccus en ses Argonautes livre second.

Quittons, o divine Uranie,
Le chant doux et melodieux
De nostre charmante harmonie
Il faut d'un ton plus furieux
Estonner les moins curieux,
En leur representant l'outrage
Dont fut enfin victorieux
Le Roy seul exempt du carnage.

Quelle horreur, quelle boucherie
Dans Lemnos arreste mes yeux!
Les femmes pleins de furie
Portent le massacre en tous lieux:
Leurs fils, leurs maris, leurs ayeux
Ne peuvent adoucir leur rage,
Dont l'excez rendit glorieux
Le Roy seul exempt du carnage.

Hypsipile en cette turie, (furie?)
Par un dessein officieux
Envers son pere et sa patrie,
Dedans le temple de ses Dieux
L'enferme, et d'un oeil gracieux
Tasche de luy donner courage,
Pour conserver au gré des Cieux
Le Roy seul exempt du carnage.

Envoy

Ce massacre prodigieux
Peint le peché contagieux:
La Vierge en ce commun dommage,

Estant parmy les vicieux
Le Roy seul exempt du carnage.[6]
G. de Belleville.

[6] *Recueil des œuvres qui ont remporté les prix sur le puy de l'Immaculeé Conception de la Vierge, en l'an 1644. Presentés à Monsieur de la Place sieur de Saint Etienne Abbé d'Eu, Prince du Puy anneé present* (Rouen, 1644), pp. 18–19.

APPENDIX II

THE SERVENTOIS

Stengel writes in Groeber's *Grundriss,* Vol. II, p. 87: "Das franz. *Serventois* des 14. u. 15. Jhs. hat nur den Namen mit der provenz. Dictungsart gemeinsam; denn es ist im wesentlichen nichts als ein refrainloser *Chant royal.*" Stengel might further have added that the *Serventois* of this period was designed to exalt the Virgin. At the outset of its career the French *serventois* was not associated with religion; it was merely one of the *poésies d'agrément.*[1] A passage in Rustebeuf, who died about 1286, has been cited[2] as containing the earliest mention of the word *serventois* as applied to religious poetry.

> "Et mes sires Phelipes et li bons cuens d'Artois,
> Et li cuens de Nevers, qui sont preu et cortois,
> Refont en lor venue a Dieu biau *serventois.*"[3]

The *serventois,* like the *ballade,* copied its system of rimes from the secular lyric of the *trouvère.* The *serventois* had no refrain, however, and had always, even in the earliest specimens that we know, an envoy. Thirteenth century

[1] From the twelfth and thirteenth centuries a few French *serventois* have survived that are like the Provençal *serventes* in that they are satirical and political in tone (See A. Scheler, *Trouvères Belges,* Vol. II, p. 74), but the French *serventois* of the later Middle Ages are wholly unlike the Provençal poems of like sounding name.

[2] See L. E. Kastner, *History of French Versification* (Oxford, 1903), p. 74.

[3] See A. Kressner, *Rustebeufs Gedichte* (Wolfenbüttel, 1885), p. 43.

lyrics other than *serventois* display the envoy, which was addressed to the judges of the *puy*, or to a brother poet, or to the deity, or to a mistress.[4] The envoy of the *serventois* was, we may suppose, one of the circumstances that led to the attachment of the envoy to both *ballade* and *chant royal.* In view of the conceivable relation of the *serventois* to the *ballade*, it will be interesting to note its characteristic features, and some of the poetic theories that circulated in regard to it. An example of the *serventois* is the following:

"Quiconques veult en haute hounour monter,
Mettre se doit à la Dame servir
En qui diex voult pour le monde sauver
D'umainne char sa deité couvrir
Et vint chaüis aparoir com homs morteuz.
Che doit chacuns savoir
Car en es flans de le Vierge Marie
De dens nuef mois prist char et sanc et vie.

Car pour ses biens à tous les bons moustrer
Voult diex son cors en la vierge nourrir;
Vierge au conchoivre et Vierge au délivrer,
Et ce ne pot ne savoir ne véir
Aucuns pour son pooir
Que femme ensi peust fruit conchevoir
Ki ains n'eust d'omme eu compagnie
Mais Diex por ce l'avoir édéfiie.

Dont doit chascuns si loiaument ouvrer
K'il puist l'amour la Vierge deservir,
Qui tous nouz puet vers celui racorder
Ki pour nous voult son cors en trois partir,

[4] H. Guy, *Essai sur la Vie et les Œuvres du Trouvère Adan de la Hale* (Paris, 1898), pp. xliii–xlviii; and A. Jeanroy, *Les Chansons Françaises Inédites du Manuscrit de Modène,* Supplement to the *Revue des Langues Romanes,* 1896.

Sen fist en chiex remanoir la Deité.
Et chaüis recevoir l'umanité.
Mort en crois à haschie,
Li Saint Espire fut la tierche partie.

Tant vaut amours, che puet—on esprouver
Ke par amouts veut diex en crois morir;
S'il nous ama nous le devons amer,
Ne nous devons point de li retolir
Quant de si très chier avoir nous racheta,
Quant il nous voult ravoir
Ke de son cors fut la debte païe
Por aquiter tout humaine lignie.

Cors pour les cuers en tous bien doctriner
Ki de vous ont vierge, le souvenir
Bien deust avoir le cuer amer
Quant vo chier fil véistes mort souffrir
Pour nous et par son vouloir.
Or consentez que chascuns son devoir
Fache si bien, Vierge mère et amie,
A vos douch fil k'ame ne soit ne soit périe.

Vierge à vous pri main et soir
Ke nouv veilliez m'ame ramentevoir
Au destroit jour où elle iert mal baillie
Se de vous n'a anvers vo fil aïe."[5 and 6]

The *Miracles de Notre Dame* abound in *serventois couronnés.* The remarks of the poetic theorists in regard to these are worth noting. Deschamps in *L'Art de Dictier* (1392) says:[7]

"*Serventois* sont faiz de cinq couples comme les *chansons*

[5 and 6] G. A. T. Hécart, *Serventois et Sottes Chansons Couronnés à Valenciennes au XIIe et XIIIe Siècles* (Paris, 1834), p. 55. This *serventois* can hardly be a thirteenth century product.

[7] Gaston Paris and Ulysse Robert, *Les Miracles de Notre Dame, Société des Anciens Textes Français* (Paris, 1899).

royaulx; et sont communement de la Vierge Marie, sur la Divinité; et n'y souloit on point faire de refrain, mais a present on les y fait, servens comme en une *balade;* et pour ce que c'est ouvrage qui se porte au *Puis d'amours,* et que nobles hommes n'ont pas acoustumé de ce faire, n'en faiz cy aucun autre exemple."[8]

Other poetic treatises either ignore the refrain, or mention it as unnecessary. LeGrand in *Des Rimes* (before 1405) declares:

"Après, en francoys nous trouvons acuns ditz qui sont nommez serventois, lesquelz, come dient aucuns, se font a plaisir, excepté que l'en doit prendre ung certain nombre de vers tel come l'en veult, mais qu'ilz soyent d'une longueur, et que lung ver responde a l'autre en bonne ryme; et lors on doit proceder en faisant autant de vers [come l'en veult], et de semblable ryme. Et ainsi tousjours."[9]

Les Règles de la Seconde Rhétorique (1411–1432) reads:

"Ou temps du dit Machault fut Brisbarre, de Douay, qui fist le livre de l'escolle de foy et le Tresor Nostre Dame, et si fist le serventoys de

S'Amours n'estoit plus poissant, que Nature,
No foy seroit legiere a condempner."[10]

Apropos of these lines, Langlois says in a footnote: "Ce serventois se retrouve, sans nom d'auteur, sous la rubrique *Serventois de Nostre Dame,* dans le manuscrit de la Bibl. Nat. fr. 1543, f. 99, qui est de la première partie du XIVe siècle; une autre pièce de même taille, sur les mêmes rimes

[8] G. Raynaud, *Œuvres Complètes de Eustache Deschamps, Société des Anciens Textes Français* (Paris, 1891), Vol. VII, p. 281.

[9] E. Langlois, *Recueil d'Arts de Seconde Rhétorique, Collection de Documents Inédits sur l'Histoire de France* (Paris, 1902), p. 9.

[10] E. Langlois, *Opus Cit.*, p. 12.

commençant par le même vers, se trouve dans le manuscrit de la Bibl. Nat., fr. 2095, f. 80 elle est intitulée *Balade.* Le 2e vers est:

Dont nos venroit la cause d'esperer.

Enfin le *Jardin de Plaisance,* éd. Vérard, en donne une troisième, toujours sur les mêmes rimes, dont voici les deux premiers vers:

Si argent n'estoit plus puissant que Nature,
Ne tout le sens qu'elle peut doctriner.

Ces trois pièces ont dû être écrites pour le même concours.''[11] . . . ''La taille des serventoys est ainsi comme il s'enssuit, excepté qu'il convient que la derraine ligne soit feminine et de 11 silabes, et la penultime ligne doit estre de 10.''[12]

Baudet Herenc wrote in *Le Doctrinal de la Seconde Rhétorique* (1432):

"Et se font ces *serventois,* a Lisle en Flandres, le premier dimanche devant l'Assumption Nostre Dame; et doibvent parler de l'Assumption Nostre Dame et de Passion Nostre Seigneur."[13]

Jean Molinet: *L'Art de Rhétorique* (1493):

"Les *serventois* servent pareillement aux puis royaulx, ausquelz il y a certaines regles que les princes desdid puis y mettent, affin de constraindre le facteur sans trop ouvrer a sa plaisance. Et avient

[11] E. Langlois, *Opus Cit.,* p. 12, note 5.

[12] E. Langlois, *Opus Cit.,* p. 26: In Note 1 on this page, Langlois says in regard to the definition of *serventois:* ''La règle peut être speciale à quelque *pui.*'' The *serventois* given consists of five stanzas riming a b a b c c d d e d e and an envoy e d e that begins with the word *Princes.*

[13] E. Langlois, *Opus Cit.,* p. 170. Herenc gives an example of the *serventois* a five-stanza poem; the rimes of each stanza are a b a b c c d d e d e, and the rimes of the envoy are d e d e.

souvent qu'il prent les terminations et premieres lignes d'une amoureuse, laquele amoureuse traitte de matiere d'amours, et contient. .v. couplès et l'envoy, sans reffrain, mais lesdis couplès de pareille consonance. Et les dis serventois le plus sont fais a l'onneur de la vierge Marie et par figure de la Bible."[14]

The *serventois* was, then, in the fourteenth and fifteenth centuries, commonly composed in the *puys* where *ballades* and *chants royaux* were also being offered. All three forms are concluded with envoys. At an earlier period than the other two forms, the *serventois,* as is shown by the Valenciennes collection, was being presented in the *puys.* For this reason, its envoy may have furnished a model to a later generation of *puy* poets composing *ballades* and *chants royaux.*

[14] E. Langlois, *Opus Cit.,* p. 245. The example that follows is composed of five stanzas and envoy, riming a b a b c c d d e d e; d e d e. Envoy begins with "*Prince.*"

APPENDIX III

THE CHANT ROYAL

A form closely related to the *ballade* also developed in the *puy,*—the *chant royal,* a refrain poem, composed of five stanzas and an envoy, in which the same rimes are continued, as in the *ballade.* It is, in fact, a *ballade* in every respect but in the number of stanzas. The word *royal* in this connection seems to refer to the fact that the poem was composed for rendering before a prince of the *puy.* In the statutes of the English *puy,* the phrase *chancon reale* occurs five times. Whether what was later known as a *chant royal* was referred to in these statutes is more than doubtful. But the statutes go to show, at any rate, that a song composed for a *puy* presided over by a prince, might well be described as "royal." The passage in the *Liber Custumarum* is plain.

"E porceoque la feste roiale du pui est maintenue e etablie principaument pur un chaunsoune reale coronner de ci cum ele est par chaunsoun honore et enhaunsier sont tint luy gentil compaignoun du pui par dreite raisoun tenuz des chauncons roiaus auancer a lur pouir et especiaument cele qe est coronne par assent des compaignouns le jour de la graunt feste du pui: par quei il est ici puruu en droit de celes chauncons qe chascun prince nouel le jour qil portera la coronne et gouernera la feste du pui. E si tost com il auera fait prendre son blasoun de ces armes en la sale ou la feste du pui serra tenue qe maintenaunt face atachee de souz son blazon de chauncoun de estoit coronnee le jour qil fur estu nouel prince, apertement et droitement escrite e saunz defaute. Kar nul chantour par droit ne doit chauncoun reale chaunter ne proffrir a la feste du puy desques a taunt qil veit la chauncoun coronnee dreinement en lan prochainement passe devaunt honoure a son droit en la manere auaundite."[1]

Unfortunately none of the lyrics honored in the English *puy* seem to have been preserved to settle the question. Perhaps some day they may come to light.

The following diverse explanations are given of the term *chant royal.* L'Infortuné in *L'Instructif de la Seconde Rhétorique* (1500) explained:

" Item il est dict champ royal, pource que de toutes especes de rithme c'est la plus royalle, noble, ou magistralle: et on l'en couche les plus graves substances. Parquoy c'est voluntiers l'espece pratiquée en puy la, ou en pleine audience, comme en chant de bataille l'en juge, le meilleur est qui est le plus digne d'avoir le prix apres que l'en a bieu batu de l'une part et d'aultre."

Sibilet (1548) wrote:

" Car le chant royal n'est autre chose qu'une balade surmontant la balade comme en nombre de coupletz et en gravité de matiere. Aussi s'appelle il chant royal de nom plus grave ou a cause de sa grandeur et majesté qu'il n'appartient estre chanté que devant les roys, ou par ce que veritablement la fin du chant royal n'est autre que de chanter les louanges, preeminences et dignities des doys tant immortelz que mortelz."

An early use of the exact term *chant royal* is to be found in *Le Dit de la Panthère d'Amours,* where the lover says:

" Car certes moult grant joie avroie,
Douce dame, se je pooie
Faire chose qui vous pleüst,
Combien que couster me deüst,
Fust ce du corps, fust de l'avoir;
Ne pour mal que je puisse avoir
Ne ferai plainte ne clamour;

[1] Folio 176. See also f. 175^{r} and f. 177^{v}.

24

Ains en merci vous et Amour,
Quant il li plest et li agree
. . . .
De vrai cuer entier et loial,
S'en dirai en cest chant royal:[2]

Then there follows a five stanza poem of Adan de la Hale which is not a *chant royal* in the later sense of the word,[3] for although the same rimes occur in every stanza, there is no refrain and no envoy. Here again the significance of the adjective *royal,* taken in connection with the fact that Adan was a member of the *puy* of Arras, is clear.[4] The *chant royal* without refrain, which was exactly like the fourteenth century *serventois,*[5] in fact, is described in *Les Règles de la Seconde Rhétorique* (1411–1432):

"Chans royaux pour porter aux puis de Nostre Dame en la ville de Dieppe sur la mer, et non ailleurs, sont de 5 couples et le Prince, qui est appellez l'Envoy. Et est de 11 lignes, chascune ligne de 10 silabes ou masculin et de 11 ou feminin."[6]

Then follows the example, a *chant royal* of five strophes and envoy; the strophe eleven lines in length, the envoy, five. The rime-scheme of the strophe is a b a b c c d d e d e; the envoy rimes d d e d e. The *chant royal* given shows no

[2] H. A. Todd, *Le Dit de la Panthère d'Amours, par Nicole de Margival* (Paris, 1883), p. 96.

[3] See XII in Table of Adan de la Hale's *Chansons* in H. Guy, *Adan de la Hale* (Paris, 1898), p. 580.

[4] Cf. also H. A. Todd, *Opus Cit.,* ll. 24466 ff.

''Si com dist Adam de la Halle,
Qui onques n'ot pensee male
Vers Amour, ne cuer desloial,
En ce ver d'un sien chant royal.''

[5] See Appendix II.

[6] E. Langlois, *Recueil d'Arts de Seconde Rhétorique, Collection de Documents Inédits sur l'Histoire de France* (Paris, 1902), p. 21.

refrain. Its subject matter is religious, dealing with the redemption. I quote one stanza to show how proper names had become a stylistic feature of such verse:

> "Vierge royaux, turtre delicieuse,
> Nous devons bien vostre venue amer,
> Car vostre nativité glorieuse
> Fist aux humains paradis recouvrer.
> De vous parloit le prophete Ysaye,
> David, Amos, Abdias, Jheremie,
> En affermant, sainte vierge prudente,
> Qu'Adam et sa compaignie dolente
> Raroit des cieux par vous le luminaire
> Ainsi que c'est vraie chose evidente,
> Deffendez nous du sathan deputaire."[7]

Another description and definition of the *Chant royal* which differentiates it not all from the *serventois* is that given by Baudet Herenc in *Le Doctrinal de la Seconde Rhétorique* (1432):

> "Cy s'ensuit la forme et taille d'ung chant royal, qui se font a Dieppe en Normandie; et s'appelle chant royal pour ce que l'on commence et fine en telle maniere que l'on veult [absurd notion]; et doibt parler de la Nativité Nostre Dame et de la Passion Nostre Seigneur et de l'Assomption Nostre Dame."[8]

The example given has five stanzas riming a b a b c c d d e d e and an envoy riming d d e d e.

An earlier authority, however, Deschamps, in his *L'Art de Dictier* (1392), gives the *chant royal* a refrain. He says:

> "Item en ladictet ballade a Envoy. Et ne les soloit on point faire anciennement fors es Chancons royaulx, qui estoient de cinq

[7] E. Langlois, *Opus Cit.*, p. 23.
[8] E. Langlois, *Opus Cit.*, p. 173.

couples, chascune couple de .x., .xi. or .xij. vers; et de tant se puelent bien faire, et non pas de plus, par droicte regle. Et doivent les envois d'icelles chancons, qui se commencent par *Princes,* estre de cinq vers entez par eulx aux rimes de la chancon sans rebrique; c'est assavoir .ij. vers premiers, et puis un pareil de la rebriche, et les .ij. autres suyans les premier deux, concluans en substance l'effect de ladicte chancon et servens a la rebriche."[9]

Molinet in the *L'Art de Rhétorique* cites a *chant royal* with a refrain that was crowned at Amiens in 1470.[10]

L'Infortuné in *L'Instructif de Seconde Rhétorique* exemplifies the form in the same way:

De vndecimo colore rethorice gallicane sciz
de campis realibus.

Souefue manne de distilation
Rassasiant substancieusement
Diffuse par fructification
De minerue scientifiquement
Est ou verger de dame rethoricque
En souefue odeur flaugrante aromatique
Sur pluseurs fleurs receuans influence
De fronesis de tresnoble science
Espanissant mainte fleur necte et pure
Mais sur toutes de tresnoble assistence
Le champ royal est de noble faicture.

Promotheus par constellation
Souuent transmet delicieusement
Dyaphanon par illustracion
Pour esclarcir substancieusement
Dong transparant ray fulgent & celique
Procedant sus maint support auctentique
Qui au verger predict fait residence
Duquel souuent par noble prouidence

9 G. Raynaud, *Œuvres Complètes de Eustache Deschamps, Société des Anciens Textes Français* (Paris, 1891), Vol. VII, p. 278.

10 E. Langlois, *Opus Cit.*, p. 242.

Mainte fleur est prodiucte clere & pure
Entre quelles de plaisance euidence
Le champ royal est de noble faicture.

Qui nous aprent melodieusement
Par sa franche descrete instruction
A bien traicter tragedieusement
Nous peult noter que pour faiz de cronique
Ou pour autre digne forme heroique
Ou doraison de bonne conuenance
Ceste forme a et grant coincidence
Pource dis ie que pour ceulx qui ont cure
De faire ditz qui aient bonne essence
Le champ royal est de noble faicture.

Du champ royal la compilation
Est en ce dit rethoricalement
Si est aussi la postillation
Et en tout dit pareil egalement
Qui cinq coupletz a dune forme vnique
Bien pareille semblable & politique
Terminaison selon ce que commence
La premiere couple sans difference
Auec aussi prince de leur figure
Ou a motie des coupletz: ainsi en ce
Le champ royal est de noble faicture.

Pluseurs gens font reduplication
De la ligne croissant secondement
Luy redoublant sa termination
Mail il souffist faire sortablement
De la sorte de ceste que iapplique
Item aucuns par forme manifique
Font en telz ditz de leur forme sequence
Double refrain par forme deloquence
Item pluseurs en mentrificature
Dyalogue sont: et en leur sentence
Le champ royal est de noble faicture.

Prince royaulx retrogradacion
Belle et noble est quant bien on le figure
Et en telz ditz fait decoration
Ainsi qui tient telle proportion
Le champ royal est de noble faicture.[11]

At least as late as Colletet, the author of *L'Escole des Muses* (1652), the theorists repeated the same formula, or approximately the same one that L'Infortuné and Molinet prescribed. The *chant royal* and the *ballade* became the favorite forms of the poets of the *puy.* Whereas the *ballade* originated outside the *puy,* and was adapted to the circumstances under which poetic contests were held, the *chant royal* seems to have been the wholly sophisticated artifice of poetic contrivers who were familiar with the *chansons* of the trouvères, with the *balletes,* and with the early *ballades.* Both the *chant royal* and the *serventois,* as we get them in the fourteenth century, are the product of conditions in the *puy.*

[11] f. biiii^{v}.

BIBLIOGRAPHIES

CHAPTER I

The Origins of the Ballade

Works, General Authorities, etc.

Aubry, Pierre. *La Chanson Populaire dans les Textes Musicaux du Moyen Âge.* Paris, 1905.

Le Roman de Fauvel (Reproduction photographique du manuscrit de la Bibliothèque Nationale, avec un index des interpolations lyriques). Paris, 1907.

Trouvères et Troubadours. Paris, 1909.

Bahlsen, L. *Adam de la Hale's Dramen und das 'Jus du Pelerin.' Ausgaben und Abhandlungen aus dem Gebiete der Romanischen Philologie,* XXVII. Marburg, 1885.

Bartsch, K. *Chréstomathie Provençale.* Marburg, 1903.

Denkmäler der Provenzalischen Literatur. Stuttgart, 1856.

Grundriss zur Geschichte der Provenzalischen Literatur. Elberfeld, 1872.

Die Provenzalische Liederhandschrift Q. Zeitschrift für Romanische Philologie, IV (1880).

Beck, J. *La Musique des Troubadours.* Paris, 1910.

Bédier, J. *Un Feuillet Récemment Retrouvé d'un Chansonnier Français du XIIIe Siècle. Mélanges de Philologie Romane et d'Histoire Littéraire Offerts à M. Wilmotte.* Paris, 1910.

Les Plus Anciennes Dances Françaises. Revue de Deux Mondes, XXX, 15 Janvier, 1906.

BIADENE, L. *La Forma Metrica de Commiato nelle Canzone Italiana dei Secoli XIII e XIV. Memoria di N. Caix e A. Canello.* Firenze, 1886.

Leggende dello Sclavo Dalmasino. 1894.

COUSSEMAKER, E. DE. *Œuvres Complètes du Trouvère Adam de la Halle.* Paris, 1872.

CRESCINI, V. *Manualetto Provenzale.* Verona-Padua, 1905.

DAVIDSON, F. J. A. *Über den Ursprung und die Geschichte der Französischen Ballade.* Halle, 1900.

DREVES, G. M., AND BLUM, C. *Analecta Hymnica Medii Ævi.* 52 vols. Leipzig, 1886, ff.

ECKERT, G. *Über die bei Altfranzösischen Dichtern Vorkommenden Bezeichnungen der Einzelnen Dictungsarten.* Heidelberg, 1895.

FARAL, EDMOND. *Les Jongleurs en France au Moyen Âge.* Paris, 1910.

FLAMINI, FRANCESCO. *Per la Storia d'Alcune Antiche Forme Poetiche Italiene e Romanze. Studi di Storia Letteraria.* Livorno, 1895.

Studi di Storia Letteraria Italiene e Portoghese. Wien, 1895.

GATIEN-ARNOULT, A. F. *Monumens de la Littérature Romane.* 4 vols. Paris-Toulouse, 1841–1849.

GENNRICH, FRIEDERICH. *Le Romans de La Dame à La Lycorne et du Biau Chevalier au Lyon. Gesellschaft für Romanische Literatur, Band XVIII.* Dresden, 1908.

Le Romans de la Dame à la Lycorne et du Biau Chevalier. Strassburg, 1908.

GROEBER, G. *Grundriss der Romanischen Philologie.* 4 vols. Strassburg, 1888, 1902.

Zu den Liederbüchern von Cortona. Zeitschrift für Romanische Philologie XI (1887), pp. 371–394.

GUY, H. *Le Trouvère Adan de la Hale.* Paris, 1898.

HÉCART, G. A. T. *Serventois et Sottes Chansons Couronnés à Valenciennes aux XIIIe et XIVe Siècles.* Paris, 1834.

HECQ, G. *La Ballade et Ses Derivés.* Bruxelles, 1891.

HESS, R. *Der Roman de Fauvel. Romanische Forschungen, XXVII.* Erlangen, 1910.

Histoire Littéraire de la France. Ouvrage commencé par des Religieux Bénédictins de la Congregation de S. Maur. Continués par des membres de l'Institut (Académie des Inscriptions et Belles-Lettres). Paris, 1733 ff.

HOEPFFNER, E. Jehan Acart de Hesdin, *La Prise Amoureuse. Gesellschaft für Romanische Literatur,* Bd. 22. Dresden, 1910.

JÄRNSTRÖM, E. *Recueil de Chansons Pieuses du XIIIe Siècle.* Helsinki, 1910.

JEANROY, A. *Les Chansons Françaises Inédites du Manuscrit de Modène.* Special issue of *Revue des Langues Romanes.* 1896.

Les Chansons Pieuses du Ms. fr. 12483 de la Bibliothèque Nationale. Mélanges de Philologie Romane et d'Histoire Littéraire Offerts à M. Maurice Wilmotte. Paris, 1910.

Modèles Profanes de Chansons Pieuses. Romania, XL (1911), p. 84.

Les Origines de la Poésie Lyrique en France au Moyen-Âge. Paris, 1904.

Review of *Recueil de Chansons Pieuses du XIII Siècle. Romania,* XL (1911), pp. 124–127.

JEANROY, A., AND GUY, H. *Chansons et Dits Artesiens du XIIIe Siècle.* Bordeaux, 1898.

JUNKER, H. P. *Grundriss zur Geschichte der Französischen Literatur.* Münster i. W., 1905.

LANGLOIS, CH. V. *La Vie en France au Moyen Age.* Paris, 1908.

LANGLOIS, E. *Les Manuscrits du Roman de la Rose. Les Travaux et Mémoires de L'Université de Lille.* 1910.

MENAGE, G. *Dictionnaire Etymologique.* 2 vols. Paris, 1750.

MEYER, P. *Les Derniers Troubadours de la Provence.* Paris, 1871.

Documents Manuscrits de l'Ancienne Littérature de la France, conservés dans les Bibliothèques de la Grande Bretagne. Paris, 1871.

Des Rapports de la Poésie des Trouvères avec celle des Troubadours. Romania, XIX (1890), p. 1–62.

MEYER, P., AND RAYNAUD, G. *Le Chansonnier Français de Saint-Germain-des-Près.* (*Bibl. Nat. 200 50*), *Reproduction Photographique,* Tome I. Paris, 1872.

MEYER, RUDOLPH ADELBERT. *Französische Lieder aus der Florentiner Handschrift Strozzi-Magliabecchiana cl. VII, 1040.* Halle, 1906.

MONTAIGLON, A. DE. *Jehannot de Lescurel. Chansons, Ballades et Rondeaux.* Paris, 1855.

NOACK, FRITZ. *Der Strophenausgang in seinem Verhältniss zum Refrain u. Strophengrundstock in der Refrainhältigen Altfranzösischen Lyrik.* Marburg, 1899.

NOVATI, FRANCESCO. *La Canzone Popolare in Francia e in Italia nel Piu Alto Medio Evo. Mélanges de Philologie Romane et d'Histoire Littéraire Offerts à M. Wilmotte.* Paris, 1910.

Le Roman de Fauvel. Histoire Litt. XXXII. Paris, 1898.

Review of Jeanroy's '*Les Origines de la Poésie Lyrique en France au Moyen Âge.' Journal des Savants* (1891). pp. 674–688; 729–742.

PETIT DE JULLEVILLE, L. *Histoire de la Langue et de la Littérature Française des Origines à 1900.* 8 vols. Paris 1896–1899.

PEY, A. *Le Roman de Fauvel. Jahrbuch für Romanische und Englische Literatur. Bd. VII.* Leipzig, 1886.

PIAGET, A. *Un Manuscrit de la Cour Amoureuse de Charles VI. Romania, XXXI* (1902), pp. 597–602.

La Cour Amoureuse, Dite de Charles VI. Romania, XX (1890), p. 415.

RAYNAUD, G. Review of Hoepffner's *La Prise Amoureuse. Romania, XL* (1911), pp. 129–131.

RÖMER, LUDWIG. *Die Volkstümlichen Dichtungsarten der Altprovenzalischen Lyrik. Ausgaben u. Abhandlungen aus dem Gebiete der Romanischen Philologie,* pt. 26. Marburg, 1884.

SCHELER, A. *Le Regret Guillaume par Jehan de la Mote.* Louvain, 1882.

STEFFENS, GEORG. *Die Altfranzösischen Lieder Ms. der Bodleiana in Oxford Douce 308. Abdruck aus Herrig's Archiv. Bd.* 97, pp. 283–308; *Bd.* 98, pp. 343–382; *Bd.* 99, pp. 77–100.

STENGEL, E. *Ableitung der Provenzalisch-französischen Dansa und der Französischen Virelay-Formen. Zeitschrift für Französische Sprache, XVI* (1894), pp. 94–101.

Die Refrains der Oxforder Ballettes. Zeitschrift für Französische Sprache, XXVIII (1905), pp. 72–78.

Der Strophenausgang in den Ältesten Französischen Balladen und sein Verhältniss zum Refrain u. Strophengrundstock. Zeitschrift für Französische Sprache, XVII (1896), pp. 85–114.

TODD, H. A. *Le Dit de la Panthère d'Amours par Nicole de Margival.* Paris, 1883.

ULRIX, E. *Les Chansons Inédites de Guillaume le Vinier. Mélanges Wilmotte.* Paris, 1910.

VOLLMÖLLER, K. *Kritischer Jahresbericht über die Fortschritte der Romanischen Philologie.* 11 vols. München, 1892–1910. (Vol 2 pub. in Leipzig.)

WARREN, F. M. *The Romance Lyric from the Standpoint of Antecedent Latin Documents. Publications Modern Language Association,* XIX (1904).

ZINGERLE, W. VON *Zu Roman de la Dame à la Lycorne et du Beau Chevalier. Philologische und Volkskundliche Arbeiten Karl Vollmöllers.* 1908.

THE PUY

Manuscripts

Bodleian Library. Ms. Douce 379.

Bibliothèque de Rouen. Ms. Y 80.

Bibliothèque de Rouen. Ms. Y 18.

Bibliothèque de Rouen. Ms. Y 48.

General Authorities, etc.

AYMARD. *Notice Relatif à l'Ancienne Confrérie de Notre Dame du Puy. Congrés Scientifique de France. 22e Session, tome 2.* Paris, 1856.

BEAUVILLE, V. DE. *Recueil de Documents Inédits Concernant la Picardie.* 3 vols. Paris, 1860–1882.

BEAUREPAIRE, E. DE R. DE. *Étude sur la Poésie Populaire en Normandie.* Paris, 1856.

Les Puys de Palinod de Rouen et de Caen. Caen, 1907.

BÉDIER, J. *Richard de Normandie. Romanic Review,* I (1910).

BREUIL. *La Confrérie de Notre-Dame-du-Puy d'Amiens.* Amiens, 1854.

Mémoires de la Société des Antiquaires de Picardie III, p. 489. Amiens, 1838 et ann. suiv.

BOURGUEVILLE, C. DE. *Les Recherches et Antiquitez de la Province de Neustrie, à present Duche de Normandie, comme des Villes remarquable d'icelles, mais plus spécialement des ville et université de Caen.* Caen, 1588.

CASENEUVE, P. DE. *Origine des Jeux Fleureux de Toulouse.* Toulouse, 1659.

DURILLET, L. *Le Poète.* See below.

GISSEY, P. O. DE. *Discours Historiques de la Trésancienne Deuotion de Nostre Dame du Puy ou du Puy Nostre Dame.* Toulouse, 1627. (This is a second edition.)

GUIOT, J. A. *Les Trois Siècles Palinodiques ou Histoire Générale des Palinods de Rouen, Dieppe, etc. Publié par la Société de l'Histoire de Normandie.*

GARDIN, L. DU. *Premieres Addresses du Chemin de Parmasse, pour Monstrer la Prosodie Françoise par les Menutez des Vers Francois Minutees en Cent Reigles.* Douay, 1610.

GRIMM, J. *Deutsche Rechtsalterthümer.* Bd. II, 800–802. Leipzig, 1899.

LA RUE, G. DE. *Essais Historiques sur les Bardes les Jongleurs et les Trouvères Normands et Anglo-Normands.* 3 Tom. Caen, 1834.

LE ROUX DE LINCY, A. J. V. *Essai Historique et Litteraire sur l'Abbaye de Fécamp.* Rouen, 1840.

MEDICIS, E. *Le Livre de Podio, Recueil des Chroniqueurs du Puy-en-Velay.* Ed. by A. Chassaing. Le-Puy-en-Velay, 1869.

MEYER, P. *Chanson de la Croisade contre les Albigeois. Société de l'Histoire de France.* 2 vols. Paris, 1875, 1879.

Palinods Présentés au Puy de Rouen. Recueil de Pierre Vidoue. (1525) Precédé par un Introduction par E. de Robillard de Beaurepaire. Rouen, 1897.

PASSY, L. *Bibliothèque de l'École, des Chartes, 4e Serie, V* (1859), 491 et suiv.

PICOT, É. *Une Querelle Littéraire aux Palinods de Dieppe au XVe Siècle. Mélanges de Philologie Romane et d'Histoire Litteraire Offerts à M. Maurice Wilmotte.* Paris, 1910.

Le Poète, Ode qui a remporté un prix aux Jeux Floraux, le 3 mai 1808, par M. L. Durillet (de Dole), membre de l'Académie de Besançon. *Moniteur, Mardi,* 7 juin, 1808.

Recueil des Œuvres qui ont remporté les prix sur le puy de l'Immaculée Conception de la Vierge, en l'an 1655. Présentées à M. de la Place sieur de Saint Estienne, Abbé d'Eu, Prince du Puy année présente. Rouen, 1643?

Riley, H. T. *Memorials of London and London Life, in the XIIIth, XIVth and XVth centuries. Being a series of extracts, local, social, and political, from the early archives of the City of London. A. D. 1270–1412.* London, 1868.

Munimenta Gildhallae Londoniensis; Liber Albus; Liber Custuarum, and Liber Horn. Vol. II, part II. London, 1859. (Vol. II, pt. I; xlviii; Vol. II, pt. II, p. 579; 708.

Roquefort, J. B. B. de. *De l'État de la Poésie Française dans les XIIe et XIIIe Siècles.* Paris, 1815.

CHAPTER II

The Ballade in France from the Middle of the Fourteenth to the End of the Seventeenth Century.

Manuscripts

Bibliothèque Nationale. Ms. Français 1707.
Bibliothèque Nationale. Ms. Français 2306.
Bibliothèque Nationale. Ms. Français 19369.
Bibliothèque Nationale. Ms. Français 24408.
British Museum *Manuscript Additional 15224.*
British Museum *Ms. Harley 4397.*

Works, General Authorities, etc.

Bartsch, K. *Chréstomathie de l'Ancien Français.* Leipzig, 1884.

Blaise d'Auriol. *Depart Damours.* Paris, 1509.

Blanchemain, P. *Œuvres Complètes de Melin de Sainct-Gelays.* 3 vols. Paris, 1873–4.

Borderie, A de la. *Jean Meschinot, sa Vie et ses Œuvres. Bibl. de l'École des Chartes.* t. IV′ (Paris, 1895. Vol. 56, pp. 99–140; 274–317; 601–638).

Bouchet, J. *Opuscelles du Trauerseur des Voyes Perilleuses. Nouvellement par lui reueuz,* etc. Poitiers, 1526.

Le Chappellet des Princes en Cinquente Rōdeaulx, et Cinq Ballades Faict et Composé par le Trauerseur des Voyes Perilleuses. Paris, 1517.

XIII Rondeaulx Differens. Avec XXV Balades Différentes. Paris, 1536.

Champion, P. *Charles d'Orléans, Joueur d'Échecs.* Paris, 1908.

Le Ms. Autographe des Poésies de Charles d'Orléans. Paris, 1907.

Champollion-Figeac, A. *Louis et Charles Ducs d'Orléans Leur Influence sur les Arts, la Littérature et l'Esprit de Leur Siècle.* Paris, 1844.

Les Poésies du Duc Charles d'Orléans. Ed. by A. Champollion-Figeac. Paris, 1842.

Chickmaref, V. Guillaume de Machaut, *Poésies Lyriques.* 2 Vols. Paris, 1909.

Collerye, R. de. *Les Œuvres de Maistre Roger de Collerye.* Paris, 1536.

Coquiliart, G. *Les Œuvres.* Paris, 1532.

Deshoulières, Mme et Mlle. *Œuvres.* 2 vols. Paris, 1803.

DUCHESNE, A. *Les Œuvres de Alain Chartier.* Paris, 1617.

EHRLICH, A. *Jean Marot's Leben u. Werke.* Leipzig, 1902.

FEHSE, E. *Sprichwort u. Sentenz bei Eustache Deschamps u. Dichtern seiner Zeit.* Berlin, 1905.

HOEPFFNER, E. *Anagramma u. Rätselgedichte bei Guillaume de Machaut. Zeitschrift für Romanische Philologie, XXX* (1906), pp. 401–413.

Eustache Deschamps, Leben u. Werke. Strassburg, 1904.

Frage- und Antwortspiele in der Französischen Literatur des 14. Jahrhunderts. Zeitschrift für Romanische Philologie, XXXIII (1909), pp. 695–710.

D'HERICAULT, C. Guillaume Coquillart: *Œuvres.* Paris, 1857.

Les Œuvres de Roger de Collerye. Paris, 1855.

JANNET, P. *Œuvres Complètes de Clément Marot.* 4 vols. Paris, 1873–1876.

KLEINERT, G. *Ueber den Streit zwischen Leib u. Seele.* Halle, 1880.

KNOBLOCH, H. *Die Streitgedichte im Provenzalischen und Altfranzösischen.* Breslau, 1886.

LA FONTAINE, J. DE. *Œuvres Complètes.* 18 vols. Paris, 1819–21.

L'ENGLET-DUFRESNOY, N. *Œuvres de Clément Marot . . . avec (t. V.) les Ouvrages de Jean Marot son Père.* 4 vols. La Haye, 1731.

LE ROUX DE LINCY, A. J. V. *Le Livre des Proverbes Français.* 2 vols. Paris, 1859.

Recueil de Chants Historiques Français. Paris, 1841–1842.

"La Bibliothèque de Charles d'Orléans à son Château de Blois (en 1427)." Bibliothèque de l'École des Chartes. Paris, 1843/4, tome V, pp. 59–82.

LETTENHOVE, K. DE. *Œuvres de Chastellain.* 8 vols. Brussels, 1863–66.

LONGNON, A. H. François Villon: *Œuvres Complètes.* Paris, 1892.

Étude Biographique sur François Villon, d'après les Documents Inédits Conservés aux Archives Nationales. Paris, 1877.

Les Deux Coquillart. *Romania,* XXIX (1900), pp. 564–569.

MAROT, CLÉMENT. See *Œuvres* below.

MENNUNG, A. *Jean-François Sarasin's Leben und Werke, Seine Zeit und Gesellschaft.* 2 vols. Halle, 1902–04.

MESCHINOT, J. *Les Lunettes des Princes.* Paris, 1539.

MEYER, P. *Documents Manuscrits de L'Ancienne Littérature de la France Conservés dans les Bibliothèques de la Grande-Bretagne. Extrait des Archives des Missions Scientifiques et Littéraires.* 2e série. Paris, 1871.

MONOD, M. B. *Guillaume de Machault, Quinze Poésies Inédits.* Versailles, 1913.

MONTAIGLON, A. DE. Jehannot de Lescurel: *Chansons, Ballades et Rondeaux.* Paris, 1855.

Recueil de Poésies Françaises des XVe et XVIe Siecles. 13 vols. Paris, 1855–78.

NEFF, T. L. *La Satire des Femmes dans la Poésie Lyrique Française du Moyen-Âge.* Paris, 1900.

Œuvres de Clement Marot . . . avec les Ouvrages de Jean Marot son père ceux de Michel Marot son Fils & les Pièces du Different de Clement avec François Sagon. 4 vols. A la Haye, 1731.

OULMONT, C. *Pierre Gringore.* Paris, 1911.

PARIS, G. *François Villon.* Paris, 1911.

PATTERSON, F. A. *The Middle English Penitential Lyric.* New York, 1911.

PIAGET, A. *Une Édition Gothique de Charles d'Orléans.*

Romania, XXI (1892), pp. 581–596; XXII (1893), pp. 254–260.

PICOT, E. *Supercherie d'Antoine Vérard. Romania*, XXII (1893), pp. 244–260.

QUEUX DE SAINT-HILAIRE, MARQUIS DE, AND RAYNAUD, G. Eustache Deschamps: *Œuvres Complètes.* 11 vols. Paris, 1878–1903.

QUICHERAT, J. *Les Vers de Maître Henri Baude.* Paris, 1856.

Henri Baude. Bibl. de l'École des Chartes. X (1848–49), pp. 93–133.

RAYNAUD, G. *Les Cent Ballades.* Paris, 1905.

REGNIER, H. *Œuvres de J. de la Fontaine.* 11 vols. Paris, 1883–1892.

RUUTZ-REES, C. *Charles de Sainte-Marthe (1512–55).* New York, 1910.

ROY, M. Christine de Pisan: *Œuvres Poétiques.* 3 vols. Paris, 1886–91.

Les Œuvres de Me. Sarasin. Amsterdam, 1694.

SCHELER, A. *Poésies de Froissart.* 3 vols. Bruxelles, 1870–72.

STECHER, J. *Œuvres Complètes de Jean Lemaire.* 4 vols. Louvain, 1882–91.

TARBE, P. Guillaume de Machault: *Œuvres.* Reims and Paris, 1849.

UBICINI, A. *Œuvres de Voiture.* Paris, 1855. Vol. II.

VOLLMÖLLER, K. *Kritischer Jahresbericht über die Fortschritte der Romanischen Philologie.* 11 vols. München, 1892–1910. (Vol. 2 pub. in Leipzig.)

VILLON, F. *Œuvres.* Editées par un Ancien Archiviste. Paris, 1911.

THE DRAMA

BRANDENBURG, M. *Die Festen Strophengebilde u. Einige Kunstleien des Mystère de Saint Barbe.* Greifswald, 1907.

CARNANDET, J. *La Vie et Passion de Monseigneur Sainct Didier, Martir et Evesque de Lengres p. Maistre Guillaume Flamang.* Paris, 1855.

CARNAHAN, D. H. *The Prologue in the Old French and Provençal Mystery.* New Haven, 1905.

CLÉDAT, L. *Le Theâtre en France au Moyen Age.* Paris, 1896.

ERLER, C. *Mystère de Saint Denis.* Marburg, 1896.

GUESSARD, F., ET DE CERTAIN, E. *Le Mistère du Siège d'Orléans.* Paris, 1862.

LANGLOIS, E. *Jean Molinet Auteur du Mystère S. Quentin. Romania,* XXII (1893), pp. 552–553.

LOHMANN, W. *Untersuchungen über Jean Louvets 12 Mysterien zu Ehren von Notre Dame de Liesse.* Greifswald, 1900.

MICHEL, F. *Le Mystère de Saint Loys, roi de France.* Westminster, 1895.

MÜLLER, L. *Das Rondel in den Französischen Mirakelspielen und Mysterien des 15 u. 16 Jahrhunderts. Ausgaben u. Abhandlungen, XXIV.* Marburg, 1884.

PARIS, G., ET RAYNAUD, G. *Le Mystère de la Passion d'Arnoul Greban.* Paris, 1878.

PARIS, G., ET ROBERT, U. *Miracles de Nostre Dame. Sociéte des Ancien Textes Françaises.* Paris, 1876, '77, '78, '79, '80, '81, '83, '93.

PETIT DE JULLEVILLE, L. *Histoire du Théatre en France; les Mystères.* 2 vols. Paris, 1880.

PICOT, É. *Le Livre et Mystère du Glorieux Seigneur et Martir Saint Adrien.* Macon, 1895.

Recueil Général des Sotties. 3 vols. Paris, 1902, 1904, 1912.

QUEDENFELDT, G. *Die Mysterien des Heiligen Sebastien, Ihre Quelle und Ihr Abhängigkeitsverhältniss.* Marburg, 1895.

ROTHSCHILD, J. DE. *Le Mistère du Viel Testament. Société des Anciens Textes Françaises.* 3 vols. Paris, 1878, '79, '81.

SEEFELDT, P. *Mystère Français de Saint Barbe en Deux Journées.* Greifswald, 1900.

SÖDERHJELM, W., ET WALLENSKÖLD, A. *Le Mystère de Saint Laurent.* Helsingfors, 1890.

STENGEL, E. *L'Istoire de la Destruction de Troye la Grant p. Maistre Jacques Milet.* Marburg u. Leipzig, 1883.

TOBLER, A. *Wechsel der Versarten in Mysterien. Zeitschrift für Romanischen Philologie,* XIX (1895).

CHAPTER III

THE THEORY OF THE BALLADE FROM DESCHAMPS TO BOILEAU.

Works, General Authorities,[1] *etc.*

ASSELINEAU, C. *Le Livre des Ballades.* Paris, 1876.

BECKER, P. A. *Autobiographisches von Jehan Molinet. Zeitscrift für Romanische Philologie, XXVI* (1902).

BRUNET, J. C. *Manuel du Libraire.* 9 vols. Paris, 1860–1880.

CHAMARD, HENRI. *Le Date et l'Auteur du "Quintil Horation." Revue d'Histoire Littéraire de la France.* 15 janvier, 1898.

CHATELAIN, A. *Recherches sur le Vers Français au XVe Siècle.* Paris, 1908.

GRASSERIE, M. DE LA. *De la Strophe et du Poème dans la Versification Française Spécialement en Vieux Français.* Paris, 1893.

[1] A sufficient bibliography of the various rhetorical treatises on versification, dealing with the *Ballade,* is given in Chapter III itself.

GOUJET, C. P. *Bibliothèque Françoise ou Histoire de la Littérature Françoise.* 18 vols. Paris, 1740–1756.

HUET, G. Langlois, *Recueil,* etc. *Le Moyen Âge,* XVI (1903), pp. 377–81.

KASTNER, L. E. *History of French Versification.* Oxford, 1903.

LANGLOIS, E. *De Artibus Rhetoricae Rhythmicae.* Paris, 1890.

Recueil d'Arts de Second Rhétorique. Paris, 1902.

MACFARLANE, J. *Antoine Vérard.* Illustrated Monographs Issued by the Bibliographical Society, VII. London, 1900.

MORF, H. Langlois, *Recueil,* etc. *Archiv für das Studium der Neueren Sprachen u. Literaturen CXII* (1904), pp. 229, 230.

PASQUIER, E. *Les Recherches de la France.* Paris, 1633.

PELLECHET, M. *Catalogue des Incunables des Bibliothèques Publiques de France.* Paris, 1897.

PELLISSIER, G. *De Sexti Decimi Saeculi in Francia Artibus Poeticis.* Paris, 1883.

PICOT, E. Langlois, *Recueil,* etc. *Romania, XXXIII* (1904), pp. 111–114.

RICHELET, P. *Versification Française.* Paris, 1677.

RIGOLEY DE JUVIGNY, J. A. *Les Bibliothèques Françoises de la Croix du Maine et Du Verdier Sieur de Vaupiras.* Paris, 1772.

STENGEL, E. Langlois, *Recueil, etc. Zeitschrift für Romanische Philologie, XXVII* (1903).

RUCKTÄSCHEL, T. *Einige Arts Poétiques aus der Zeit Ronsard's u. Malherbes.* London, 1889.

TOBLER, A. *Vom Französischen Versbau Alter und Neuer Zeit.* Leipzig, 1903.

VILLEY, P. *Les Sources Italiennes de la Deffense et Illustration de la Langue Française.* Paris, 1909.

VIOLLET-LE-DUC, E. L. N. *Catalogue des Livres Composant sa Bibliothèque Poétique.* 2 vols. Paris, 1843–47.

WENDEROTH, G. *Estienne Pasquier's Poetische Theorien und Seine Tätigkeit als Literarhistoriker. Romanische Forschungen, XIX,* pp. 1–75. Erlangen, 1905.

ZSCHALIG, H. *Die Verslehren von Fabri, Du Pont und Sibilet.* Leipzig, 1884.

CHAPTER IV

THE MIDDLE ENGLISH BALLADE

Manuscripts

Bodleian *Ms. Fairfax 16.*

Bodleian *Ms. Tanner 346.*

Bodleian *Ms. 648.*

British Museum *Ms. Arundel 26.*

British Museum *Ms. Lansdowne 380.*

British Museum *Ms. Lansdowne 699.*

British Museum *Ms. Harley 7333.*

British Museum *Ms. 16165.*

Cambridge University Library *Ms. Ff. 1. 6.*

Trinity College Cambridge *Ms. R. 14. 5.*

Trinity College Cambridge *Ms. R. 3. 20.*

Works, General Authorities, etc.

BATESON, M. *George Ashby's Poems. Early English Text Society.* Extra Series 76. London, 1899.

BOCK, F. *Metrische Studien zu Thomas Hoccleves Werken.* München, 1900.

BOLLE, W. *Zu Lyrik der Rawlinson Ms. C. 813. Anglia, XXII, Neue Folge* (1911), p. 273.

BULLRICH, G. *Uber Charles d'Orléans und die ihm Zugeschiebenen Englischen Übersetzungen seiner Dichtungen.* Berlin, 1893.

CHAMBERS, E. K., AND SIDGWICK, E. *Early English Lyrics, Amourous, Divine, Moral and Trivial.* London, 1897.

CHAMPOLLION-FIGEAC, A. *Poésies du Duc Charles d'Orléans.* Paris, 1842.

Louis et Charles Ducs d'Orléans. Paris, 1844.

COTGRAVE, R. *A Dictionarie of the French and English Tongues.* London, 1611.

CUNLIFFE, J. W. *Gascoigne's The Glasse of Governement and Other Works.* Cambridge, 1910.

Gascoigne's The Posies. Cambridge, 1907.

DOUGLAS, G. *The Palice of Honour.* Edinburgh, 1827.

FLÜGEL, E. *Chaucer's Kleinere Gedichte. Anglia, IX, X, XI,* Neue Folge (1899, 1901).

FURNIVALL, F. J. *Hoccleve's Regement of Princes. Early English Text Society.* Extra Series 72. London, 1897.

Hoccleve's Minor Poems. Early English Text Society, Extra Series 61. London, 1892.

A Balade or Two by Chaucer, in Tyl of Brentford's Testament, etc. Printed for Private Circulation. London, 1871.

Political, Religious and Love Poems. Early English Text Society, 15. London, 1866.

Parallel Text Edition of Chaucer's Minor Poems. 3 pts. in 2 vols. London, 1871–79.

Minor Poems of the Vernon Ms. Pt. II. *Early English Text Society.* 107.

Trial Forewords. London, 1871.

GALPIN, S. L. *"Fortune's Wheel in the Roman de la Rose." Publications of the Modern Language Association, XXIV* (1909), p. 332.

LYDGATE, J. *Minor Poems. The Two Nightingale Poems.*

Ed. O. Glauning. Early English Text Society. Extra Series 80. London, 1900.

HAMMOND, E. P. *Omissions from the Selections of Chaucer. Modern Language Notes,* XIX (1904), 35–38.

Two British Museum Manuscripts. A Contribution to the Bibliography of John Lydgate. Anglia, Neue Folge, XVI (1905).

Chaucer: A Bibliographical Manual. New York, 1908.

Ashmole 59 and Other Shirley Manuscripts. Anglia XXX Neue Folge (1907), pp. 320–348.

Lydgate and the Duchess of Gloucester. Anglia, XXVII Neue Folge (1904), pp. 381–398.

HENLEY, W. E. *English Lyrics.* London, 1897.

HORSTMANN, C. *Sammlung Altenglischer Legenden.* Heilbronn, 1881.

HULME, W. A. *The Middle English Harrowing of Hell and Gospel of Nicodemus. Early English Text Society.* Extra Series 100. London, 1907.

JAMES, M. R. *The Western Manuscripts in the Library of Trinity College, Cambridge.* 4 vols. Cambridge, 1911.

JAMES VI OF SCOTLAND, I OF ENGLAND. *Essayes of a Prentice, in the Divine Art of Poesie.* London, 1569.

KITTREDGE, G. L. *Chaucer and Some of His Friends. Modern Philology,* I (1903–1904), pp. 1–18.

Chauceriania. Modern Philology, VII (1910). *Englische Studien, XIII* (1889), 24 f.

KOCH, J. *Chronology of Chaucer's Writings.* London, 1890.

KÖPPEL, E. *Gowers Französischen Balladen und Chaucer. Englische Studien* XX (1895), p. 154.

Chauceriania: Jehan de Meung. 1. *Le Roman de la Rose. Anglia, XIV* Neue Folge (1891), pp. 238–267.

LOWES, J. L. *The Chaucerian 'Merciles Beaute' and Three Poems of Deschamps. Modern Language Review,* V (1910), p. 33.

The Prologue to the Legend of Good Women Considered in its Chronological Relations. Publications of the Modern Language Association, XX (1905), p. 749.

The Prologue to the Legend of Good Women as Related to the French Marguerite Poems and the Filostrato. Publications of the Modern Language Association, XIX (1904), p. 593.

Illustrations of Chaucer. Drawn chiefly from Deschamps. Romanic Review, II (1911), p. 113.

Macaulay, G. C. *John Gower, Complete Works.* 4 vols. Oxford, 1899–02.

Froissart. Macmillan's Magazine, LXXI (1895).

MacCracken, H. N. *The Minor Poems of John Lydgate. Early English Text Society.* Extra Series 107. London, 1911.

A New Poem by Lydgate. Anglia, XXII, Neue Folge (1910), pp. 283–286.

Quixley's Ballades Royal. Yorkshire Archaeological Journal, XX, pp. 33–50.

Earl of Warwick's Virelai. Publications of the Modern Language Associations, XXII, p. 597. Baltimore, 1907.

Additional Light on the Temple of Glas. Publications of the Modern Language Association, XXIII (1908), p. 128.

King James' Claim to Rhyme Royal. Modern Language Notes, XXIV, p. 31. January, 1909.

Hoccleve and the Poems from De Guileville. The Nation, LXXXV (1907), p. 280.

An English Friend of Charles of Orleans. Publications of the Modern Language Association, XXVI (1911).

Lydgate's Serpent of Division. Oxford, 1910.

Marsh, G. L. *The Flower and the Leaf. Modern Philology,* IV (1906–07).

PADELFORD, F. M. *Early Sixteenth Century Lyrics.* New York, 1907.

The Songs in Manuscript Rawlinson C 813. Anglia, XVIII, Neue Folge (1908), pp. 309–397.

Ms. Rawlinson 813 Again. Anglia, XXIII, Neue Folge (1912).

PIAGET, A. *Oton de Granson. Romania, XIX* (1882), pp. 237–259; 403–408.

PROTHERO, G. W. *A Memoir of Henry Bradshaw.* London, 1888.

Retrospective Review. Second Series, London, 1827, p. 147. *Article: Early English Poetry.*

ROBINSON, F. N. *Two Mss. of Lydgate's Guy of Warwick. Harvard Studies,* V. Boston, 1896.

SANDRAS, E. C. *Étude sur Chaucer Consideré comme Imitateur de Trouvères.* Paris, 1859.

SCHELER, A. *Dits et Contes de Baudouin de Condé et de son Fils Jean de Condé.* 3 vols. Bruxelles, 1867.

SCHICK, J. *Lydgate's Temple of Glas. Early English Text Society,* Extra Series, 40. London, 1891.

SCHIPPER, J. *Englische Metrik.* 2 vols. Bonn, 1881–88.

SHERZER, J. B. *Isle of Ladies.* Berlin, 1903.

SKEAT, W. W. *An Unknown Poem by Chaucer. Athenaeum,* 1891, No. 3310, pp. 440, 472 ff.

James I of Scotland. London, 1884.

Chaucer's Virelays. Athenaeum, 1893, No. 3410, p. 281.

The Complete Works of Geoffrey Chaucer. 7 vols. Oxford, 1894.

A Complaint, Possibly by Chaucer. Athenaeum, 1894, No. 3482, p. 98; No. 3484, p. 162.

Chaucer's "Balade" in the Legend of Good Women. Academy, 1891, II, No. 1022, p. 504.

SKEAT, W. W., AND POLLARD, A. W. *An Unknown Balade by Chaucer. Athenaeum,* 1894, No. 3476, p. 742; No.

3477, pp. 773 ff.; No. 3478, p. 805 ff.; No. 3479, p. 837 ff.

Smith, G. G. *Elizabethan Critical Essays:* Vol. I: Gascoigne, pp. 46–57; Webbe, pp. 226–302. 2 vols. Oxford, 1902.

Stengel, E. *Gower's Minnesang und Ehezucht Büchlein,* p. 28. Marburg, 1886.

Tanner, T. *Bibliotheca Britannico-Hibernica, sive de scriptoribus, Qui in Anglia, Scotia, et Hibernia ad sacculi XVII. initium floruerunt literarum ordine juxta familiarum nomina dispositis commentarius.* London, 1748.

Tatlock, J. S. P. *Chaucer and Dante. Modern Philology,* III (1904–05), p. 369.

Development and Chronology of Chaucer's Works. Chaucer Society. London, 1907.

Tarbé, P. *Œuvres de Guillaume de Machault.* Rheims, 1849.

Taylor, G. W. *Poems Written in English by Charles Duke of Orleans.* Roxburghe Club, 1827.

A Treatise excellent and compendious, shewing and declaring, in maner of Tragedye, the falles of sondry most notable Princes and Princesses, etc. Translated by Don John Lidgate, etc.

Triggs, O. L. *The Assembly of Gods by John Lydgate. Early English Text Society.* Extra Series 69. London, 1896.

Ward, A. W., and Waller, A. R. *The Cambridge History of English Literature,* Vol. II. *The End of the Middle Ages.* Cambridge, 1908.

Warner, G. F. *Illuminated Manuscripts in the British Museum.* London, 1903.

Warton, T. *History of English Poetry.* 4 vols. London, 1871.

CHAPTER V

The Ballade in the Nineteenth Century

Works, General Authorities, etc.

Adams, W. D. *Latter Day Lyrics.* London, 1898.

Banville, T. de. *Gringoire.* Paris, 1877.

Petit Traité de Poésie Française. Paris, 1909.

Odes Funambulesques. Paris, 1859.

Poésies Occidentales, Rimes Dorées, Rondels. Paris, 1875.

Poésies, Odes Funambulesques. Paris, 1880.

Bergerat, Émile. *Ballades et Sonnets.* Paris, 1910.

Besant, Walter. *Studies in Early French Poetry.* London, 1868.

Coppée, François. *Poésies,* 1864–1887. Paris, no date.

Costello, Louisa S. *Specimens of the Early Poetry of France, from the Time of the Troubadours and Trouvères to the Reign of Henri Quatre.* London, 1835.

Dobson, A. *Collected Poems.* London, 1909.

Dowden, E. *On Some French Writers of Verse. Cornhill Magazine,* XXXVI, 1877.

Gosse, E. *A Plea for Certain Exotic Forms of Verse. Cornhill Magazine,* XXXVI, 1877.

French Profiles. New York, 1905.

In Russet & Silver. London, 1894.

New Poems. London, 1879.

Henley, W. E. *London Voluntaries and Other Poems.* Portland, 1910.

Lazare, Job. *Albert Glatigny Sa Vie, Son Œuvre.* Paris, 1870.

Lang, Andrew. *Essays in Little.* New York, 1891.

Books and Bookmen. London, 1887.

Ban and Arrière Ban. London, 1894.

Ballads and Lyrics of Old France. Portland, 1898.

XXXII Ballades in Blue China. London, 1888.

Rhymes à la Mode. London, 1887.

LEMAÎTRE, JULES. *Les Contemporains*. 4 vols. Paris, 1890.

MATTHEWS, BRANDER. *A Study of Versification*. New York, 1911.

MURRAY, F. E. *A Bibliography of Austin Dobson*. Derby, 1900.

NOYES, ALFRED. *The Poems of Edmund Gosse*. *Fortnightly Review*, XCII. August, 1912.

PAYNE, JOHN. *The Poems of Master François Villon of Paris*. London, 1892.

PROTHERO, R. E. *Théodore de Banville*. *Nineteenth Century*, XXX. 1891.

RABACHE, G. *Austin Dobson, Poète*. *Revue Germanique*, IX. 1913.

RICHEPIN, JEAN. *Les Caresses*. Paris, 1898.

ROLLINAT, MAURICE. *Les Névroses*. Paris, 1907.

ROSSETTI, D. G. *Poetical Works*. 2 vols. Boston, 1899.

ROSTAND, EDMOND. *Les Musardises*. Paris, 1911.

SAINTE-BEUVE, C. *Poésies Complètes*. Paris, 1879.

SCOLLARD, CLINTON. *Pictures in Song*. New York, 1884.

SHERMAN, F. D. *Madrigals and Catches*. New York, 1887.

STEVENSON, R. L. *Familiar Studies of Men and Books*. New York, 1900.

STRONG, A. T. *The Ballades of Théodore de Banville*. London, 1913.

SWINBURNE, A. C. *Poems*. Philadelphia, 1910.

TAILHADE, L. *Au Pays de Mufle*. Paris, 1891.

The Poems of François Villon. Translated by H. De Vere Staepoole. London, 1913.

VIGIER, H. *François Villon en Angleterre*. *Revue Germanique*, IX. 1913.

WHITE, G. *Ballades and Rondeaux*. London, 1887.

WRIGHT, C. H. C. *A History of French Literature*. New York and London, 1912.

INDEX

SUNY Geneseo College Libraries
3 0260 00388134 3